Understand Accounting!

Claude Hitching FCMA
Derek Stone BA, FCA

Pitman

PITMAN PUBLISHING
128 Long Acre, London WC2E 9AN

First published in Great Britain 1984
Reprinted 1987, 1988

British Library Cataloguing in Publication Data
Hitching, Claude
Understand accounting!
1. Accounting
I. Title II. Stone, Derek
657 HF5635

ISBN 0–273–01883–3

Text set in 10½ on 13 pt Plantin Roman
Printed and bound in Great Britain at The Bath Press, Avon

Contents

Preface and acknowledgements

Background

Some time ago, we each had the good fortune to become involved in the development and presentation of a series of in-house training courses for Roche Products Ltd, one as the internal accountant responsible for internal organization and liaison, and the other as the external course consultant and lecturer.

One of the things which helped to make these courses so successful and enjoyable was the degree of commitment that they received from the top. Bill Gerard, Managing Director of Roche, gave every sort of support imaginable to the company's Management Development Programme, of which these courses formed a part. As well as the valuable lecture presentations contributed by senior finance managers from both the UK and the Swiss parent company, Bill and his fellow directors were always ready and available to take part in one of our role-playing case studies. In fact, it even got to the point where we had to make up a rota for the allocation of roles—and we couldn't have asked for a greater commitment than that!

One of the main objectives of the courses was to try to stimulate a general interest in the subject of business finance and commercial awareness among people who really ought to be concerned with it, but probably felt that the subject was either too dull, too specialized, or too complicated for them. So we decided at the outset that a light, palatable form of presentation was needed, and that we should avoid, at all costs, the use of the words 'accountancy' or 'finance' in the title of the course!

And yet a basic knowledge of the elements of finance is an essential part of any manager's mental equipment, because finance is the common denominator through which managers from all functional backgrounds can *communicate* with each other. The ability to communicate with his colleagues is absolutely essential to any manager in business who wishes to *stay* in business. This is a point which is inevitably going to be emphasized several times throughout the book.

So we have a very important message to try to get across. It is important, not only to the accountant, but also to his colleagues from all walks of corporate life—or to the director of a small business who tries to fulfil most of the functional roles himself. It is also important to the managers of the future—the young people who are perhaps in need of a general background knowledge of accountancy and business finance against which to develop their own specialized training, whether this be in the accountancy profession itself, or in some other field where 'accounting' may be a secondary subject.

The path ahead

This is not intended to be a syllabus text aimed at coaching a student through to a specified professional examination level. It is intended to provide a broad background of understanding against which more detailed study can be undertaken as required. We have consequently tried to incorporate a practical approach within a light-weight frame, and we have decided to start at the very beginning! We have assumed that the reader will be starting off with absolutely no knowledge at all of finance or accounting, and we shall limber up in the first chapter with a brief discussion on the problems of communication that need to be recognized and overcome within any business organization. We shall then move on to a topic that is near and dear to all our hearts, and to the very heart of all our business lives—the functions of *money*!—into which we shall introduce some basic terminology through the use of a simple example. A few pages on cost behaviour are also included here in order to provide a familiar base to which some people will be able to relate, and from which, hopefully, they will be able to proceed with confidence to our discussion of the basic financial structure of a business, and the need for a formal presentation of financial information.

This leads us to a study of the conventions which lie behind the presentation of the balance sheet and the profit and loss statement, and to a few words about the need for profit in business, and the function of taxation in our economy. We are then ready to tackle the methods by which the financial transactions of a company are recorded in its books of account, and this will lead us on to the source and application of funds statement and the cash flow forecast.

By this time, our thoughts will have gradually moved from the recording and interpretation of historically-based data to the formulation of financially evaluated plans and budgets for the future. A manager can only hope to lead his company forward if he is looking in the direction in which he is hoping to go, but he will need to have access to reliable and relevant information from the past in order to be able to assess which is likely to be the most potentially successful strategy out of a number of possible alternatives.

One way of looking at management information is via the use of ratios. We shall be studying some of the more common of these in some detail and examine the ways in which they can be used as reliable bases for decision making. This is the part that is likely to be of most practical interest to a manager, although it would be impossible to appreciate fully the points at issue here without first understanding the basic principles behind the figures. Conversely, to read a book confined solely to basics would be like walking down a cul-de-sac, or learning the rules of a game without ever getting a chance to play it—and this is why finance is also called 'The Rules of the Business Game'.

We have followed the same reasoning in delaying our brief discussion of the legal obligations of companies to display financial information until the very end of the book, after we have delved into the basic principles of Added Value and Inflation Accounting. Although the balance sheet and profit and loss examples that we shall be using throughout the book have all been built around the formats prescribed in the Companies Act of 1981, it seemed pointless to divert into the statutory aspects of these statements too soon. By the time you get through to Chapter 16, however, these formats should be familiar enough for you to follow the reasoning behind the requirements of the Act quite easily.

The book is rounded off with a comprehensive glossary of all the terms encountered throughout the course of the book. However, it should perhaps be pointed out here that some of the definitions used at the ends of the earlier chapters will not be quite so comprehensive as the ones used in the Glossary. This is because we want to avoid jumping in too quickly at the deep end, and there will be some cases where a definition will be gradually expanded as we go along.

We have also included definitions or cross references for about fifty or so additional or 'alternative' terms that the reader may encounter in practice, and we are indebted to Kenneth Harry of the Kingston Regional Management Centre for his suggestions and assistance in the compilation of this list. Some of these terms are the American 'equivalents' of the UK terminology used throughout the text, and there are also some definitions of terms which we decided not to bring into our general discussions because of the risk of introducing unnecessary clutter and confusion. It should, however, be readily possible to appreciate the implications of these additional topics once you have read the main text, and they may well prove to be useful as a future point of reference.

In order to provide an easy-reference round-up of all the case study material, we have also included an appendix in which this has been assembled into two complete sets of financial statements—primarily in order to provide you with a convenient point of reference *after* you've read the book, as distinct from a convenient point of reference as you are trying to work out the figures for yourself!

Acknowledgements

Our acknowledgements and thanks are due to a number of people and organizations without whose help and encouragement the completion of this project would have been a very daunting task. As we have already explained, this book was born out of a series of in-house management training courses with which we had the pleasure to be associated. A number of training packages were sampled during our initial period of research and preparation, and many of these contained some very sound ideas, but did not completely comply with our own particular requirements.

The outcome was almost inevitable. Various basic ideas were 'borrowed' from these sources, and remoulded into the programme that was considered to be most appropriate to our needs. One such package was a video learning programme entitled 'Minding Our Own Business', produced by ICI Plastics Division, and now marketed by Vision, Communications in AV/TV, in conjunction with Training Films International Ltd. The finance and economics consultant for this package was Mr H. S. Corlett, of Resource Planning Ltd. The first three modules of this package set out to explain the use of money, and how it is made to work and grow in both domestic and commercial situations.

A theme was developed which illustrated a person winning some money, and then using the money to buy a car with which to start his own taxi business. This seemed a particularly good way in which to build the foundations for the rest of our course—especially since it also slotted in very nicely with another source of training material in which we were interested.

Video Arts Ltd had produced two excellent films which we decided to use as the 'main frame' around which the course presentations and case studies would be built. These were 'The Balance Sheet Barrier' and 'The Control of Working Capital', both of which featured John Cleese and Ronnie Corbett. Both films, and their supporting booklets, were written by Ernest Jones and Antony Jay, and produced by Video Arts. They are based on the structure of the course 'Finance for the Non-Financial Manager', devised by Ernest Jones of Mobile Training and Exhibitions Ltd. These sources provided inspiration for a basic approach to cash movement and the financial statements, the close analogies that can be drawn between the human and the corporate body, and the development of a balance sheet from a financial model. They also used horse-racing as an illustrative parallel: this provided the link to the ICI 'M.O.O.B.' package referred to above and the idea of Andrew Coe, one of our central characters, came from this.

Having built up, and progressively modified, all the ideas and data that we needed to cover the ground of our course, we found that we nearly had sufficient material available from which to compile a useful book on the subject of the preparation and interpretation of company accounts. This seemed to be a sensible idea, although the problems were immediately obvious, because we had never started out with the intention of writing anything completely original from start to finish—even if such a thing had been possible in the first place. Natural modesty does not forbid us to admit that at least some of the ideas and case study development is completely original, although we are nevertheless greatly indebted to all the people and organizations mentioned above for the inspiration provided by their work, and for their permission for the adaptations that have been made from their copyright material.

This applies also to Thomson McLintock & Co., whose excellent booklet on the understanding and application of the 1981 Companies Act proved to be a most valuable reference for our own chapter on this subject. Our special acknowledgement is also due to the invaluable advice and infinitely patient co-operation of Michael McFee, a tax partner with Thomson McLintock & Co, for his guidance through the complexities of taxation topics. Brian Earle, Computer Manager of Inter Company Comparisons Ltd, has also been a tremendous help to us in the provision of data from his Company's files—only a fraction of which we have been able to use in this book. Reference has also been made to a number of tax changes prescribed in the 1984 budget and, to the best of our knowledge and belief, the book is—for all practical purposes—'up to date' at the time of writing. We must, however, add the inevitable disclaimer that none of the people referred to above are responsible for any of the views expressed which are our own.

We are extremely grateful to the directors of Roche for their agreement to our adaptation and development of their course material in this way, and for the many facilities that they have very generously put at our disposal throughout the preparation and reproduction of the completed typescript. Our sincere thanks are also due to Nick Bond, Fraser Goodall, Lynda Howell, Alban Kissane, Veronica Wootliff and Jack Wright for their patience and diligence in checking through the proofs of the typescript and the numbers in the case studies, and for their valuable initial feed-back.

And finally . . .

. . . our thanks are due to Andrew Coe and Matthew Grimble, without whose involvement this book would never have taken shape. They are both fictional characters who bear nothing but a purely coincidental resemblance to any person, alive or dead, although we have to admit that we have grown to know them both pretty well by now.

We used to meet Andrew occasionally at our local hostelry, where the conversation would sometimes turn to matters of a financial nature. He started off by working for someone else, and then he had a stroke of luck, won some money, and started up his own Andycab taxi business. This did quite well, and, after a while, he decided to launch his own manufacturing company under the name of Andco Ltd.

Matthew Grimble had a slightly easier start to life than Andrew, and, by the time we meet him, his business had already been established for about five years. He had invented a fantastic little product which had completely taken over the old widget market, and it was quite natural that these 'midget miracles' should very quickly become affectionately named after their creator. The 'grimble' revolution had arrived!

This is not intended to be as gimmicky as it may sound, because every company makes grimbles—even your company makes grimbles. They are just another name for whichever product it is that your company is in business to sell—whether it be chemicals, textiles, jam, garden furniture or combine harvesters. If you can accept this definition, you should find it much easier to translate our examples into your own environment than if we had used a title like 'The Walter Wall Carpet Co. Ltd'. If we had done that, there would inevitably have been a carpet specialist out there somewhere who would have got hold of our examples, and immediately disputed all the figures.

Anyway, that brings us up to date with the origins and background of the book. We can now set out on our journey of discovery together, and we look forward to the pleasure of your company along the way, in the hope that you will receive as much enjoyment out of reading our book as we have obtained from writing it.

Let's get down to business by trying to learn something about the 'Language of Business' . . ..

Summer 1984

Claude Hitching
and
Derek Stone

1 The language of business

Introduction

Never ask of money spent
Where the spender thinks it went.
Nobody was ever meant
To remember or invent
What he did with every cent.

So said Robert Frost, the American poet who manages to convey the impression in these few short lines that he was a little out of touch with the world of finance. Perhaps he was someone who preferred to leave the control of money to those who were trained and paid to do it for him—the accountants.

A lot of people would agree with him, largely because they don't really understand the weird mumbo-jumbo that they have heard accountants use. They probably couldn't care less whether or not fixed assets are always the things that are nailed down, or whether or not an unpaid electricity bill should be classified as a current liability.

But think what the accountant has to put up with! He has to listen to builders going on about their bending moments, flashing, and relieving arches, and to engineers trying to explain the difference between a grub screw and an endless belt. Or he might have to discuss inter-grade differentials with the personnel manager, or try and appreciate the shipping manager's concern over deviation claims, lay days, CIF, and Section 7 Relief. And then, while all this is going on, the data processing manager is rushing around making sure that nobody has got their bits mixed up with their bytes, or their ROMs confused with their RAMs, and that they have all remembered to 'boot' their disks before settling down with their micros!

In fact, while we are on the subject of data processing jargon, how about this sample extract from a set of instructions recently issued with a 'software package'?

> The options in the file are processed as though they replace the OPTIONS option. Consequently, the OPTIONS option in one option file can refer to another option file. Options files can be chained together in this manner. Alternatively, the OPTIONS option in the SCRIPT command line might refer to a file that contains a list of OPTIONS options, each of which points to a different options file . . ..

Faced with all that, the only thing the accountant wants to do is to escape back to his own office and browse quietly among his debits and credits. He does not really want to be a nuisance to anybody . . ..

The need for communication

All managers and specialists have their own particular jargon which they use as a means of communication. This is fine when they are communicating with someone who understands the same sort of language, but it is not so good when they are trying to get a message across to someone who doesn't.

Two things can sometimes happen. The specialist may assume that his audience understands every word he says, whereas they don't, but don't like to admit it. And also, it is not unknown for specialists to deliberately try to get out of tricky situations by blinding their audiences with science, and hoping that they won't be honest enough to admit that they didn't get the point—often only to find that one of them did!

Either way, things could very quickly degenerate into a situation where a state of mutual embarrassment and mistrust brings on the withdrawal symptoms that push people further and further back into their own functional and departmental corners, cutting the lines of communication as they go.

This must be wrong. It is counter-productive, and a sure recipe for disaster. A successful business depends on a cohesive management team—and teamwork depends on *Communication*. The ability to communicate depends entirely upon the availability and the universal understanding of a common language—and this is where the accountant has the golden opportunity to come into his own, because finance really can be claimed to be the 'language of

business'. Almost every business situation is capable of financial evaluation, and most situations should therefore be capable of being related through this common denominator.

It is consequently extremely important that all managers should have a full and confident knowledge and understanding of the financial and commercial implications and consequences of the actions and decisions with which they may be involved, or for which they may be responsible. This sense of commercial awareness is an essential quality for all managers who hope to be able to make an effective contribution to the work of their management team, or to the future success of their company. The secret is to ensure that their accountant provides them with all the information they need to enable them to make the best and safest judgements possible in the circumstances that prevail.

One of the main objectives of this book is to help non-financial managers—and others—to learn the 'language of finance', and to help them identify and interpret the sort of information they will need in order to perform their management function more effectively.

The person who prepares this information for them is the accountant, who, according to the *Oxford Dictionary* definition, is the 'professional keeper and inspector of accounts'. This is not the only definition that we could quote, and you may well care to suggest a number of others, some of which may not be quite so complimentary as the Oxford Dictionary! In any event, and however we may choose to define his responsibilities, it must be accepted that the accountant has a key role to play as a member of the management team. Part of his time will also be taken up with the preparation of the company accounts to send to the company's shareholders, and looking after the company's financial relationship with the outside world—a role which involves making sure its customers pay their accounts on time, and that there is enough cash in the bank with which to pay the company's suppliers and its employees' wages, and so on.

But we don't need to dwell on this side of the accountant's duties too much here. We are more concerned with his (or her) 'management accounting' responsibilities, which can be very briefly summarized as follows:

1 To assist colleagues in the planning and co-ordination of company budgets and forecasts, and to ensure that these are both reasonable and acceptable.

2 To prepare timely, relevant and accurate management reports and accounts.
3 To hold regular performance reviews with management colleagues, and to help them interpret past results and update future forecasts and strategies.
4 To play a consultative role by advising colleagues on the possible financial implications of actions and decisions for which they may be responsible.

Summary

Throughout this book, we shall be concentrating mainly on building up an understanding of the accountant's jargon: the way in which he prepares his reports, what his financial statements mean, and how his work integrates with that of his colleagues in the company's management team.

His role can be compared to that of a GP advising on his company's health and well-being; a referee keeping a record of the score in the 'game of business'; or an interpreter translating opinions, judgements, actions or decisions into the common language of commercial finance. Part of this latter function must also be to ensure that his colleagues are able to recognize, understand and appreciate the signs and messages of this common language. So, if you ever see an advertisement for an accountant who is required to be qualified in medicine, hold a referee's certificate, and speak several foreign languages, then you'll know that at least one other person has read this book apart from yourself!

2 Who needs money?

What is money?

Many people have defined money in their own particular way. Oscar Wilde once said, 'When I was young, I used to think that money was the most important thing in the world. Now that I am old, I know it is!', while 200 years ago Benjamin Franklin said: 'The use of money is all the advantage there is of having it. If you would like to know the value of money, go and try to borrow some'. James Baldwin, on the other hand, thought that money was rather like sex 'You thought of nothing else if you didn't have it, and of other things if you did', which makes you wonder what they used to think about before money was invented . . ..

In those days, people could only exchange, or barter, their own goods or labour for the goods or labour of others. The shopping list of the average working man might have read:

1 Cow = 3 Sheep
= 10 Days' work
etc., etc.

This meant that traders had to carry wagonloads of goods around with them, or herd their animals around until they found somebody with whom they could arrange some mutually satisfactory barter. They eventually decided to make things easier by using less bulky, but more rare and valuable things, like measures of gold and silver, which were of an agreed and recognizable value, and which they could exchange for other goods of equivalent value.

Then, about 700 years BC, the Lydians of Asia Minor began to make coins of fixed values which they could use as tokens of exchange. The idea caught on very well, because coins of gold, silver and copper were used for over 2,500 years before the Americans started using paper money in large quantities, and then, in 1914, the Europeans started to do the same.

Paper money and coinage have no great value in themselves. Their value depends on what they can be exchanged for; so a country could not get rich simply by printing lots of paper money. If there were not enough goods being produced to be exchanged for the money, the money itself would be worthless.

What do we need to know about money?

Nowadays, we all tend to take money for granted—unless we haven't got any. But we are going to concentrate for the moment on what money means to us, as individuals.

There are basically two things that we need to know about money. Where it comes from, and where it goes to—or how we can get our hands on it, and what we can do with it once we've got it. These two things need to be thought about together, because you can't very well spend money before you are reasonably certain that you are going to have some to spend, and, conversely, money isn't very much good to you unless you use it. It's nice to know you've got some, but if you just stash it away in a safe, it will gradually lose its purchasing power as inflation pushes up the cost of goods and services, so you need to keep it moving if it's really going to be of any 'value' to you. In other words, it has to *flow* in order to maintain or increase its value.

Where does money come from?

As individuals, we can obtain money in several ways. We earn wages and salaries from our jobs, receive interest or dividends from investments made in the past, obtain revenue from the sales that we make in our shop—or maybe we have just been lucky enough to inherit a fortune.

Where does money go to?

Once we've got some, we can then decide what we are going to do with it, and consider what it is useful for.

We immediately find that we have achieved a degree of flexibility that barter could never provide. We are able to make a choice about the way we use our money. For example, we can spend it or save it. We can store—or invest—the results of our labours at one time or period, and obtain the benefits from them at some other time in the future. Conversely, money also enables us to obtain goods or services on credit, and to pay for them out of our future income.

There are also a number of different areas in which we can decide to allocate our money. These include:

(a) Essentials, such as housing, clothing and food.
(b) Consumer durables/luxuries, such as a car, a television, or a washing machine.
(c) Consumables, such as food, drink, tobacco and leisure pursuits, on which expenditure is mainly a matter of choice.

Money as a measure

As well as thinking about money from the viewpoint of its function as a useful means of exchange, we must also consider its use as a measure. For instance, money can help us to form opinions or judgements, and to take decisions, such as:

(a) The relative cost, and value for money, of one lawnmower compared with another.
(b) Which building society offers the best rate of interest on the money we deposit with them.
(c) Which assurance company offers the best value in life policies.
(d) Whether or not we can afford to buy and run a car.

In exactly the same sort of way, managers in business can use money measures to help them decide:

(a) Whether or not they should invest money in a new factory or piece of machiney, or in the promotion of a new product.
(b) Whether one project is 'better' or 'worse' than another.
(c) Whether or not they are trading profitably or wisely.

Savings and investment

Having thought about some of the ways in which we can obtain money, and about some of the things we can spend it on once we've got it—or, in some cases, even before we've got it—let us now suppose that we have been lucky enough to earn or obtain more money than we actually need to spend on the things that we happen to want at the moment. We have a surplus—so what do we propose to do with it?

We can either save it or invest it. We can store it in a piggy-bank, stuff it under the mattress or under the clock on the mantel-piece, or we can put it into a bank, post-office or building society account, where we hope and trust that it will attract more money to itself in the form of interest—and so increase in value over time.

This is quite commonly all lumped together under the general heading of 'Saving', but we ought really to be a bit more specific in our definitions. We shall therefore define 'saving' as merely holding on to our money for use at some future date without adding any value in the form of accrued interest—in other words, the 'mattress' or the 'piggy-bank' approach. The storage of money in any place where it can attract, or *earn*, interest—such as a bank deposit or a building society account—must be defined as an *investment* in just the same way that money can be invested in property, shares, coins, stamps, pictures, or any other article that the investor considers will increase in value over time.

What is investment?

Investment is therefore a way of making money work, and can be simply defined as

An outlay of cash or its equivalent, in the anticipation of obtaining a net profit at some time in the future.

If, for instance, we were lucky enough to inherit £30,000, we could 'save' it under the mattress so that it would always be available for a rainy day. But not many people would do this for the simple reason that, while it is under the mattress, it is not *doing* anything. It is not working, or earning any interest.

We are much more likely to put it on deposit in a bank, or into the Proverbial Building Society, where we are confident that it will be safe, and where it is almost guaranteed to earn a known rate of interest. This interest would be our 'return on investment' or 'return on capital employed'—terms that we shall encounter quite a lot later on.

There are not many places 'safer' than a building society in which we could invest our money because there is hardly any risk that we shall lose it, or fail to accumulate interest on it as the years go by. The rate of return that we would expect will not therefore be particularly exciting—perhaps 10 per cent after tax—but will be the sort of return that we would expect from a 'low-risk' investment. The £30,000 invested in a building society at this rate would therefore be worth about £48,300 after five years.

The important thing to consider is our freedom of choice. No one is going to *make* us put our money into the building society, because it is *our* money, and it is entirely up to us to do what we like with it, and, if we are anything like the other 99 people out of a hundred in a similar situation, the investment that we shall look for is the one that we feel is likely to attract the highest rate of return commensurate with the degree of risk involved.

Risk and judgement

The next question we have to ask is who is going to quantify the degree of risk for us? Well, this is something that must depend on our judgement, and our judgement alone. There are all sorts of 'experts' about who will be only too happy to advise us on any aspect of investment and risk that we care to think of, but they can never make us do anything against our 'better judgement'. Therefore we are always ultimately responsible for the 'management' of our own money.

Perhaps we may feel that we would like to invest our £30,000 in stamps, or in property. We might regard either of these as just about as 'safe' as the building society, so what sort of 'return' would they be likely to yield? A philatelic expert may advise us that a £30,000 collection of stamps could very well be worth about £50,000 in five years' time, and an estate agent or surveyor may estimate that a house costing £30,000 now could easily be worth £52,000 by then. Both of these amounts are more than we expect from the building society, so, assuming that we have just about equal faith in each of these expert assessments, we are likely to go for property, because our sources of information tell us that this is the way in which we shall obtain the greatest 'growth' from our money over the next five years.

Of course, there is always the chance that our information could have been wrong. There is no way of knowing, until the five years are up, just how accurate the forecasts were. Perhaps, after all, we have not made the right choice. That will be our own hard luck! Nobody made us make the wrong decision—in the end, it was the result of our own *mis*judgement, which may have been absolutely sound and valid at the time, but eventually turned against us. This could very likely have arisen out of a change of circumstances over time—probably circumstances over which we had no control at all, so that, in reality, our investment was nothing more nor less than speculation.

A risky business

Suppose you have been longing to start up your own business. That £30,000 that has just come your way may be just what you have been waiting for, because not many businesses can be launched without any capital being available. Or maybe you have a friend who wants to start a business, and he has heard about this £30,000, and asked you to invest your new-found wealth in that. You have the money that he needs, and he is prepared to pay you for the use of it.

If you considered that this might be a risk worth taking, and agreed to lend him your money for a certain number of years, he might guarantee to pay you 20 per cent per annum for it—twice as much as you would expect to get from the building society—or he might perhaps offer you a 'share' in the business, where the return you get would depend entirely upon the degree of success or failure that he achieved. This may consequently be more or less than the 20 per cent he promised you in return for the loan of your money, but the choice is yours. It would be up to you to assess the degree of risk that would be involved, and whether or not you are prepared to take that risk in order to earn a possibly higher rate of return from your money than you would expect to get from the many other 'safer' options that are likely to be available at lower rates of return. The final decision will depend upon your own final judgement.

However, whatever you decide, your friend will still need to find money from somewhere if he is going to get his business started. He will need it because investment is fundamental to business, and this is another concept of investment that we need to keep very firmly in our minds. The other—as we have already explained—is that investment is essentially speculative by nature, because it is based on the principle that money is being spent or committed today in the hope of yielding a 'return', or profit, at some time in the uncertain future.

Information

So how uncertain is the future? Is there any way in which we can predict what is likely to happen tomorrow, next week, or over the next few years with any reasonable degree of accuracy?

Some people might consult the stars and their horoscopes, but others would tend to shrug this off as being far too unrealistic to be used as a practical base for forecasting purposes, even though the astrological charts and tables have been built up painstakingly over centuries of observation and measurement. Most people, however, accept the view that what happens today is in some way an extension or progression of what happened yesterday, and that, consequently, what happens tomorrow will be a sort of extrapolation of the same chain of events.

Everything would be nice and simple if we could take one thing at a time and consider it in complete isolation from everything else, but reality is never as simple as that. While food-shopping, for example, we are unlikely to look at the price of potatoes in the supermarket and think to ourselves that, if a given quantity costs 70p today, and the same quantity cost 80p last month, then it is likely that they will cost 60p next month—and nothing in seven months' time! What we might do is to relate this month's price to the price of potatoes exactly a year ago, and then to forecast next month's price by applying the same relationship to the price that ruled twelve months prior to that—assuming, of course, that we could remember what it was.

In other words, in order to make our forecast, we would be mentally acknowledging the existence of seasonal variations in the price of potatoes, and be superimposing this on to the general underlying trend or pattern of price movements over a given period of time in the past. In order to quantify the future, however, we have to be in a position of being able to quantify the past—we already know how much potatoes cost today, but, in order to estimate how much they are likely to cost next month, we now want to know how much they cost twelve months ago, and how much they cost eleven months ago. We need historical *information*.

In this respect, an investor is no different from the food-shopper. He also needs to have information about what has happened in the past in order to enable him to assess the sort of risk that might be involved, and the amount of return that he might reasonably expect to receive in the future as a result of the outlay of a certain sum of money at the present time. If he is thinking of spending his money on physical things of value, such as stamps or antiques, he will want to know how prices for these things have moved over the past few years, and, if he is considering putting his money into an established company, the sort of information that he needs will be found in the balance sheets and profit and loss statements of that company for the last few years.

We shall be devoting quite a lot of time to these and other financial records of a company in later chapters, but let us just say for now that the balance sheet will help him assess the degree of *risk* that is likely to be associated with his investment, and that the profit and loss statement will help him assess the sort of *return* that he might expect to receive from the use of his money.

This would be an appropriate point at which to pause and to summarize the points that we have covered so far.

Summary

The value of money lies only in what it can be exchanged for, and it has to move—or *flow*—in order to maintain or increase its value, or purchasing power. It provides flexibility of choice about the way in which it is used, and it can also be used as a relative measure.

Investment is a speculative outlay of cash or its equivalent, in the hope of obtaining a net inflow of cash or its equivalent—or a net profit—at some time in the future.

The choice of investment will depend upon the investor's own assessment of the relative risks from the range of choices available, commensurate with his assessment of the possible rates of return that he might expect from the use of his money. Normally, the higher the degree of risk involved, the higher the rate of return that will be required by the investor.

In order to assess the level of risk involved, and the possible rate of return that might be expected, the investor will need to have access to specialized information. This information will be based on records of historical events and performances, and he will then need to judge how these past performances might be expected to extrapolate into the future. 'Now' is only one single moment in time during the course of a continuing stream of events, and the important things to know are:

- what information you need,
- where to find it, and
- how to analyse and interpret it once you have found it.

This brings us right back to the *Oxford Dictionary*'s definition of an accountant—'The professional keeper and inspector of accounts'. The accountant is the person to go to for information relating to the past financial and commercial performance of a company, and, as we have already seen, he is the person who should be qualified and capable of interpreting these records for the guidance and assistance of his colleagues in the management team.

3 Assets, expenses and costs

Coming to terms with the jargon

In all the examples that we have examined so far, there has been one common factor—the movement or transfer of resources:

— one cow being exchanged for three sheep
— goods being exchanged for labour
— goods being sold for money
— interest being earned on money invested.

One of the main functions of money is therefore to stimulate activity. It can either be used as a direct reward for labour, or it can be used for investment in goods or services which will later be converted back into more money. Either way, it acts as a motivating influence—just like the petrol in a car engine, or the heart in a human body. This does not necessarily mean that the spending of money will always result in the earning of a profit—as most of us who have had to be careful not to live 'beyond our means' will know—although it is certainly true that no-one ever earned a profit out of nothing, even though it may not have been their own money that was spent—or invested—in the first place. This is the Story of Business, and we shall be looking at a number of different aspects of this story before we reach 'The End'.

Let us start the story by introducing you to Andrew Coe, who, some years ago, used to regard himself as an investor. In those days, he didn't know much about stamp-collecting, property and balance sheets—his speciality was horse-racing. He used to glean all the historical information and market forecasts that he needed from the form pages of his daily newspapers, after which he would apply his own judgement to assess which contestants he considered would stand the best chance of winning a particular race.

His favourite tale relates to Derby Day, 1980, when he was watching the racing on television. There were four races due to be televised, so he studied the form, made his selections, and placed one of those rather complicated multiple bets with his turf accountant which ensured he would get back at least some of his money even if only one of his horses won—and considerably more if they all did.

Luck—as well as good judgement—was obviously on his side that day, because all four horses won. His fourth winner hadn't even had time to get back to the unsaddling enclosure before Andy had worked out that he had won £5,700, and he was on his way round to the bookie's before that generally rather amiable gentleman had a chance to discuss the possibilities of emigration with his travel agent.

Andy certainly wasted no time in deciding what to do with the money he'd won that day, because, for some time now, he had wanted a new car. He knew exactly which one he wanted, and where to get it. It was a smart new model, costing £5,150, so he collected his money, wished the bookmaker a happy holiday, and set off for the showroom, where he handed over the cash and completed the formalities. In accounting terms, he had just purchased a fixed asset.

But, before he could use his new car, he had to pay road tax of £50, and insurance of £150—remember, incidentally, that this was a few years ago now! These could be classified as advance payments, because he had to pay in advance for the tax and insurance cover that he needed to last him for a whole year ahead.

This means that, after spending £5,150 on his fixed asset, and £200 on his advance payments, he still had (5,700 − 5,150 − 200 =) £350 cash left out of his original winnings of £5,700. To an accountant, this would be known as a current asset. This is a term that covers, in effect, all those things which make the wheels of business go round, such as the stocks of materials that are used to manufacture a finished product. They are termed 'current assets' because they are generally readily convertible to some other form of current asset. It didn't take Andy long to realize that he needed to convert some of his current-asset cash into some current-asset petrol before he would be able to make his own wheels go round.

If we assume that he bought £10 worth of petrol, we can list all the transactions mentioned so far in the form of a very basic financial statement:

		£	£
Fixed asset:	1 Car		5,150
Advance payments:	Road tax	50	
	Insurance	150	
			200
Current assets:	Stocks (Petrol)	10	
	Cash	340	
			350
Total assets			5,700
Financed by:	Winnings		5,700

Andy's winnings could also be called his 'risk capital', because that is the money that he committed to buying and running his new car.

This very simple statement in rather formal financial terms answers the two basic questions with which we started our previous chapter—'Where did the money come from?' and 'Where did it go to?' The only difference is that we have now switched the questions around; this statement tells us first of all where Andrew's money went to, or how it was used (his car, and the advance payments and current assets that he needed to keep it going), followed by details of where it came from (his winnings).

We could look at this in another way—in the form of a simple equation—by listing all his assets on one side of the 'equals' sign, and his risk capital on the other:

Fixed assets		Advance payments		Current assets	=	Risk capital
5,150	+	200	+	350	=	5,700

Running a car

Having purchased, taxed and insured his car, and put some petrol into the tank, Andy was then able to drive it on the roads. So how much did it cost him to do that? His actual 'running' costs will depend upon how far he drives, and these can consequently be called his 'variable costs'—probably working out at about 5.0p per mile on average.

But that isn't all. His tax and insurance payments are going to come up for renewal year after year, however many miles he drives, and he is also inevitably going to have to put aside—or 'reserve'—some money each year to cover his maintenance expenses. Andrew reckoned that these would amount to about £250 per annum. All of these costs can be called fixed costs, because, generally speaking, they are linked to a time base rather than to a level of activity. For the purpose of this very basic illustration, therefore, the fixed costs will stay the same, however many miles are travelled, whereas the variable costs will increase in direct proportion to the number of miles travelled.

We are consequently beginning to build up a picture of Andy's spending pattern on his car, although, if you are talking to an accountant, you may hear him refer to it as his cash flow. But we haven't quite finished yet, because, from the point of view of assessing the expenses incurred year by year in running his car, we have to make one or two adjustments to these figures. (One thing that we ought to point out here, incidentally, is that you must never ever let your accountant hear you suggest that any of his figures are 'fiddled'—the correct professional term is 'adjusted'!)

The important point here is that Andy spent £5,150 on his car *at one particular moment in time*, and this accountant of ours has got a very convenient way of calling this point 'Year 0' because every successive year of usage can then be numbered quite naturally from 'Year 1' onwards.

But it wouldn't be fair to regard the whole of this £5,150 as a legitimate charge against the day, week, or even the year during which the car was bought. Andy is likely to have the use of that car for quite a few years, by the end of which time he will trade it in for a new one. If you were to ask him to say exactly how many years this was likely to be, he is most unlikely to be very specific about it—his best estimate would be 'About five—give or take a few!'

Depreciation

The next question that we would want to ask him is how much he thinks the car might be worth when he trades it in at the end of his estimated five years, and the chances are that he won't be too sure about that either—if only because he isn't a second-hand car dealer by trade. But he is a great one for making inspired guesses, as he would have been the first to admit on that Derby Day, so he'd be likely to come up with 'Something in the order of £1,150'.

This may sound quite precise, and consequently scientifically accurate and 100 per cent reliable, although he probably related his estimated trade-in price to the original purchase price of £5,150, so that the difference between the two figures works out at a nice, tidy, round £4,000. But we should be the last ones to complain about that. We are the ones who are going to be doing the sums, and, from what Andy has just told us, we can conclude that that nice, tidy, round £4,000 can be taken as being the (estimated) cost of using his car during its (estimated) useful life of five years.

For accounting purposes, this 'using up' cost is referred to as depreciation, and one of the accountant's responsibilities is to ensure that the net costs of all fixed assets are 'used up', or amortized, or 'depreciated' equitably throughout their working lives. There are several ways in which this can be done, but the usual way would be to charge an equal portion to each year, so that, in the case of Andrew's car, the annual cost of depreciation would be (4,000/5 =) £800.

There are two very important things to remember about depreciation, the first of which is that there is no cash involved in the transaction. Andrew spent the whole of his £5,150 in Year 0, and hoped to get £1,150 back in Year 5; so what we have done is to say that the net usage cost of £4,000 should be spread evenly over the five years at the rate of £800 per year. The second thing to remember is that, even though the £800 is not represented by any actual outflow of cash from his bank, it is still just as much a part of his *costs* as is the petrol or the maintenance bills.

It should also be noted that this calculated cost of depreciation can, by its very nature, only be an approximation because it is based on somebody's estimation of two uncertain future events. The first is the length of time over which the net cost of the asset should be spread. The second is the amount of money that is likely to be obtained when it is eventually traded in at the end of that time—and we all saw how scientifically Andrew applied his judgement to those two questions!

You may also encounter one definition of depreciation which represents it as being the 'loss in value of an asset over a period of time', but this, in our opinion, is unhelpful. It is better to think of depreciation as being concerned with the apportionment of cost, and cost is not necessarily synonymous with value.

Fixed and variable cost behaviour

Before we leave the subject of costs and cost behaviour, let's just see where we've got to. We have taken care of just about all the costs that will be associated with the running of Andrew's new car, so the next thing we want to do is to build them up into a simple cost profile that will enable us to visualize a pattern of cost behaviour over a period of time. We have now gathered together sufficient data to enable us to do this quite easily:

		£ p.a.
(a) Fixed costs:	Tax and insurance	200
	Maintenance	250
	Total:	450
	Depreciation	800
Total fixed costs		1,250

(b) Variable costs: Petrol @ 5.0p per mile

As we have already noted, the fixed costs are geared to a time base, which means that they will remain substantially the same over a wide range of mileage that might be travelled during the year, whereas the variable costs will vary in proportion to the distance travelled.

The cost profile for this set of data is illustrated in Figure 3.1 and we can see clearly from this that the average cost per mile will decrease as the number of miles travelled goes up. This is obviously because the fixed costs of £1,250 can be divided by an increasingly high denominator.

This fairly innocent statement of the mathematically obvious actually happens to be an example of how easy it can be to get our definitions confused if we are not careful. We have defined the petrol costs as 'variable' because they vary in proportion to the total number of miles travelled, but they could conversely be thought of as 'fixed', inasmuch as the cost of every individual mile travelled is 'fixed' at 5.0p, so that we must always remember that costs are defined from an overview concept, rather than from an average unit point of view.

Similarly, if we were to think of the fixed costs of £1,250 in terms of an average cost per mile, we would find—as we have just pointed out—that they would 'vary' inversely with the number of miles travelled: from 25p at 5,000 miles per year to 4.2p at 30,000 miles per year. But it is again the total overview concept that we must bear in mind, because these are the fixed costs that have to be borne each year, however many miles are travelled.

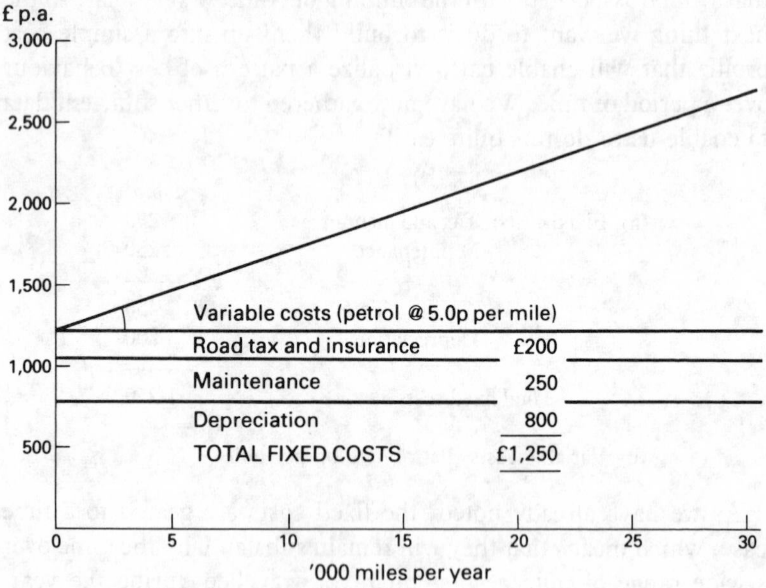

Fig 3.1 The cost profile of running a car

Costs and cash flow

We have already stressed the point that costs and cash flow are not necessarily the same. In Andrew's case, this is principally because depreciation—whilst being an inseparable element of his costs—does not involve any movement of cash. His cash flow started at the end of Year 0 with an outlay of the £5,150 that he paid for his car. He then planned to spend £200 per year on tax and insurance, plus another £250 on maintenance bills, adding up to a total of £450 per year over the five-year life of the car, and expected to end up with £1,150 from the sale of the car at the beginning of Year 6. On the other hand, we will have to spread his net 'usage cost' of £4,000 over the five years' useful life of the car, and the resulting depreciation cost of £800 will have to be added to his other fixed costs of £450, thus adding up to £1,250 in all. The *net* result is the same, but the two profiles are completely different, as we can see quite clearly from Figure 3.2.

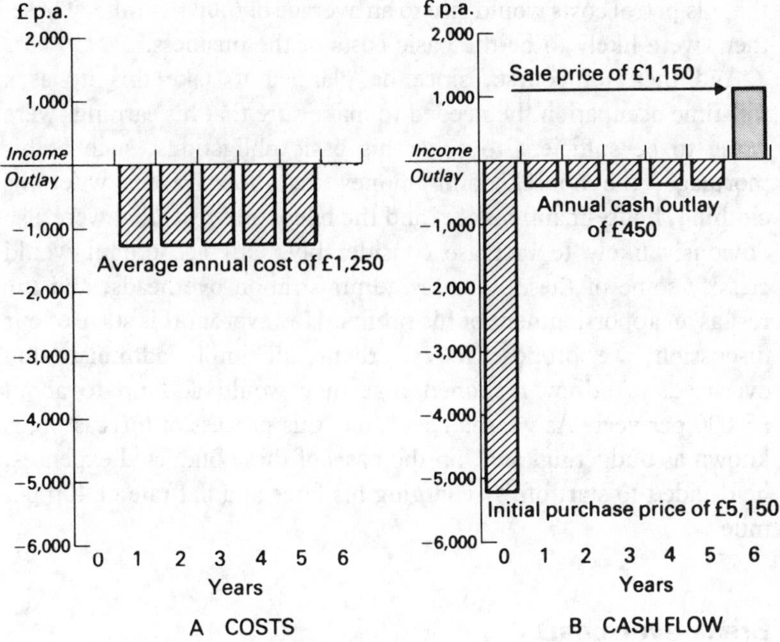

Fig 3.2 The difference between costs and cash flow

Making money work—Andrew Coe's taxi business

Quite often, when people buy cars, they regard them just as something that will enable them to get to and from work, and to be completely flexible and independent when it comes to planning their holidays. Andrew's new car was going to be much more closely associated with his work than that, however. He decided to put it to use as a taxi, and the first Andycab took to the road. This immediately made his financial situation much closer to that of an ordinary business, since he was now entering a typical commercial situation where there is, we hope, an income as well as an outlay. But there were obviously some changes to be made to the ground rules. For the sake of simplicity, we shall ignore for the time being such complications as taxation, but, faced with the prospects of a far higher mileage and wear and tear, he decided that it would be more realistic to charge £1,000 per annum to his new business for depreciation, and £1,200 for tax, insurance and maintenance, which added up to £2,200 for his fixed business costs. With a probable high proportion of short journeys to be covered, he also estimated that his petrol costs would rise to an average of 6.0p per mile. These, then, were likely to be the basic costs of the business.

And then, of course, since he planned to take this up as a full-time occupation, he needed to make sure that his earnings were going to be sufficient to cover his basic obligations, such as his mortgage, the housekeeping money that he gave his wife, his clothing, house-maintenance, and the telephone costs that were also obviously likely to increase considerably. Our accountant would classify some of these items as administration overheads, and the rest as an apportionment of his profits. However, at this stage of our discussion, we propose to call them all simply administration overheads. Andrew reckoned that they would add up to about £5,000 per year. As we shall see later, this process of forecasting is known as budgeting, and, on the basis of these budgeted expenses, he decided to start off by charging his fares at a flat rate of 40p per mile.

Break-even charts

These forecasts obviously made a very significant difference to his cost profile, mainly because it now had a much higher base than the

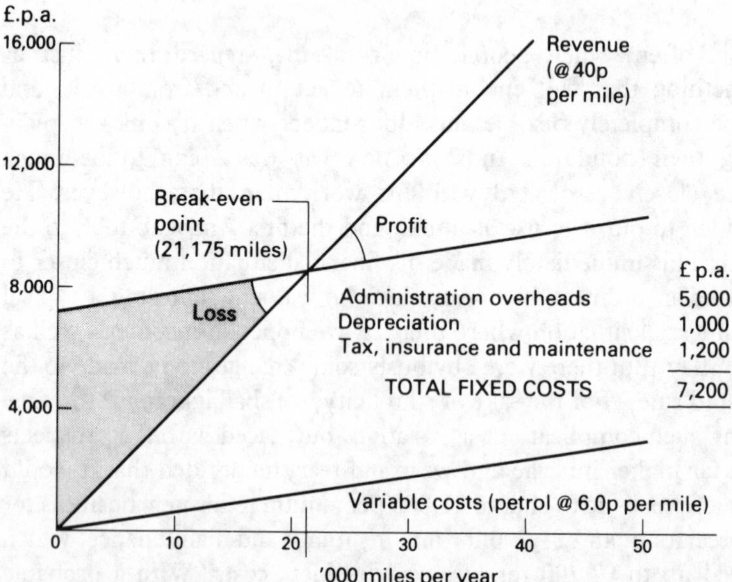

Fig 3.3 The Andycab break-even chart

one we prepared to represent his domestic costs. But there is also another major difference: this time we have an additional line which represents his revenue, or income. We can see from Figure 3.3 that Andrew had to travel 21,175 miles during the year before his total revenue reached the level of his total costs. This is the level of activity at which his business 'breaks even', and this sort of profile is consequently called a 'break-even chart'.

There are two ways of drawing these charts: one with the fixed costs forming a base, and with the 'variable' slope above, and the other with the variable costs as the base, and with the fixed costs above. We have chosen the latter version because, as we shall now demonstrate, it illustrates more easily how the break-even point can be calculated.

The contribution concept

First of all, we have a revenue figure of 40p per mile. By definition this must be a variable element in our calculations, because it varies in direct proportion to the number of miles travelled. We also have a variable cost of 6p per mile for the petrol. This means that, for every mile travelled, the variable revenue exceeds the variable cost by (40 – 6 =) 34p. This difference is known as a contribution because, for every mile travelled, a contribution of 34p is being made towards the recovery of Andrew's fixed costs and profit.

It is not unknown for some people to jump to completely wrong conclusions from a set of figures such as these, so once again we need to be careful. They might look at our present figures and conclude that the Andycab business makes 34p profit out of every mile that it operates, but we can now see that this takes no account at all of the fixed costs. What the 34p actually does is to make a *contribution* towards the recovery of these fixed costs, and then, only when these have been fully recovered, does it start to make a contribution towards profit.

In order to calculate the break-even point, one simply needs to divide the total fixed costs by the rate of contribution per unit of output. In our Andycab example, where we have fixed costs of £7,200 and a contribution of 34p per mile, the break-even point is (7,200/0.34 =) 21,175 miles.

The 'contribution concept' is consequently another, and very fundamental, concept of cost behaviour. It enables us to simplify our break-even chart even further. Instead of charting both full costs and revenue, we can deduct the common element of variable costs from both lines, and show just the fixed costs and the contribution, as illustrated in Figure 3.4, which demonstrates that

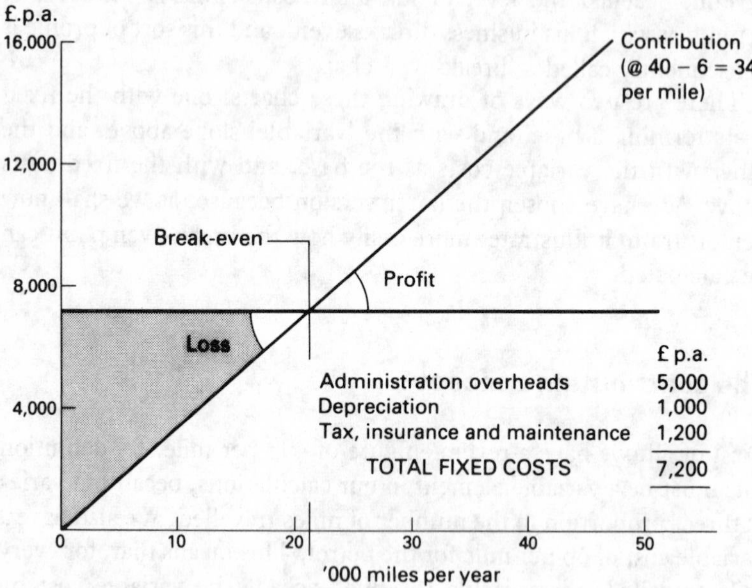

Fig 3.4 The Andycab contribution chart

the break-even point is still the same under this method of calculation as it was in Figure 3.3. The 'contribution' chart is the more concise of the two, and, once the concept has been grasped, is generally more readily understood—and consequently more often used—than the 'full cost' presentation.

However, whichever sort of chart we prefer, it didn't take Andrew long to realize that his Andycab was going to have to take quite a lot of fares before his business was going to start making a profit—and, if there was anything that he needed more than anything else in the first year in order to help provide a cushion against possible hard times in the future, it was *profit*!

Summary

This simple exercise of preparing a cost and revenue forecast—or budget—certainly helped Andrew to appreciate a number of very important basic facts about how a business works:

1 Capital, in the form of cash, has to be invested in a business before it can begin to operate.
2 The cash is needed to buy equipment—or fixed assets—with which to convert consumable items—or current assets—back into cash.
3 The net cost of fixed assets—their purchase price less their anticipated scrap value or trade-in price—should be spread over the period of their anticipated useful working lives as a 'usage cost' called depreciation.
4 Although depreciation is an essential element of cost, it has nothing at all to do with an outflow of cash—this takes place at the time of the original purchase.
5 Depreciation is one of the 'fixed' costs of a business, and this term is used to describe those costs which are geared to a time base, rather than to a level of activity. Other examples would be rent, rates, insurance etc.
6 Variable costs are those which are linked more or less in direct proportion to the level of activity, such as the cost of the petrol used in Andrew's Andycab business.
7 The difference between revenue and variable costs is called 'contribution'. By definition, this also must vary with the level of activity.
8 The level of activity at which the total revenue equals the total costs of the business—or at which the total contribution equals the total fixed costs—is called the 'break-even' point.
9 A successful business needs to generate sufficient revenue to cover all of its costs—or sufficient contribution to cover all of its fixed costs—before it starts making a profit. Profit is essential to enable the business to build up 'reserves' from which to finance future expansion, or to cushion possible future contingencies.

Happily, the Andycab more than covered its costs during its first and subsequent years of operation. The business expanded, and Andrew Coe was able to branch out and explore other avenues of interest, as you will see if you stay around for the next few chapters.

4 Some fundamental facts of business life

Introduction

How many of us have at some time or another dreamed about starting up a business of our own? Somewhere where we could be our own master, and organize things in just the way that we think they should be done—after all, who was it who once said that 'Nobody ever got rich by working for somebody else!'? That may well be true, but, as we have already said, it generally takes money to start a business. Not everyone has the good fortune to have direct access to the sort of money that they would need to take the plunge—or the courage to borrow someone else's money, and then to risk the possibility of losing it all for them.

Andrew Coe got off to a flying start, but then, he was lucky, and he would be the first to admit it. 'I was lucky—and I'd be the first to admit it!', he used to say, recalling that famous winning bet of his on Derby Day, 1980, when a horse called Pontin Lad apparently 'started it all' by helping him to win enough money to buy himself a new car. He then decided to use this car to start his own taxi business, which went from strength to strength, and, as far as we know, is still going as strong as ever.

Raising the money

But not many of us could expect to be as lucky as Andrew. One of the first problems we would need to solve if we wanted to start our own business would be where—and how—to raise the money. There are two main sources that we would have available:

(1) ourselves, in the form of an investment, or
(2) somebody else, in the form of a loan.

We might have a friend or a relative who is interested in coming into the business with us, in which case we could form a partnership. Then both of us would be investing money in the business, as risk capital in a speculative venture. This would be regarded as an 'unlimited' investment because, if the business failed, we would be jointly responsible for the settlement of all the business debts—even if we had to sell up our homes and our other possessions in order to do so.

Or we might decide to register a limited company. From a legal point of view, this is rather like giving birth to a new person. The company would have a completely separate identity for trading purposes, and would be 'born' by the investment of a certain amount of capital in its 'shares', together with some additional 'loan capital', if this was required. This is consequently just like lending to, or investing money in, another person, and the amount of the company's capital represents its 'liability' to its investors or lenders. The main significance of this is that the company's liability in case of failure is *limited* to the amount of capital, or money, that it has available under its own name. When that has gone, it is bankrupt—just like any ordinary individual.

Share capital and loan capital

Money invested speculatively, or at risk, is known as share capital, while loans from people who generally prefer a 'safer', or more guaranteed return from the use of their money are called loan capital, and there are a number of very important distinctions between share capital and loan capital that must be appreciated:

(1) Loans are generally of a long-term nature, and at a fixed rate of interest. The rate of interest may perhaps be geared to the bank lending rate, but the term, or life, of the loan will be fixed by arrangement. Once fixed, the lender cannot reclaim his money until the termination of that period, and this is a provision which safeguards the borrower against a possible demand for repayment at a time when he may just not have the funds available from which to repay. In recent years, an ever-increasing number of companies have also started life with the

help of short-term overdraft 'loans' from banks. These loans are likely to be at a comparatively high rate of interest and are repayable as and when sufficient funds become available.

(2) The payment of interest on loan capital is a prime legal charge against the trading operations of a company, and has to be paid whatever the trading profits may be.

(3) The shareholders' funds are what is left after all debts and liabilities have been met. They are made up of the share capital that they initially invested in the business, plus any trading profits that they may have subsequently decided to re-invest, or 'reserve' in the business. This is consequently the part of the business capital which stands to gain or lose, according to the trading fortunes of the company. This is where the *risk* lies, and shareholders are not automatically entitled to any return, or interest, on their investment. They own everything that is left after all debts (including loan interest), outstanding bills and taxes have been paid. They can decide how much of this balance should be retained in the business as reserves, or divided up amongst themselves in proportion to the number of shares they hold. We shall have more to say about 'reserves' later on.

(4) Shareholders cannot take their money out of a business whenever they feel like it. They can only sell their shares if they are able to find somebody else who is prepared to buy them, and, even then, they can only sell them for whatever price that person is prepared to pay for them. This consequently leads to a situation where a company may quote its share capital as, for example, '800,000 shares at £1 each = £800,000', while the 'quoted' exchange price may be £1.80 each. This means that prospective purchasers would be prepared to pay £1.80 for each nominal £1 share—or for each 1/800,000th part of the company's risk capital. As far as the company itself is concerned, it never receives any of the money that changes hands during these share transactions, so its share capital will remain at £800,000 unless or until any further shares are issued.

Equity

Let's stop here for a moment, and consider two points which arise from this. The first concerns shareholders' funds, or 'what is left after all debts and liabilities have been met'. Another word for this is equity.

Think of it from the point of view of a mortgage. Maybe you have a house, and want to move to another one, and you know that you will be able to get £40,000 from the sale of the one you're in. This will be the total capital that will be realized from the sale—but it won't all be yours if you still have £10,000 outstanding on your present mortgage. Only £30,000 will be yours—the rest belongs to the building society.

In effect, their £10,000 represents your loan capital, and the rest is your equity, or 'the amount that is left after all debts and liabilities have been met'.

Gearing

The second point that arises from this discussion concerns the amount, or the proportion of total capital employed, that ought to be represented by loan capital, as distinct from equity capital. The relationship between the two is known as the company's debt ratio, or gearing, for which there are a number of different definitions. The one we shall use is the proportion of a company's total capital employed that is represented by loan capital, although it is quite often defined as the relationship between loan capital and equity. Both calculations are equally legitimate, and it does not matter which one is used, provided that all comparisons are made from a consistent base.

'Gearing' is one of those rather intriguing terms that is used by accountants in this context, and it is just the sort of term that might make an engineer sit up and take notice because, all of a sudden, he can see what is going on. It is a piece of jargon that has been lifted straight out of his own vocabulary.

Capital gearing is best illustrated by taking two rather extreme examples, and who better to provide them than Andrew Coe? Andrew had always had this ambition to launch his own taxi business, even before he won all that money, and he was the sort who wanted to be able to go into it in a really *big* way. He used to dream of running this fleet of about ten limousines, all with two-way radios, hooked up to an office with a secretary/operator, and all the trimmings. He could really see himself running an outfit like that! 'Weddings and Race Meetings a Speciality', and all that sort of thing!

Well, the amount of capital that would have been required for 'all that sort of thing' would have been about £100,000, but, as we saw, his current assets after he'd bought that car were only about £350. To this we could probably add another £650 that he had put aside in the bank; so let's say that he would have been able to lay his hands on £1,000. This means that he would have needed to borrow the rest; so, in order to keep our example in round figures, we shall assume that he successfully managed to negotiate a loan for £100,000—and still managed to call his business his own! In that situation, his capital structure would have been:

	£
Share capital (equity)	1,000
Loan capital	100,000
Total capital employed	101,000

This would be known as a very 'highly-geared' situation, because his capital employed contained such a relatively high proportion of loan capital. If we now assume that his trading profit in the first year was £16,000, and that the rate of interest on the loan was 15 per cent, his own net profit would have been:

	£
Trading profit	16,000
Less: Loan interest @ 15% on £100,000	15,000
Net profit	1,000

That £15,000 loan interest charge made a massive great hole in the £16,000 trading profit made by the business, but the lenders of the loan capital would have got their 15 per cent, and Andrew would, after all, have only risked £1,000 of his own money, so £1,000 net profit out of a capital outlay of only £1,000 can't be bad! Andrew would have doubled his money in one year—so why don't we all do it?

Well, before we start making appointments with our Friendly Bank Managers, let's just think about what could happen if things were to change. Not by much—just by a fraction . . ..

Suppose, for instance, that the interest rate on the loan capital was linked to the bank lending rate, and that—possibly as a result of a political crisis in another country—it were to be increased without any warning by a mere 2 per cent to 17 per cent. Or perhaps the trading profit had only been £14,000, instead of £16,000. Neither of these changes would have been particularly significant in themselves, but their impact on Andrew would have been drastic, because he would have seen his £1,000 profit change abruptly into a £1,000 loss, and that would have wiped out the whole of the £1,000 capital with which he had started. All of which helps to explain why equity is often called 'risk capital'.

On the other hand, if he had got plenty of money and had been able to raise the £100,000 himself, and for some reason or other needed to raise another £1,000 from somewhere else, the capital structure of his business would have been identical, but reversed:

	£
Share capital (equity)	100,000
Loan capital	1,000
Total capital employed	101,000

This would be regarded as a very low-geared situation, because his total capital employed contained such a *low* proportion of loan capital, and the effects of the same changes that were suggested above would be minimal. A change of £2,000 in the trading profit is hardly going to make any difference to his ability to pay the £150 that would have been due in loan interest, and a 2 per cent change in the rate of that would not have had too much effect on his profit figure.

The message here is that highly-geared businesses are much more susceptible to outside influences that are quite beyond their own control, and care has consequently to be taken to ensure that gearing does not get too high. The maximum level beyond which it should not be allowed to rise is not easy to define, and is also likely to vary between one business and another, one industry and another, and between one country and another. It all depends on the degree of certainty with which we feel that we can depend on the maintenance of the income stream out of which the interest on the loan capital will have to be paid.

Using the money

Assuming that we have managed to raise the money needed to start our own business, what are we going to do with it? We now know where the money came from, but where is it going to? Which part of the business are we going to spend it on?

Andrew was lucky in more ways than one. Apart from getting off to such a good financial start, he basically only needed his car and a base from which to operate his Andycab business. We might well need much more than that in order to fulfil our lifetime ambition. We might need to buy or lease a factory, for instance, with plant and machinery to manufacture a product that we hoped to sell. In that case, we would have plenty of things to spend our money on, such as:

— Buildings
— Raw materials
— Labour
— Land
— Advertising
— Insurance
— Plant and machinery
— Delivery vehicles
— Office equipment
  and so on . . .

If we look at this list carefully, we can see that it is possible to divide these items up into the same broad categories that our accountant used when Andy first bought his new car, namely:

— Fixed assets The things that we intend to use in the business for several years, and
— Current assets The things that we have every intention of converting into services or products, and then selling and converting back into cash.

Money invested in fixed assets is fully committed, and is consequently no longer available for further use. This type of expenditure is called capital expenditure, as opposed to 'revenue expenditure' because their net cost has to be spread equitably over the period of their anticipated useful working lives. We shall come back to this distinction later.

In our case, these items would be:

— Buildings
— Land
— Plant and machinery

— Delivery vehicles
— Office equipment

The items that we would include under the heading of current assets are:

— Raw materials, together with any part-finished work-in-progress, or finished products.
— Any cash that we may have in the bank or in the office safe.
— Any money that might be owed to us by some of our customers for goods or services that have already been delivered to them, but for which they have not yet paid.

The fixed costs that we shall incur as a result of our operation—some of which will have to be paid for in advance—may include insurance, rent and rates, most of our wages and salary costs, heating and lighting and so on, while the variable costs might include such things as power, plant maintenance, some labour costs, delivery and postage charges etc.

For the purposes of our present discussion, these fixed and variable costs should all be regarded as part of our current assets, which may seem rather strange and confusing at first sight. Andrew found it rather difficult at first to see how anyone could think of such things as labour, advertising and insurance costs as assets—current or otherwise. 'And yet, when you come to think about it,' he said, 'I suppose you could regard them as just as much ingredients of a finished saleable product as the bought-in-raw materials that you can see stacked away in the warehouse.'

He was obviously beginning to get the message. 'Well, think of it this way,' he said, 'Suppose that I wanted to make teaspoons. A roll of alloy strip isn't suddenly going to turn itself into a set of teaspoons all on its own—somebody will have to load it into a machine, pay for the power to run the machine, insure the machine against damage, and so on. And there isn't much point in producing a mountain of teaspoons unless someone—who also needs to get paid a salary—has advertised the fact that I have a load of teaspoons available for sale to a public that is anxiously waiting to buy them. How about that, then?'

Not at all bad, Andy! The clue is to regard all available resources as assets—whether they are fixed assets or current assets—and on the use of these resources as costs. This type of expenditure is called revenue expenditure, because it will eventually end up by being charged against the trading revenue for a period. The other thing to remember is that the fixed assets are the things with which we intend to convert the current assets back into cash, and thus enable us to buy more fixed assets, if we need them, and more raw materials, labour, and other current assets that we shall need in order to keep the wheels turning so that we can stay in business. It all boils down to *circulation*!

That takes us right back to where we started. Can you imagine what would happen if, just because you happened to make teaspoons, you tried to persuade your supplier of alloy strip to let you have another consignment in exchange for a couple of cases of spoons? And what about your production workers, and the Post Office, or the Electricity Board? Teaspoons won't do for them—they all want *cash*! The Lydians probably never realized what they were starting all those years ago in Asia Minor when they thought up this idea of using exchange tokens in place of barter.

In fact, this is another example of the way in which the function of cash in business is very similar to that of the petrol in Andrew's car. Quite a lot is initially needed in order to get the engine started, and then a continual flow is needed in order to keep it running.

Outside investments

If you're lucky more money flows in than flows out, and after a while you may start to accumulate more than you will need in order to keep the business going.

The Andycab business was a bit like that. Andrew did very well, and it didn't take more than a few years to expand the scope of his operations right up to—and even beyond—the level of which he had dreamed for so long. He achieved this ambition by reinvesting most of his profits back into the business, even though this was actually more than he needed in order to keep it going. Some of the surplus cash was placed on deposit with the bank, where it earned about 12 per cent interest, and his bank manager put him on to someone who was able to advise him on which shares to buy on a short-term basis. These didn't do too badly, either—he actually got about 16 per cent on that investment by the time he was ready to sell them.

By that time he had a fleet of four cars and was really beginning to need an office for a base. Since he had a realistic proposition to discuss with his bank manager, he didn't expect to encounter any problems here. He would be able to realize his investments, and only need to borrow from the bank the balance of the sum that he needed to put down on the office that he had found. It suited his purpose right down to the ground.

So, even when he had some spare cash that was actually surplus to his immediate requirements, Andy didn't let it rest and do nothing. His was not the 'stuff it under the mattress' approach. He looked around for somewhere for it to work during the time that he didn't actually want to use it himself, and he chose the place where he felt he stood to earn the highest return from its use. There is nothing unusual about that—it's just one more example of the sort of thing that we were discussing earlier.

Debtors and creditors

Having stressed the need to keep money on the move, we should now turn our thoughts to the *rate* of flow, because the speed at which cash flows through a business is important too. If your customers don't pay up quickly enough, you won't be able to pay your own bills. Your supplies of alloy strip, labour, and all the other goods and services you need to keep your business running will soon dry up unless you can persuade your suppliers to wait for their money—or can find or borrow some more to put into the business in order to keep things moving.

This doesn't mean that everything has to be paid for on the nail. When we buy something for the business, like raw materials or services, the chances are that we shall not pay for it immediately in cash. There will be a time delay while our suppliers prepare and submit their invoices, and while we check the goods received against the invoices, approve the payment, and send off our cheque. During the period between receiving and paying for the goods and services, the suppliers are our creditors, because they are in credit with—or are owed money by—our business. Similarly, our own customers are our debtors—they owe us money, or are in debt to us—during the period between our despatch of the goods, and our receipt of the payment for them.

Some people like to think of debtors and creditors as acting rather like a brake and an accelerator on the flow of cash circulating around the business 'engine'. If we need to speed up the circulation of cash in order to produce more goods, we shall have to find more money to purchase more material and to pay more wages. We can do this, within limits, by pressing the accelerator marked 'Creditors', and asking our suppliers for more time to pay. But we also need to remember that, if our own customers wish to do the same thing themselves, and ask *us* to extend further credit to *them*, then they will be putting their great big feet on the brake marked 'Debtors', and so slow down the rate of the cash coming in.

So the speed and regularity with which cash circulates through or around the business is not only very relevant, but absolutely vital to its health and survival—in just the same way that the circulation of blood through our veins is essential to the health and survival of our own human bodies.

Working capital

We have already discussed current assets, and defined them as being the materials and resources in our possession that will be used for conversion into the goods or services that we intend to sell.

Some assets are more 'current' than others. Cash can be immediately converted, or exchanged, into anything we like. So, within reason, can the money owed to us by our debtors, or the money invested outside the company on short-term loan—like the shares that Andrew bought on the advice of that friend of his bank manager. These readily-convertible items are called liquid assets.

Stock is generally rather different, because it may take some time to shift, and there is no absolute guarantee that you will sell all of it anyway. Even if you do, you may not be sure of getting the price that you would want. So, if we think of this in mathematical terms, we get the equation:

$$\text{Current assets} - \text{Stocks} = \text{Liquid assets}$$

And then we have to think about the money that we owe to our creditors: our suppliers, the taxman, the shareholders, or whoever. The total of these outstanding debts is called our current liabilities, and we must obviously take these into consideration when we are assessing our general financial situation.

The main difference between what we own in the form of current assets, and what we owe in the form of current liabilities is known as working capital, and this—as we shall see later—is what we can almost regard as the heart of the business. So this is just one more of those physiological analogies that can be found scattered right through this book, and we shall be discussing later how a company should be kept 'fit' by trimming off all its surplus 'fat'. One of the ways in which it can do this is to keep the level of working capital as low as is practically possible and feasible, because only in this way can it achieve the major objective of maximizing the return—or profit—earned out of every pound invested in it.

Later on in the book, when we get around to talking about inflation accounting, we shall also be using the term 'monetary working capital', and it should be fairly easy to work out what this term means. It is the net value of the 'monetary' items—i.e. liquid assets less current liabilities.

A financial model

We shall now try to consolidate the points that we have made so far with the aid of a financial model, as illustrated in Figure 4.1.

This model shows us, above the horizontal line, where the company's money came from—the shareholders' funds and the loan capital, which together make up its capital employed. This is the extent of the company's total liability to its shareholders and others who have invested money in, or who have lent money to, the business.

Basically, this capital starts off as cash, and, below the line, we can see how the cash can be spent—or where the money goes to. It can go into fixed assets, like buildings, plant and machinery, or it can go into the working capital area which, as we have just seen, includes materials, labour and service costs, as well as the money owed to us by our debtors, less the money owed by us to our creditors.

The model also illustrates how the working capital area can be thought of as a circulating system—or 'Money-go-Round', as it has been called. Cash flows out of the centre into materials, labour, and all the other costs associated with the production of our finished goods, and then flows back in again when the goods are sold. The speed with which the cash goes out is regulated by the speed with which we pay our creditors, while the speed with which it flows back in again is regulated by the speed with which our debtors pay us.

. Hopefully, over a period of time, more cash comes in than goes out. If it does, you're in business, because—like Andrew—you will have enough money to put aside for future expansion, or for that rainy day which might just happen to come along when you least want it to. On the other hand, if less cash comes in than goes out, and the cash flow slows down until it eventually dries up altogether,

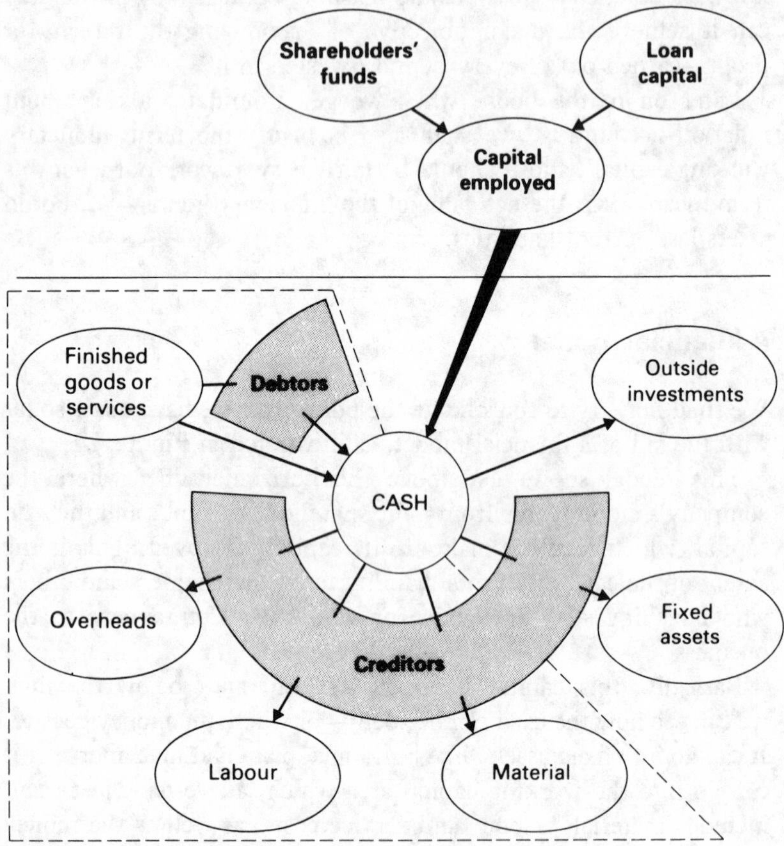

Fig 4.1 Illustration of a financial model. The dotted line encloses the working capital area—the things that we mean to sell or convert into saleable goods and services

you're 'dead'! Which brings us right back to our blood circulation analogy once again.

If the business is healthy and has a good cash flow, but has no immediate reinvestment or expansion plans, the shareholders can either take out more for themselves in the form of higher dividends on their invested stake in the company's fortunes or they can invest it outside the company. They might put money into a subsidiary business in the form of a long-term loan, in which case the loan would be regarded as fully-committed in the same way as if it were a fixed asset. Alternatively, if they just wanted the surplus cash to do some work until they needed it again later to help finance their expansion plans, they might invest it speculatively in another company on a short-term basis rather than just stashing it away under the proverbial mattress. In this case, it would be recoverable at short notice, and would consequently be regarded as a current asset. The financial model illustrated in Figure 4.1 assumes that 'outside investments' have been classified as long-term ('fixed') loans in this particular instance.

But, fixed or current, outside investments are just like all the other things that appear below the line in our financial model. They are all assets, and the total value of all of a company's assets is called its 'total assets'. This figure will, in turn, be the same in value as its 'total liabilities', since everything it owns must have been paid for with money that it obtained from somewhere.

Or has it? What about the things that it hasn't paid for at all yet? Those raw materials that were delivered last week, but have not yet been invoiced, or the dividends on last year's profits that have not yet been sent out to the shareholders, or the tax that has still to be handed over to the Inland Revenue? These are all current liabilities, as distinct from the company's long-term liability to its shareholders or the lenders of its loan capital, so that it could be argued that it would be more useful to separate out the current liabilities, and regard these as part of the company's ongoing trading activities. In this way, it would then be possible to relate the capital resources—as distinct from the unpaid bills—to the *net* assets, and thereby obtain a more meaningful picture of how these resources have been utilized.

This is quite a legitimate argument, although it is one of those situations where one has to accept that it all depends on what you are looking at—or looking for. There are some situations where one would be much more interested in the 'gross' picture of total assets and total liabilities—such as the assessment of liquidity or possible insolvency—and there are other situations where the 'net' figures are more relevant. We shan't be concerning ourselves too much with insolvency during the course of this particular book, so our tendency will consequently be biased towards the net figures.

Before we move on, though, let us try to illustrate how all these things link together in diagrammatic form. This is shown in Figure 4.2.

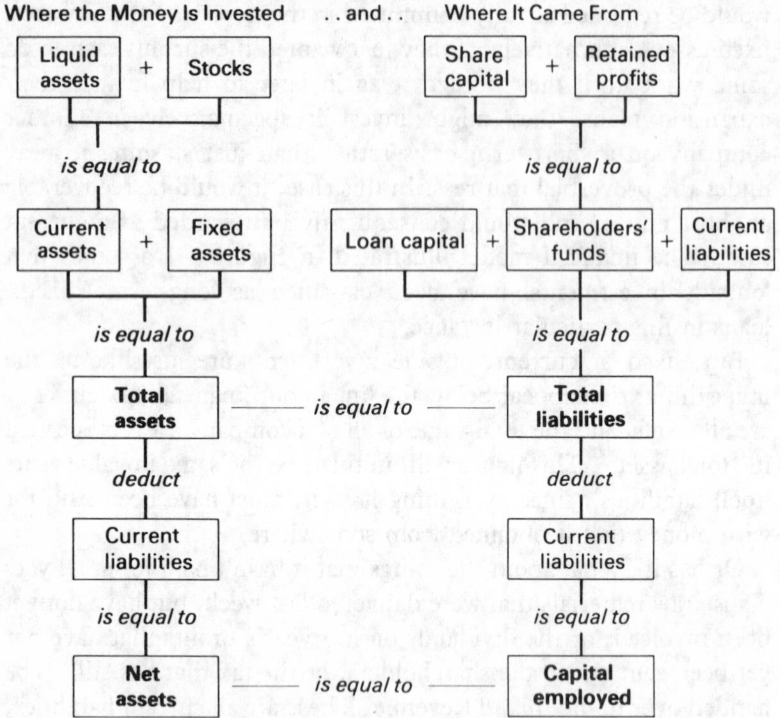

Fig 4.2 Interrelationship of asset and liability classifications

The need for formal presentation of financial information

Every company has a legal, as well as a moral responsibility to keep a record of what it has done with the money invested in it by its shareholders, or loaned to it on a fixed-term agreement.

It has to record every financial transaction in its accounts, and, every year, the auditors come round to ensure that this has been done properly, and that the final accounting summaries represent a 'true and fair view' of its financial situation.

This means that the final statements have to be prepared in a formal and conventional manner. The financial model that we looked at in Figure 4.1 was all very well for the purposes of illustration, but, unfortunately, it hardly fills the bill when it really comes down to the satisfaction of these sorts of requirements—the reason being that it is a bit like an artist's impression of a static situation. It conveys the 'feel' of where a company's money came from, and the areas in which it could have been used, but it would not suit your average auditor at all! He would not be used to seeing this sort of information displayed in this particular way—and neither would anybody else who is used to reading and interpreting financial information.

Auditors are not the only ones who need to be able to obtain this information. In fact, they tend to work as agents on behalf of others who do—people such as the investor, who needs access to the information in order to be able to assess the degree of *risk* and the rate of *return* that is likely to be associated with the use of his money. He will be looking at the information from the *outside*, while, from the *inside*, the company's management team will be looking at it with a view to assessing how effectively they are managing the resources for which they are responsible, and what decisions they should take in order to optimize their future business strategies.

So the display of information in their financial statements and reports serves exactly the same basic purpose for them as Andrew Coe's race-cards served for him. All of the facts that are available for presentation must of necessity be historical, but their interpretation is intended to provide the basis for a decision relating to a future course of action, or to a judgement relating to the possible outcome of a future series of events.

The financial information provided by a company must consequently contain sufficient details of past performance to enable these assessments to be made, and the details must be presented in a formalized way so that the analyst knows exactly where to find what he is looking for. This principle is so fundamentally important that all of these details—and the precise way in which they are to be displayed—is actually enshrined in statute via Companies Acts, which are individually identified by the years in which they are published. The current Act was published in 1981, and we shall be summarizing some of its main provisions in Chapter 16. Although this will virtually be our final subject for discussion, the presentations that we shall use in our examples and case studies will conform as far as is appropriate with this legislation.

There are two main financial statements that every company has to prepare in order to satisfy these requirements. The first of these is the balance sheet, which—rather like our financial model—shows us where the company's funds came from, and where they are invested at a particular moment in time—which is normally at the end of the 'financial year'. This helps an investor to assess *risk*, but studying a series of annual balance sheets would be rather like taking a number of still frames at five-minute intervals out of a cine or video film—it would have been nice to know what happened in between!

So, although the balance sheet shows us where a company is, another document is required to show us how it got there—to summarize the events that happened since the previous balance sheet was prepared. This is what the profit and loss statement does, and this is what the investor will use to enable him to assess the possible *return* that he might expect to receive on any money that he may be thinking of putting at *risk* in the company.

Summary

Let us now summarize the ground that we have covered so far. We have been basically talking about money, and of how it has to keep circulating in order to generate more money. We have discussed the basic principles of investment—of the risk that is involved, and of the return that is needed from the money that is invested—and we have looked at the reasons why the circulation of money is so relevant and vital to the commercial health and stability of a business.

The need to define and understand exactly what we are talking about at each step of our journey into the realms of Business Finance and Commercial Awareness cannot be over-emphasized, so this would be an appropriate time to take another look at some of the basic definitions that we have used so far.

- *Investment* An expenditure in cash or its equivalent in one time period or periods in the anticipation of obtaining a net inflow of cash or its equivalent in some future time period or periods. It is speculative by nature.
- *Share capital* The amount of money invested in a company by its risk-taking shareholders.
- *Shareholders' funds* The part of a company's capital that is owned by its shareholders. It is made up of share capital plus any trading profits that may have been re-invested—or 'reserved'—in the business.
- *Equity* Shareholders' funds: what is left after all debts and liabilities have been met.

- *Loan capital* Money that has been loaned to the company on a long-term basis at a pre-arranged rate of interest to help finance the operations of the business.
- *Gearing* The proportion of a company's capital employed that is represented by loan capital. This term is also often used to define the relationship between loan capital and equity, although we shall use the former definition. Both ratios are equally valid, but the essential thing is to ensure that all comparisons are made against a consistent base.
- *Capital employed* The total funds invested in a business, made up of shareholders' funds and loan capital. It is consequently 'owed' by the company to the investors and the lenders of the capital, and represents a measure of the company's 'limited liability'. It is the same in value as the company's net assets.
- *Fixed assets* Things that we intend to use in the business for several years, such as land, buildings, plant and machinery, furniture, etc.
- *Current assets* Things of value that are moving back into cash, or are readily convertible into cash, such as stocks, debtors, cash and bank balances etc.
- *Liquid assets* Things that are almost immediately convertible into cash, such as cash itself, bank and debtors' balances—but *not* stocks. Liquid assets are consequently the same as current assets minus stocks.
- *Outside investments* Money invested outside the company in order to earn interest on the cash available. The short-term investment of temporarily surplus funds would be regarded as a current asset, while long-term supportive investments or loans would be classified as fixed assets.
- *Debtors* Customers who owe a company money for goods received but not yet paid for.
- *Creditors* Suppliers to whom a company owes money for goods received but not yet paid for.
- *Current liabilities* Debts that are currently owed to other people.
- *Working capital* The net value of current assets and current liabilities.

- *Net assets* The total of fixed assets, working capital and outside investments, representing where the total funds of the business are invested. Equal in value to capital employed.
- *Sales/Revenue/Income* They all mean the same thing.

Finally, we mentioned the company balance sheet and the profit and loss statement, and the fact that these statements are prepared in accordance with established and logical conventions. The principles upon which these conventions are based are so fundamentally important that they are statutorily defined in the Companies Acts.

We can now examine each of these financial statements in turn, and establish just what the conventions are, and how we can interpret the *information* that they contain.

We shall start with the balance sheet . . ..

5 The balance sheet

Introduction

In Chapter 4, we described a balance sheet as the source of information that enables us to assess the degree of *risk* associated with money invested in a business, and we now have to think about how this can be done. We must be careful not to go too fast, though, because a balance sheet contains a lot of different pieces of information, and it will be necessary to ensure that we are able to understand the significance of each piece before we can expect to be able to assess the picture as a whole.

We were talking to Andrew about this some time ago, and he saw the point immediately. He remembered how baffled he used to be when he was a lad, and used to see his father's racing papers lying around the place, filled with all that gibberish and hieroglyphics which were supposed to tell the story of a horse's 'form'. He can understand it all quite easily nowadays, of course, although he still has trouble with those diagrams and codes that they use to record the moves in a game of bridge or chess.

He probably isn't the only one, although we don't need to get involved with chess notations now, so let's start right at the beginning—with the definition that we shall be using throughout the book:

A balance sheet is a statement which will tell us where the company's money is invested, and where it came from, so that we can assess for ourselves what we consider the risk to be.

You will have noticed how this thing called risk keeps cropping up. As Andrew would tell you, the concept of risk refers to something we expect to encounter at some time in the uncertain future, so no set of historical figures can be expected to forecast exactly what the future may hold. As we were saying earlier, we have to use our own judgement about the possible outcome of present and future events, and the likely extent of the risks we anticipate may be associated with these events. In this sense, the balance sheet has to be used as a springboard for questions, rather than as an answer to them.

Some basic concepts of the balance sheet

We took a brief glimpse at the end of the last chapter at the sort of information displayed in a balance sheet, and we saw that there were two possible versions of it. One version included a list of all of the company's assets—showing how all the company's money had been used—balanced off by a list of all its liabilities—showing where all the money came from. This version is called the 'grossed-up' balance sheet, because the total values of assets and liabilities are gross values. Also, of course, both of these total values are the same, which is one good reason why this statement is called a 'balance' sheet.

The second version is called the 'net' balance sheet, because the value of current liabilities is deducted from both 'sides' of the equation in order to restrict the items under the heading of liabilities to those which can be legitimately classified as capital employed. These, in turn, 'balance' with net assets, and this 'net' version is the one with which we shall generally be concerned in this volume.

You will recall that, at the end of the last chapter, we explained that a balance sheet shows us where the company's funds came from, and where they are invested, at a particular moment in time. There are two points to note here—the first being that, when we use the word 'invested' in this context, we are talking about how the money has been used. It could have been spent on fixed assets or on working capital, and, either way, any purchase could be regarded as a mini-investment in its own right.

The second point is rather more conceptual, but, nevertheless, absolutely fundamental to the discussion that we shall develop. A balance sheet is, in effect, a *snapshot* of the company's financial situation, taken *at a particular moment in time*. This point in time very often happens to be the 31 December, because so many companies find it convenient for their trading year to coincide with the calendar year, but there is nothing particularly magical or sacred about that date—it could, in fact, be any date.

Now let us think about snapshots for a moment. Imagine a photographer being asked to take one of the local football team. Almost invariably, he will arrange the players in two or three rows, standing along the back, and perhaps kneeling on one knee in the front row. There might be two goal keepers, and they will generally be found in the middle of the back row, while a couple of track-suited trainers will be standing proudly, with their arms folded, one at each end of the middle or back row—presumably to make sure that the rest of them don't fall over sideways. The empty stands in the background help to indicate to us that this is not their 'natural' position on the football pitch—these 'snapshots' are taken in this way because it is *conventional* for football teams to pose like this for that particular purpose, or on those particular occasions.

But are they *representative* occasions? Are the players likely to be lined up like that on a Saturday afternoon? Just imagine what would happen if they strung themselves out like a double row of tailor's dummies throughout the ninety minutes of a league match! Then we really would have empty football stands all the time! In other words, a conventional 'snapshot' should not necessarily be interpreted as representing a 'normal' situation.

The balance sheet is arranged in a conventional manner, too, and although it represents a legitimate picture of a company's financial situation at a particular moment in time, we have to remember that this may not necessarily be a *representative* moment in time, and that, consequently, the picture that we see may not necessarily be a representative picture. Care is therefore called for in its interpretation.

Construction of a balance sheet

In Figure 4.1, we illustrated a financial model, which showed cash coming into the business in the form of capital invested, and then being used—or being reinvested in turn by the company—on fixed assets and working capital. This information is exactly the same as we said we would expect to find in a balance sheet; so it should be readily possible to translate the details from one to the other.

In order to illustrate this, we have asked Andrew to let us have a look at Last Year's balance sheet for his latest venture, Andco Ltd.

Having done so well with the Andycab business, he was able to hand over the management of this to his wife, while he got together with a few friends of his in this enterprising manufacturing venture.

He certainly knew where to find the right sort of friends. Between them, they were able to raise no less than £800,000 of share capital, to which it was none too difficult to add a further £200,000 of loan capital, which they managed to negotiate at an interest rate of 10 per

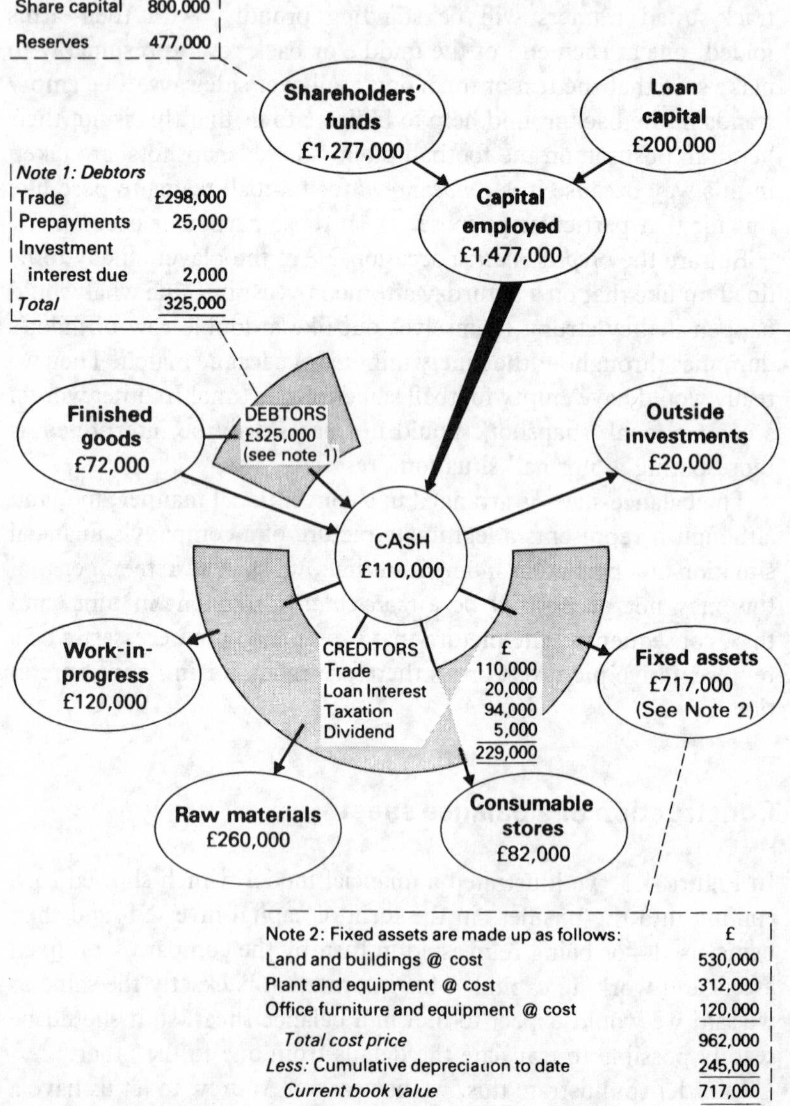

Fig 5.1 Andco Ltd financial model as at 31 December, Last Year

cent. We don't need to go into details about what they make at the moment, but there are whispers that they may have something new and quite exciting in the pipeline. Great things are evidently expected of the future, but getting any definite clues out of Andy about what this might be is just like asking him to give you the name of next year's Derby winner—he will only tell you afterwards, just in case he's wrong!

Figure 5.1 shows the financial model for the year just ended, while Figure 5.2 shows how this information would be translated into either a 'grossed-up' balance sheet, or a 'net' balance sheet. For the sake of convenience, we have constructed these balance sheet formats in the same basic sequence as the financial model—that is, with the liabilities at the top, followed by the assets at the bottom. This makes it easier to grasp the 'where the money came from/where it went to' concept, although we shall switch things round before we get to the end of the chapter.

For the time being, let's take the presentations in Figure 5.2 at their face value. Although the 'grossed up' and 'net' formats are different, and have different balancing totals, you will be able to see that the content is identical. The only difference between the two is the place where the current liabilities are shown—a significant difference which enables us to introduce some additional terms for subtotals and totals in the figures which all have their own particular meaning and uses, depending upon the sort of information you wish to obtain.

Some of these terms and headings do not appear in the financial model, because these are items which did not happen to apply to Andco Ltd last year. The values are consequently zero, and we shall not spend too much time on them, but it will nevertheless be useful to give them a mention in order that we can establish a reference back as and when this may be needed later on.

Reserves—the third source of capital

We discussed the difference between share capital and loan capital in Chapter 4, and, during that discussion of the various sources of capital from which a company can fund its operations, we also mentioned the term 'reserves'.

Reserves are effectively a third source of capital. It is admittedly rather a strange word to use (some people even consider it to be

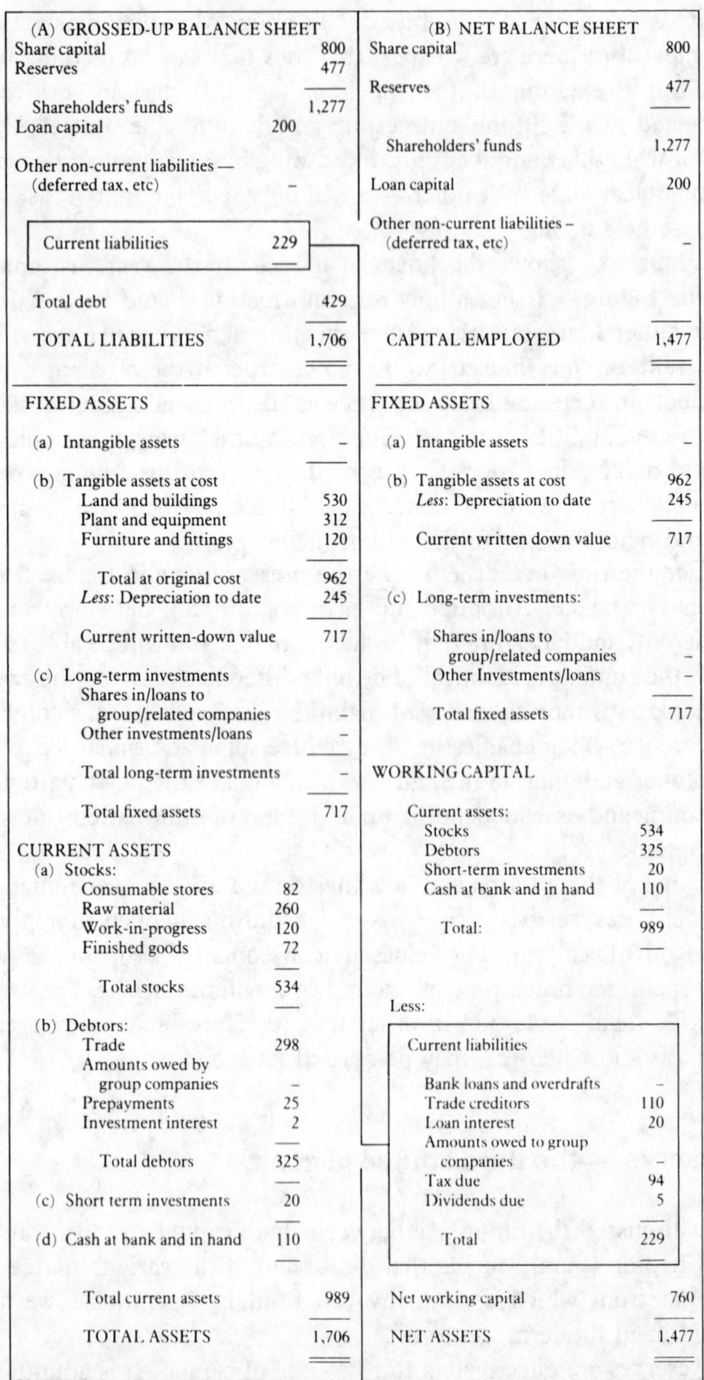

(A) GROSSED-UP BALANCE SHEET

Share capital		800
Reserves		477
Shareholders' funds		1,277
Loan capital	200	
Other non-current liabilities — (deferred tax, etc)	–	
Current liabilities	229	
Total debt		429
TOTAL LIABILITIES		1,706
FIXED ASSETS		
(a) Intangible assets		–
(b) Tangible assets at cost		
Land and buildings		530
Plant and equipment		312
Furniture and fittings		120
Total at original cost		962
Less: Depreciation to date		245
Current written-down value		717
(c) Long-term investments		
Shares in/loans to group/related companies		–
Other investments/loans		–
Total long-term investments		–
Total fixed assets		717
CURRENT ASSETS		
(a) Stocks:		
Consumable stores	82	
Raw material	260	
Work-in-progress	120	
Finished goods	72	
Total stocks	534	
(b) Debtors:		
Trade	298	
Amounts owed by group companies	–	
Prepayments	25	
Investment interest	2	
Total debtors	325	
(c) Short term investments	20	
(d) Cash at bank and in hand	110	
Total current assets		989
TOTAL ASSETS		1,706

(B) NET BALANCE SHEET

Share capital		800
Reserves		477
Shareholders' funds		1,277
Loan capital		200
Other non-current liabilities – (deferred tax, etc)		–
CAPITAL EMPLOYED		1,477
FIXED ASSETS		
(a) Intangible assets		–
(b) Tangible assets at cost		962
Less: Depreciation to date		245
Current written down value		717
(c) Long-term investments:		
Shares in/loans to group/related companies		–
Other Investments/loans		–
Total fixed assets		717
WORKING CAPITAL		
Current assets:		
Stocks	534	
Debtors	325	
Short-term investments	20	
Cash at bank and in hand	110	
Total:	989	
Less:		
Current liabilities		
Bank loans and overdrafts	–	
Trade creditors	110	
Loan interest	20	
Amounts owed to group companies	–	
Tax due	94	
Dividends due	5	
Total	229	
Net working capital		760
NET ASSETS		1,477

Fig 5.2 Andco Ltd balance sheet as at 31 December, Last Year

misleading) but its meaning in this context is *retained profits*. In other words, it is part of the trading profits that the shareholders have decided to put back into the business since it was originally founded, instead of taking it out in the form of dividends. Over the years during which Andrew's company has been trading, these reinvested profits have added up to the grand sum of £477,000.

This does not mean that the £477,000 has been locked up in the safe, though. As we can see, the total amount of actual cash on 31 December Last Year was only £110,000. It will, in fact, have been used in exactly the same way as any other capital—in the purchase of fixed assets, or in the working capital area of the business—so that profits put back into the business in the form of reserves are just as much a part of capital as the original money that was invested by the shareholders. It will have been the shareholders themselves, through their appointed directors, who decided how much of the trading profits should be 'reserved' in the business in this way, instead of being distributed to them in the form of dividends or as a 'return' on the money that they invested in the company. So it does, in reality, 'belong' to them, and is consequently combined in the balance sheet, together with share capital, in order to arrive at the total amount shown as shareholders' funds.

The total funds 'owed' by Andco Ltd to its shareholders on 31 December Last Year was therefore made up of the £800,000 that they invested in the company in the first place, plus the reinvested reserves of £477,000, making £1,277,000 in all. These figures can be transferred directly to both versions of the balance sheet in Figure 5.2.

The loan capital of £200,000 can also be transferred, and, since the company had no other long-term liabilities, such as deferred tax etc, there is nothing to enter on the balance sheet against this item. We don't need to go into the technicalities of deferred taxation at the moment, because we shall be dealing with the general subject of taxation in Chapter 7. So let's just say at this stage of our discussion that we do not include it as a current liability because it is not due to be paid within one year.

The total capital employed by Andco last year was consequently (1,277,000 + 200,000 =) £1,477,000, as shown quite clearly in the financial model, and this can be slotted in to the net balance sheet, where it is now one of the two main balancing totals.

The current liabilities' total of £229,000 is made up of £110,000 owed to trade creditors: £20,000 in interest to the lenders of the loan capital, £94,000 to the Inland Revenue in respect of Last Year's tax, and £5,000 to the shareholders in respect of the dividends that have been declared on Last Year's profits. These items are listed individually on the net balance sheet, where they are deducted in total to arrive at the figure for Net Working Capital. For our own convenience, and in order to save space, these items are included only in total in the 'grossed-up' version, where they form part of the company's 'total debt'.

This is another term that we don't need to pursue too far here. However, it is still quite useful to show, because we can see, by arranging the figures in this way, that the company's total liability of £1,706,000 was divided between the shareholders' funds of £1,277,000, and total debts to non-shareholders—or to the outside world—of £429,000. This sort of split is interesting if one is looking at the financial stability of a company, because, if its total debt ever gets to a point where it passes—or even approaches—the level of shareholders' funds, the question immediately arises as to who really owns the company—its shareholders or its creditors? And that's generally the point where the creditors invite the Receiver to start taking an interest!

Subclassifications of fixed assets

However, Andco were nowhere near that sort of situation, so we can now turn our attention to tabulating exactly how the company had used all of the £1,706,000 they obtained, by one means or another, from their shareholders and other creditors.

This is all set out in the lower half of the financial model, but we now have to be much more careful about the way in which the company's assets are classified. We have already explained how outside investments have to be split, if appropriate, between long-term and short-term investments. Long-term investments would not be readily convertible back into cash, and must consequently be regarded as 'fixed' assets, whereas short-term investments which *are* readily convertible back into cash can be regarded as 'current' assets. As it happens, Andco didn't have any long-term outside investments, but if they had had, it would have been necessary to distinguish between shares held in, or loans made to, companies with which they had particular trading association (called associated companies), and 'other' investments and loans.

Another subheading under 'fixed assets' with which Andco had no concern is 'intangible assets'. This term relates to something for which the company may have had to pay, but for which there are no physical or tangible things to see. It could cover such things as patents, trade marks, research and development costs which have yet to be written off, or amortized. 'Goodwill' is another type of intangible asset, and a rather complicated one. It is created when one company buys another—a subsidiary—and pays more for it than the figures shown in the balance sheet for its net tangible assets. These items all have to be accounted for as part of a company's assets, and, since they cannot be regarded as readily convertible to cash, there is no alternative but to regard them as 'fixed'.

The other subclassification under 'fixed assets' is the solid bricks-and-mortar stuff of land and buildings, plant and machinery, and office equipment, etc. All of these play their part in the conversion process that enables raw materials to be turned into finished products which can be sold and turned back again into cash. We have already been through that story before, but the point to note here is that Andco's Last Year valuation of £717,000 doesn't tell us the whole story, because it is also necessary to show on a balance sheet how much the assets originally cost, and how much has so far been depreciated—or charged against trading profits for the 'using up' of the assets concerned—in order to arrive at this 'net' value. Luckily, in Andrew's case, this information has all been set out in the financial model, so we are able to transfer everything that is needed over to the balance sheet.

Subclassifications of current assets

Next we come to current assets, which are subdivided between stocks, debtors, short-term investments and cash. Details of the various categories of stocks are contained in the peripheral boxes around the lower and left-hand sides of the financial model. These can be easily transferred over to the balance sheets, where we have included the analysed details in the grossed-up version, but only the total value in the 'net' version—again, solely in order to save space by avoiding unnecessary duplication.

Debtors are dealt with in the same way, and you will notice here that any debts owed by any associated companies need to be shown separately from trading debts. This is no problem for Andco, since they don't have any associated companies.

Then we come to short-term investments of a speculative nature, which is exactly where that £20,000 of Andco's fits, and, finally, we arrive at the cash which didn't actually happen to be doing anything special on 31 December Last Year, apart from sitting in the bank or the office safe waiting for its next call to action stations.

Andco's total current assets at that date were consequently made up of:

	£'000
Stocks	534
Debtors	325
Short-term investments	20
Cash at bank/in hand	110
Total:	989

This, together with fixed assets of £717,000, gives us the total assets of £1,706,000 that we need to balance off the total liabilities.

In the net balance sheet, we need to deduct the current liabilities from the current assets in order to get the value for net working capital. We have already looked at current liabilities, and know how the total value of £229,000 is made up. If we deduct this from the current assets total, we arrive at a working capital valuation of (989,000 – 229,000 =) £760,000. This figure, when added to the fixed assets total of £717,000, gives us a net assets valuation of (760,000 + 717,000 =) £1,477,000—which is exactly what we want in order to balance with the capital employed of £1,477,000. So we've made it on both counts!

Now that we have seen how the figures have been transposed from the financial model to the balance sheets, it is quite clear which presentation has the advantage. The model is useful enough in illustrating the overall conceptual scheme of things, but would be quite impractical for formal interpretation. The balance sheet, on the other hand, presents a concise, orderly summary of the origins and distribution of the company's capital.

Another way in which these figures could be presented is in the form of a simple equation—just like the one we used earlier to illustrate the way in which Andrew spent his Derby winnings on his new car. This is done in Figure 5.3.

This equation lists all of the Andco asset balances on the left of the equals sign, and demonstrates that the total of all these is equal to the total of the liabilities listed on the right. These totals are equivalent to those shown in the grossed-up balance sheet, since the current liabilities are included with all of the long-term liabilities on the right-hand side of the equation, instead of being netted off against the current assets on the left-hand side.

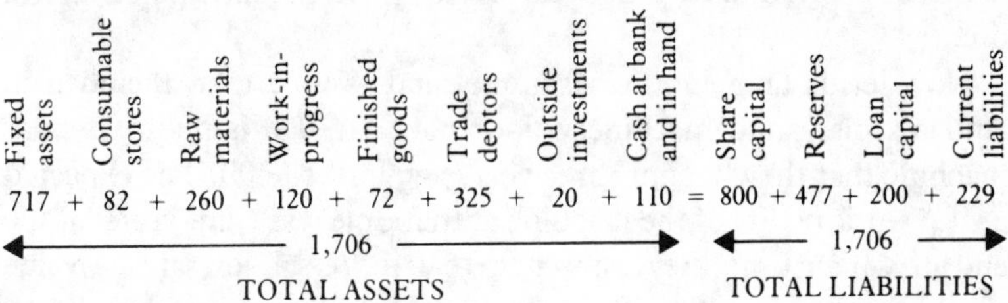

Fig 5.3 The balance sheet equation

Conventional valuation of fixed assets

We have already studied the various ways in which capital can get into a business, so let us now turn our attention to its assets, and think about how we should interpret the valuations that we are given, and the various conventions that are associated with them. We shall think a little about what we mean by 'value' later, but, for the time being, we shall be concentrating on historical cost. Our present terms of reference are still, after all, based upon the equation:

'Where the money went to = Where the money came from'

so we intend to avoid any diversions into the realms of 'How much is it worth?' at the present time.

The conventional way of arriving at the historical balance sheet valuation of fixed assets is to take the original purchase price, and deduct the accumulated depreciation to date. As we have already seen, depreciation is an accounting transaction which charges the 'usage cost' of the fixed assets against the trading operations of a period, and thus effectively reduces their 'value' in the balance sheet. It is important to stress once again that *no cash* is involved in this transaction, so that a charge against profits in respect of depreciation does not magically create funds out of which a company can go out and buy new machinery, or pay higher wages to its staff.

There are, as we indicated earlier, a number of different ways of calculating depreciation. Some methods charge more to earlier years than later, in order to compensate for increasing maintenance costs as the years go by, but the most general and readily-understood method is the 'straight-line' calculation that we used to spread the usage cost of Andrew's new car evenly over its anticipated useful life.

Now let us take another example, and assume that, included in Andco's plant and machinery figure of £312,000 is one particular machine that they bought three years ago for £18,000. The expected useful working life of the machine at that time was eight years, at the end of which time they estimated that its re-sale or salvage value would be about £2,000. The value at which this machine would be shown in the company's books at the end of its third year would be calculated as follows:

	£
Cost when new	18,000
Estimated salvage value	2,000
Net usage cost	16,000
Annual depreciation (over 8 years)	2,000
Balance sheet valuation at the end of Year 3:	
Cost when new	18,000
Less 3 years' depreciation @ £2,000	6,000
Written-down value at end of Year 3	12,000

This valuation is consequently based on a readily-understood convention, and can be taken to represent the 'book value' of the asset that remains to be 'used up' over the remainder of its life—assuming that it will continue in use, and that the business can fairly be regarded as 'a going concern' throughout this period.

Valuation of outside investments

These are very similar to fixed assets from the point of view of the way in which they are treated in the balance sheet. In other words, they are normally valued at cost, unless there is a subsequent change in their market value which is considered to be of long-term effect. Short-term fluctuations in value would be ignored.

In the case of our Andco example, we can see that provision has been made under 'Debtors' for investment interest of £2,000 which is due, but has not yet been received. Andrew tells us that this is a whole year's interest, which means that it is equivalent to a rate of 10 per cent on their outside investments of £20,000. This is the same rate of interest that they negotiated on their loan capital, although this does not necessarily mean that they originally borrowed more than they needed. You have to remember that they negotiated that loan a few years ago—apparently when they needed the extra money—and that they had to organize it on a long-term, fixed rate basis.

From the look of their reserves, they have obviously been making some pretty respectable profits since they started the business, and the cash balance of £110,000 at the end of the year seems to be rather high. One would imagine that they might have used some of this cash to increase their outside investments, although, from the sound of things, there is obviously something rather significant going on at the moment. There could well be a situation on the horizon that is about to involve the purchase of some new assets, so they may have decided to keep some of their ready cash resources immediately available for that.

The balance between the amount of cash held inside a company, compared with the amount invested outside is very much a 'value judgement', and, who knows, it could even be that, on 29 December, the amount of cash available inside the company could have been £30,000, and the value of outside investments £100,000. This is something that the balance sheet will not tell us.

Valuation of working capital

Working capital has already been defined as the things we mean to sell, or to convert into saleable goods or services. It is made up of current assets (the things of value that are moving back into cash) minus current liabilities (the things that are currently owed by the company to other people).

If we refer to Andco's balance sheet, we can see that 'Stocks' have been subdivided into four categories and that the valuation of each of them is based on different conventions. Under 'historical cost' conventions, consumable stores and raw materials would be valued at the lower of cost or realizable market value, while, under the recently-introduced current cost accounting guidelines, they would be shown at the lower of their *current* replacement cost or realizable value. The 'historical' market value, and the 'current' realizable value are obviously two different ways of saying the same thing, although there is a real difference between 'historical' cost and 'current replacement' cost. This is something about which we shall have quite a lot to say later on.

Work-in-progress (WIP) and finished goods would be shown at a cost which includes any expenditure that has been incurred during the normal course of business in bringing the product or service to its present location and condition. Such costs include all related production overheads, including depreciation, even though some of these may have accrued on a time basis. The emphasis here is on 'production' overheads, and the resulting valuation must in no case exceed net realizable value—it being understood, of course, that any such work-in-progress will eventually be transformed into a saleable finished product.

Debtors are valued at the value that we believe will be paid to us by the people who owe us the money. Andco had trade debtors of £298,000, for instance, although this does not necessarily mean that this is the total of the unpaid bills still owing to them. This might have been £305,000, but, if they felt that £7,000 of this was never likely to be paid, they would reduce the balance to £298,000 in their balance sheet, and write the £7,000 off against their profit for the year.

Cash and bank balances are the one area where absolute accuracy should be assured, because cash is a physical thing that can be actually counted and measured in value.

Trade creditors are simple enough to evaluate, because this figure represents the value of goods or services received but not yet paid for. It could still happen, however, that some goods or services that have been received may be under dispute regarding quality, so that the 'true' value of creditors may be slightly different from the total of suppliers' balances—in just the same way that potential bad debts may reduce the total debtors' balance.

Loan interest due to be paid will be a predetermined figure, and the amount of dividends payable will almost certainly be known by the time the balance sheet is prepared. So should the amount of tax due to the Inland Revenue.

Bank overdrafts, if any, would also be regarded as current liabilities. It is possible for a company to list both an overdraft and cash in hand in their balance sheet, so that if, for example, Andco had happened to have an overdraft of £50,000, and had shown this in the balance sheet, together with a 'cash' balance of £12,000, their actual overdrawn position would have been £38,000, with £12,000 still available.

A diagrammatic form of presentation

Most things can be looked at from several points of view—even balance sheets. We have already looked at a simple model representation, and at two 'normal formal' formats, but there has been a strong movement over recent years towards the production of employee reports, and the presentation of the financial statements of companies in illustrative chart form. This had led to a lot of very resourceful and imaginative creations—some of which have been excellent, and some of which have been downright awful. The trouble is that beauty is so often in the eye of the beholder, and the sort of presentation that rings a bell with one person might easily leave another stone cold. Quite a lot of companies go for pie charts, for example, or for diagrams of their own particular product dissected into small pieces to represent the relative proportions of various elements.

One such company is Matthew Grimble Ltd, so now would seem to be as good a time as any to introduce you to them. Matthew is another very good friend of ours, who set up his company of Matthew Grimble Ltd some five years ago to manufacture a range of new component products that he had just invented. These were aimed at completely revolutionizing the legendary widget market, and it was quite natural that these components should be named after their creator.

The 'grimbles' had arrived, and there is almost nothing for which they cannot be adapted or used—from Balaclava helmets to deep-sea mining gear, or from aeroplane elastic to wurgle-fasteners. You will soon be able to judge for yourself just how far this company has gone over its last—or its first—five years, after which we shall be taking a rather critical look at what the whole grimbling future appears to hold in store.

But that's still some way ahead—let's take a look at one of his

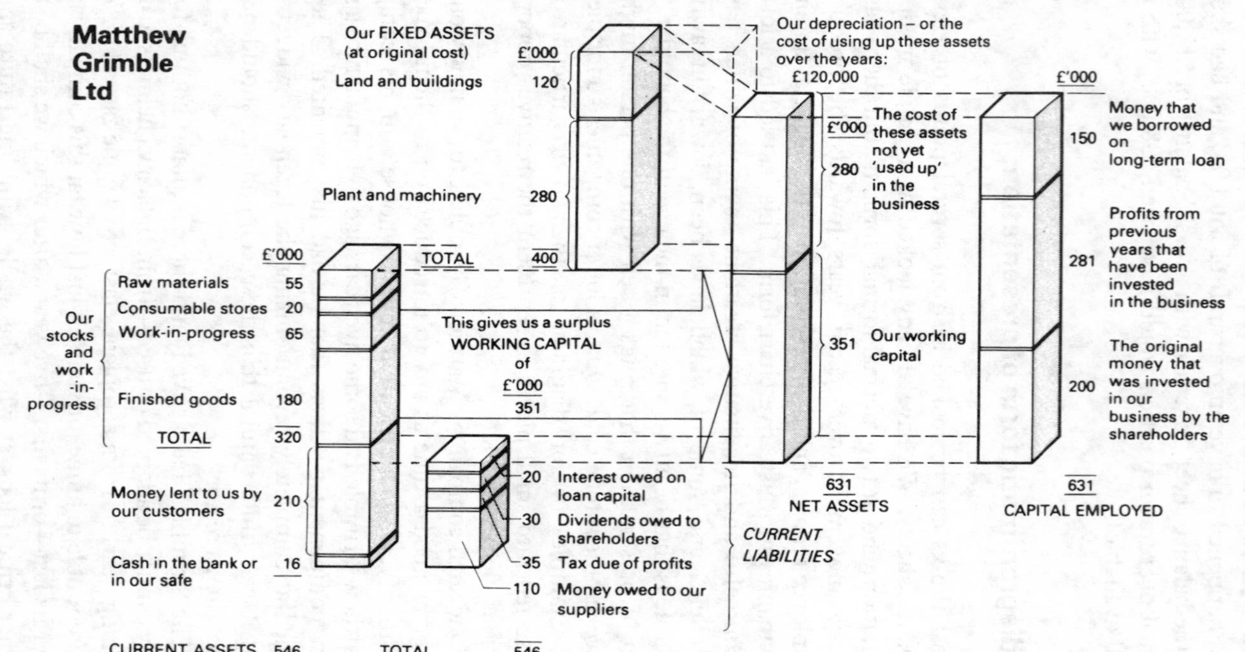
Our BALANCE SHEET. The 'Financial Snapshot' of Our Company, taken at 31st December, Year 5
This is how we used our money.... and .... This is where it came from
Matthew Grimble Ltd
Our FIXED ASSETS (at original cost)
£'000
Land and buildings 120
Plant and machinery 280
TOTAL 400
Our depreciation – or the cost of using up these assets over the years: £120,000
£'000
280 The cost of these assets not yet 'used up' in the business
351 Our working capital
631
NET ASSETS
£'000
150 Money that we borrowed on long-term loan
281 Profits from previous years that have been invested in the business
200 The original money that was invested in our business by the shareholders
631
CAPITAL EMPLOYED
Our stocks and work-in-progress
£'000
Raw materials 55
Consumable stores 20
Work-in-progress 65
Finished goods 180
TOTAL 320
Money lent to us by our customers 210
Cash in the bank or in our safe 16
CURRENT ASSETS 546
This gives us a surplus WORKING CAPITAL of £'000 351
20 Interest owed on loan capital
30 Dividends owed to shareholders
35 Tax due of profits
110 Money owed to our suppliers
CURRENT LIABILITIES
TOTAL 546

Fig 5.4 A diagrammatic view of the balance sheet for Matthew Grimble Ltd, as at the end of Year 5

£'000		Year 5
Fixed assets at cost:		
Land and buildings		
Plant and machinery		
Total cost		
Less: Depreciation to date		
Written-down book value		
Stocks:		
Consumable stores		
Raw materials		
Work-in-progress		
Finished goods		
Total stocks		
Trade debtors		
Cash/Bank		
Current assets		
Trade creditors		
Tax due		
Share dividends due		
Loan interest due		
Current liabilities		
NET WORKING CAPITAL		
NET ASSETS		
Share capital		
Reserves		
Shareholders' funds		
Loan capital		
CAPITAL EMPLOYED		

Fig 5.5 The balance sheet of Matthew Grimble Ltd as at the end of Year 5

balance sheets first. Matthew has been kind enough to lend us a copy of the Employees' Report that he produced for Year 5 of his company's trading operations, and we have reproduced the balance sheet representation in Figure 5.4.

You will see that he has headed his chart with 'This is how we used our Money . . . and . . . This is where it came from', thus following the general principle established in our Transaction Equation of Figure 5.3, in which the assets are shown on the left, and the liabilities on the right. He has then illustrated his evaluation of working capital by netting off the current liabilities against the current assets, and this is then built up into net assets by adding in the current book value of the fixed assets. The original analysed purchase cost of the fixed assets is shown, together with the cumulative amount by which they have been depreciated, and we can also see the way in which the net assets total corresponds with that of capital employed. This probably looks rather prettier than the formal presentations, but it is still, after all, only another snapshot taken at a particular moment in time.

Figure 5.5 provides you with the opportunity to transpose the figures from his diagram onto the more conventional (net) balance sheet format that we have been discussing during the course of this chapter. This time—as we warned at the beginning of this discussion—we have switched the assets and the liabilities around, so that your transposition of the numbers from Matthew's diagram will follow more naturally than they would if we had retained the sequence that we used in Figure 5.2.

There are obviously a number of ways in which it would be possible to present this same information, and, up to a few years ago, it would not have mattered very much which way round we wanted to present a balance sheet. Indeed, the 'old' way actually used to be to show the liabilities on the left, and the assets on the right, although we don't need to waste time going into that now! The fact is that, in 1978, the EEC issued its 'Fourth Directive', and this stipulated quite precisely what information had to be detailed in published company accounts, and how it was to be displayed. Member countries were asked to legislate for these requirements to be incorporated into Company Law, and the UK Companies Act of 1981 did just that. As we shall see later on (in Chapter 16), one of the stipulations is that the balance sheet should be presented with the assets at the top, followed by the liabilities at the bottom—so this is the format that we shall stay with from now on.

Summary

We have now covered most of the main points connected with the balance sheet, and looked at some of the conventions associated with the two main formats in which it can be presented—as well as one or two diagrammatic illustrations. The historical conventions of valuation have also been mentioned, and we have picked up a number of new terms, so this is the point where we ought to pause in order to bring these definitions together.

- *Balance sheet* A financial statement which will tell us where the company's money is invested, and where it came from, so that we can assess for ourselves what we consider the risk to be. It is a 'snapshot' of the financial situation taken at a (not necessarily representative) moment in time. A balance sheet can be prepared at any time, but one will always be prepared to represent the financial situation as at midnight on the final day of each financial year.
- *Reserves* Profit which has been retained, or reinvested in the business. It is just as much a part of the company's capital as the original money invested by the shareholders, or placed at their disposal by the lenders of the loan capital.
- *Deferred tax* A long-term tax liability, the payment of which is not expected to become due during the next full year. This is defined more fully in Chapter 7.
- *Total debt* The total of all of a company's liabilities to the 'outside world': the lenders of its loan capital, other long-term liabilities (such as deferred tax), and its current liabilities. Equivalent in value to total liabilities minus shareholders' funds.
- *Intangible assets* Non-physical things, such as goodwill, patents, trade marks, and unamortized research and development costs, which are regarded as having some trading value to a company. These items all have to be accounted for as part of a company's assets, and, since they cannot be regarded as readily convertible into cash, there is no alternative but to regard them as 'fixed'.
- *Goodwill* The difference between the price paid for the acquisition of a company as a 'going concern', and the total value of its net tangible assets, as shown in its balance sheet.

6 The profit and loss statement

Introduction

There is a saying that can often be heard quoted around the Stock Exchange: 'No one was ever ruined by making a profit'. 'Profit' is one of those words that make most people sit up on the edge of their chairs and take notice. They may not be too keen on trying to define it, but they would have absolutely no doubt that they would want to be first in the queue when it was being handed around. The dictionary gets away with it quite nicely in five words by defining profit as 'excess of returns over expenditure', but—even if this may be quite true—we feel that we should take a rather closer look at it.

As you might imagine by now, Andrew Coe is a person who has some very definite ideas on this sort of subject. We were talking to him once about the money that he put on those horses, and asked him what happened to it. As usual, he hit the nail right on the head, and said that it 'grew', because, on that particular Derby Day, his selections all won. He got his stake money back, plus his winnings—or his profit—of £5,700, whereas, if they had lost, he would have lost his stake money, and his cash balance would have shrunk by that amount.

All businesses do the same sort of thing with their money: they invest their funds continually in fixed assets, raw materials, labour and overheads, and hope that their returns are going to exceed their expenditure, or that their resources are going to grow instead of shrink over time. The time span over which they will want to measure this growth will be longer than Andrew's because he only had to wait a couple of hours or so for the results of his races, but the principle is the same.

So we can define profit and loss as 'The measurement of growth or shrinkage arising out of the operational activities of a business for whatever period of time we choose'. Businesses can also 'grow' as a result of takeovers, or the issue of more share capital, and so on, but items such as these will not appear in the profit and loss statement, so it is important to remember the qualification about 'trading operations' when one thinks about 'profit' in terms of 'growth'.

The company's history book

We described the balance sheet as a snapshot of a business taken at a particular moment in time. In a similar sort of way, the profit and loss statement is rather like a history book which shows how the business has grown or shrunk over a period of time. It is also similar to the balance sheet in that it is normally presented in accordance with certain established conventions, and Figure 6.1 shows the sort of presentation that you would normally expect to find. Once again, we can look to Andco's figures for Last Year in order to illustrate the points which need to be made.

We have once again included a couple of items which do not apply directly to Andco in order to make our list of definitions rather more comprehensive without complicating the figures too much. Most of these figures are self-explanatory, although it will do no harm to run through them briefly.

Sales

This is the revenue that has been earned from the trading activities of the company, and would normally be net of any returns, discounts allowed, or commission paid to agents etc. It must not be confused with cash coming in, though, because, as we have seen, the debtors' 'barrier' will intercept the flow of money coming into the business, and 'sales' are therefore the net invoiced value of the goods supplied or services rendered during a trading period.

Cost of sales

The cost at which goods sold are valued will be the cost at which they are priced in the stock records, and at which they appear in the balance sheet. Andco were using the historic-cost conventions at the time these accounts were prepared, which means that both stocks

£'000		*Last Year*
Sales turnover		1,770
Less: Cost of sales		1,358
Gross profit/(loss)		412
Selling, distribution, and administration costs	277	
Depreciation—(non-production)	10	
Total fixed costs		287
Operating profit/(loss)		125
Interest received from short-term outside investments		2
Profit before interest and tax		127
Interest payable on loan capital		20
Profit before tax		107
Tax on operational activities		94
Profit after tax		13
Extraordinary income/(expenses)	:	
Tax on extraordinary items	:	
Net profit/(loss) on extraordinary items	:	
Share dividends		5
Retained profit		8

Fig 6.1 Andco's profit and loss statement for Last Year

and stock movements were based on 'average actual' rates—or on the prices actually paid for the materials when they were purchased, and on the costs actually incurred during their production.

Having explained that the value of sales is not necessarily the same as the value of the cash received from customers over the same span of time, we now have to face the fact that the cost of sales is not necessarily the same as the cost of production and this time the answer is to be found in any variations that there may be between the values of the opening and closing stocks. Last year's situation at Andco Ltd is a good case in point, because their closing stock balances were £218,000 less than their opening balances, as shown in Figure 6.2, which means that their cost of production must have

£'000	*Opening stock*	*Closing stock**
Consumable stores	82	82
Raw materials	120	260
Work-in-progress	123	120
Finished goods	427	72
Total	752	534
Net decrease in stock	:	218

**Note:* The closing stock figures can be checked against Last Year's balance sheet in Figure 5.2

Fig 6.2 Andco's opening and closing stock balances for Last Year

been £218,000 *less* than their cost of sales. If their stock values had *increased* over the year, then their cost of production would have been *more* than their cost of sales.

Stock movements and cost of goods sold schedule

A useful way of finding out what went on 'on the inside' is to prepare a stock movements and cost of goods sold schedule, as we have done in Figure 6.3. This schedule traces the movement of stocks progressively through from consumable and raw materials, via work-in-progress to finished goods, so that we can see how much Andco spent on materials, labour and production costs—including the amount of depreciation charged to the production activities of the business. The opening and closing stock balances that we have just listed can also be picked out, and we can see how and why the variations arose.

This presentation also enables us to summarize the cost of production by listing the outgoing expenses—the purchases of consumable and raw materials, and the cost of labour and overheads—and to link this to the cost of sales via the variations in stock levels, as we have demonstrated in Figure 6.4.

Gross profit/(loss)

This is the difference between sales revenue and the cost of sales, but has to have the time-based (or 'period') costs deducted before we can see by how much the business has grown or shrunk during the period under review.

£'000		Last Year
(a) CONSUMABLE STORES		
Opening stock		82
Purchases		57
Total available		139
Less: Closing stock		82
Usages (Transfers to work-in-progress)		57
(b) RAW MATERIALS		
Opening stock		120
Purchases		589
Total available		709
Less: Closing stock		260
Usages (Transfers to work-in-progress)		449
(c) WORK-IN-PROGRESS		
Direct labour		245
Production overheads:		
Indirect labour	95	
Power and light	70	
Depreciation	64	
Rates and insurance	20	
Consumable stores (b/d)	57	
Total:		306
Charges during year (Activity)		1,000
Opening stock		123
Total available		1,123
Less: Closing stock		120
Cost of goods manufactured		1,003
(d) FINISHED GOODS		
Opening stock		427
Total available		1,430
Less: Closing stock		72
Cost of goods sold		1,358

Fig 6.3 Stock movements and cost of goods sold schedule

£'000	Last Year
Purchases: Consumable stores	57
Raw materials	589
Direct production labour	245
Production overheads	249
Total cost of production ('Activity') during year	1,140
Plus: Net decrease in stock (Fig. 6.2)	218
Cost of goods sold during year	1,358

Fig 6.4 Reconciliation between Andco's cost of production and cost of goods sold

Selling, distribution and administration costs

These would include all of the selling, distribution and administration overheads, such as the wages and salaries of these functional areas, the advertising and promotional expenses, telephone, postage, rent, rates and insurance, travel, office stationery etc.

Depreciation

In this particular example, we have already included production-related depreciation charges in the cost of production, so the only amount to be charged separately under the business administration costs will be the balance applicable to this function.

Operating profit/(loss)

This is the profit or loss arising out of the purely operational activities of the business, as distinct from any 'non-operational' income or expenditure which may also be incurred or received. The interest that Andco received on their outside investments must consequently be shown independently from their sales revenue.

Profit before interest and tax

This is a very significant profit figure—out of the several 'levels' of profit that are listed in the profit and loss statement—since it can be interpreted as the profit arising out of the actual trading operations of the 'business'. The principle here is that the business, as a separate trading entity, is not concerned with its capital structure as such. This is the responsibility of its shareholders and its loan-lenders: its measure of performance is the level of profit that it achieves *before* the deduction of any financing costs (such as loan interest), and taxation.

There are three main measures that are based on this level of profit: 'profitability', 'return on capital employed' and 'profit margin'. It is not our intention to jump ahead and delve too deeply into the implications of these ratios right now, because we shall be discussing management information ratios in some detail in Chapter 12. However, now that the subject has been raised, let us just say here that 'profitability' in this context is measured by relating Profit Before Interest and Tax (P.B.I.T.) to total assets, in order to assess the amount of profit that has been generated out of each pound invested in the total assets of the company. Similarly, the return on capital employed is measured by relating P.B.I.T. to capital employed, in order to find the amount of profit generated by each pound invested in its capital employed, and the profit margin relates P.B.I.T. to sales revenue, in order to assess how much profit has been generated out of each pound of sales revenue achieved.

Loan interest

Here we have the financing costs which have to be deducted from the company's operational profit, in order to arrive at the amount of profit before tax attributable to its shareholders.

Profit before tax (net profit)

This is the level of profit generated by the business after all financing costs have been deducted, so that we are now looking at its performance from the 'outside'—or from the point of view of the shareholders and loan-lenders.

Tax on 'ordinary' activities

This one speaks for itself, although it probably seems strange—not to say downright unfair—to see that, in our example, Andco had no less than £94,000 deducted last year in respect of tax, out of a net profit of £107,000. There happens to be a very good reason for this, which we promise to explain in our next chapter, but, for the time being, let us just accept that these figures are indeed correct.

Profit after tax

This is the net profit left to the shareholders after all operational and financing costs, plus the taxation associated with the company's routine trading activities, have been deducted. They could, if they wished, distribute the whole of this amount out among themselves, or they could hold some back for reinvestment in the company as reserves.

Extraordinary items of income and expense

There may sometimes be occasions when a company incurs some expense, or receives some income, which has no direct relevance to the current trading year. Perhaps the previous year's stock valuation has since proved to be far too high as a result of unexpected obsolescence, or some expense which had previously been capitalized has been found to have no positive value, and consequently needs to be written off completely, rather than being depreciated over a number of years, or perhaps the company has disposed of some of its fixed assets at a handsome profit. None of these events would come under the heading of normal trading activities, but must nevertheless be shown in the company's profit and loss statement, so the place to show them would be as Extraordianry Items.

Dividends

This is the share of the profit after tax that the shareholders, on the advice of their Board of Directors, decide to take out of the business as a return on their investment in the company. In Andco's case, this only amounted to £5,000 Last Year, or 0.6 per cent on their original investment of £800,000. All in all, they don't seem to have had too much to get excited about, and it's a good job that Andrew has so much confidence in these new expansion plans of his. We can only hope that his confidence is fully justified.

This return of 0.6 per cent must not be confused with the Return on Capital Employed (ROCE) that is so often used as a measure of a company's performance. That relates the profit figure *before* the deduction of loan interest and tax—the 'operational profit of the business' that we have just mentioned—to its total capital employed, whereas we are now looking at the relationship between the dividends actually paid out to the shareholders, and the nominal value of their original share capital.

Retained profit

This is the amount that is left by the shareholders for reinvestment in the business after they have taken out the dividends to which they feel reasonably entitled. Andco's retained profit of £8,000 last year will be included in the figure of £477,000 in the balance sheet (Figure 5.2) under Reserves.

It may be useful here to reiterate that 'Reserves' is not necessarily represented by cash in a bank vault. Money is continually flowing through a business, and can be used for investment either within the fixed assets or the working capital areas inside the company—or in another business outside the company if preferred. The retained profit figure in the profit and loss statement is a measure of the net growth or shrinkage that has taken place as a result of the trading operations of the business throughout the trading period, after all the revenues and expenses that are recorded above it have been taken into account.

At the end of the trading period, this amount will be transferred to Reserves, so it follows from this that the profit and loss statement could be regarded as an analysis of all the movements which have taken place within the 'Reserves' portion of the shareholders' funds between the successive moments at which the balance sheet 'snapshots' were taken. If a profit is made, it should consequently be regarded as an additional 'liability' that the company owes to its shareholders, whereas a loss would serve to reduce this liability.

Bias in the profit and loss statement

We have defined profit and loss as 'the measurement of growth or shrinkage in a business arising out of its trading activities over a period of time', and we have also seen that there are two main areas in a business in which money can be invested: namely fixed assets or working capital.

Working capital is the area in which we are mainly interested, because this is the area through which the business is hoping to grow. It is quite true that we could possibly make a profit by selling some of our assets, and that, if we did, this profit would have to be recorded in the profit and loss statement as an extraordinary income, but we are not in business to sell off our fixed assets. We need these to convert the items in the working capital 'money-go-round' back into cash, and it is consequently the working capital area upon which our interests are mainly focused. To this extent, one could argue that the presentation of the profit and loss statement will be biased towards that area.

Profit and loss period

The normal period over which the growth or shrinkage that has arisen out of the trading activities of a business is measured is one year, partly because company law and Inland Revenue requirements are such that accounts have to be prepared on an annual basis. That would obviously be a good enough reason in itself, but it is also convenient in most business situations, because a year is an appropriate period to apply in order to smooth out the seasonal peaks and troughs of the normal annual trading cycle.

Profit and loss statements for shorter periods, such as one month, are often prepared for internal management control purposes, but these do not generally reflect a fully representative trading period, and managers should be aware that these should only be regarded as progress reports, and that they may not necessarily be indicative of the final year's figures—in much the same way that the scores for the first hole are not necessarily indicative of the outcome of a round of golf. The general message is that, the shorter the period, the more violent the fluctuations may appear, and this could be even more evident if a short period is isolated out of the middle of a long-term project, such as a research and development programme, for example.

The difference between profit and cash

We have already discussed how growth (or profit) in business is achieved by putting cash to work in those areas where it can earn the highest rate of return. The profit after tax figure shown in the profit and loss statement is what is left after all expenses *for a period* have been deducted from all receipts or revenues. It is important here to emphasize 'for a period', because sales are taken as being the realizable revenue from goods despatched to customers during the period—whether or not the cash payment for them has yet been received. Similarly, all goods received are taken into account as purchases, or expenses, whether or not the goods or services involved have yet been paid for by the end of the period. Debtors and creditors consequently affect a company's *cash* balance, but not their *profit*, so that profit and cash need not necessarily be synonymous.

We have also just demonstrated that the cost of sales is not necessarily the same as the cost of production. It is the cost of *sales* that is charged against the trading revenue for the period, not the cost of *production*, which is the total of all the costs incurred in production during the period.

We can go back to our Andco example to demonstrate this:

	£'000
Opening stock as at 1 January Last Year	752
Cost of production (Fig. 6.4)	1,140
Total available	1,892
Less: Cost of goods sold (Fig. 6.1)	1,358
Closing stock as at 31 December (Fig. 6.2)	534

This shows us that, although the actual cost of production for the year was £1,140,000, Andco were able to charge £1,358,000 against their sales revenue for the period, because they had run down their stocks by the difference of £218,000. In this case, cash is affected by the outflow of £1,140,000—give or take any difference that there might have been between their opening and closing creditors' balances—whereas profit is affected by the charge of £1,358,000.

The fallibility of judgement

During our discussion of the balance sheet, we spent some time talking about the different bases of valuation that are commonly used for the various classifications of assets. Under the historical-cost conventions that we have been mainly using so far, these generally amounted to a question of purchase price, less the deduction of any 'usage costs' by which the fixed assets may have been depreciated to the date of the balance sheet.

We have already indicated that these valuations may be open to some degree of error, and we shall have more to say about that later when we get around to the subject of current cost accounting, but two good reasons why the figures could be slightly less than 'accurate' are the judgements upon which the valuations are based. On the one hand, there is the estimated scrap or salvage value that should be netted off against the original purchase price in order to arrive at the net usage cost of the asset, and, on the other hand, there is the anticipated number of years' useful working life over which this cost should be amortized.

If either of these judgements is wrong, then the amount of depreciation charged against the trading operations for the period will be wrong, and, if that is wrong, then the resulting profit figures will be wrong. And then, if the profit figures are wrong, the dividends actually paid to the shareholders could also be 'wrong' to the extent that perhaps the dividend could have been more—or possibly should never have been paid at all—and those performance ratios that we mentioned just now will also be inaccurate.

And, talking about accuracy, how 'accurate' are the stock valuations recorded in the balance sheet? Are we absolutely sure that all the stock quantities were counted correctly, and that they were realistically valued? Could there have been any obsolete stock included at full value which should have been reduced, or even written off altogether? When it really comes down to it, the figures that we read in the balance sheet and the profit and loss statement can only be as accurate as the judgement of the people who compiled the basic information and bases of valuation in the first place.

Those people were not all accountants. They couldn't have been, because the knowledge and expertise of the Production Manager, the Chief Engineer, Warehouse Manager, and the Sales Manager would all have been required in order to arrive at the valuations. So our Accountant of Many Parts now has another role to play—that of an interpreter who has to bring together the knowledge and judgement of his fellow managers, and to translate all this into the common language of the financial statements. But it is the responsibility of the whole management team to ensure that the judgements upon which these statements are based are as realistic as possible in the circumstances that prevail, in order that the interpretations that are later made of the resulting figures are not misleading. It is the old story of 'garbage in/garbage out'—with everyone carrying the can!

DANGER!—Misinterpretation

Before we conclude these notes on the profit and loss statement, we should also consider what other limitations it may have. Look at it not so much from the point of view of what you can see, but think also of what you can't see—rather like trying to visualize the other side of the moon. For example, the main elements of Andco's profit and loss statement were:

	£'000
Sales	1,770
Less: Cost of sales	1,358
Gross profit	412
Fixed costs (including interest paid and received)	305
Net profit before tax	107
Taxation	94
Profit after tax	13

Let us go through this summary one point at a time:

1 The profit before tax of £107,000 represents a margin of (107/1,770 =) 6.0 per cent of sales. This doesn't seem to be too good, although we haven't been told what Andco make, so we can't be too sure about this.
2 We can't see from the profit and loss statement alone what the profit after tax of £13,000 represents in terms of a return on investment, because this statement does not tell us how much capital is invested in the business. If this had been £50,000, the rate of return would have been 26 per cent, which seems quite reasonable, but we have to refer to the balance sheet to find that, in fact, the share capital was £800,000. The rate of return on this original investment was only about 1.6 per cent. Not quite so impressive!
3 These figures give us no comparison with previous years, and we would need to look at those figures in order to identify a trend.

4 Nothing is revealed about how the company's money has been spent, or what future commitments may still be outstanding. We have admittedly heard whispers about some exciting new expansion plans that Andrew has in mind, but that is 'inside information' to which casual observers would not have access.

These points will illustrate that it is impossible to use the profit and loss statement as the sole source of financial information about a company, because the picture cannot be completed without also making reference to the balance sheet.

A graphical presentation

We closed Chapter 5 with a diagrammatic presentation of Matthew Grimble's balance sheet for Year 5, which he allowed us to reproduce from his Employees' Report. This report was quite a comprehensive document, in which he also represented his stock movements and cost of goods sold schedule and profit and loss statement in a similar sort of form. These are reproduced in Figures 6.5 and 6.7, and blank versions of the more conventional formats are given in Figures 6.6 and 6.8, so that you can once again transpose the information for yourself.

Summary

We have defined the profit and loss statement as a sort of history book which shows us the extent to which the operational activities of a business have caused it to grow or shrink over a period of time—as distinct from the balance sheet, which provides a 'snapshot' of the business taken at a particular point or moment in time.

We have examined each of the main headings that normally appear in a profit and loss statement, and demonstrated via a stock movements schedule that the outgoing costs of production are not necessarily the same as the cost of goods sold, and that profit is not necessarily synonymous with cash.

The period of measurement of a published profit and loss statement is normally one year, although these statements are often prepared for much shorter periods for the purposes of internal management control. The area of the business in which we are most

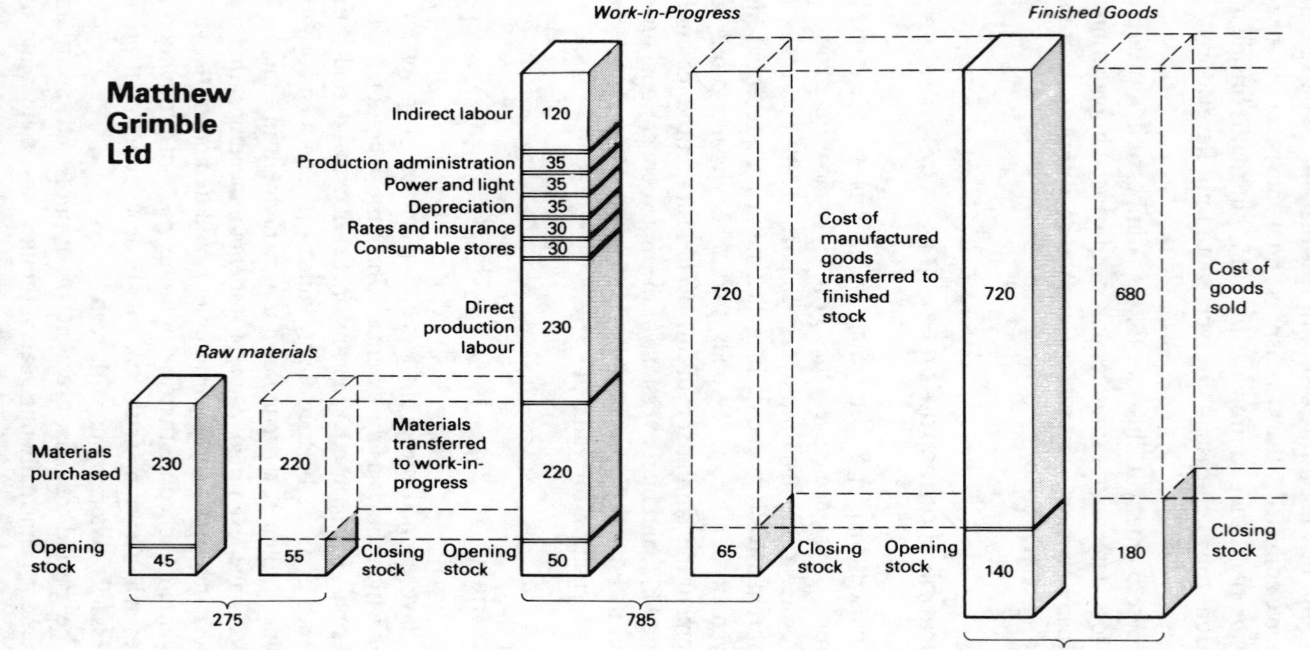

Fig 6.5 The diagrammatic version of Matthew Grimble's stock movements and cost of goods sold schedule for Year 5

	(£'000) Year 5
(a) Consumable stores	
Opening stock	15
Purchases	35
Total available	
Less: Closing stock	
Usages (to W.I.P.)	
(b) Raw materials	
Opening stock	
Purchases	
Total available	
Less: Closing stock	
Usages (to W.I.P.)	
(c) Work-in-progress	
Direct labour	
Overheads:	
Indirect labour	
Production administration	
Power and light	
Depreciation	
Rates and insurance	
Consumable stores	
Total	
Charges during year ('Activity')	
Opening stock b/fd	
Total available	
Less: Closing stock c/fd	
COST OF GOODS MANUFACTURED	
(d) Finished goods	
Opening stock b/fd	
Total available	
Less: Closing stock c/fd	
COST OF GOODS SOLD	

Fig 6.6 Matthew Grimble's stock movements and cost of goods sold schedule for Year 5

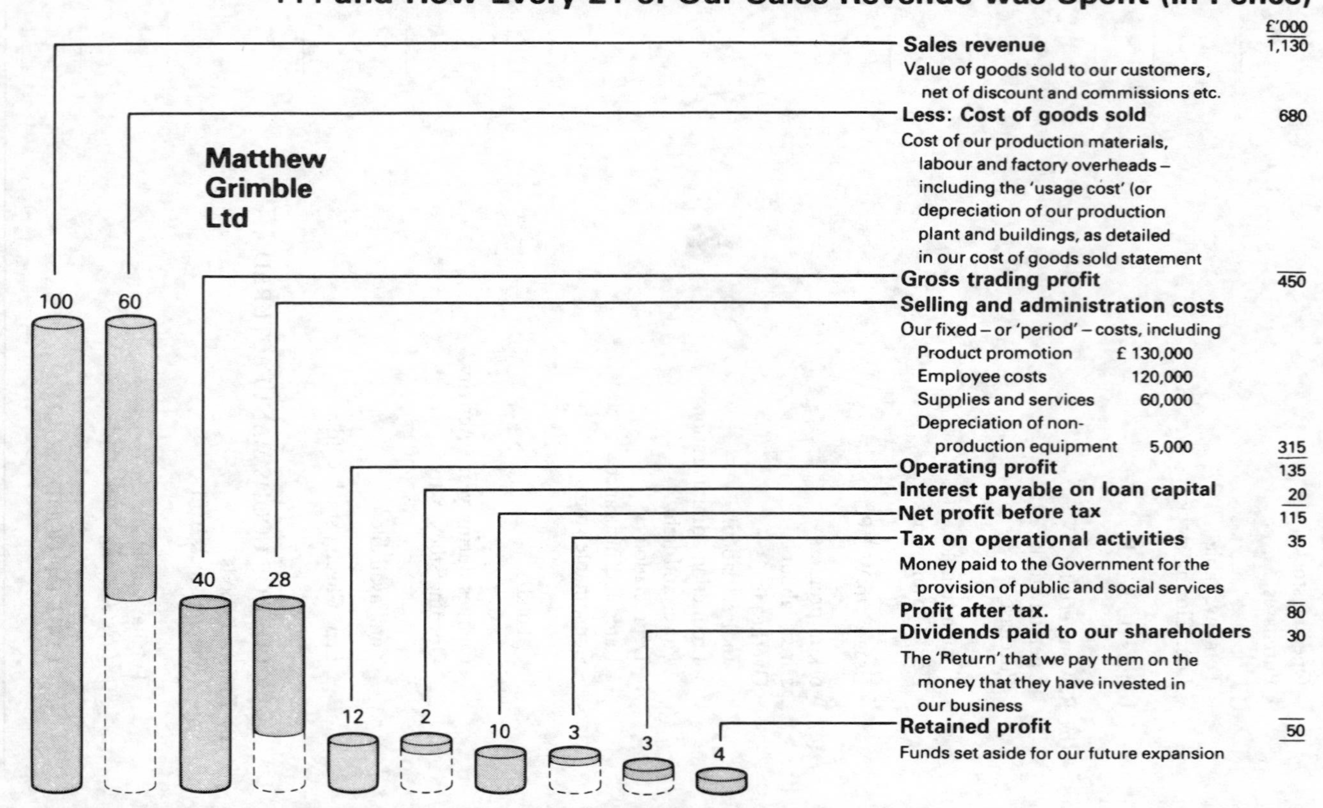
Our profit and loss statement for year 5 . . .
. . . and How Every £1 of Our Sales Revenue was Spent (in Pence)
Matthew Grimble Ltd
£'000
Sales revenue 1,130
Value of goods sold to our customers, net of discount and commissions etc.
Less: Cost of goods sold 680
Cost of our production materials, labour and factory overheads – including the 'usage cost' (or depreciation of our production plant and buildings, as detailed in our cost of goods sold statement
Gross trading profit 450
Selling and administration costs
Our fixed – or 'period' – costs, including
Product promotion £ 130,000
Employee costs 120,000
Supplies and services 60,000
Depreciation of non-production equipment 5,000
315
Operating profit 135
Interest payable on loan capital 20
Net profit before tax 115
Tax on operational activities 35
Money paid to the Government for the provision of public and social services
Profit after tax. 80
Dividends paid to our shareholders 30
The 'Return' that we pay them on the money that they have invested in our business
Retained profit 50
Funds set aside for our future expansion
100
60
40
28
12
2
10
3
3
4

(£'000) Year 5	
Sales	
Less: Cost of goods sold	
Gross trading profit	
Product promotion	
Selling and administration	
Employee costs	
Third party costs	
Depreciation (non-production)	
Total fixed costs	
Operating profit/(loss) before interest and tax	
Interest payable on loan capital	
NET PROFIT BEFORE TAX	
Taxation	
Profit after tax	
Share dividends	
RETAINED PROFIT	

Fig 6.8 Matthew Grimble's profit and loss statement for Year 5

interested is the working capital area, since this is the operational area of the business that has the greatest influence on its growth or shrinkage over time. To this extent, therefore, we can claim that the profit and loss statement is biased towards this area.

It has to be admitted that some of the figures cannot be interpreted as being strictly precise. This is particularly true of depreciation, which (as we have illustrated) is generally split between production-related and 'other' usage costs. This is because their evaluation depends upon so many facets of judgement by, in some cases, so many different people, and any one or more of these judgements could be subject to error or subsequently changing circumstances. There are also a number of very important things that the profit and loss statement does *not* tell you, and reference must also be made to the balance sheet in order to obtain a clear perspective of a company's affairs.

The profit and loss statement can be regarded as an analysis of all the movements that take place within the reserves portion of the shareholders' funds between the successive moments in time at which the balance sheet 'snapshots' are taken, so that any profit made will increase the company's liability to its shareholders by a corresponding amount, while any loss will have the opposite effect.

The terms and definitions which have been introduced during the course of this chapter are summarized below:

- *Profit and loss* The measurement of growth or shrinkage arising out of the operational activities of a business for whatever period of time we choose.
- *Sales revenue* The revenue that has been earned from the trading activities of the business. It must not be confused with cash coming into the business, because this will be interrupted by the 'debtors barrier'.
- *Cost of sales* The cost to the company of all goods or services sold during a trading period. It is not necessarily the same as the cost of production, since a business may manufacture more, or less, in a period than it actually sells.
- *Cost of production* The outgoing costs of producing goods or services for sale during a trading period. This is not necessarily the same as the cost of goods sold (or cost of sales) since the company may manufacture more, or less, in a period than it actually sells.
- *Gross profit/(loss)* The difference between sales revenue and the cost of goods sold, before the deduction of any time-based costs, such as selling, distribution, administration, research and development, etc.
- *Operating profit/(loss)* Profit (or loss) arising out of the purely operational activities of a business, but excluding any non-operational expenditure or income, such as investment or loan interest, they may incur or receive.
- *Profit before interest and tax* The profit arising out of the operational activities of a business, which, as a separate entity, is not concerned with its capital structure. This is the 'level' that is used to measure the company's profitability, return on capital employed, and profit margin.

- *Profit before tax* Net profit (or loss) arising out of the trading operations of a business, *before* the deduction of tax, but *following* the deduction of all expenses, including any non-operational finance costs, such as loan interest etc., which may be involved.
- *Profit after tax* Net profit attributable to the shareholders of a company, after all operational, non-operational and finance costs, and taxation have been deducted. This is the amount that is left for allocation between the amount of dividends paid to the shareholders, and the amount of profit retained in the business as reserves.
- *Dividends* The amount of profit distributed to shareholders in proportion to the number of shares that they hold in the business.
- *Retained profit* The amount of profit held back for reinvestment in the business by the shareholders as reserves.

7 Profit, taxation and interest

The need for profit

Profit, as we have defined it, is the measure of growth arising out of the operational activities of a business over a period of time. We have looked at it from more than one point of view: we started off by imagining that we had been lucky enough to inherit £30,000, and considered how we might select a place for investing the money. And then, of course, we have heard all about Andrew's Derby Day bet—several times! Thanks partly to a horse called Pontin Lad, who started it all, he was able to win enough money to invest in a car with which he could start up a taxi business. And finally, in our previous chapter, we looked at two profit and loss statements relating to his more recent venture of Andco Ltd.

All these examples had one thing in common: the motivation of maximizing the return that could be obtained on the initial investment. This return, or excess of revenue over expenses, is called profit, and is an absolutely essential ingredient to the survival of any person, business or community.

For instance, it is essential for each of us to earn or receive more wages, salaries or pension than the total amount of money that we spend out on food, clothes, and all the other things we need in order to maintain our 'standard of living'. This also means that we have to look for a rise every now and then in order to keep pace with the way in which prices have gone up since the last time we had one—plus, if possible, a bit extra with which we can improve our 'standards', and perhaps put aside some savings for the future. The person that we hope is going to be able to provide us with this money is our employer, who, in turn, has to generate more money from the goods or services that he sells than he pays for the goods and services that he purchases in order to have enough left over to put in our wage packet.

The 'small businessman', like Andrew Coe with his taxi, or a builder or decorator who either works on his own or perhaps employs one or two men to help him, has to generate enough revenue out of his business activities to enable him to meet all his business debts—*plus* enough extra money to meet his own personal living needs. If he is lucky enough to have any profit left after dealing with all these requirements, he may decide to reinvest some (or all) of it in his business in order to keep it going—or even expanding. This is absolutely no different from a larger company, like Andco or one of our leading industrial giants, who have to make sure that they generate sufficient revenue from their trading operations to cover all their costs, pay a dividend to their shareholders as a return on the money that they have invested in the company, and then to have some profit left over to plough back into the business as reserves.

Later on, we shall be turning our attention to the question of 'value', and to current cost accounting. We shall see that it is quite unrealistic to assume that all of the profit that is reinvested in the business in this way can be used for 'expansion'. Some of it will be needed to *maintain* the value of the company's assets during periods of inflation. A business *needs* profit—even in order to stand still!

We don't want to digress too far into this topic now, but let us just take one example to illustrate the sort of thing that we mean. If we take a look at Andco's balance sheet for Last Year in Figure 5.2, we can see that the total value of their fixed assets Last Year was £962,000 *at original cost*. The usage costs of these assets that was charged against their trading operations for Last Year can be ascertained from the stock movements schedule in Figure 6.3: which shows £64,000 charged as production overheads, and from the profit and loss statement in Figure 6.1, which shows a depreciation charge of £10,000 under 'Administration'. This makes a total of (64,000 + 10,000 =) £74,000, or (74/962 =) 7.7 per cent of the original cost of the assets.

Purely for the sake of argument, we shall now assume that Andco had a fire on 1 January Last Year, and had to replace every single one of their fixed assets from scratch. They were happily able to do so, and get straight back into production on the very same day. However, the price that they had to pay to replace all those assets, in exactly the same state of repair that the old ones were in on the night before the fire, was the *current*, or *replacement* cost, and this was obviously somewhat higher than the prices they paid when they originally purchased the items over the last few years. The comparisons might have been something like this:

(£'000)	*Historic cost (Fig. 5.2)*	*Current replacement cost*
Land and buildings	530	800
Plant and machinery	312	462
Office furniture and equipment	120	150
Total:	962	1,412

Assuming that Andco's original estimates of relative scrap values and estimated working life spans were realistic, they would still be justified in charging an overall 7.7 per cent of the total cost as a depreciation charge against profits. The only trouble is that, this time, they would have to take 7.7 per cent of the substantially higher current replacement cost, which would be (7.7% × 1,412,000 =) £109,000, instead of the £74,000 that they charged based on their 'historic' cost.

So where would that have left them? The answer is quite simply that it would have left them with (109,000 – 74,000 =) £35,000 less profit than they showed in their profit and loss statement for Last Year. Considering that their profit after tax was only £13,000, this wouldn't have left them with a great deal out of which to pay those dividends, even if they did only add up to £5,000! This example also demonstrates that in the circumstances that we have described Andco effectively needed at least £35,000 profit Last Year in order to reinstate the original *value* of their assets. That's on top of the £74,000 that they charged to their operational activities for using them!

This is really no different from that 'standard of living' we were talking about just now. We all know that if a business continually makes losses there will eventually be no business left. We are now saying that even if it 'breaks even', the continually increasing costs of materials, services, labour and equipment caused by the effects of inflation will mean that it will gradually be able to buy less and less for the same amount of money. This means that when it needs to replace an essential piece of equipment, more cash than before will be needed to buy the replacement asset, and appreciably more depreciation will have to be charged against future profits for its use. Effectively, therefore, every business needs a regular 'rise' to cover the effects of inflation. In our present example, the conclusion must be that £35,000 should be appropriated out of Andco's profits as being the amount that would have been necessary to *maintain* the physical structure and operational ability of the business at its present level. Anything less than that would eventually have the same effect as an 'historic cost loss', so, all in all, the £8,000 they retained Last Year could hardly have been regarded as 'an aid to future expansion'!

Well, you can imagine Andrew's reaction when we put this hypothesis to him! He had great difficulty in accepting that his company could be *shown* to have made a loss Last Year when his accounts told him that he had *actually* made a profit of £13,000. He didn't have time to stay and discuss the situation, because he was just on his way to keep an appointment with his tax consultant, but, as he was getting himself poised for the 'off', we could hear him muttering something about the sort of odds that he would be likely to get on the taxman letting him off paying any tax at all just because he had suddenly decided to change over to a system of current cost accounting . . ..

The need for taxation

He was obviously quite upset, but then, Andrew never did look forward to discussing how much tax he was going to have to pay. As far as he could see, the taxmen were the people who stood around while you did all the work, and then—as soon as you started to make a profit—stepped in and took some of it away from you. And here we were trying to convince him that it still didn't make any difference, even if you did decide to change your system in order to show a current cost accounting loss!

Perhaps we had better pause for a moment, and consider why taxation is necessary. We all need schools, hospitals, a police force, motorways, rubbish collection, street lighting, sewage disposal and countless other amenities in order to support our standard of living, and these all have to be provided by the state, or by the local administrative authority.

These administrations have to be organized just like any other business. All the services they provide have to be funded from somewhere, and that 'somewhere' is the tax and insurance contributions paid by ourselves, as individuals, out of the salaries we earn, and by the companies or organizations for whom we work. The taxman is the one who has to ensure that all the money that is due for collection by the state is paid as and when it becomes due—just like the credit control manager of any business, or the 'small businessman' who has to collect any outstanding debts from his customers.

Corporation Tax

We are all only too aware of our own personal taxes and national insurance contributions which are deducted from our wages and salaries before we even see them—and then we have to pay local taxes in the form of rates to our local authorities. But the level on which we want to concentrate here is company taxation, and, for the moment, we shall be discussing the tax that a company pays on the profit that it makes—Corporation Tax.

There are several different 'facets' of Corporation Tax, and it would take many pages of tightly-packed text to cover them all in detail. We have decided to avoid the challenge, partly because it would require far more specialist expertise than we are able to provide, and partly because we feel that those who are especially interested in the finer points of detail would be advised to consult a more specialized book on the subject. It should also be remembered that these details can be amended at any time by the Chancellor of the Exchequer—and his 1984 Budget was no exception! But we cannot duck the issue entirely, because some basic knowledge of the principles of taxation is essential to our general understanding of accounting.

Corporation Tax is levied on the amount of taxable profit that a company makes each year, so the first thing to define is what we mean by 'taxable profit'. This is the net profit made by a company, after all operational and financing costs have been deducted, and after certain items have been added back. The only 'added back' item with which we need to be concerned is depreciation, and the reason why this was not regarded as an 'allowable expense' was because almost all expenditure on fixed assets qualified for special tax allowances, called capital allowances.

Capital allowances

Various types of capital allowances were made, depending on the general category under which the investment was classified. Plant and machinery qualified for 100 per cent 'first year allowances', for instance, whilst industrial buildings qualified for a 75 per cent 'initial allowance', coupled with a 'writing down allowance' of 4 per cent per annum—the general idea being to provide an incentive to industry for capital investment through the medium of these allowances. If the total allowances to which a company became entitled in any one year was greater than the tax liability calculated on its taxable profits, then the excess allowances could be 'set off' against future tax liabilities.

In the 1984 Budget, the Chancellor changed these rules, with a view to phasing out capital allowances over the next few years. For the sake of simplicity and illustration, however, we have retained the pre-1984 allowances in our case studies, together with the pre-1984 rate of Corporation Tax—52 per cent. The Glossary contains up-to-date details of the tax situation as at the time of writing.

Andco's net tax liability for Last Year

During our last chapter we promised to explain how it was that Andco had a tax liability of £94,000 Last Year, deductable from a net profit of £107,000. At the time, it probably seemed an enormously unfair amount of tax to pay—those were not exactly the words that Andrew used, but the general gist was the same—but we can now explain how this figure was calculated.

We have just established that Andco's total charge for depreciation during Last Year was £74,000, and, since they had purchased no fixed assets over the previous few years, they had no capital allowances to set off against this figure. The calculation of their taxable profit and Corporation Tax liability is therefore as shown in Figure 7.1:

	£'000
Profit before tax (Loan interest has already been deducted)	107
Depreciation added back	74
TAXABLE PROFIT	181
Corporation Tax @ 52%	94

Fig 7.1 Calculation of Andco's taxable profit and Corporation Tax liability for Last Year

This explains why the tax calculation of £94,000 was correct Last Year, even though the profit before tax was only £107,000. The fact was that the profit before tax wasn't very much more than the amount of depreciation which had to be added back.

It was a pity that Andrew had to leave as quickly as he did, because, if he hadn't been so short of time, we could have explained to him why the taxman would not have been too impressed with his story about current cost losses. We had calculated that Andco should probably have charged an additional £35,000 in usage costs against last year's trading operations, even though this would have transformed their profit after tax of £13,000 into a loss of £22,000. Let us now have a look at the effects of such an adjustment in Figure 7.2.

(£'000)	*Original historic cost*				*Current cost revaluation*
Profit before tax	107	–	35	=	72
Depreciation added back	74	+	35	=	109
Taxable profit	181				181
Corporation Tax @ 52%	94				94

Fig 7.2 Calculation of Corporation Tax on Andco's current cost profits for Last Year

This demonstrates that, since depreciation has to be added back in order to translate the profit before tax into a taxable profit figure, the actual amount of depreciation charged does not affect the level of profit upon which the tax liability is calculated.

Other grants and reliefs

The basic idea behind the UK system of capital allowances was that they provided an investment incentive to industry. Many countries base their tax computations on the net profit made by companies *after* the deduction of fixed asset depreciation at agreed rates, whereas the UK method effectively allowed a company to depreciate the whole, or at least the greater part of, the investment in the year of purchase. This 'accelerated depreciation' calculation was only made for the purposes of arriving at the tax liability, however; the 'accounting' profit before tax figure always having to be net of depreciation, calculated in accordance with the normal conventions described earlier in this book.

There are a number of other tax incentives and allowances available which we should perhaps mention in passing. One of the major ones is the Development Grant, which is a cash grant made to companies investing in certain designated 'development areas' around the country.

'Small' companies, defined in the Finance Act of 1978 as being companies earning taxable profits 'not exceeding £60,000', may be entitled to pay Corporation Tax at a lower rate than larger companies, and there was also a 'stock relief' introduced in the mid-1970s—finally abolished in the 1984 Budget—to help 'cushion' companies against the effects of the ever-increasing costs of stockholding. Some of these measures are relatively short-lived, or are often modified, so there is no point in pursuing them here. This is not meant to imply that taxation is unimportant, but it is certainly a subject on which you should consult a specialist in order to obtain relevant and up to date advice.

Advance Corporation Tax

It can be assumed that, as a general rule, companies will normally expect to pay most of their net tax liability about nine months after the end of their financial year. 'Most' is admittedly a generalization, but the implication is that it should be interpreted to read 'most—but not necessarily all of . . .'.

The reason for this is that some tax will be payable in advance of the 'mainstream' amount at the time at which dividends are paid out to shareholders, and it is hardly surprising that the amount paid in this way is called Advance Corporation Tax. The idea was that all dividends should be declared (and paid) as if they had already had tax deducted at the standard personal rate—currently 30 per cent. If they had been paid as 'gross' amounts, then the Inland Revenue would be faced with the task of collecting the tax back individually from the shareholders. In order to avoid this, the total amount of tax, calculated at a rate of 3/7ths of the dividends paid, is 'imputed' by the company at source, and paid over to the tax authorities in one lump sum. The amount of tax payable 'in advance' in this way can then be deducted from the mainstream amount when that eventually becomes due for payment.

That was the original idea, although another major consideration is that nowadays a very considerable proportion of shares are held by institutions, such as pension funds, and so on. These bodies are not liable to pay income tax on the dividends that they receive, and can consequently claim a refund of the tax that has been 'deducted' at source. Well, no Government is likely to be too happy about paying back refunds on tax that it hasn't even collected yet, so this situation has tended to underline their need for this 'dividend tax' to be paid over in advance of the companies' mainstream liability—they would regard this as an almost essential source of revenue out of which to pay the refunds!

One could argue, of course, that this rather rapid circulation of tax payments and refunds must surely defeat the original object of the system. It will be clear by now, that after all these various liabilities, allowances, grants and reliefs have been taken into account, and the net amount payable has been split between 'advance' and 'mainstream' payments, the actual phasing between the accounting liability and its eventual settlement can be quite significantly distorted, and there can often be an extremely long time before a company's mainstream tax liability actually becomes due for payment. This must presumably have been the thinking behind the changes introduced by the 1984 Budget.

Deferred tax

This takes us quite a long way back to an earlier chapter, Chapter 2, when we were talking about the need for *information* which can be properly and reliably *interpreted*. Our contention then was that people needing information for whatever purpose should be entitled to know exactly where to go for it, and how to interpret what they find. In the case of a company's financial statements, it is understandable that its reported taxation liability should be related to its reported profit, since the profit after tax figure is such a critical indicator of performance, representing as it does the fund of earnings which supports—or perhaps does not support—the distribution of profit by way of dividends.

As we have explained, however, the purpose of the system of capital allowances was to reduce considerably such a calculated tax liability, and it used to be the case that companies would 'bridge the gap' by incorporating a deferred tax element into their tax calculation—hence the appearance in the balance sheet of the deferred tax liability that we mentioned in Chapter 5. But then, over the years, as companies were continually investing in new fixed assets and clocking up more and more capital allowances, it was found that their 'deferred' tax liability got bigger and bigger, to the extent that the eventual 'settlement date' could no longer be regarded as being in 'the foreseeable future'. So, in line with the practical nature of the accounting process, the system was changed again. Nowadays, companies can, if they wish, simply declare as their tax liability the amount that the taxman actually requires them to pay.

Having straightened that one out, the only problem that they then had to solve was where to put the balance that they had accumulated on their deferred tax liability account. So where do you think they decided to put it? No!—not where Andrew suggested, but right back into the shareholders' funds where it belongs!

The general strategy of taxation

And now you can see why we didn't want to go too deeply into this subject. We have tried to restrict ourselves to the development of an understanding of the strong and vital links that exist between a company's tax liability and its cash flow. A lot more has yet to be said concerning the importance of cash flow forecasting and control, but it should now be clear that the various aspects of tax legislation that we have discussed can have very erratic effects on its timing. Some sort of general appreciation of the subject is therefore essential.

By far the greatest proportion of tax income comes from payroll and personal income taxes, and from added-value, or 'turnover' taxes. This is just one good commercial reason why a strong, healthy economy depends upon full employment and efficient, profitable business and commercial enterprise. If we, on a personal level, try to spend more than we earn, we soon run into debt, and must expect to have the bank manager after us. If we then persuade him to let us have an overdraft, but our expenses still exceed our income, we shall not only get deeper into debt, but have to pay interest on the overdrawn balance as well, which can only make the situation progressively worse.

A matter of increasing interest

Let's think about interest rates for a moment, and the effect that they can have on overdrafts. This can often be the time when we suddenly realize that there is more than one 'class' of interest rate. You could almost say that there are three—the first of which is by far the best, because it is the interest that we receive on our investments, and the higher the rate, the better we like it. The second class isn't all that bad, either, even though it is a bit of a nuisance, but at least we are generally able to plan for it well in advance.

This is the interest that we pay on long-term loans, so that we know what we are letting ourselves in for when we enter into the initial negotiations. The rate of interest applicable to these loans is generally likely to fluctuate in phase with bank rates, of course, and this can sometimes cause problems—as all of us with mortgages to repay will know only too well!

The class of interest to beware, though, is the third 'class'—the one which sneaks up on you unawares just when you don't want to know about it! This is the one that we were just talking about—the interest that you are charged on those unexpected and unwanted overdrafts which arise when the amount of cash coming in is exceeded by the amount of cash going out, and it can be quite frightening to see the way in which the rate of interest can affect your ability to recover. This is even more relevant now that the banks charge interest on overdrawn accounts on a quarterly basis.

Let us take an example to illustrate this, and assume that our expenses exceed our income by £1,000 per annum consistently over a period of five years. If we start off with nothing, and the rate of interest is zero, we would be £5,000 overdrawn by the end of the five years—but how much overdrawn would we be if the rate of interest charged quarterly on our average overdrawn balance was 8 per cent, 12 per cent, 16 per cent and 20 per cent?

Since we would be overspending by £250 per quarter, the average balance on which the interest would be calculated would be £125 above the opening balance brought forward. The quarterly calculations for the first year are as shown in Figure 7.3, and the five-year profiles are charted in Figure 7.4.

All interest charges have a compound effect which gets progressively worse from the borrower's point of view as time goes by. As you can see from the chart, the higher the rate of interest, the steeper the line becomes, and the more difficult it becomes to keep the situation under control. By the end of Year 5, for instance, the overdrawn balances in our example range from £6,130 at 8 per cent to £8,470 at 20 per cent—or nearly 70 per cent higher than the £5,000 related to a nil rate of interest—so it is consequently essential to make every effort to avoid living or trading beyond our means.

	Annual rate of interest			
	8%	*12%*	*16%*	*20%*
Q1 Balance b/fd	0.0	0.0	0.0	0.0
Quarterly overspend	250.0	250.0	250.0	250.0
Interest on (Q1 + 125)	2.5	3.7	5.0	7.5
Q2 Balance b/fd	252.5	253.7	255.0	257.5
Quarterly overspend	250.0	250.0	250.0	250.0
Interest on (Q2 + 125)	7.5	11.3	15.2	19.1
Q3 Balance b/fd	510.0	515.0	520.2	526.6
Quarterly overspend	250.0	250.0	250.0	250.0
Interest on (Q3 + 125)	12.7	19.2	25.8	32.5
Q4 Balance b/fd	772.7	784.2	796.0	809.1
Quarterly overspend	250.0	250.0	250.0	250.0
Interest on (Q4 + 125)	17.9	27.2	36.8	46.7
Q5 Balance b/fd	1,040.6	1,061.4	1,082.8	1,105.8

Fig 7.3 Effects of different rates of interest on a steady overspend of £250 per quarter over one year

A similar message applies at a national level, at which it is also imperative to keep down the rate of inflation, since this is the basic economic factor that influences interest rates. No one is going to invest money at a rate of return lower than the rate of inflation—they will go out and spend the money now while they are able to buy more for each pound they spend. So, whichever way you look at it, a business or a national economy must be successful to survive. Success means profit, and profit—if we remember correctly—is a measure of *growth* over a period of time.

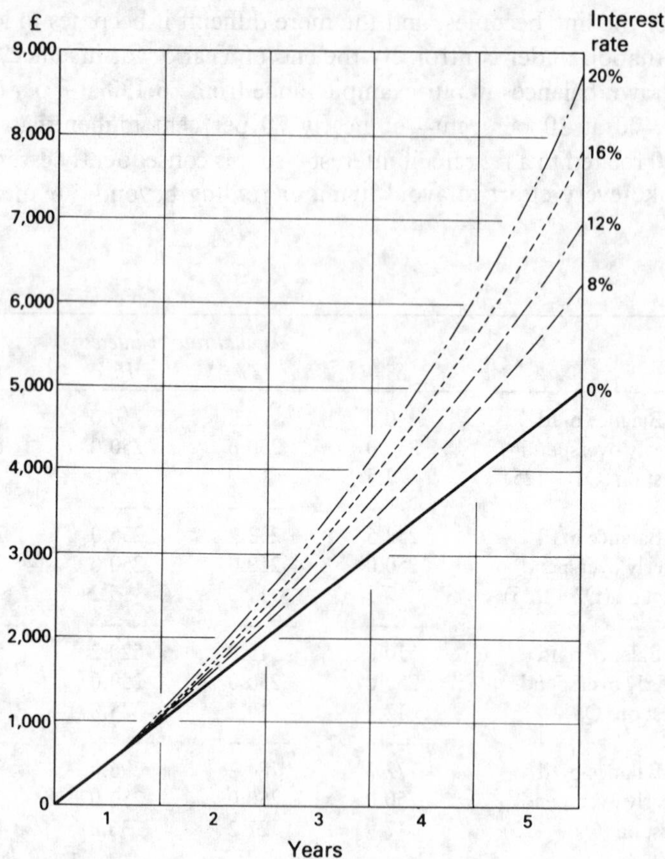

Fig 7.4 Profiles of overdraft patterns based on a quarterly overspend of £250 over five years at a range of Interest rates

Summary

Our first definition of profit was 'the excess of revenue over expenses', and we have discussed how we all need profit in order to live and survive—at all levels. This means as individual members of society, through industrial, commercial and service organizations to the local, national and international levels of society itself.

Taxation is a means by which some of these profits are diverted for the local and national services and amenities which—by their very nature—we all have to share, and cannot pay for individually. We have looked briefly at some of the various forms of corporate taxation that fall generally within the context of this book, and have concluded that the principal sources of national tax income are from personal and payroll taxes, and from value added, or 'turnover' taxes—a most important concept which will be dealt with in some detail in Chapter 14.

Prior to the eventual phasing in of the effects of the 1984 Budget, the amount of tax actually paid by a company was affected by the level of capital allowances available, which were in turn geared to its investment programme. The timing of these payments was accelerated by the payment of Advance Corporation Tax, which is linked to the timing of dividend payments—so it was consequently very important to keep a watchful eye on the way in which these 'due dates' affected the company's cash flow pattern.

As in our previous chapters, we shall close this section with a summary of the new terms and definitions which have been introduced during the course of this discussion. Some of these definitions will be rather more specific—or 'legitimate'—than the general references made in the text, but it must be remembered that any or all of the rates quoted as 'current' at the time of writing could be changed at any time.

- *Corporation Tax* The tax levied on the accounts profit of a company after it has been adjusted for income and expenses or allowances recognized or ignored for tax purposes, but not for accounts purposes. The 'mainstream' Corporation Tax is generally payable nine months after the company's year-end, but payment of part of that tax may be accelerated if dividends are paid. The Advance Corporation Tax linked to the dividend payment may be offset against the mainstream liability. The rate of Corporation Tax prior to the 1984 Budget was 52 per cent of the company's taxable profit, but was reduced to 50 per cent with effect from the date of that legislation—consequently applicable to the 1983 tax year—with a view to further and progressive reductions in successive years: i.e. to 45 per cent for the 1984 tax year, 40 per cent for 1985, and to 35 per cent for 1986. The ultimate objective of these changes was consequently to transfer the tax/allowance motivation for companies from a policy of continuing capital investment to one of profit stimulus.
- *Advance Corporation Tax* A tax which is linked to, and paid shortly after, dividends are distributed to shareholders. The rate is currently 3/7ths of the dividend paid. ACT can be offset against a company's mainstream Corporation Tax liability for

the year in which the dividend is paid, subject to certain restrictions. Any amount of ACT which cannot be set off against that year's mainstream Corporation Tax liability may be carried back or forward as appropriate.

- *Mainstream Corporation Tax* *See* Corporation Tax.
- *Capital allowances* These allowances, which are computed by reference to the level of capital expenditure undertaken, are deducted from a company's accounts profit when computing its taxable profit. A phasing-out of these allowances was initiated by the Chancellor in his 1984 Budget, but they were of three main types—namely 'first year allowances' in respect of plant and machinery, 'initial allowances' in respect of industrial buildings, and 'writing-down allowances' in respect of industrial buildings and certain types of equipment not eligible for first year allowances. Fuller details of each of these allowances may be found under their respective headings.
- *First year allowance* One of the three types of capital allowance, applicable to investments in plant and machinery. Prior to the 1984 Budget legislation, these allowances used to be 100 per cent of the cost of all such investments, allowable—as the name implies—in the actual year of investment. The 1984 Budget reduced this rate to 75 per cent with immediate effect—i.e. as from the 1983 tax year—with further planned reductions to 50 per cent for the 1984 tax year, and to nil thereafter.
- *Initial allowance* The first, and major, capital allowance that used to be available in respect of investments in industrial buildings. The pre-1984 rate of this allowance was 75 per cent, granted in the year in which the cost was incurred, but this was reduced to 50 per cent for the 1983 tax year, with further projected reductions through 25 per cent to nil in successive years.
- *Writing-down allowance* The writing-down allowance on industrial buildings is currently 4 per cent, available from the date of investment. This allowance was not affected by the 1984 Budget, and is also given on plant and machinery which does not qualify for first year allowances. The rate of allowance for qualifying plant and equipment is 25 per cent, calculated on the reducing balance.

- *Development grants* Cash grants made by the Government to help defray the cost of capital investment made in certain designated areas of the United Kingdom.
- *Stock relief* An allowance against taxable profits introduced in the mid-1970s to help defray the cost of holding increasing levels of stock during periods of high inflation. This relief was finally abolished in the 1984 Budget.
- *Small companies relief* Relief granted to companies earning 'small' profits—defined in the Finance Act of 1978 as 'not exceeding £60,000'—by means of a reduced rate of Corporation Tax. This rate was adjusted to 30 per cent in the 1984 Budget, but may obviously be changed again at any time.
- *Deferred tax* A provision charged separately against accounting profits to reflect the difference between tax actually payable, and tax which would have been payable if the charge had been based solely on accounting profits. Not every difference between 'accounting' tax and tax deducted would be reflected in the deferred tax provision, however, and the need to make such a provision is no longer obligatory.

8 The transaction equation

Introduction

We have now made a fairly detailed study of the two main financial statements that accountants produce, and have started to see how to interpret them, but we have not yet explained how the recording system actually works. This should not be interpreted as an intention to shroud the practical aspects of the accountants' profession in mystery. On the contrary, we would be the last to pretend that the accountant should be depicted as a sort of magician, producing figures out of thin air with the facility of a conjurer producing rabbits out of a hat. While it is certainly true that the professional ranks do actually contain people who also happen to be members of the Magic Circle, this is purely coincidental, and our job now is to draw aside the veils and take a closer look at some of the 'tricks of the trade'.

Not that the 'expert' is always the best person to ask, of course! For example, if you ask a gardener or a geologist to explain his basic skills in a few simple words, he will probably tell you that 'the secret's in the soil!' Ask a carpenter or a plumber, and he'll say that you have got to learn how to use the basic tools. An engineer will talk about nuts and bolts, and a builder about sand and cement, while a musician or an athlete will insist that only practice can perfect the skills they possess.

If you ask an accountant, he will almost certainly start talking about debits and credits, and begin drawing 'T'-shapes all over the nearest piece of paper, or flip-chart or marker-board. But that's not much good to us, so we shall start off by going right back to simple basics. We can think about debits and credits and 'T-Accounts' later on.

How it all began

The recording system used by accountants today originated in Italy about five hundred years ago. A monk named Paccioli actually started it all in 1494, when he wrote a book on algebra, and incorporated an appendix on the subject of double-entry book-keeping. (Andrew immediately reacted to this piece of information by calculating that this was just four hundred and eighty-six years before that other front runner, Pontin Lad, also 'started it all' by winning the two o'clock at Epsom!)

However, back to Paccioli. Being interested in algebra, it is hardly surprising that he should think of most problems in terms of equations, and it does not stretch the imagination too far to think through the way in which he might have developed the system to its present level of complexity. Let's take it step by step.

Some way back, in Chapter 3, we introduced the idea that balance sheets can really be thought of as simple equations, and we set out the opening balance sheet equation of the Andycab business like this:

←	ASSETS	→		= ← LIABILITIES →
Fixed assets	Advance payments	Current assets		Capital
5,150 +	200 +	350	=	5,700

Now let's see how Andrew got to that position. First of all, thanks to that little bit of help provided by Pontin Lad and a few other four-legged friends, he raised £5,700 cash. Then he bought a car, paid the road tax and insurance to cover his first year's motoring, and bought some petrol to put in his tank. All of these transactions involved a reduction in his cash balance, in exchange for a corresponding increase in the value of another asset, and can be recorded, using our equation of:

$$\text{Assets} = \text{Liabilities}$$

in the manner illustrated in Figure 8.1.

This balance sheet equation represents the financial situation of the Andycab business just before it began to trade. But it wasn't going to stay like that for long, because Andrew wanted to start work—he wanted to generate some revenue out of his trading activities, and he wanted to ensure that this revenue was greater than the expenses he incurred. He wanted to make a profit.

	← ASSETS			→	= LIABILITIES
	Fixed assets	*Advance payments*	*Stock*	*Cash*	*Capital*
(1) Set up business				5,700 =	5,700
(2) Buy car	5,150			−5,150 =	0
(3) Pay road tax etc.		200		− 200 =	0
(4) Buy petrol			10	− 10 =	0
Total	5,150	200	10	340 =	5,700

Fig 8.1 Background to the Andycab opening balance sheet equation

Any profit that is made by a business will naturally have to be shown in the financial records of that business, but, as we have already explained, that doesn't mean that any surplus money actually *belongs* to the business. It may be *held* by the business, but it *belongs* to its owner—and, in our case, the owner was Andrew.

So one of the things that he will want to know—at least once a year, if not more often—is how much money is available for him to take out of the business for his own use. In order to do that, he must be able to work out how much profit or loss the business has made on his behalf. This is something that we can cater for very easily in our equation by simply adding another column, thus:

←	ASSETS		→	=	← LIABILITIES →	
Fixed assets	Advance payments	Stock	Cash		Capital	Profit and loss account
5,150 +	200 +	10 +	340	=	5,700 +	0

As he has still not started to trade, the opening balance of the profit and loss column will be zero.

The only potential problem with this is that both revenue and expenses would appear in the same column. This might cause some confusion, once we start writing in some figures, so, while we're at it, why don't we divide this up into two separate columns before we start? There is no great shortage of columns, so our headings now become:

←	ASSETS		→	=	← LIABILITIES		→
Fixed assets	Advance payments	Stock	Cash		Capital	Revenue	Expenses
5,150 +	200 +	10 +	340	=	5,700 +	0 −	0

This is the sort of logical progression that Paccioli followed all those years ago, and this was one of the points at which a slight frown began to furrow his learned brow. Like almost every accountant since those long bygone days, he had an aversion to seeing his equations being cluttered up with minus signs. Even today, practitioners of this most honourable profession will put numbers in brackets, circle them, write them in red, lean them over sideways—or even write 'less' next to them. Anything to avoid a minus sign!

So Paccioli had to find a way of removing the minus sign that had now been introduced. This was no problem to him, because, as a mathematician, he knew that all he had to do was to add 'Expenses' to both sides of the equation. This would effectively cancel the negative figure on the right of the equals sign, and move it over to the left as a positive number:

←	ASSETS			→	=	← LIABILITIES →	
Fixed assets	Advance payments	Stock	Cash	Expenses		Capital	Revenue
5,150 +	200 +	10 +	340 +	0	=	5,700 +	0

The transaction equation work-sheet

We shall now apply these basic principles to the transactions relating to the first year of the Andycab business. In that year, Andrew's taxi travelled 35,000 miles, for which he charged 40p per mile. All his fares were paid in cash at the end of each journey, so his revenue was (35,000 × 0.40 =) £14,000. He had to travel an additional 5,000 miles in order to collect his passengers and so on, so his total variable costs at 6p per mile were (40,000 × 0.06 =) £2,400. These were mostly petrol costs, for which he still owed his garage £300 at the end of the year.

His road tax, insurance and maintenance costs came to £1,200, as budgeted, and, at the year end, he had already paid £250 in advance for insurance in respect of the following year. His depreciation charge was £1,000, and his administration overheads came to £5,600—or £600 more than his original forecast, unfortunately!—out of which he had only paid £4,800 by the year-end.

The work sheet on which these transactions are recorded is shown in Figure 8.2, so let us now go through them all one by one.

		ASSETS and EXPENSES								=	LIABILITIES and REVENUES		
		Fixed assets	*Advance payments*	*Stock*	*Cash*	*Variable costs*	*Road tax, insurance & maintenance*	*Depreciation expense*	*Admin. overheads*	=	*Capital*	*Creditors*	*Revenue*
1	Opening balances	5,150	200	10	340	0	0	0	0	=	5,700	0	0
2	Revenue				14,000					=			14,000
3	Variable costs incurred					2,400				=		2,400	
4	Road tax, insurance/ maintenance				−1,250		1,250						
5	Settlement of advance payments		−200				200						
6	Depreciation	−1,000						1,000					
7	Administration overheads								5,600	=		5,600	
8	Variable costs paid				−2,100					=		−2,100	
9	Administration costs paid for				−4,800					=		−4,800	
10	Payments in advance		250				−250						
11	TRIAL BALANCE (1)	4,150	250	10	6,190	2,400	1,200	1,000	5,600	=	5,700	1,100	14,000

Fig 8.2 The Andycab transaction work-sheet

1 *Opening balances*
The opening balances are taken from the opening balance sheet equation in Figure 8.1, but the other column headings have been put in at this stage because we know that we shall need them to record our later transactions.

2 *Revenue*
Since Andrew's revenue was always in cash, this item must have the effect of increasing the balance in his Cash column, and the balancing entry is in the Revenue column. Our opening balance equation has now been supplemented by a transaction equation which states that +14,000 = +14,000. There can be no doubt about the arithmetical accuracy of that statement, so the overall balance is still preserved.

3 *Variable costs incurred*
We have assumed here that all of Andrew's variable costs were credit transactions. In practice, some of these expenses would have been paid for in cash, but, since we were not told how much these were, we have been unable to make a split, and have balanced the total of £2,400 by an entry of the same amount in the Creditors column. Once again, this equation tells us quite truthfully that +2,400 = +2,400, so we must still be 'in balance'.

4 *Road tax, insurance and maintenance*
The implication here is that these items were paid in cash. Hence the entry, which decreases Cash, and increases the appropriate Expenses columns to show that the business had incurred this expense. You will see that we have entered the total amount of £1,250 at this stage, although we are told that £250 of this actually relates to an advance payment in respect of the following year. We shall deal with this in Line 10, but the net effect of our present entry is to balance out an increase in Expenses with a decrease in Assets. Both entries are consequently made on the left-hand side of the equals sign, so that, in this case, our transaction equation will tell us that −1,250 + 1,250 = 0. Still no problem!

5 *Settlement of advance payments*
The reference to advance payments leads us to the £200 in our opening equation, relating to the road tax and insurance that Andrew had to pay before he could even get his taxi on the road. This will have been 'used up' during the year, so we can transfer this from Advance Payments to the column for road tax, insurance and

maintenance expenses, and, since both of these columns are on the left-hand side of the equation, there is once again no entry to make on the right. This is similar to our previous equation – we are told that $-200 + 200 = 0$, and the right-hand side is not affected.

6 *Depreciation*
Remember that this is the cost to the business for the 'using up' of the original cost of Andrew's taxi. The equation to record this must consequently reduce the value of Fixed Assets, and increase the Depreciation expense. We shall see later that it is often helpful to keep the Fixed Asset column in gross terms, which can be achieved quite easily by inserting a new column called something like 'Accumulated Depreciation'. We have not bothered to do that in this example, but, if we had, it would have looked like this:

←	ASSETS	→	=	← LIABILITIES →
Gross fixed assets	Accumulated depreciation	Depreciation expense		Capital
5,150	0	0	=	5,150
	−1,000	1,000	=	0

But more of that later. We have expressed this transaction in the algebraic form of $-1{,}000 + 1{,}000 = 0$, so that, once again, nothing has happened to disturb our equilibrium.

7 *Administration overheads*
These costs were incurred, but not necessarily paid for, during the year, so the entry to cover this transaction must be to increase both the Administration Overheads and the Creditors' columns. We now have two positive amounts in our equation, but, since they are presented in the form of $+5{,}600 = +5{,}600$, our balance must still be intact.

8 *Variable costs paid*
We are told that, out of the £2,400 of Variable Costs incurred by Andrew's taxi business during its first year, recorded in Line 3, £300 was still owed at the year-end. This means that ($2{,}400 - 300 =$) £2,100 must have actually been paid for in cash, so the effect of this must have been to decrease both the Cash balance and the amount owing to Creditors. In this case, we have an equation which tells us that $-2{,}100 = -2{,}100$.

9 *Administration costs paid for*
The same comments apply here as for Line 8. £4,800 of the total administration costs of £5,600 were actually paid for during the year, so that both Cash and Creditors are reduced by this amount, and our equation is $-4{,}800 = -4{,}800$.

10 *Payments in advance*
We have already referred to this item under Line 4. Only £1,000 of the total £1,250 paid out during the year in respect of road tax, insurance and maintenance actually related to the current year, the remaining £250 being in respect of the following year. This means that this figure will have to be transferred from (or out of) road tax, insurance and maintenance, and into the Advance payments column. This time, our equation says quite simply that $+250 - 250 = 0$.

11 *The 'trial balance'*
We are now in a position to total all of our columns, and assess the cumulative effect of all of our transactions on the opening balances with which we started in Line 1. We have checked the individual mathematical integrity of all our transaction equations as we went along, so that, if we total the figures in each of the columns and then add them across, we should find that the total of the assets still 'balance' with the total of the liabilities. If they don't, then we must have made a mistake somewhere, and shall have to check the figures again! This list of totals in Line 11 consequently represents an intermediate balance equation, or 'trial balance', as it would normally be called.

Now we can continue our exercise, and establish whether or not Andrew's taxi business made a profit during that first year of operation. In order to do so, we must first reinstate the Profit and Loss Account column on the work sheet. It will be placed on the Liabilities side of the equation, since any profit that the business may have made will be 'owed' by the business to its owners—and the owner, in this case, is Andrew. Once this column has been reopened, we can transfer the balances on the expense and revenue accounts to it, as illustrated in Figure 8.3.

Each individual transaction equation must be mathematically valid, just as they were in the preceding lines of this example, so we shall transfer the revenue in Line 12 by entering $-14{,}000$ under Revenue, and $+14{,}000$ under Profit and Loss. This equation is

		← ASSETS and EXPENSES							→		← LIABILITIES and REVENUES				→
		Fixed assets	*Advance payments*	*Stock*	*Cash*	*Variable costs*	*Road tax, insurance and maintenance*	*Depreciation expense*	*Administration overheads*	=	*Capital*	*Creditors*	*Revenue*	*Tax due*	*Profit and loss*
1	Opening balances	5,150	200	10	340	0	0	0	0	=	5,700	0	0	0	0
2	Revenue				14,000					=			14,000		
3	Variable costs incurred					2,400				=		2,400			
4	Road tax, insurance/ maintenance				−1,250		1,250								
5	Settlement of advance payments		−200				200								
6	Depreciation	−1,000						1,000							
7	Administration overheads								5,600	=		5,600			
8	Variable costs paid				2,100					=		−2,100			
9	Administration costs paid for				−4,800					=		−4,800			
10	Payments in advance		250				−250								
11	TRIAL BALANCE (1)	4,150	250	10	6,190	2,400	1,200	1,000	5,600	=	5,700	1,100	14,000	0	0
	Transfers to profit and loss														
12	Revenue												−14,000		14,000
13	Variable costs					−2,400				=					−2,400
14	Road tax, insurance/ maintenance						−1,200			=					−1,200
15	Depreciation							−1,000		=					−1,000
16	Administration overheads								−5,600	=					−5,600
17	TRIAL BALANCE (2)	4,150	250	10	6,190	0	0	0	0	=	5,700	1,100	0	0	3,800
18	Tax due									=				1,500	−1,500
19	CLOSING BALANCES	4,150	250	10	6,190	0	0	0	0	=	5,700	1,100	0	1,500	2,300

Fig 8.3 The Andycab closing balance sheet equation

consequently in the form of $-14{,}000 + 14{,}000 = 0$. Similarly, the expenses associated with variable costs, road tax and insurance, depreciation and administration costs are transferred in Lines 13 to 16, so that, when we sub-total the columns into a second Trial Balance in Line 17, all of these expense and revenue columns cancel out to zero.

If we now look at the total in the Profit and Loss column, we can see that the gross profit made by the Andycab business during the year was £3,800. This is not quite the end of the story, however. Like any other business, this gross profit will be subject to the deduction of Corporation Tax. We have already discussed the implications of this in Chapter 7 and we know that the payment of this tax will not actually become due until some time during the following year. We don't need to bother about an exact calculation here, but we can assume that it will be something in the order of £1,500—which is more than enough for Andrew's peace of mind, thank you very much! This will be an outstanding liability at the end of the year, but all we have to do in order to cater for this situation is to open up yet another column under the title of 'Tax Due'. The transfer is recorded in Line 18, and the (final) closing balance equation is shown in Line 19. The Andycab business apparently ended up with a net profit of £2,300 over the year.

Our work sheet now contains all the information we need in order to prepare Andrew's annual accounts. The profit and loss column shows the profit position, the first and final lines show the opening and closing balance sheets, and the Cash column shows where the cash came from, and where it went to. We are able to see quite easily how his business 'moved' from one balance sheet position to the other.

You will also be able to see how the cash balance 'moved' from £340 at the beginning of the year to £6,190 at the end—an increase of (6,190 – 340 =) £5,850. His net profit was only £2,300, though, so this is just one more example of the point that we must continually stress: profit and cash are *not* necessarily the same thing.

Debits and credits and T-Accounts

There is no point in trying to be modest—Andrew was really quite impressed! He studied our work sheet for a few minutes and said 'It all seems quite logical to me, but, if it really is as simple as you say, then why do accountants spend so much time talking about debits and credits and "T-Accounts"? Why do they always seem to get so technical about things?'

'Would you really like to know, Andrew?' we asked. We wanted to give him every opportunity to back out if he wanted to, so we offered another life-line: 'It is really rather a complicated story!'

'That's all right,' he said, 'I don't imagine that I need to know all the technical details, but I would be rather interested to know how modern double-entry book-keeping developed out of Paccioli's algebraic equations.'

It was time for a deep breath and a shallow draught—so we took both! 'Well, you see, Andy, it's just like we've been saying all along' we began. 'In business, things come in and things go out. Nothing ever stands still—they have to move all the time, or else the business might just as well be dead! It's exactly the same as the blood flowing through our veins—and it's also true of all the columns on that work-sheet of ours. It's especially true of the Cash column, of course, since it is vitally important to any business to know how much cash comes in, in total, and how much goes out.'

Paccioli was very well aware of this, even in those days, so, in order to provide this information, he decided to split each of his columns into two: one side to show increases, and the other to show decreases, thus:

Cash		Capital	
increase	decrease	increase	decrease
+	−	+	−

Using this form of presentation, he would have set up the opening balance sheet equation of the Andycab business in the following way:

	← ASSETS								→		=	LIABILITIES			
	Fixed assets		Advance payments		Stock		Cash		Exp.			Capital		Rev.	
	+	−	+	−	+	−	+	−	+	−		+	−	+	−
(1)							5,700				=	5,700			
(2)	5,150							5,150							
(3)			200					200							
(4)					10			10							
	5,150	0	200	0	10	0	5,700	5,360	0	0	=	5,700	0	0	0

So far, so good. Even though half the columns have negative values associated with them, Paccioli had made them all look like positives: simply by moving the minus signs to the top of the columns! But he hadn't quite got there yet. He didn't need to be a great mathematician to see that the Cash column had a net balance of (5,700 – 5,360 =) £340, but, being a bit of a perfectionist, he wanted to isolate this figure. The easiest way would be to subtract £5,360 from each side:

	Cash	
	+	–
Totals	5,700	5,360
	–5,360	–5,360
Balance	340	0

The only trouble with this idea was that minus signs had cropped up again, so Paccioli decided to get round this by adding the difference, or balance, to both sides, and to use this balance as the carry-forward figure into the next period, instead of carrying down the gross totals. This may seem a bit weird, but it is exactly what accountants do to this day!

		Cash	
		+	–
Period 1	Totals	5,700	5,360
	Balance c/fd		340
		5,700	5,700
Period 2	Balance b/fd	340	

And then there was the question of the equals sign. Paccioli couldn't quite see that it would be practical to keep a set of accounts in equation form, but that didn't pose too much of a problem, because he knew that:

$$\text{If } A = L, \qquad \text{then} \qquad A - L = 0$$

Or had he forgotten those positive and negative values again? Remember that 'A – L' really looks like this:

$$\left\{\frac{\text{Assets}}{+ \quad -}\right\} - \left\{\frac{\text{Liabilities}}{+ \quad -}\right\}$$

He now had to play his last card! He decided that, since '−Liabilities' should really be written as:

$$-1\left\{\frac{\text{Liabilities}}{+ \qquad -}\right\}$$

then he would have to multiply the contents of the bracket by −1 in order to remove it.

$$-1\left\{\frac{\text{Liabilities}}{+ \qquad -}\right\} \text{ consequently became } +1\left\{\frac{\text{Liabilities}}{- \qquad +}\right\}$$

and the equation became:

$$\frac{\text{Assets}}{+ \qquad -} + \frac{\text{Liabilities}}{- \qquad +} = 0$$

Under this convention, Andrew's very first transaction would be recorded as follows:

$$\begin{array}{cc|cc|c}
\multicolumn{2}{c}{\text{ASSETS}} & \multicolumn{2}{c}{+\ \text{LIABILITIES}} & \\
\hline
\multicolumn{2}{c}{\text{Cash}} & \multicolumn{2}{c}{\text{Capital}} & \\
\hline
+ & - & - & + & \\
5{,}700 & & & 5{,}700 & = 0
\end{array}$$

This may look rather odd at first sight, for we seem to have created a situation in which two numbers of +5,700 equal zero! Well, we have to remember that we are still in Paccioli's land of equations, and, in order to add or subtract numbers, they have to be on the same side of the account. Since the T-Account

$$+1\left\{\frac{\text{Liabilities}}{\begin{array}{cc} - & + \\ & 5{,}700 \end{array}}\right\} \text{ is the same as } -1\left\{\frac{\text{Liabilities}}{\begin{array}{cc} + & - \\ 5{,}700 & \end{array}}\right\}$$

this means that we have, in effect:

$$\left\{\begin{array}{cc} \multicolumn{2}{c}{\text{ASSETS}} \\ \hline \multicolumn{2}{c}{\text{Cash}} \\ \hline + & - \\ 5{,}700 & \end{array}\right\} - 1 \left\{\begin{array}{cc} \multicolumn{2}{c}{\text{LIABILITIES}} \\ \hline \multicolumn{2}{c}{\text{Share capital}} \\ \hline + & - \\ 5{,}700 & \end{array}\right\} = 0$$

The whole of Andrew's initial transactions would consequently have been recorded under Paccioli's double-entry system of book-keeping in the way illustrated in Figure 8.4.

	← ASSETS							→			← LIABILITIES →			
	Fixed assets		*Advance payments*		*Stock*		*Cash*		*Exp.*		*Capital*		*Rev.*	
	+	−	+	−	+	−	+	−	+	−	−	+	−	+
(1) Start							5,700					5,700		
(2) Car	5,150							5,150						
(3) Advance payments			200					200						
(4) Petrol					10			10						
	5,150		200		10		5,700	5,360	0	0		5,700	0	0
Balance c/fd		5,150		200		10		340		0	5,700		0	
	5,150	5,150	200	200	10	10	5,700	5,700	0	0	5,700	5,700	0	0
Balance b/fd	5,150		200		10		340		0			5,700		0

Fig 8.4 The Andycab opening account entries

It all looks a lot more complicated than our simple, basic transaction equation method. In fact, it is more complicated, but Paccioli then proceeded to make things even worse! You will have noticed that the accounts which were on the left-hand side of the original equation all increase on the (positive) left, and decrease on the (negative) right, while those that were on the right-hand side do the opposite: they increase on the (positive) right, and decrease on the (negative) left.

Well, even Paccioli recognized the confusion that could be caused by this, so he decided to introduce technical names that would enable him to instruct his pupils in his new-found art of double-entry book-keeping. He defined all left-hand entries as 'debits', and spoke of 'debiting' the accounts, and he defined all right-hand entries as 'credits', and spoke of 'crediting' the accounts. So:

Debit = left-hand side
Credit = right-hand side

And that's all there is to it—but you can see how confusing it had all become! Andrew could, anyway! What it boils down to is that debits increase assets and expense accounts, and decrease liabilities and revenue accounts, while credits decrease assets and expenses, and increase liabilities and revenues.

Now you can see why it takes accountants so long to learn the system. This is the traditional double-entry method that you hear so much about. It is a logical system based on simple mathematics, but—like so many professional techniques these days—it is confused by its terminology. All you really have to remember are the three golden rules:

(1) Debits increase assets and expense accounts, and decrease liabilities and revenue accounts.
(2) Credits decrease assets and expense accounts, and increase liabilities and revenue accounts.
(3) Every debit has to have a corresponding credit in order to retain the 'balance', step by step.

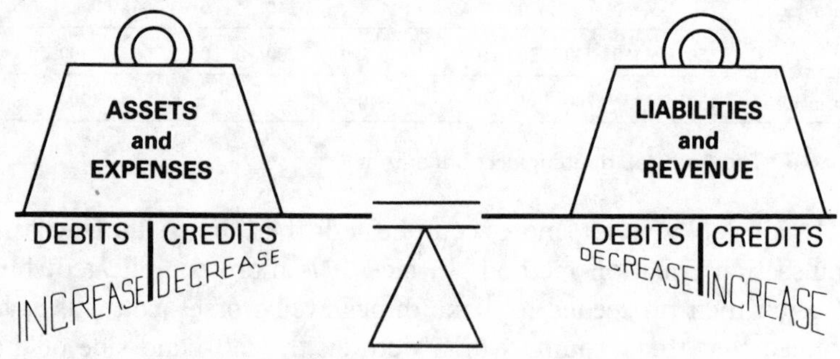

Fig 8.5 The transaction equation

The accountant would tell you to 'debit the account which receives, and credit the one that gives'. This is quite true—but it is also important to understand *why* it works that way. Perhaps our illustration of the transaction equation in Figure 8.5 will help you to memorize these rules.

Practice makes perfect

'Right!' said Andrew, when he had taken a few moments to study the diagram. 'By the time you've got the next round of drinks organized, I shall have drawn up my first T-Account, and be ready to start talking about debits and credits!'

This promised to be too good to miss, so, since it was our turn anyway, we collected the drinks, and returned to find that he had drawn a large T-shape on a piece of paper.

Dr	Cr

'That's my first T-Account,' he said, 'and now I'm going to write up those basic transaction equation examples in true double-entry style!'

He started off with the first year's Andycab revenue of £14,000, and drew up the two T-Accounts in which to record the transaction:

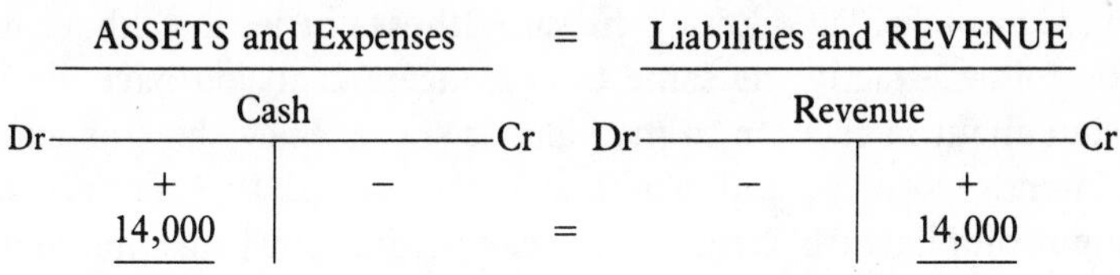

The increase in assets is balanced by the increase in liabilities, and the debit entry is balanced by the credit, so, as far as Andrew could see, all the rules had been satisfied.

He then looked at the transaction relating to the variable costs that had been incurred during that first year:

Assets and EXPENSES		=	LIABILITIES and Revenue	
Variable costs			Creditors	
Dr	Cr		Dr	Cr
+	–		–	+
2,400		=		2,400

Once again, both the expenses and the liabilities are increased by the £2,400 costs that were incurred, and the debit entry is again balanced by the credit, so he had scored another bullseye.

The next example was slightly different, but that didn't seem to worry him now. His confidence was obviously getting stronger all the time, because he was able to show us how to handle the payment of road tax and insurance costs.

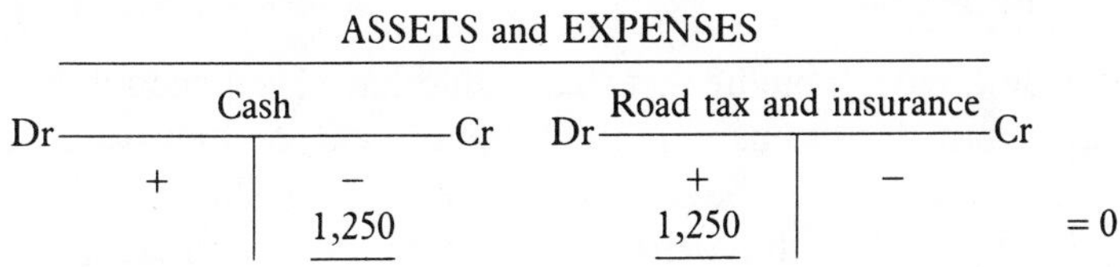

In this case, liabilities were not affected, so the two entries had to cancel each other out within the asset and expense accounts. This they did, and the debit entry was still balanced by the credit.

Closing account balances

Three out of three was a very encouraging start, and Andrew had every right to be pleased with himself: so we decided to skip the rest of the entries and join him in the appropriate celebration.

He then wanted to pursue a new line of thought that had just occurred to him. 'You know,' he said, 'those entries that I have just made follow exactly the same basic concept that you have always spoken about in relation to the balance sheet. They show us where the money goes to, and where it comes from. I've never really thought of a balance sheet in this way before, but I imagine that it would be possible to produce it in the form of a set of T-Account balances, if you wanted to. After all, the balance sheet is really nothing more nor less than a list of account balances extracted from the company's books at a particular moment in time, is it?'

Yes, indeed it is: which is another very good reason for it to be called a balance sheet. He had made quite an interesting point, and we were obviously delighted at this fresh evidence of enlightenment. In order to bring our examples just a little more up to date, we decided to try this idea out on his Andco balance sheet for Last Year. You will remember that we reproduced the equation for this in Figure 5.3, but, in order to simplify things a bit, we have copied this into Figure 8.6, together with the translation of these balances into the form that he had suggested.

The asset account balances are shown on the left, and the liabilities are shown on the right. This enables us to see clearly how the asset accounts have debit balances, and the liabilities have credit balances. In fact, the term 'normal sign' is often used to indicate that a person would *expect* to see a debit balance on an asset account, and a credit balance on a liability account.

Thinking ahead

You would have thought that that would have been enough for one evening, but all this business about transaction equations and debits and credits seemed to have fired Andrew's imagination.

'I'll tell you one thing that I liked about your transaction work sheet,' he said, 'and that's the sense of perspective that it provides. I think the point you made about "movement" is important, too—you know, when you explained the way in which it shows how a business has "moved" from one balance sheet position to another. I know you

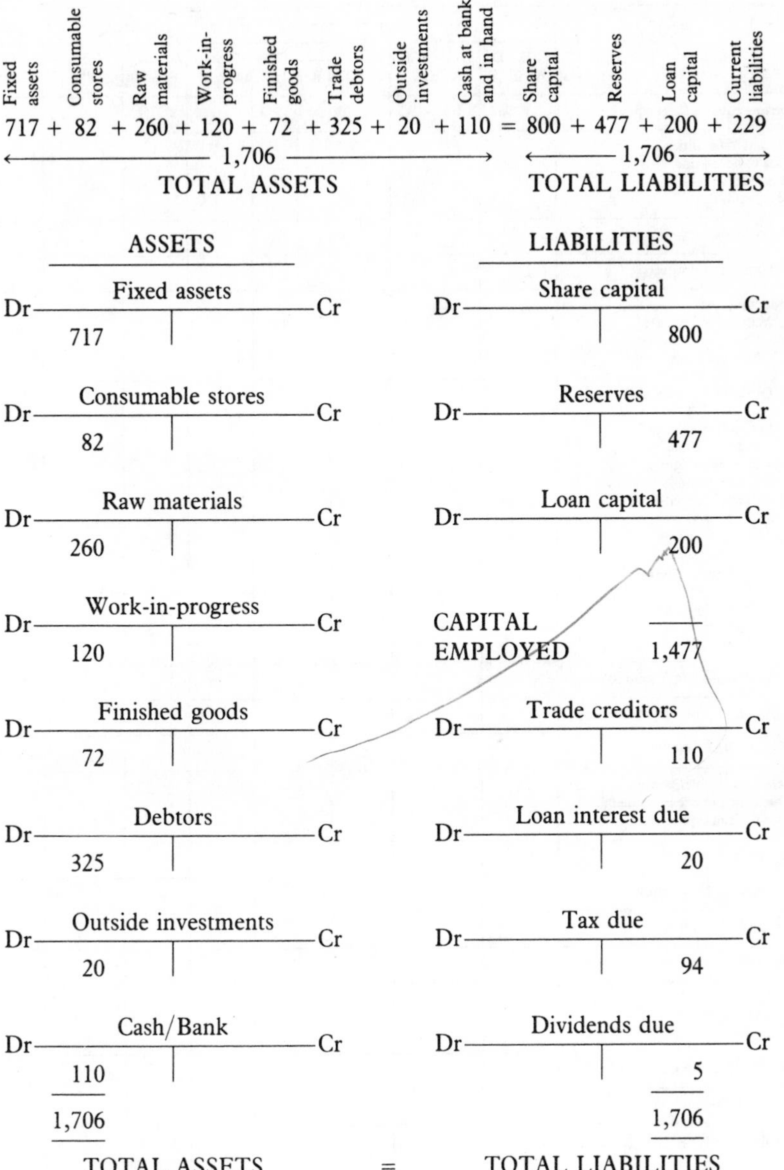

Fig 8.6 Andco's closing account balances for Last Year

illustrated the technique by taking some historical data relating to my Andycab business, but it could also be a useful way of plotting the effects of forecasts into the future. Suppose we started with my Andco balance sheet for Last Year, for instance, and I gave you

(£'000)	ASSETS							
	FIXED ASSETS	DEPRECI-ATION	STOCKS CONS.	STOCKS R. MTLS	STOCKS W. I. P.	STOCKS F. GDS	O'SIDE INV'MTS	TRADE DEBTORS
1 Opening balance sheet equation	962	−245	82	260	120	72	20	29
2 Payment of liabilities – Loan interest due – Tax due – Dividends due								
3 Sales revenue								2098
4 Investment interest received								
5 Production costs (A) Materials purchased – Consumable items – Raw materials			65	640				
(B) Direct production labour					365			
(C) Production overheads – Indirect labour – Power and light – Depreciation – Rates, lease, insurance		-77			144 110 77 25			
(D) Materials used – Raw materials – Consumable stores			-92	-715	715 92			
6 Cost of goods manufactured					-1421	1421		
7 Cost of goods sold						-1293		
8 Selling, distribution & administration								
9 Depreciation – (non-production)		-10						
10 TRIAL BALANCE (1)	962	-332	55	185	227	200	20	2396
11 Interest receivable/payable – Due from outside investment – Due on loan capital								
12 Purchase of new plant	133							
13 Cash received from debtors								-2155
14 Cash paid to creditors								
15 Leasehold pre-payments								
16 Dividends – Interim paid – Final due								
17 TRIAL BALANCE (2)	1095	-332	55	185	227	200	20	241
18 Estimated tax due								
19 Transfer to reserves								
20 Closing balance sheet equation								

Fig 8.7 The Andco transaction equation work sheet for This Year

				LIABILITIES							
RE-NTS	INV'MT INT.DUE	CASH/ BANK	=	SHARE CAPITAL	RESERVES	LOAN CAPITAL	TRADE CRED'RS	LOAN INT.DUE	TAX DUE	DIV'DNDS DUE	PROFIT & LOSS
25	2	110	=	800	477	200	110	20	94	5	0
		-20 -94 -5						-20	-94	-5	
											2098
	-2	2									
							65 640				
		-365									
25		-144					110				
											-1293
		-151					191				-342
											-10
5	0	-667		800	477	200	1116	0	0	0	453
	2										2
								20			-20
							133				
		2155									
		-1154					-1154				
30		-30									
		-20								30	-20 -30
30	2	284		800	477	200	95	20	0	30	385
									202		-202
					183						-183
					660				202		0

details of the way in which I see things happening This Year. We presumably ought to be able to build up a work-sheet from which I could extract my forecast balance sheet, stock movements, profit and loss statement, and cash position as at the end of This Year. Isn't that right?'

Yes, it was absolutely right, and he had once again touched on one of the great merits of this technique. The best way to prove it will be to let you check this out for yourself by working through his forecast transactions as he gave them to us. A blank work sheet is provided in Figure 8.7, and, when you have entered all the transactions, and checked all the totals, you should be able to transfer the relevant details into the forecast balance sheet, the stock movements and cost of goods sold schedule, and the profit and loss forecast in Figures 8.8 to 8.10. Copies of the completed documents are reproduced in Figures 8.11 to 8.14, but remember that, in order to get the maximum possible benefit from this exercise, you should only refer to these when you have completed your own entries. If you get stuck on any points during the course of the exercise, then it would be far better to refer back to the relevant explanatory text rather than copy details from an unexplained answer about which you may be unsure. Your ability to cope confidently with the topics that follow will depend very largely upon the ease with which you are able to handle this particular exercise.

The Andco projections for This Year

Anyway, let's get on with Andrew's projections for This Year. If you turn to Figure 8.7, you will see that we have set up the work sheet with all the columns and line headings that you will need. The only concession that we have made towards saving space is to leave out specific columns for expenses and revenue, since the entries to be made in these would be relatively few, and you should by now have grasped the principles involved. The items which would have affected these columns can consequently be entered directly into the Profit and Loss column.

1 *Opening balance sheet equation*

We have started you off with all the opening balances already filled in, since you probably know all these off by heart already! Notice that we have split fixed assets and cumulative depreciation into separate, but adjoining columns, in order to facilitate your preparation of the balance sheet.

2 *Payment of liabilities*
The first thing Andrew told us was that he had already paid the loan interest, tax and dividends which had been outstanding at the beginning of the year.

3 *Sales revenue*
His forecast for this was £2,098,000, and all of his sales would be on normal credit terms.

4 *Investment interest received*
He had just received the £2,000 that was due at the end of Last Year.

5 *Production costs*
Estimates for these could be split under four main headings:

(a) Materials purchased—This would amount to £65,000 for consumable items, and to £640,000 in respect of raw materials. Here again, he would assume that all purchases would be on normal credit terms.

(b) Direct production labour—This would amount to £365,000 during This Year, and would all be paid in cash. The charge will be to work-in-progress.

(c) Production overheads—These costs would also be charged direct to work-in-progress, and would be as follows:

Indirect labour	£144,000 paid in cash
Power and light	£110,000 credit terms
Depreciation	£77,000
Rates, lease and insurance	£25,000 paid Last Year

(d) Materials used—The value of raw materials used in production would be £715,000, and there would also be £92,000 of consumable items used.

6 *Cost of goods manufactured*
These would be worth £1,421,000 by the end of the year.

7 *Cost of goods sold*
The cost of goods sold will be £1,293,000.

8 *Selling, distribution and administration costs*
Andrew thought that these would total £342,000 during the year, out of which £151,000 would be employee costs, and the rest would

be regarded as normal 'third party' credit transactions. This is consequently an item which could be posted as two separate transactions: one to cover the employee costs, and the other to cover the 'third party' element. But there is no reason why it could not be treated as one composite equation, in which £−151,000 is entered under Cash, £+191,000 under Creditors, and £−342,000 under Profit and Loss. Try it—it will still balance.

9 *Depreciation (non-production)*
There will be £10,000 to be charged This Year in respect of the depreciation of fixed assets not connected with production uses.

10 *Trial balance (1)*
Andrew had now accounted for all of his anticipated operational items, so this is a useful point at which to sub-total the columns, and to check that they still balance across. The sub-total in the Profit and Loss column at this point should be the anticipated operating profit (or loss) for the year.

11 *Interest receivable/payable*
The amount of interest due from outside investments should again be £2,000. It will not be received until Next Year, although the £20,000 interest due on his loan capital will not be payable until Next Year, either.

12 *Purchase of new plant*
Andrew had already mentioned that he had arranged to buy some new plant This Year. In fact, it was almost installed and ready to go, and the cost—on credit, of course—was going to be £133,000.

13 *Cash received from debtors*
This should amount to £2,155,000 by the end of the year.

14 *Cash paid to creditors*
This would be £1,154,000, give or take a copper or two.

15 *Leasehold prepayments*
This will be going up to £30,000, and will all be in respect of Next Year's operations.

16 *Dividends*
Andrew forecast that his company would be paying £50,000 in dividends This Year. £20,000 of this would be paid as an interim dividend before the end of the year: and the rest wouldn't.

£'000	*Last Year*			*This Year*		
FIXED ASSETS						
Land and buildings			530			
Plant and machinery			312			
Office furniture and equipment			120			
Total at original cost			962			
Less: Depreciation to date			245			
Current written-down value			717			
WORKING CAPITAL						
Current assets:						
(a) Stocks						
Consumable stores	82					
Raw materials	260					
Work-in-progress	120					
Finished goods	72					
Total:	534					
(b) Debtors						
Trade	298					
Prepayments	25					
Investment interest	2					
Total:	325					
(c) Short-term investments	20					
(d) Cash at bank and in hand	110					
Total current assets		989				
Current liabilities						
Trade creditors	110					
Loan interest due	20					
Taxation due	94					
Dividends due	5					
Total current liabilities		229				
NET WORKING CAPITAL			760			
NET ASSETS			1,477			
Share capital			800			
Reserves			477			
Shareholders' funds			1,277			
Loan capital			200			
CAPITAL EMPLOYED			1,477			

Fig 8.8 Andco's forecast balance sheet for This Year

£'000	*Last Year*		*This Year*	
(a) CONSUMABLE STORES				
Opening stock		82		
Purchases		57		
Total available		139		
Less: Closing stock		82		
Usages (Transfers to WIP)		57		
(b) RAW MATERIALS				
Opening stock		120		
Purchases		589		
Total available		709		
Less: Closing stock		260		
Usages (Transfers to WIP)		449		
(c) WORK-IN-PROGRESS				
Direct labour		245		
Production overheads:				
Indirect labour	95			
Power and light	70			
Depreciation	64			
Rates and insurance	20			
Consumable stores (b/d)	57			
Total:		306		
Charges during year (Activity)		1,000		
Opening stock		123		
Total available		1,123		
Less: Closing stock		120		
Cost of goods manufactured		1,003		
(d) FINISHED GOODS				
Opening stock		427		
Total available		1,430		
Less: Closing stock		72		
Cost of goods sold		1,358		

Fig 8.9 Andco's forecast stock movements and cost of goods sold schedule for This Year

17 *Trial balance (2)*
This would take us down to the profit before tax position.

18 *Estimated tax due*
We reckoned that the amount of tax due on This Year's net profit, payable during Next Year, would be £202,000.

19 *Transfer to reserves*
This now only left us with the job of transferring the retained profit to reserves.

20 *Closing balance sheet equation*
This should be it! Andrew's forecast balance sheet as at the end of This Year.

£'000	*Last Year*		*This Year*	
Sales revenue		1,770		
Less: Cost of sales		1,358		
Gross profit/(loss)		412		
Selling, distribution and administration costs	277			
Depreciation (non-production)	10			
Total fixed costs		287		
Operating profit/(loss)		125		
Interest received from short-term outside investments		2		
Profit before interest and tax		127		
Interest payable on loan capital		20		
Profit before tax		107		
Tax on operational activities		94		
Profit after tax		13		
Dividends		5		
Retained profit		8		

Fig 8.10 Andco's forecast profit and loss statement for This Year

(£'000)	← ASSETS							
	FIXED ASSETS	DEPRECI-ATION	STOCKS CONS.	R. MTLS	W. I. P.	F. GDS	O'SIDE INV'MTS	TRADE DEBTORS
1 Opening balance sheet equation	962	−245	82	260	120	72	20	298
2 Payment of liabilities								
Loan interest due								
Tax due								
Dividends due								
3 Sales revenue								2,098
4 Investment interest received								
5 Production costs								
(A) Materials purchased								
Consumable items			65					
Raw materials				640				
(B) Direct production labour					365			
(C) Production overheads								
Indirect labour					144			
Power and light					110			
Depreciation		−77			77			
Rates, lease, insurance					25			
(D) Materials used								
Raw materials				−715	715			
Consumable stores			−92		92			
6 Cost of goods manufactured					−1,421	1,421		
7 Cost of goods sold						−1,293		
8 Selling, distribution & administration								
9 Depreciation – (non-production)		−10						
10 TRIAL BALANCE (1)	962	−332	55	185	227	200	20	2,396
11 Interest receivable/payable								
Due from outside investment								
Due on loan capital								
12 Purchase of new plant	133							
13 Cash received from debtors								−2,155
14 Cash paid to creditors								
15 Leasehold pre-payments								
16 Dividends								
Interim paid								
Final due								
17 TRIAL BALANCE (2)	1,095	−332	55	185	227	200	20	241
18 Estimated tax due								
19 Transfer to reserves								
20 Closing balance sheet equation	1,095	−332	55	185	227	200	20	241

Fig 8.11 The Andco transaction equation work sheet for This Year

------------→			=	←----------	LIABILITIES						----------→
PRE- P'MNTS	INV'MT INT.DUE	CASH/ BANK		SHARE CAPITAL	RESERVES	LOAN CAPITAL	TRADE CRED'RS	LOAN INT.DUE	TAX DUE	DIV'DNDS DUE	PROFIT & LOSS
25	2	110	=	800	477	200	110	20	94	5	0
: : :	: : :	−20 −94 −5	= = =	: : :	: : :	: : :	: : :	−20 : :	: −94 :	: : −5	: : :
:	:	:	=	:	:	:	:	:	:	:	2,098
:	−2	2		:	:	:	:	:	:	:	:
: :	: :	: :	= =	: :	: :	: :	65 640	: :	: :	: :	: :
:	:	−365		:	:	:	:	:	:	:	:
: : : −25	: : : :	−144 : : :	 = 	: : : :	: : : :	: : : :	: 110 : :	: : : :	: : : :	: : : :	: : : :
: :	: :	: :		: :	: :	: :	: :	: :	: :	: :	: :
:	:	:		:	:	:	:	:	:	:	:
:	:	:	=	:	:	:	:	:	:	:	−1,293
:	:	−151	=	:	:	:	191	:	:	:	−342
:	:	:	=	:	:	:	:	:	:	:	−10
0	0	−667	=	800	477	200	1,116	0	0	0	453
: :	2 :	: :	=	: :	: :	: :	: :	: 20	: :	: :	2 −20
:	:	:	=	:	:	:	133	:	:	:	:
:	:	2,155		:	:	:	:	:	:	:	:
:	:	−1,154	=	:	:	:	−1,154	:	:	:	:
30	:	−30		:	:	:	:	:	:	:	:
: :	: :	−20 :	=	: :	: :	: :	: :	: :	: :	: 30	−20 −30
30	2	284	=	800	477	200	95	20	0	30	385
:	:	:		:	:	:	:	:	202	:	−202
:	:	:		:	183	:	:	:	:	:	−183
30	2	284	=	800	660	200	95	20	202	30	0

£'000	Last Year			This Year		
FIXED ASSETS						
Land and buildings			530			530
Plant and machinery			312			445
Office furniture and equipment			120			120
Total at original cost			962			1,095
Less: Depreciation to date			245			332
Current written-down value			717			763
WORKING CAPITAL						
Current assets:						
(a) Stocks						
Consumable stores	82			53		
Raw materials	260			185		
Work-in-progress	120			227		
Finished goods	72			200		
Total	534			667		
(b) Debtors						
Trade	298			241		
Prepayments	25			30		
Investment interest	2			2		
Total	325			273		
(c) Short-term investments	20			20		
(d) Cash at bank and in hand	110			284		
Total current assets		989			1,244	
Current liabilities						
Trade creditors	110			95		
Loan interest due	20			20		
Taxation due	94			202		
Dividends due	5			30		
Total current liabilities		229			347	
NET WORKING CAPITAL			760			897
NET ASSETS			1,477			1,660
Share capital			800			800
Reserves			477			660
Shareholders' funds			1,277			1,460
Loan capital			200			200
CAPITAL EMPLOYED			1,477			1,660

Fig 8.12 Andco's forecast balance sheet for This Year

£'000	*Last Year*		*This Year*	
(a) CONSUMABLE STORES				
Opening stock		82		82
Purchases		57		65
Total available		139		147
Less: Closing stock		82		55
Usages (transfers to WIP)		57		92
(b) RAW MATERIALS				
Opening stock		120		260
Purchases		589		640
Total available		709		900
Less: Closing stock		260		185
Usages (Transfers to WIP)		449		715
(c) WORK-IN-PROGRESS				
Direct labour		245		365
Production overheads:				
Indirect labour	95		144	
Power and light	70		110	
Depreciation	64		77	
Rates and insurance	20		25	
Consumable stores (b/d)	57		92	
Total		306		448
Charges during year (Activity)		1,000		1,528
Opening stock		123		120
Total available		1,123		1,648
Less: Closing stock		120		227
Cost of goods manufactured		1,003		1,421
(d) FINISHED GOODS				
Opening stock		427		72
Total available		1,430		1,493
Less: Closing stock		72		200
Cost of goods sold		1,358		1,293

Fig 8.13 Andco's forecast stock movements and cost of goods sold schedule for This Year

£'000	Last Year		This Year	
Sales revenue		1,770		2,098
Less: Cost of sales		1,358		1,293
Gross profit/(loss)		412		805
Selling, distribution and administration costs	277		342	
Depreciation (non-production)	10		10	
Total fixed costs		287		352
Operating profit/(loss)		125		453
Interest received from short-term outside investments		2		2
Profit before interest and tax		127		455
Interest payable on loan capital		20		20
Profit before tax		107		435
Tax on operational activities		94		202
Profit after tax		13		233
Dividends		5		50
Retained profit		8		183

Fig 8.14 Andco's forecast profit and loss statement for This Year

By the time we had worked through all these figures, we had also worked our way through quite a lot of paper, and Andrew could now understand why it was that accountants were so often inclined to take up the noble art of graffiti in their spare time. 'Yes,' he said, 'I feel much happier about all this than I did when we started, but I think that I would have to agree with your view that the transaction equation is far easier for a beginner to follow than the fully-fledged Paccioli method. After all,' he concluded, 'what's a minus sign and an equals sign between friends?'.

There is nothing very startling or difficult about the concept of transaction equations. Perhaps the most surprising thing is that this method of double-entry book-keeping is not more widely taught, for it is of such fundamental importance and significance to everything that follows that we really do have to do our best to ensure that the basic principles are well documented. If you can grasp this simple technique which enables us to record the monetary aspect involved in every financial or commercial transaction, we're in business! . . ..

Summary

There are two 'sides' to every transaction: a 'giving' side and a 'receiving' side. In accounting terms, the creditor, or provider of the goods or services, is credited with the value of the goods, and the debtor, or receiver, is debited. The three 'golden rules' to remember are:

1 Debits increase assets and expense accounts, and decrease liabilities and revenue accounts.
2 Credits decrease assets and expense accounts, and increase liabilities and revenue accounts.
3 Every debit entry has to have a corresponding credit entry in order to retain the 'balance', step by step.

Both sides of the transaction have to be recorded in a 'double-entry' accounting system in such a way that every debit entry is 'balanced' by a credit entry. This can be done by means of a transaction equation in which all asset and expense accounts are placed on the left-hand side of an equals sign, and all liabilities and revenue accounts are placed on the right.

If a sheet of analysis paper is set up with a series of columns, one headed up for each of the company's accounts and with the assets divided from the liabilities by an equals sign, and if the first line contains the figures for the 'opening balance sheet equation', it is possible to compile a 'trial balance' after any transaction equation or series of transaction equations has been entered. This can be done simply by sub-totalling or totalling the columns down to the point required. The completed work sheet thus enables us to see how a business 'moved' from one balance sheet position to another.

We haven't introduced many new terms or definitions during the course of this chapter, since we are now beginning to get down to discussing matters of practical application, as distinct from 'learning the language'. However, the three that we have mentioned are of very basic importance, so we must define them here.

- *Debit* To charge. An accounting entry which records the value of goods or services supplied in the account of the debtor, or receiver of the benefit of the goods or services provided or supplied. The debit entry is always made on the left-hand side of the account, and represents an increase in the value of a company's assets or expenses, or a decrease in the value of its liabilities or income.

- *Credit* To acknowledge the receipt of services rendered. An accounting entry which records the value of goods or services received in the account of the creditor, or provider of the goods or services received. The credit entry is always recorded on the right-hand side of the account, and represents a decrease in the value of a company's assets or expenses, or an increase in the value of its liabilities or income.
- *Double-entry book-keeping* The method by which a company records details of each and every financial transaction that takes place between itself and the 'outside world', and often between different sections of its own organization. An 'account', or transaction record, is maintained for every supplier, every customer, and every asset and liability owned by the company. Every transaction is recorded twice: the creditor (or *provider* of the goods or services received) is credited with the value of the transaction, and the debtor (or *receiver*) is debited, so that every debit is balanced by a corresponding credit, and vice versa.

9 The source and application of funds

Introduction

Between them, the balance sheet and the profit and loss statement show the amount of profit made by a company during a year, and the disposition of the company's resources at the beginning and at the end of the year. What they do not show us, however, are the movements that have taken place during the year which affect the company's assets, liabilities and capital. They do not answer such questions as:

— 'How has the company financed its investments in fixed assets?'
— 'How much did it raise from the disposal of any assets that it may have sold?'
— 'What became of the proceeds from the recent issue of shares?'

Answers to questions such as these would help to provide a better understanding of how the company manages its affairs, or finances its operations. With this objective in view, the Accounting Standards Committee produced in 1975 a Statement of Standard Accounting Practice—SSAP 10—relating to the Source and Application of Funds. This defined the information that was required to be published by a company concerning the ways in which it had raised and used its cash resources during the financial year, and the way in which this information should be presented.

This was certainly a move in the right direction, and proved, if nothing else, that the heart of the accountancy profession was in the right place; although, in Andrew's opinion, the accountants could have ended up with a clearer and more meaningful presentation of the Source and Application of Funds. That's jumping ahead a bit, but it does mean that we have two things to do in this chapter. The first is to look at the 'official' Statement, as prescribed in the SSAP, and the second is to suggest a way in which it might have been improved.

What do we mean by 'funds'?

The first thing that we must do is to make absolutely certain that we know what we mean by 'Funds'. Let's do this by thinking back to our balance sheet equation, which—in its simple, basic form—states that:

Assets = Liabilities

If we analyse these two 'main' headings into the subclassifications that we have already defined, we can rewrite this as:

← TOTAL ASSETS →			=	←—— TOTAL LIABILITIES ——→				
Fixed assets	+	Current assets	=	Shareholders' funds	+	Long term debt	+	Current liabilities

These are the headings under which the details of a 'grossed up' balance sheet would be listed. If we now think instead of the 'net' version, then these headings would be switched around slightly, like this:

←—— NET ASSETS ——→					=	← CAPITAL EMPLOYED →		
		←— *Working Capital* —→						
Fixed assets	+ (	Current assets	−	Current liabilities)	=	Shareholders' funds	+	Long term debt

Now let us consider the effect that some typical transactions would have on this net balance sheet equation.

1 Suppose that we buy some fixed assets. However the deal is arranged, it is obvious that fixed assets will increase. If we pay in cash, current assets will decrease, while, if we buy on credit, creditors—current liabilities—will increase; so that, either way, working capital will decrease. Capital employed will not be affected.
2 If we want to borrow more money, long-term debt will increase, and this will be balanced by a corresponding increase in the cash area of working capital.
3 If we use some cash to pay creditors, then both cash and creditors will be reduced, which means that the net value of working capital will remain unchanged. Similarly, if we receive

cash from customers, then cash increases and debtors decrease, but the net value of working capital remains the same.

Any transaction which leads to a change in the net value of working capital is called a *funds transaction*, so that we can say that changes in working capital will either increase or decrease *funds*. The first two of our three examples can consequently be defined as funds transactions, whilst the third one cannot.

Circulating capital

This leads us back to the concept of 'circulating capital'. We have already referred to working capital as being the part of the business which keeps it on the move, because all of the operational activities circulate around it. Let us take a very basic example to illustrate this:

1 Raw materials are purchased on credit, so that the value of both stocks and creditors is increased. The net value of working capital is not affected.
2 The creditors are paid in cash; so that, as we said just now, both cash and creditors are reduced, but the net value of working capital is not affected.
3 The materials are converted into finished goods by the employment of labour and services, which are paid for in cash or on credit. The value of stocks is increased, and this is balanced by a decrease in cash and/or an increase in creditors.
4 The finished goods are sold to customers on credit, so that the value of stocks goes down, and the value of debtors goes up; but the net value of working capital does not change.
5 The customers pay for their goods, so that cash is increased, and the value of debtors goes down; but the net value of working capital stays as it was.

If a business happened to receive exactly the same amount of money in for the goods that it sold, as it actually spent on producing them, then its net working capital—its funds—would remain unchanged. The funds would literally be just circulating around the operational system in order to keep it 'ticking over'. The 'source' of funds would be exactly balanced by the uses—or 'applications'—to which they are put.

If less money comes in than is spent in keeping the wheels turning, then the funds will gradually shrink until the wheels stop turning altogether. But if, on the other hand, more money comes in than needs to be spent on generating this revenue, then the (working capital) funds will gradually grow as the business makes a profit.

This is a very simplified model, of course. In reality, we would have to allow for the depreciation of the company's fixed assets to be charged as part of the operational costs, in order to arrive at the operating profit, but, although this may affect the calculated value of stocks if the beginning and end-of-term values happen to be significantly different, it would not be regarded as a funds transaction.

There are, however, one or two 'extraneous' items which do qualify as funds transactions, and these are consequently of special interest. They are the 'non-operational' expenses, such as the interest to be paid on loan capital, which will be siphoned out of the cash resources, in the same way as the cash that may be required to settle any tax liability which may arise. And then, of course, one would always hope that dividends will be payable to the shareholders, and this will create another drain on cash assets.

When you think about it, the funds transactions are the ones which are of most interest when you are studying the accounts of a company from the outside. We are not so concerned with the recirculating working capital as we are with the way in which the net growth or shrinkage within the business can be accounted for. We are interested in the extent by which the funds have grown, and the way in which they have been used—their source and their application.

The interpretation of published accounts

Our studies of the basic financial statements in earlier chapters have been quite detailed, and we have assumed that complete sets of data have been available for our analyses. In a sense, we have been looking at the 'internal' accounts of a company, compiled from a complete set of internal records.

Unfortunately, published accounts will not be quite so comprehensive. For one thing, the stock movements and costs of goods sold schedule will not be included. This is partly for the reasons that we have just mentioned, but one also has to accept that companies, in general, will have a natural reluctance to publish more detail in their accounts than they are absolutely obliged to. Andrew, for one, would certainly not be too keen on all and sundry—especially his competitors—having access to all the details from which we built up his forecast statements for This Year in our last chapter. It's lucky for him that he can trust us not to spread it around!

The Companies Act of 1981 is very much more specific than its predecessors about the amount of detail that has to be disclosed in both shareholders' and published company accounts, as we shall see when we get through to Chapter 16. It is also specific about the formats in which these details are to be displayed, and those illustrated in Figures 9.1 and 9.2 follow the 'first' of the permitted formats for both the balance sheet and the profit and loss statement.

ANDCO LTD
Balance Sheet as at 31 December This Year

Last Year		*£'000*	*This Year*	
	717	Fixed assets (Note 1)		763
		Current assets		
534		Stocks	667	
325		Debtors	273	
20		Short term investments	20	
110		Cash	284	
989			1,244	
229		*Less:* Current liabilities (2)	347	
	760	Net working capital		897
	1,477	NET ASSETS		1,660
		Represented by:		
	800	Share capital (Note 3)		800
	477	Reserves (Note 4)		660
	1,277	Shareholders' funds		1,460
	200	Loan capital		200
	1,477	CAPITAL EMPLOYED		1,660

Fig 9.1 Andco's published balance sheet for This Year supported by comparative details for Last Year

You will see, for example, that the balance sheet in Figure 9.1 contains only the net values of the fixed assets and the current liabilities, although a lot of the background details relating to the accounting principles which have been applied have to be spelled out in either the Notes to the Accounts or Directors' Report which are appended to the accounts. Extracts from the Notes are shown in Figure 9.3, while Figure 9.2 provides the profit and loss details.

ANDCO LTD
Profit and Loss Statement for This Year

Last Year	*£'000*	*This Year*
1,770	Sales revenue	2,098
1,358	Cost of sales	1,293
412	Gross profit	805
287	Distribution and administration expenses	352
125	Operating profit	453
2	Interest received from short-term investments	2
127	Profit before interest and tax	455
20	Interest payable on long-term debt	20
107	Profit before tax	435
94	Tax on operational activities	202
13	Profit after tax	233
5	Dividends paid and proposed	50
8	Retained profit	183

Fig 9.2 Andco's published profit and loss statement for This Year

These are almost identical to the profit and loss format that we used in Figure 8.14, although we are repeating them here for ease of reference.

It is interesting to note, however, that, under the requirements of the Companies Acts of 1948 to 1980, companies did not have to show how they arrived at their profit figures—there was a 'gap' between revenue and trading profit of which the majority of companies were only too pleased to take advantage!

ANDCO LTD
Notes on The Published Accounts for This Year

Note 1—Fixed Assets

£'000	*Land and Buildings*	*Plant and Equip't*	*Office F. and E.*	*Total*
Assets at cost				
as at Last Year	530	312	120	962
additions during year	:	133	:	133
as at This Year	530	445	120	1,095
Accumulated depreciation				
as at Last Year	:	205	40	245
charge for This Year	:	77	10	87
as at This Year	:	282	50	332
Net value as at 31 December This Year	530	163	70	763

Note 2—Current Liabilities	*Last Year*	*This Year*
Trade creditors	110	95
Interest on loan capital	20	20
Taxation	94	202
Dividends	5	30
	229	347

Note 3—Share Capital (Both Years)	*Authorized*	*Issued*
800,000 Shares @ £1 each	800	800

Note 4—Reserves	*£'000*
Balance as at 31 December Last Year	477
Retained profit for This Year	183
Balance as at 31 December This Year	660

Fig 9.3 Notes appended to Andco's published accounts for This Year

Tracing the movement of funds

What we now want to do is to pretend that this is the first time that we have seen Andco's figures. These published statements represent our first introduction to Andco Ltd, and it is a company about which we should like to learn more. We should like to know how they raised their funds, and what they did with them, because this will give us some insight into the sort of policies pursued by the management. We shall even pretend that we can't find the 'official' source and application of funds statement that is supposed to support the balance sheet and profit and loss statement—or perhaps, at this stage, we wouldn't even recognize it if we saw it!

It is time to don our deer-stalker, pick up our transaction equations, and get busy with our work sheet again, although, this time, we shall be working in the opposite direction to the one we took in our last chapter. We now have the final statements, but want to work backwards to the details of the fund movements which lie behind them.

One of the things we will not be able to do is to identify the exact nature of some of the transactions. We shall not be able to tell

	← - - - - - - - - - - - - - - ASSETS - - - - - - - - - -					
(£'000)	FIXED ASSETS	DEPRECI-ATION	STOCKS	DEBTORS	O'SIDE INV'MTS	CASH BANK
1 Opening balance sheet equation	962	−245	534	325	20	11
2 Transfer to reserves	:	:	:	:	:	:
3 Dividends paid	:	:	:	:	:	:
4 Tax due	:	:	:	:	:	:
5 Interest receivable/payable Due from outside investment Due on loan capital	 : :	 : :	 : :	 : :	 : :	 :
6 Depreciation of fixed assets	:	−87	:	:	:	:
7 Purchase of new plant	133	:	:	:	:	:
8 TRIAL BALANCE (1)	1095	−332	534	325	20	11
9 Net funds generated from operations	:	:	:	:	:	:
10 Increase in stocks	:	:	133	:	:	:
11 Decrease in debtors	:	:	:	−52	:	:
12 Increase in cash	:	:	:	:	:	17
13 Decrease in trade creditors	:	:	:	:	:	:
14 Payment of last year's tax	:	:	:	:	:	:
15 Payment of dividends	:	:	:	:	:	:
16 Closing balance sheet equation	1095	−332	667	273	20	28

Fig 9.4 Transaction equation work sheet compiled from details extracted from Andco's published accounts for This Year

whether they were in cash or on credit, for example, but, since we have established that Cash, Debtors and Creditors are all part of the funds area of the business, all we need to do is to open an extra column on our work sheet under the heading of 'Funds'. This is shown in Figure 9.4, in which we have started in Line 1 with a rather condensed version of the Andco opening balance sheet equation. We are now only able to show one column for Stocks, and one for Debtors, but have added Funds as an asset classification.

Since this is a reconstruction exercise, our primary objective is to piece together the first part of our picture by working through the profit and loss statement, and, in this example, we shall even work through it backwards! Not that we necessarily have to nowadays, since the 1981 Act has made things considerably simpler for us in this respect, but this is the way things used to be before 1981, when there was nothing more than a gaping hole between 'Sales Revenue'

--→	=	←------ LIABILITIES						------→
FUNDS		SHARE CAPITAL	RESERVES	LOAN CAPITAL	TRADE CRED'RS	LOAN INT.DUE	TAX DUE	DIV'DNDS DUE	PROFIT & LOSS
0	=	800	477	200	110	20	94	5	0
:		:	183	:	:	:	:	:	−183
:		:	:	:	:	:	:	50	−50
:		:	:	:	:	:	202	:	−202
2 −20	= =	: :	: :	: :	: :	: :	: :	: :	2 −20
:	=	:	:	:	:	:	:	:	−87
−133		:	:	:	:	:	:	:	:
−151	=	800	660	200	110	20	296	55	−540
540	=	:	:	:	:	:	:	:	540
−133		:	:	:	:	:	:	:	:
52		:	:	:	:	:	:	:	:
−174		:	:	:	:	:	:	:	:
−15	=	:	:	:	−15	:	:	:	:
−94	=	:	:	:	:	:	−94	:	:
−25	=	:	:	:	:	:	:	−25	:
0	=	800	660	200	95	20	202	30	0

and 'Trading Profit' in most published accounts. Now that this hole has been plugged, it does not make much difference whether you start reconstructing the movements of funds from Sales Revenue or from Retained Profit, but we might as well work our way up from the bottom, since that is what you will have to do should you wish to reconstruct some pre-1981 accounts in real life. This means that the first transaction in our example (Line 2) will pick up the £183,000 that was transferred from Profit and Loss to Reserves. No funds are involved here, so the transaction will be:

	ASSETS	=	← LIABILITIES →	
			Reserves	*P & L*
(2) Transfer to reserves	0	=	183	−183

We then have to transfer the dividends declared, and the calculated tax liability out of Profit and Loss into Dividends Due and Tax Due respectively. Neither of these commitments will be paid until Next Year, so that Funds will still not be affected. The transactions will be as shown in Lines 3 and 4.

	ASSETS	=	←— LIABILITIES —→		
			Tax Due	*Dividends Due*	*Profit & Loss*
(3) Dividends declared	0	=		50	−50
(4) Transfer of tax due	0	=	202		−202

Moving further up the profit and loss statement, we come to interest received and payable. We have no positive indication concerning the dates of receipt and payment, although that is not really a material factor, as you will see in a few lines' time. We shall assume here that these amounts will, sooner or later, be transacted in cash. They can therefore be regarded as legitimate funds transactions. Line 5 shows the transfers between Profit and Loss and Funds:

	ASSETS	=	LIABILITIES
	Funds		*P & L*
(5) Interest receivable/payable			
Due from outside investments	+2	=	+2
Due on loan capital	−20	=	−20

This takes us up to the Operating Profit line of the profit and loss statement, and things could now start to get a bit tricky if we had been hoping to analyse all of the transactions which make up cost of sales, stock movements, and so on. However, we have already decided that this will not be necessary now that we have opened our 'Funds bag'.

One item that we can and must pick up, though, is depreciation, because its very nature makes it different from all the others. It is part of the year's costs, but has nothing to do with funds, and we can see from Note 1 to the accounts that the charge for this year was £87,000. Our next transaction will therefore be:

	ASSETS	=	LIABILITIES
	Depreciation		*P & L*
(6) Depreciation of fixed assets	−87	=	−87

Note 1 of the Report also tells us that £133,000 was spent on plant and machinery this year, so this is another transaction that we can post in our work sheet. This time, we are increasing the value of Fixed Assets, and reducing Funds.

	← ASSETS →		=	LIABILITIES
	Fixed Assets	*Funds*		
(7) Purchase of new plant	133	−133	=	0

There are no other transactions that are specifically identified in the accounts, so we should now subtotal the columns on our work sheet, and extract a trial balance. This will enable us to check how close we are to the balances on the closing balance sheet, since that is the target that we are trying to reach.

The subtotals in Line 8 tell us quite clearly that we still have some way to go. The first figure to catch our eye is the minus 540 in the Profit and Loss column, and at first sight this might appear rather strange. It is really quite simple, though. It represents the total of the amounts that we have just been transferring *out* of the Profit and Loss column to cover the tax, dividends, retained profit etc which have been charged against the profit for the year. Since the closing balance in this column has to be zero, then plus 540 must represent the net amount of funds which were generated out of the company's trading operations during the year. This can be checked very easily from the profit and loss statement and directors' report:

	£'000
Operating profit	453
Depreciation added back (Line 6)	87
Net funds generated from trading operations	540

We can consequently transfer this figure straight from the Profit and Loss column to Funds, as shown in Line 9:

	ASSETS	=	LIABILITIES
	Funds		*P & L*
(9) Net funds generated from trading operations	540	=	540

This will clear down the Profit and Loss column, but it still will not make the other individual column totals agree with the ones in the closing balance sheet. However, since we know that we are now thinking entirely in terms of the operational area of the business, we can quite legitimately conclude that we can reconcile the columns by transferring the necessary balancing amounts into the Funds column. All we are doing is to transfer the *differences* between the opening and closing balances: Lines 10 to 13 in Figure 9.4 show how this has been done to Stocks, Debtors, Cash and Creditors.

Now we are only left with the Tax and Dividends Due, which show in our trial balance in Line 8 as £296,000 and £55,000 respectively. Since Note 2 in the report tells us that these items should only be £202,000 and £30,000 respectively, it must follow that payments of (296,000 – 202,000 =) £94,000—the brought forward tax liability—and (55,000 – 30,000 =) £25,000 must have been paid out (of funds) during the year. These transactions are recorded in Lines 14 and 15, and, if we now re-total our columns, we shall find that the closing balance sheet figures all appear in Line 16. The Profit and Loss column adds up to zero, as we knew it should, and so does the Funds column; which proves that we must have accounted for all the sources and uses of funds during the year.

Presentation of the sources and application of funds statement

This is exactly what we set out to do, so the thing to decide now is how this information should be summarized. Well, the answers are all in the funds column of our work sheet, so the best way to start is to list these items in some logical sequence. One way to do this would be to list the (positive) sources first, followed by the (negative) uses, as illustrated in Figure 9.5.

This, then, is a summary of how Andco raised its funds this year, and of what it did with them. We can see that the items listed in

	£'000
Sources of funds	
Interest received from investments	2
Net funds generated from operations	540
Increase in debtors	52
Total:	594
Uses of funds	
Interest paid on loan capital	20
Purchase of new plant	133
Increase in stocks	133
Increase in cash	174
Decrease in creditors	15
Payment of tax in respect of last year	94
Payment of dividends	25
Total:	594

Fig 9.5 Summary of Andco's sources and uses of funds for This Year

Figure 9.5 could be easily rearranged to show separate groupings of:

— those which appear in the profit and loss statement
— those which only affect increases or decreases in working capital (funds) items, and
— those which are of a capital nature.

Our work sheet shows clearly how the profit and loss items link into the company's funds, and we can also—once again!—see that profit, at any level, need not necessarily be synonymous with funds.

Now we can shuffle the figures around a bit into the format needed for the source and application of funds statement. Since this is now a statutory document, just like the balance sheet and the profit and loss statement, we need to get it right; but now that we've got this far, the rest of it is really quite easy.

The headings under which the funds flow details have to be reported are:

(1) Sources of funds
(2) Application of funds
(3) Increases/Decreases in working capital

For the sake of clarity and continuity, we shall examine each of these headings in turn.

Sources of funds

'Sources of funds' has to be split between trading operations and 'other sources', which is exactly what we did in the profit and loss statement in Figure 9.2, when we separated out the £2,000 investment interest from the operating profit. This should consequently cause no problems.

Application of funds

This heading covers the items of loan interest, dividends and tax which were all part of the outgoings from funds this year, together with details of any cash spent on the purchase of new capital equipment etc.

Increases/decreases in working capital

This section summarizes the various net movements which have taken place within the working capital area of the business, and is exactly what we did in Lines 10 to 13 of our work sheet. So, once again, we have already extracted the figures: all we have to do now is to present them in the prescribed format. You can see what this looks like in Figure 9.6.

How Andco used their money

So, starting off with only the details provided by the balance sheet and the profit and loss statement, we have been able to use our transaction equation technique to build up a completely new document which adds considerably to our knowledge of the company. It shows us exactly how Andco earned their money during this year, and what they did with it. We now have some insight into the trading and investment policies that they pursue.

We can see, for instance, that almost exactly half of the total funds generated during the year was allocated to the expansion of working capital, although the greater part of that was admittedly still available in liquid (cash) form. Almost exactly half of what was left was soaked up by non-operational expenses, and the remaining quarter was spent on new plant. As Andrew pointed out when we were tracing all these figures through with him, you can see an analogy between the complete set of financial statements and his

	£'000	£'000
SOURCES OF FUNDS		
Operating profit before interest and tax		453
Adjustments for items not involving the movement of funds:		
Depreciation		87
		—
Total generated from trading operations		540
Funds from other sources:		
Interest received from outside investments		2
		—
Total funds generated		542
APPLICATION OF FUNDS		
Interest on loan capital	20	
Dividends paid:	25	
Tax paid	94	
Purchase of new plant	133	
	—	272
		—
		270
INCREASE/DECREASE IN WORKING CAPITAL		
Increase in stocks	133	
Reduction in creditors	15	
(Decrease) in debtors	−52	
Increase in net liquid funds (110 to 284)	174	
	—	270

Fig 9.6 Andco's source and application of funds statement for This Year

Andycab operations. The balance sheets are like pictures of the car taken at two separate moments in time; the profit and loss statement is like his log book which tells you how far it has travelled between the two dates, while the source and application of funds statement is rather like a model of the engine showing you how much petrol it used, and how this was converted into the energy needed to make the car travel that distance.

Another way of looking at it

Turning back to the source and application of fund statements that we had just completed, Andrew scratched his head thoughtfully, and said, 'You know, it's a funny thing, but I was quite happy about all this until we got to the final product! Now that you have explained it to me, I can understand what it is supposed to be trying to tell me—but don't you think it's rather an odd way to present this sort of information? I mean!—what are those balancing figures of £270,000 supposed to represent?'

We explained that this showed the net increase in the funds' resources, as represented by the working capital area of the company, but he was not very enthusiastic about that explanation. 'Yes, I can see that,' he said, 'but surely it would be more useful and relevant to place the emphasis more on the funds required and used for long-term investment, rather than on the circulating funds. Of course, I accept that the control of working capital is important—we have talked about that already, and I wouldn't be surprised if we talked about it again!—but I think that I would prefer to see the figures changed around.

'For instance, why couldn't we draw up a statement which starts, like the profit and loss statement, with sales revenue, from which the operational costs are deducted in order to get the net funds generated from operations? In our case, the sales revenue would be £2,098,000, and we know that the net funds generated from operations were £540,000, which means that the operational costs must have been (2,098,000 – 540,000 =) £1,558,000. You could then deduct the financing costs—the interest, tax and dividends—in order to arrive at a figure which showed the net funds available for "use" within the business.

'Then the movements in circulating capital could be deducted in order to isolate the amount of funds generated from operations that was available for long-term investment in fixed assets. Investments actually made in this area would be deducted next, and the result of that would tell you how this expenditure had been financed. You would never have a positive figure here, since any surplus funds would be shown as an increase in circulating funds, but you might well get a negative figure. This would mean that the company had actually over-spent the funds generated from trading during the period, and had had to obtain additional capital in order to finance its activities. You could also see how much of this additional capital had been needed to replenish its circulating funds, as distinct from financing its longer-term plans. This is surely the point where the focus ought to be.'

Well, this certainly was another—very valid—way of looking at the whole question of the source and application of funds. In fact,

Andrew was so sure about the message that he was trying to convey, that he redrafted his figures for This Year into the sort of format he had in mind. It certainly looked sensible enough to us; in fact, we decided to adopt it! We will let you form your own judgement from his example, reproduced in Figure 9.7.

£'000		*This Year*
Sales revenue		2,098
Operational expenditure		1,558
Funds generated from trading operations		540
Interest received from outside investments		2
Total funds generated		542
Financing costs		
Interest paid on loan capital	20	
Tax paid on last year's operations	94	
Dividends paid	25	
		139
Net funds available for use		403
Net movements in circulating capital		
Increase in stocks	133	
Decrease in debtors	−52	
Decrease in creditors	15	
Increase in cash	174	
		270
Operating funds available for long-term use		133
Investment in new plant		−133
Additional funds required for investment		0

Fig 9.7 Andco's source and application of funds statement for This Year, prepared in accordance with the way in which we consider the SSAP should have been drafted

He was quite proud of this effort. 'I know this layout isn't really a great deal different from the "official" one,' he said, 'but I think that it conveys a much clearer picture, because I can now see what funds were generated out of my business operations; how much it has cost me to finance them, and how much I had left for re-allocation around the business. The extent to which I have had to lock up more—or less—circulating capital in order to generate this business

Year 4		£'000		Year 5
	230	FIXED ASSETS (Note 1)		280
		Current assets:		
250		Stocks	320	
175		Trade debtors	210	
88		Cash/Bank	16	
513		Total current assets	546	
162		*Less:* Current liabilities (2)	195	
	351	Net current assets		351
	581	NET ASSETS		631
	200	Share capital (Note 3)		200
	231	Reserves (Note 4)		281
	431	Shareholders' funds		481
	150	Loan Capital		150
	581	CAPITAL EMPLOYED		631

Fig 9.8 Matthew Grimble's balance sheets for Years 4 and 5

£'000	Year 5
Sales revenue	1,130
Less: Cost of goods sold	680
Gross trading profit	450
Less: Total fixed costs	315
Operating profit before interest and tax	135
Interest payable on long-term loan capital	20
Net profit before tax	115
Taxation	35
Profit after tax	80
Dividends	30
RETAINED PROFIT	50

(*Note:* Total depreciation included above = £40,000)

Fig 9.9 Matthew Grimble's profit and loss statement for Year 5

MATTHEW GRIMBLE LTD
Notes on the published accounts for This Year

Note 1—Fixed Assets

(£'000)	*Land and buildings*	*Plant and equipment*	*Total*
Assets at cost			
as at Last Year	85	225	310
additions during year	35	55	90
as at This Year	120	280	400
Accumulated depreciation			
as at Last Year	:	80	80
charge for This Year	:	40	40
as at This Year	:	120	120
Net value as at 31 December This Year	120	160	280

Note 2—Current Liabilities

	Last Year	*This Year*
Trade creditors	80	110
Interest on loan capital	20	20
Taxation	32	35
Dividends	30	30
	162	195

Note 3—Share Capital (both years)

	Authorized	*Issued*
200,000 shares @ £1 each	200	200

Note 4—Reserves

	£'000
Balance as at 31 December Last Year	231
Retained profit for This Year	50
Balance as at 31 December This Year	281

Fig 9.10 Notes appended to Matthew Grimble's published accounts for Year 5

comes next, followed by the amount of capital expenditure that has been invested in the longer-term future of my company. If this investment has been financed out of my operational profits and

(£'000)	ASSETS					
	FIXED ASSETS	DEPRECI-ATION	STOCKS	DEBTORS	CASH/ BANK	FUNDS
1 Opening balance sheet equation	310	80	250	175	88	0
2 Transfer to reserves						50
3 Dividends due					-30	-30
4 Tax due					-35	-35
5 Interest due on loan capital					-20	
6 Depreciation of fixed assets		40				40
7 Purchase of new buildings/plant	90					-90
8 TRIAL BALANCE (1)						
9 Net funds generated from operations						
10 Increase in stocks						
11 Increase in debtors						
12 Decrease in cash						
13 Increase in trade creditors						
14 Payment of last year's tax						
15 Payment of dividends						
16 Payment of loan interest						
17 Closing balance sheet equation	400	120	320	210	16	0

Fig 9.11 Matthew Grimble's transaction equation work sheet for Year 5

available funds, well and good. If not, then you can see exactly how much additional capital investment was required in order to finance my expansion plans—right on the bottom line, where it really matters!'

The Matthew Grimble statements

As in previous chapters, we propose to close by taking another look at the Matthew Grimble operations, and once again we shall leave you to complete the figures for yourself. We shall be looking once more at his Year 5 figures, with which you are already somewhat familiar.

=	LIABILITIES							
	SHARE CAPITAL	RESERVES	LOAN CAPITAL	TRADE CRED'RS	LOAN INT.DUE	TAX DUE	DIV'DNDS DUE	PROFIT & LOSS
	200	231	150	80	20	32	30	
		50						
							-30	
						-35		
								-20
								-40
	200	281	150	110	20	35	30	

Figure 9.8 gives you the balance sheet for Years 4 and 5; the profit and loss statement for Year 5 is reproduced in Figure 9.9, and extracts from the directors' report are contained in Figure 9.10. A blank work sheet is provided in Figure 9.11, and blanks of both the 'SSAP' and recommended versions of the source and application of funds statement are given in Figures 9.12 and 9.13. A completed work sheet and statements are provided for check purposes in Figures 9.14 to 9.16, while Figure 9.17 is a reproduction of Matthew's representation of this statement from his employees' report. He thought you might like this to make up the set.

£'000	Year 5
Sources of funds:	
Operating profit before interest and tax	
Add back: Total depreciation	——
TOTAL FUNDS GENERATED	——
Application of funds:	
Interest paid on loan capital	
Share dividends paid	
Tax paid on Year 4's operations	
Purchase of fixed assets	——
Total:	——
Increases/(Decreases) in working capital	
Increases in stocks	
Increase in debtors	
(Decrease) in cash	
(Increase) in creditors	——
Net increase:	——
TOTAL APPLICATION OF FUNDS	══

Fig 9.12 Matthew Grimble's source and application of funds statement for Year 5—SSAP version (skeleton)

(£'000)	ASSETS					
	FIXED ASSETS	DEPRECI-ATION	STOCKS	DEBTORS	CASH/ BANK	FUN
1 Opening balance sheet equation	310	−80	250	175	88	
2 Transfer to reserves	:	:	:	:	:	
3 Dividends due	:	:	:	:	:	
4 Tax due	:	:	:	:	:	
5 Interest due on loan capital	:	:	:	:	:	
6 Depreciation of fixed assets	:	−40	:	:	:	
7 Purchase of new buildings/plant	90	:	:	:	:	
8 TRIAL BALANCE (1)	400	−120	250	175	88	
9 Net funds generated from operations	:	:	:	:	:	
10 Increase in stocks	:	:	70	:	:	
11 Increase in debtors	:	:	:	35	:	
12 Decrease in cash	:	:	:	:	−72	
13 Increase in trade creditors	:	:	:	:	:	
14 Payment of last year's tax	:	:	:	:	:	
15 Payment of dividends	:	:	:	:	:	
16 Payment of loan interest	:	:	:	:	:	
17 Closing balance sheet equation	400	−120	320	210	16	

Fig 9.14 Matthew Grimble's transaction equation work sheet for Year 5

£'000		Year 5
Sales revenue		
Operational expenditure		——
Funds generated from trading operations		
Financing costs		
Interest paid on loan capital		
Tax paid on Year 4's operations		
Dividends paid	——	
		——
Net funds available for use		
Net movements in circulating capital		
Increase in stocks		
Increase in debtors		
(Decrease) in cash		
(Increase) in creditors	——	
		——
Operating funds available for long-term investment		
Investment in new Buildings and plant		——
Additional capital required for investment		
		══

Fig 9.13 Matthew Grimble's source and application of funds statement for Year 5—'recommended' version (skeleton)

=	← LIABILITIES →							
	SHARE CAPITAL	RESERVES	LOAN CAPITAL	TRADE CRED'RS	LOAN INT.DUE	TAX DUE	DIV'DNDS DUE	PROFIT & LOSS
=	200	231	150	80	20	32	30	0
	:	50	:	:	:	:	:	−50
	:	:	:	:	:	:	30	−30
	:	:	:	:	:	35	:	−35
	:	:	:	:	20	:	:	−20
=	:	:	:	:	:	:	:	−40
	:	:	:	:	:	:	:	:
=	200	281	150	80	40	67	60	−175
=	:	:	:	:	:	:	:	175
	:	:	:	:	:	:	:	:
	:	:	:	:	:	:	:	:
	:	:	:	:	:	:	:	:
=	:	:	:	30	:	:	:	:
=	:	:	:	:	:	−32	:	:
=	:	:	:	:	:	:	−30	:
=	:	:	:	:	−20	:	:	:
=	200	281	150	110	20	35	30	0

£'000		Year 5
Sources of funds:		
Operating profit before interest and tax		135
Add back: Total depreciation		40
TOTAL FUNDS GENERATED		175
Application of funds:		
Interest paid on loan capital	20	
Dividends paid	30	
Tax paid on Year 4's operations	32	
Purchase of fixed assets	90	
Total:		172
Increases/Decreases in working capital		
Increase in stocks	70	
Increase in debtors	35	
(Decrease) in cash	−72	
(Increase) in creditors	−30	
Net increase:		3
TOTAL APPLICATION OF FUNDS:		175

Fig 9.15 Matthew Grimble's source and application of funds statement for Year 5—SSAP version (completed)

£'000		Year 5
Sales revenue		1,130
Operational expenditure		955
Funds generated from trading operations		175
Financing costs		
Interest paid on loan capital	20	
Tax paid on Year 4's operations	32	
Dividends paid	30	
		82
Net funds available for use		93
Net movements in circulating capital		
Increase in stocks	70	
Increase in debtors	35	
(Decrease) in cash	−72	
(Increase) in creditors	−30	
		3
Operating funds available for long-term investment		90
Investment in new buildings and plant		−90
Additional capital required for investment		0

Fig 9.16 Matthew Grimble's source and application of funds statement for Year 5—'recommended' version (completed)

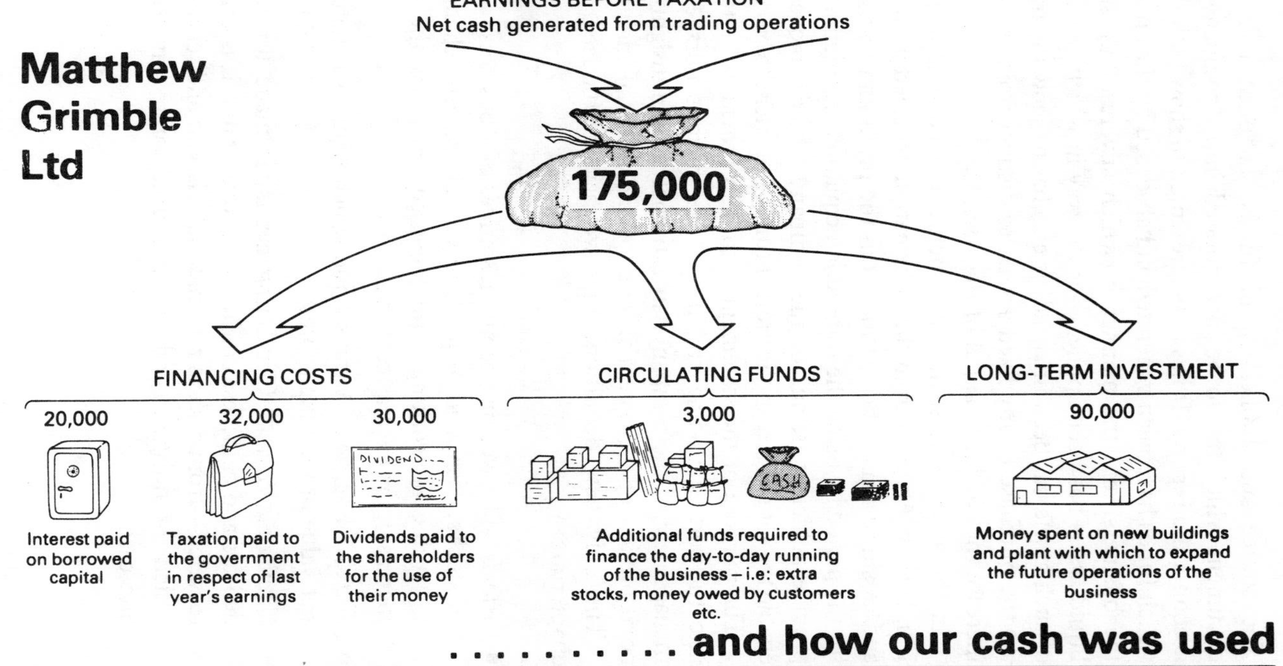

Fig 9.17 Matthew Grimble's diagrammatic representation of his source and application of funds statement for Year 5

Summary

The source and application of funds statement is a statutory document which has to be incorporated into a company's annual accounts and reports. It has to be presented to show both the way in which funds have been generated and absorbed by the operations of the business, and the manner in which any resulting surplus of liquid assets has been applied—or the way in which any deficiency of such assets has been financed. It also has to show the funds used for the purchase of any fixed assets, as distinct from those used to increase the working capital of the company.

In the absence of such a statement, it is possible to prepare a Funds Flow Analysis from the information provided in the opening and closing balance sheets, and from the profit and loss statement for the period by using the transaction equation technique. This will provide sufficient details of the company's funds' movements to enable the source and application of funds statement to be compiled.

The purpose of the statement is to help provide a better insight into the sort of trading and investment policies pursued by the management of the company: an extremely useful insight from the point of view of the potential investor and financial analyst.

The only new definitions that we have introduced into this chapter are:

- *Funds* The working capital resources of a business, consisting of stocks, cash, and debtors, less creditors. Any change to the net value of working capital consequently has the effect of increasing or decreasing funds.
- *Funds transaction* A transaction which leads to a change in the net value of working capital.
- *Circulating capital* Circulating capital is made up of stocks, debtors and cash, less creditors and overdrafts. It is continually recycled—from cash to raw materials, labour and services, from which the finished goods are produced for reconversion back into cash.

10 The cash flow forecast

Introduction

We have now completed our studies of the three statutory financial statements that every company has to file in respect of its performance. The balance sheet tells us where the company's money came from, and where it was represented at the particular moment in time at which the statement was prepared; the profit and loss statement gives us information about the degree of growth or shrinkage that has taken place within the company during the trading period; and the source and application of funds statement shows us how the company raised its funds, and how it used them.

This all adds up to a pretty comprehensive picture, and it's fine as far as it goes. Looking at a company from the outside, this is really as much as anyone could expect, because no company is going to publish its detailed plans for the future. All it will do is give some general indications of potential growth or development in the Directors' report which accompanies the accounts. But once you walk over the threshold, and start looking at the company from the inside, you realize that this isn't really quite enough. You've now got to start looking at things from the point of view of the management of the company, and it isn't long before you realize that managers can't be expected to fulfil their function properly if they only know how much they had in the kitty on 31 December last year, how much they earned last year, and where it came from. That would be just about as productive as trying to drive a car with a shattered windscreen down a busy street, with nothing to guide you but the rear-view mirror!

The need for financial planning and control

Management is concerned with the future: with defining, evaluating, comparing and selecting strategies which are considered likely to be of the greatest potential benefit to their company, and no one can manage what happened yesterday, last week, or last year. It is already too late for that; the only events that we are in a position to influence are the ones that lie ahead sometime in the future.

No one will deny that the ability to make sound commercial decisions depends to a great extent upon being able to obtain and interpret historical and current financial *information*. One of the main objectives of this book is to provide a better degree of understanding among managers and students that will enable them to do just that—but we can't just leave it there. Historical information is an essential base upon which to build our future plans and strategies; but first of all we have to do our best to ensure that there *is* a future—and the one thing you need in business in order to do that is *cash*. After all, there's no great future in planning a future if you can't find the cash to finance it!

So, in order to plan, we have to prepare budgets and evaluate our strategies; and in order to do that, we must know how much money we shall need, and how, or where, we are going to get hold of it. We shall need to forecast our *cash flow*, by means of a Cash Flow Forecast. This happens to be a very accurate description of the document because, as we have seen from our earlier discussions, something happens to cash that doesn't happen to anything else in business. It *flows*, and the continued health of a company depends on its ability to maintain that flow as steadily and as regularly as possible.

In our last chapter, we considered the concept of 'circulating capital', and of how our interest was focused on the way in which a company's funds had 'grown' or 'shrunk' during a trading period. We are now going to sharpen our focus even further, and concentrate on the cash element of funds, because, as we said back in Chapter 4, cash is the essential fuel which enables the 'funds engine' to keep circulating.

The circulation of cash is the very essence of business. It moves in from investors, out into fixed assets or working capital, and in again through sales, but the important thing to remember is that it has to be available to pay the bills as and when they become due. It is absolutely essential for a manager to know exactly *how much* he has—or will have—available at any particular point in time, whether that time is now, or at any forecast time in the future.

One of the things he also needs to remember is that money rarely moves regularly and smoothly in business, because of the cyclic patterns of trade. As we have already seen, cash is not really synonymous with anything: it is not synonymous with sales, because of the barrier created by debtors, and it is not synonymous with purchases, because of the barrier inserted by the company between itself and its creditors. Nor is it synonymous with profit, because it is not at all unusual for a business making a profit to be drastically short of cash, or even for it to be seemingly rolling in money, and yet be making a loss.

Consider, on the one hand, a manufacturer of fireworks who has to pay for his materials, labour and overheads over a long period before he sells his products. A retailer of Coronation programmes may find himself in the same difficulties; but, at the other extreme, a package tour operator will often be collecting cash from his customers for quite a while before his hotel bills have to be paid. It is therefore essential for management to be aware of the company's cash flow patterns, and to make sure that they are properly controlled.

How good was your budget?

There is nothing revolutionary about forecasting cash flow patterns. In fact, many people like to sit down and plan their household budget in the same sort of way. This quite often happens around Christmas time, when we have just been told how much of a rise we have been awarded for next year, and we want to work out what sort of holiday we can afford. The sort of figures that we might come up with would be somewhat like those illustrated in Figure 10.1. They look fine. We only have £100 to start off with, but all the expenses, including provision for a holiday, seem to be safely covered, and, provided that nothing unforeseen happens, we might even end up with more in the bank than we started with.

So that's our budget—but what about our Cash Flow Forecast? Before we get too carried away, perhaps we ought to have a closer look at these figures to see just how they are likely to move from our opening balance of £100 to our closing balance of £250.

	£'000
Balance b/fd on 1 January	100
Annual net salary	6,750
Total available for use	6,850
Mortgage payments	1,350
Rates and insurance	700
Heat, light and telephone	500
Housekeeping	1,500
Car	600
Family—clothing, etc	400
Repairs and renewals	300
Holiday	850
Miscellaneous	400
Total expenses	6,600
Balance c/fd at 31 December	250

Fig 10.1 Our personal annual expenditure budget

— *Monthly salary:* This is obviously the main ingredient, because, without this, we wouldn't be able to pay for anything. £6,750 seems to be quite adequate to cover all our anticipated expenses, but we have to remember that it won't be coming in in regular monthly instalments, because we are lucky enough—from one point of view—to have both a summer and a Christmas bonus. This means that our usual monthly pay cheque is likely to yield about £500, while June could be up to £750, and December £1,000. Roll on Christmas!

— *Mortgage, rates and insurance:* Assuming that interest rates remain fairly stable, our mortgage repayments should be nicely predictable. We pay £110 per month at the moment, so let us assume that this might go up to £120 around next October. We also pay our rates by monthly standing order—the rates being on a 10-month May–February cycle; while property insurance becomes due in November.

— *Heat, light and telephone:* Electricity charges are covered by a monthly budget plan, the gas is paid quarterly, and the telephone bills are paid every two months as and when they arrive. The winter quarters are obviously going to be comparatively expensive because of the gas bills.

— *Housekeeping and car maintenance:* We shall probably allow for some extra housekeeping money to coincide with our June and December bonuses, but the car costs are much more difficult to forecast. Car maintenance bills are always unpredictable—and always expensive—but May and August could be the most likely months when these will be highest, so we can allow for extra expenditure then.

— *Family clothing:* No one really expects you to spend a regular £15 a month on clothing, but the overall year's total is fairly predictable. We have already planned the January 'sales raid', and the children will need to be kitted out for the new school term in September, so we shall have to allow for these items at the appropriate times.

— *Repairs and maintenance:* There is quite a lot of decorating to be done around the house, and we hope to get this done in the spring.

— *Miscellaneous:* Apart from Christmas presents in November, this is really a contingency item, and can be fairly evenly spread through the year.

— *Holiday:* Assuming that we can still afford to have one, we are planning to take our holiday in August, and then send off a deposit in December for next year's holiday.

	Jan	Feb	Mar	Apr	May	Jun	Jul	Aug	Sep	Oct	Nov	Dec	Total
Balance b/fd	100	115	180	300	230	165	450	(200)	(190)	(235)	(170)	(175)	100
Monthly salary	500	500	500	500	500	750	500	500	500	500	500	1,000	6,750
Total available	600	615	680	800	730	915	950	300	310	265	330	825	6,850
Mortgage repayments	110	110	110	110	110	110	110	110	110	120	120	120	1,350
Rates and insurance	60	30	30	60	60	60	60	60	60	60	100	60	700
Heat, light and telephone	15	80	15	35	90	40	15	65	15	40	50	40	500
Housekeeping	120	120	120	120	120	150	120	120	120	120	120	150	1,500
Car	40	40	40	40	100	40	40	80	40	40	60	40	600
Family, clothing etc	100	15	15	15	15	15	15	15	150	15	15	15	400
Repairs and renewals	10	10	10	160	40	10	10	10	10	10	10	10	300
Holiday	–	–	–	–	–	–	750	–	–	–	–	100	850
Miscellaneous	30	30	40	30	30	40	30	30	40	30	30	40	400
Total expenses	485	435	380	570	565	465	1,150	490	545	435	505	575	6,600
Balance c/fd	115	180	300	230	165	450	(200)	(190)	(235)	(170)	(175)	250	250

Fig 10.2 Our annual cash flow forecast

So there we are. The Total column in Figure 10.2 is identical to our original budget in Figure 10.1, but something rather unpleasant seems to have crept into the figures during the course of our phasing process. From the look of things, we can expect to be broke, or at least resorting to a credit card, for five months out of the twelve, despite the optimism generated by our original annual budget—unless, of course, we revise our plans, get promoted, or phone our Friendly Bank Manager before he phones us! Not that he would be particularly worried, provided that we could explain the overall situation to him; and this situation would basically be that we were planning to have rather an expensive holiday at the beginning of August, which had to be paid for in July, in anticipation of a bonus that we weren't going to receive until December.

Even at this level, it is easy to see how essential it is to plan our cash flow carefully, because the more warning we have that cash is likely to run short on us, the more we shall be able to take the necessary corrective action, or to plan an appropriate strategy to overcome our anticipated difficulties.

The dangers of success

A lot of people think that the way they run their personal lives has nothing to do with the world of business, but the few examples that we have already used in this book will illustrate that there are many parallels to be found. Cash flow control is one such example, and one of the reasons why so many firms, particularly the smaller ones, go to the wall is that their managers fail to appreciate its importance. The sad, paradoxical truth of the matter is that so many cash flow problems arise out of success!

Take the case of a small builder-cum-decorator, for example. He will no doubt have worked extremely hard over several years to build up a reputation for good-quality workmanship, and now employs two men to help him. He will have ploughed his profits back into his business in order to buy a van, ladders, and all the equipment he needs to enable him to take on some of the better jobs further afield, as his reputation spreads.

But is he pricing out his jobs correctly to make sure that he is going to cover all his fixed expenses, like the depreciation on his new van? He will obviously be doing his best to get the jobs he wants to do, but he must nevertheless be very careful to watch that he is not keeping his quotations down below those of his competitors *at all costs*. If he does this too often, he might end up by getting the work at a price below which none of his competitors would consider it worth while to quote.

And then, of course, he has to get the money in from his customers, and that generally means paperwork! As we have already seen, though, time is money—especially if he has an overdraft—because, for every week that he allows his customers to owe him money for the work he has finished, the bank will be charging him interest on the money he owes them. They will have to, because that is the way their business works. What our builder will have to remember is that the money on which he is paying interest is money that ought to be in his own account anyway, and not in the account of that dear old couple in the next village who have just had their house painted.

If all goes well, and his reputation spreads, this builder might find that he is invited to quote for bigger and better jobs: perhaps for someone who wants four cottages converted into one nice luxurious residence, for example. This could be a very prestigious contract from which he could easily earn an extra margin of profit—when he finally gets paid for it. Because it is a big job, and likely to keep both him and his two lads busy for the best part of the summer, it may be six months before he sees a penny, and in the meantime he has got his men to pay, his materials to buy, and his own family to keep. It may not be so much a question of whether or not he can afford to turn the job down, but rather one of whether or not he can afford to accept it.

There are a number of things that he could do in a situation like this. He might suggest to his new client that he would like to be paid by instalments, as each portion of the contract is completed; or he could sit down and work out a realistic cash flow forecast, and take this along to discuss quite frankly and openly with his bank manager. After all, the bank's job is to help and advise its clients in any practical way it can. What banks will not do, if they can help it, is to encourage their clients to take on anything that may stand too great a risk of leading them into financial difficulties from which they might be unable to recover.

Anyway, assuming that this builder did prepare his forecast, and did consult his bank manager, who did agree to allow him overdraft facilities, the next thing that he must *not* do is go out right away and buy all the supplies that he is likely to need over the next six months. He must plan his purchases well ahead so that he knows exactly how much of which material he will need by what time, and then shop around for the best terms available from his suppliers. This may not just mean the lowest prices, but will also take credit terms into consideration, so that he can stretch his commitments out as far as possible to match his income.

Preparing the Andco cash flow forecast for This Year

The same underlying philosophy applies to all businesses, large or small, and it can also be true to say that the bigger they are, the harder they fall. Even companies like Andco have to be careful, as Andrew would be the first to admit, and one of the problems is that, as companies get larger, cash flow forecasting gets much more complex.

As a matter of fact, we were chatting to Andrew about this quite recently—soon after we had built up his forecast balance sheet and profit and loss statement for This Year, actually—and he was really quite smug about it all. He happened to have our original working papers in his pocket at the time, so he pulled out the work sheet—the one you will remember from either Figure 8.7 or Figure 8.11—spread it out on the table, and pointed triumphantly to the cash column.

Line Ref (Figure 8.11)		*£'000*	
1	Opening balance		110
2	Payment of liabilities from last year		
	Loan interest		−20
	Tax		−94
	Dividends		−5
4	Investment interest received		2
	Employee costs		
5B	Direct production labour	−365	
5C	Indirect labour	−144	
8	Selling and administration labour	−151	
	Total		−660
13	Cash received from debtors		2,155
14	Cash paid to creditors		−1,154
15	Leasehold pre-payments for next year		−30
16	Interim dividends (this year)		−20
20	Forecast closing balance		284

Fig 10.3 Andco's cash movements summary for This Year

'There you are!' he said, 'Look at that! I started off this year with £110,000 in the bank, and expect to end up with £284,000. You can't dispute it, because you helped me work out the figures yourself! And then, if you look at the profit and loss forecast, you can see a profit after tax of £233,000, compared with only £13,000 last year. And, out of that, I hope to take out £50,000 in dividends—no less than *ten times as much* as last year!'

As you might imagine, his verbal and visual presentation of all these facts and figures was somewhat spectacular; and to give him his due, he had got them all right—as you can check for yourself by looking back to Figure 8.14. By the time he had finished, he had managed to convince himself that he had every reason to consider that this called for a celebration, and now seemed to be as good a time as any! So, since it would have been far too churlish and ungracious to argue with a proposition like that, and it happened to be his round, anyway. . . .

When that had all been organized, we settled down again to study that cash column on his work sheet a bit more closely. What we decided to do was to take each item in turn, and phase it as nearly as we could over the four quarters of the year. In order to make this easier to follow, we have extracted the figures from this column into Figure 10.3.

Yes, these were the figures that Andrew had looked at, and had felt so pleased about. But had he ever sat down and phased them out over individual monthly or quarterly periods? Well, er, no he hadn't but he'd hardly considered that to be necessary—or, to be perfectly honest, when he came to think about it, he'd never actually thought about it! Perhaps we could just go through the motions, if only to prove that he needn't have bothered, anyway?

Well, that served us right for raising the question in the first place, but we were only too happy to help if we could, so we decided to prepare a quarterly cash flow forecast from his figures. This consequently meant that we now had to go through each of his summarized transactions with him in turn, so that he could tell us how the various annual amounts should be phased over the four quarters.

It was probably just as easy to work down from the top of his cash movements summary as to take any other sequence, so that's what we decided to do. Perhaps you would like to fill the figures into a blank cash flow forecast as we go along. We have set one up for you in Figure 10.4, and you will see that we have entered the annual totals into the annual column for you, so all you have to do at this stage is to make sure that you enter the figures into the correct quarterly column, and then make sure that they cross-cast to this annual figure.

Line Ref.	*(£'000)*	*Q.1*	*Q.2*	*Q.3*	*Q.4*	*Total*
1	Opening balance					110
2	B/fd liabilities					
	Loan interest					−20
	Tax					−94
	Dividends					−5
4	Investment interest received					2
5/8	Employee costs					−660
13	Cash received from debtors					2155
14	Cash paid to creditors					
	New plant & equipment					−133
	Trade creditors					−1021
15	Pre-payments for next year					−30
16	Interim dividends (this year)					−20
20	Forecast closing balance					284

Fig 10.4 Andco's cash flow work-sheet for This Year

The first item (Line 2) relates to the payment of liabilities brought forward from Last Year, and as far as Andrew was concerned, these presented no problem. Loan interest was payable during the first quarter, dividends during the second, and tax during the third. The interest receivable from outside investments (Line 4) would come in during the third quarter.

We agreed to combine the employee costs from Lines 5 and 8 into one composite figure of £660,000, since they were fairly predictable, and there were no credit terms involved to complicate things. His present level of employee costs was around £135,000 per quarter, but he was already recruiting for the extra staff that he needed for the autumn launch, so we reckoned that these costs would go up to around £175,000 per quarter from the second quarter onwards. We worked out that this would amount to (135,000 + 175,000 +

175,000 + 175,000 =) £660,000 over the year. So how was that for a nice scientific piece of forecasting, then?

The next item was cash received from debtors in Line 13, obviously a matter of particular interest to Andrew. He reckoned that Andco could not really expect to see any significant additional benefit from their new project until later in the year, and that their income would remain pretty steady at its present level of around £450,000 over the first two quarters. The third quarter should see them beginning to move more goods into the pipeline, although they would then have to allow a few weeks for the cash actually to start coming in. Having taken all that into account, he estimated that this should mean third-quarter receipts of about £520,000, thus leaving (2,155,000 – 450,000 – 450,000 – 520,000 =) £735,000 in the fourth.

That seemed to be just about the target that they were aiming for, and Andrew was beginning to find all this mental exercise quite stimulating. So we decided to press straight on with the cash that he had to pay out to his creditors: that £1,154,000 in Line 14. £133,000 of this related to the new plant which had already been installed, and was practically ready for testing. This was obviously down as a first-quarter commitment.

That left (1,154,000 – 133,000 =) £1,021,000 to be paid to normal trade creditors, and here the pattern was going to be rather different from the pattern of cash received from debtors. Andrew had already started ordering the materials that he would need to get production under way as soon as the new plant was ready to go, and he suggested that, allowing for his normal 5–6 weeks' credit from suppliers, his payment would probably work out at around £320,000 in the first quarter, £270,000 in the second, and £240,000 in the third. That would leave (1,021,000 – 320,000 – 270,000 – 240,000 =) £191,000 in the fourth and final quarter.

Well, we were nearly down to the last line now, so we pressed on with the leasehold pre-payment (Line 15) and the interim dividends (Line 16) that he hoped to pay out—just in time for Christmas. Both items would be paid in the fourth quarter.

The final phased forecast

Andrew had now given us all the breakdowns we needed; so he went off to collect some well-earned liquid refreshment while we totalled each quarter's column, and carried the closing balances forward to the top of the next column, just as we did in the household budget we prepared in Figure 10.2. If you have already done this for yourself, you will have started off with the opening balance of £110,000 at the beginning of Quarter 1, and ended up with £284,000 as the closing balance at the end of Quarter 4.

Line Ref	*£'000*	*Q.1*	*Q.2*	*Q.3*	*Q.4*	*Total*
1	Opening balance	110	−48	−48	−35	110
2	Brought forward liabilities					
	Loan interest	−20	:	:	:	−20
	Tax	:	:	−94	:	−94
	Dividends	:	−5	:	:	−5
4	Investment interest received	:	:	2	:	2
5/8	Employee costs	−135	−175	−175	−175	−660
13	Cash received from debtors	450	450	520	735	2,155
14	Cash paid to creditors					
	New plant and equipment	−133	:	:	:	−133
	Trade creditors	−320	−270	−240	−191	−1,021
15	Pre-payments for Next Year	:	:	:	−30	−30
16	Interim dividends (This Year)	:	:	:	−20	−20
20	Forecast closing balance	−48	−48	−35	284	284

Fig 10.5 Andco's cash flow forecast for This Year

You can check your final results in Figure 10.5—and you can imagine Andrew's reaction when he returned from the bar and saw these figures! We then proceeded to add insult to injury by enquiring whether or not he had discussed his impending overdrawn situation with his bank manager, and he was so aghast at the mere suggestion of such a thing that he forgot all about his hard-earned refreshment and proceeded to double-check all of the figures himself. And then he decided that he really did need that drink!

He wanted to know what he could do, and, when it came down to it, there wasn't all that much that he could do. It was almost a classic case of death by success. He had a good product, and a better one was on its way. The trouble was that it was going to take time to get the new one into the market-place, and, in the meantime, he needed to spend more money than he had available in order to get it there. He needed the new plant in order to produce the product, and he needed extra materials from which to make it. He also needed some extra staff to help cope with the extra work, and then he had to spend money on promotional campaigns so that all those potential customers out there knew that something new and wonderful was on its way. They wouldn't be able to live without it once it was there, but in the meantime. . . .

We explained to him that the first thing he must do was to watch his cash flow like a hawk. Try to get his customers to pay sooner, while trying to persuade his suppliers to grant longer credit. Watch his stock position, and really convince himself that he *needed* to increase his stocks by £133,000 during the year. In other words, move in and get to grips with his working capital, and make sure that every pound invested in that area was working as hard as it could for its living. If he did that, and was confident enough about the outcome of his expansion plans, there was little doubt that his bank manager would be happy enough to accommodate a temporary overdraft facility—at a price. He still had £20,000 on the sidelines in outside investments, anyway, so his security was sound enough, but we had still given him a bit of a fright, for all that! He had obviously set his sights on the crock of gold at the end of that distant rainbow, but hadn't even noticed that he had to cross the Grand Canyon in order to reach it!

He was lucky to have that £110,000 to start off with, too. Suppose he'd only had £10,000: the same cash flow pattern would have ended up eventually with a very comfortable £184,000 at the end of the year, but it would have had to go through quarter-end overdraft levels of £148,000, £148,000 and £135,000 before it got there, and the interest charges on those figures at a rate of 12 per cent per annum would have been around £12,000!—assuming, of course, that his bank manager had had sufficient faith and confidence in his potential success to grant him the overdraft facilities in the first place.

If he had not been able to raise the funds to finance this expansion, he might have had to face the choice of staying as he was, if he could, or of going out of business, which would have been a very sad reward for all the effort that he had put into building his business up to its present level. There was nothing strange about all this; Andrew knew it all the time really, but he just had not sat down and worked out all the figures. He knew exactly where he was going, but he had not worked out how he was going to get there. He even went as far as admitting that it all sounded rather reminiscent of some of his early trips with his Andycab!

We all need money

This just goes to show how careful we all have to be with money. We can only use it once, and while it is comparatively easy to see what is happening with your own money, or in your own small business, things get much more complicated in a large company, where everyone wants to spend it—and it does not always occur to them that someone else might need some as well. In many ways it is much easier for a manager in a big company to authorize expenditure, because it is not his own money that he is spending. After all, the managers, all specialists in their own areas, enjoy the professional satisfaction of doing a good job, and of making that essential and effective contribution to the continued success of their company as a member of the management team.

They didn't have to read a book like this to realize that team effort was needed to achieve this continued success, or even to realize that success meant profit. But they were employed as specialists, and it would not be too difficult for any of them to make out a case for the spending of more money in their own particular area of influence. For instance:

— The Personnel Manager would like better restaurant facilities for the staff, and more luxurious interview rooms that would create a better impression for potential new employees.

— The Data Processing Manager would like a bigger and better computer to enable him to provide faster and better information for his management colleagues.

— The Sales Manager would like to spend more money on promotion, and have sufficient stocks of every product available on the shelf to enable him to satisfy any conceivable customer requirement—immediately!

— The Production Manager would like long, uninterrupted runs of one product at a time so that he did not have to keep cleaning down and resetting his machines, although he does appreciate that this might cause the sales manager a problem in the event of some products running out of stock while he is producing a long run of something else. Well, he does realize that they are all interdependent in this business, so the best thing that he could do would be to produce long runs of everything!

And what has the Accountant been doing while all this has been going on? He would have been running out of hair almost as quickly as the Warehouse Manager would have been running out of space, when he saw how much money was being tied up in masses of stocks that would take quite a long time to sell—just at the time when extra money is being asked for by the Research and Development Manager in order to fund the research that is essential to the long-term benefit of the company.

And then what would happen if something went wrong? Suppose one of the major products suddenly became obsolete and there were still hundreds of units left on the shelves, unlikely ever to recover the cost of their production? What would the Production Manager do with the people committed to those particular long, continuous runs—assuming, of course, that his machines had not fallen apart in the meantime because the engineers hadn't been able to get near them while they were busy?

The Accountant is in a better position than most to see what is going on, simply because he is the one who has to make sure that the bills are paid. But there is not much that he can do on his own to control the situation while all his fellow managers are out there, tucked away in their own little departmental boxes, spending the company's money like there's no tomorrow. All doing their own particular thing to the best of their ability, but seemingly oblivious of the effect that they may be having on the company's general financial situation, or of what anyone else in any of the other little departmental boxes is up to. . . .

Summary

The main financial statements that we have studied in our earlier chapters have all related to the reflection or representation of past events expressed in financial terms. This is all that external investors or analysts could expect to see, but the job of the management team inside the company is to develop and co-ordinate commercial strategies which can steer the company on a successful course into the future.

It certainly needs historical information upon which to base its judgements, but it also has to evaluate its future strategies in financial terms. This means forecasting, or budgeting, and part of this process must involve the forecasting of likely cash flow patterns, because there is not a great deal of point in planning for things which cannot be paid for.

It is a very sad, hard, economic fact of business life that, during periods of severe depression, many companies fail and go out of business. Still, depressions do not last forever, and, when the upturn finally arrives, the opportunities for growth and expansion will be really tremendous for the companies that have been fortunate enough to survive. These will inevitably be the ones which have had the ability and foresight to preserve their cash flow intact. It all comes back to the old story of 'when the circulation stops—you're dead!'

A long-range forecast may look perfectly healthy and satisfactory when considered in overall terms, but its analysis into shorter time segments may well reveal dangerous gaps in the company's potential ability to survive, and detailed cash forecasting is essential in every business, large or small.

Cash control involves the whole company. Everyone has a responsibility to co-operate and participate in cash planning. It cannot be done exclusively by the accountant, although it is his job to monitor and review what is happening to cash as quickly and as effectively as possible. In larger companies, where functional responsibility is split between a number of specialist managers, it is also essential for them to work as a cohesive team—and that means *communication*. So here we are again at the point where we can all join in the chorus: 'The ability to communicate depends upon the existence of a common language, *and the common language of business is finance*'.

Once again, we have not introduced many new terms in the course of this chapter, but we should nevertheless not ignore the ones which have been used:

- *Cash flow forecast* A statement which analyses all cash receipts and payments over the periods during which the transactions are expected to take place, in order to anticipate any potential shortages before they actually arise, and thus give sufficient time for appropriate remedial action to be taken.
- *Employee costs* Wages, salaries, insurance, pensions and all other associated costs incurred in connection with the payment of employed labour.

11 The evaluation and co-ordination of a budget

Introduction

The function of management can be likened very closely to that of the captain of a ship. He needs to know exactly where he is at this very moment, where he is going to, and how to chart the shortest and safest course that will ensure his timely arrival at his planned destination. The going may not always be easy, and in addition to keeping a sharp look-out for any possible obstacles or dangers in his immediate or short-term vicinity, he will also keep an ear open for the long-range weather forecasts, so that he can make adequate provision and preparations for whatever may lie ahead beyond the medium-term horizon, and into the longer-term future.

We have just seen how cash-flow forecasting is one of the key strategic factors with which the management of every company must be vitally concerned. We have also referred briefly to the wider concept of budgeting, and to how essential it is that every member of the management team should be directly involved in its operation. In fact, to try and pretend that a manager has no part to play in the budgeting process is tantamount to claiming that he needs no goal to aim for, no indication of the ultimate destination that he is expected to reach, nor any guidance concerning the best way to get there.

This is obviously not on, because a collection of so-called 'managers' who are all going their own way, and doing their own thing, could never be regarded as a team, and no company can expect to survive for long without a cohesive management strategy, or policy. After all, a team of managers in a large company is nothing more nor less than a scaled-up version of the one-person manager of a small business. It must therefore follow directly from this that, if a company is going to have any hope of following that 'shortest and safest course' to its chosen destination, then its management team will have to be able to work as one co-ordinated unit.

Where are we now?

One way of illustrating the kind of situations and problems that can be included in the context of our present discussion is to go step by step through the simulated process of actually evaluating and co-ordinating a company budget. We have already prepared Andco's forecast financial statements for This Year, and broken these figures down into a cash flow forecast, so we are now going to have a look at Matthew Grimble's 'departmentalized' organization, where we shall need to draw upon the expertise and knowledge of the various specialist managers involved.

Some way back, at the end of Chapter 5, we asked you to compile a 'standard' balance sheet format from a set of data presented in the form of a financial model. Then, in Chapter 9, you prepared his source and application of funds statement for Year 5, so you already know something about his figures for that year. Since we shall now be devoting our thoughts to his managers' forecasts for Year 6, the Year 5 balance sheet would be a very appropriate point from which to start. In order to make the references easier, the next few pages contain a complete set of financial statements for Year 5, and you may well find it helpful to refresh your memory by tracing the various figures through from one document to another. All the explanations and guidance you need have been covered in previous chapters, so we shall only be skimming briefly through the main points during the actual compilation of the budgets. This will nevertheless be a useful opportunity to consolidate those topics, and to convince yourself that you are satisfied with your level of understanding and appreciation so far.

Figure 11.1 gives you the full balance sheet details for both Year 4 and Year 5. The stock movements and cost of goods sold schedule is in Figure 11.2, the profit and loss statement is in Figure 11.3, and the source and application of funds statement is in Figure 11.4.

This should not just be an exercise in moving figures around from one piece of paper to another, though; we should also take this opportunity to try and visualize what the figures mean. How do the

£'000	*Year 4*		*Year 5*	
Fixed assets at cost:				
Land and buildings		85		120
Plant and machinery		225		280
Total cost		310		400
Less: Depreciation to date		80		120
Written down book value		230		280
Stocks:				
Consumable stores	15		20	
Raw materials	45		55	
Work-in-progress	50		65	
Finished goods	140		180	
Total stocks	250		320	
Trade debtors	175		210	
Cash/bank	88		16	
Current assets	513		546	
Trade creditors	80		110	
Tax due	32		35	
Dividends due	30		30	
Loan interest due	20		20	
Current liabilities	162		195	
NET WORKING CAPITAL		351		351
NET ASSETS		581		631
Share capital		200		200
Reserves		231		281
Shareholders' funds		431		481
Loan capital		150		150
CAPITAL EMPLOYED		581		631

Fig 11.1 Matthew Grimble's balance sheets for Years 4 and 5

sales revenue figures compare with the cost of goods sold, for example. By what sort of proportion, if any, has the value of fixed assets increased during the year? Has the value of stocks increased,

£'000		*Year 5*
(a) CONSUMABLE STORES		
Opening stock		15
Purchases		35
		50
Less: Closing stock		20
Usages (to W.I.P.)		30
(b) RAW MATERIALS		
Opening stock		45
Purchases		230
		275
Less: Closing stock		55
Usages (to W.I.P.)		220
(c) WORK-IN-PROGRESS		
Direct labour		230
Overheads:		
Indirect labour	120	
Production administration	35	
Power and light	35	
Depreciation	35	
Rates and insurance	30	
Consumable stores	30	
Total		285
Charges during year ('activity')		735
Opening stock b/fd		50
		785
Less: Closing stock c/fd		65
COST OF GOODS MANUFACTURED		720
(d) FINISHED GOODS		
Opening stock b/fd		140
		860
Less: Closing stock c/fd		180
COST OF GOODS SOLD		680

Fig 11.2 Matthew Grimble's stock movements and cost of goods sold schedule for Year 5

£'000		*Year 5*
Sales		1,130
Less: Cost of goods sold		680
Gross trading profit		450
Product promotion	130	
Selling and administration		
Employee costs	120	
Third party costs	60	
Depreciation (non-production)	5	
Total selling and administration costs		315
Operating profit/(loss) before interest and tax		135
Interest payable on loan capital		20
NET PROFIT BEFORE TAX		115
Taxation		35
Profit after tax		80
Dividends		30
RETAINED PROFIT		50
Number of Employees		73

Fig 11.3 Matthew Grimble's profit and loss forecast for Year 5

and is there more cash in the bank than there was a year ago? This is the sort of approach that will help to keep the figures in perspective, because we are not just looking at numbers—we are trying to interpret *information*.

It is a little unfortunate that Matthew happens to be away on business at the moment with his Chief Accountant, so we shall have to do our best to sort out all the details we need in order to co-ordinate the Year 6 budget details into a set of forecast financial statements. We shall be able to do this from the individual functional forecasts that have been prepared by the Sales Manager and the Production Manager, together with a few notes produced by the Accountant before he left on his trip with Matthew. These forecasts are all reproduced on the following pages.

We shall start with the sales budget, because this represents the 'front end' of the business: the part from which everything else

£'000		Year 5
SOURCES OF FUNDS		
Operating profit before interest and tax		135
Add back: Total depreciation		40
Total funds generated from trading operations		175
Additional share capital	:	
Additional loan capital	:	
Total funds from other sources		:
TOTAL FUNDS GENERATED		175
APPLICATION OF FUNDS		
Interest on loan capital	20	
Dividends paid	30	
Tax paid	32	
Purchase of fixed assets	90	
Total		172
INCREASE/(DECREASE) IN WORKING CAPITAL		
Increase/(Decrease) in stocks	70	
Increase/(Decrease) in debtors	35	
Increase/(Decrease) in cash	−72	
(Increase)/Decrease in creditors	−30	
Net Increase/(Decrease)		3
TOTAL APPLICATION OF FUNDS		175

Fig 11.4 Matthew Grimble's source and application of funds statement for Year 5

develops. It is not until he knows how much is expected to be sold that the production manager can plan his stock requirements and production schedules; similarly, it is only when these have been finalized that the Purchasing Manager can negotiate his contracts, and the Chief Engineer can organize his maintenance programme.

The Sales budget for Year 6

S.1 We propose to increase our list prices of all items by an average 10 per cent from the beginning of Year 6, but, despite this, still expect to see our sales volumes increasing steadily throughout the year to finish up 16 per cent ahead of Year 5. This means that our sales revenue should be about 28 per cent up on Year 5, at about £1.45 m. All of this will be via credit sales, so that our debtors are likely to increase by roughly the same amount: say to £265,000 by the end of the year.

S.2 We shall have to spend more on product promotion in order to sustain this growth. We therefore plan to spend £160,000 on advertising, and shall need a further £20,000 to cover the salaries of one additional sales representative, and another order clerk. An additional £5,000 will also be needed to cover our increased sales administration (third party) costs.

The Production budget for Year 6

P.1 Our current expansion programme is now almost complete, and we shall have ample capacity available to cope with the increased demand of 16 per cent that is forecast by the sales manager. Higher stock levels of raw materials, consumables and finished units will be required, although work-in-progress stocks should be adequate at their present levels. Allowing for higher prices of purchased materials and services, and for the anticipated 11.5 per cent overall increase in labour rates, the stock values at the end of Year 6 should be:

	£'000
Consumable stores	25
Raw materials	65
Work-in-progress	70
Finished goods	210
Total	370

P.2 Our production costs are likely to be made up as follows:

	Annual budget £'000
2.1 *Raw materials*—at the same average price per unit as in Year 5, due to increased levels of production efficiency, coupled with product mix	255
2.2 *Direct labour.* Allowing for the increased labour rates mentioned above, some overtime, and provision for one additional operator from Q.2 onwards, our direct labour costs will be £60,000 in Q.1, £65,000 in Q.2, and £70,000 per quarter from then on.	265

		Annual budget *£'000*
2.3	*Indirect labour*. One more production supervisor, and one more person in the progress control office will be required, so our indirect labour costs will go up from £35,000 in the first quarter to £40,000 per quarter thereafter.	155
2.4	*Production administration* (third-party) costs. There will be a general increase of about one-third in the level of these costs: say of £10,000 on the Year 5 total of £35,000	45
2.5	*Power and light*. Increased demand and prices are going to increase the cost of this item quite significantly.	50
2.6	*Usages of consumable stores* will be about £5,000 higher than Year 5	35

A summary of the accountant's notes

A.1 The loan interest for Year 5 becomes due for payment in February, and the dividends should be payable in May. This means that the Advance Corporation Tax of £13,000 associated with these will be payable in July, and the Year 5 mainstream Corporation Tax is due in October.

A.2 It is anticipated that our balance of outstanding trade creditors will increase by £30,000 to £140,000 by the end of the year. Our outgoing commitments are unfortunately likely to be heaviest during the early part of the year, due to the need to procure supplies, and to manufacture products, in anticipation of the increased sales demands; so Q.1 is likely to call for £180,000, and Q.2 for £170,000, while Q.3 should drop to £145,000. There is also £90,000 still outstanding on the completion stage of our expansion programme, and this will be subject to fairly prompt payment terms: £70,000 during Q.1, and the rest in Q.2.

A.3 The breakdown of the above capital investment is £20,000 in respect of industrial buildings, and £70,000 in respect of plant and machinery, office furniture and equipment; and we shall be eligible for the usual capital allowances on these items.

A.4 From the look of the Sales Manager's predictions, it seems that we should anticipate settlement of our debtors' accounts in progressively increasing amounts, although our normal credit terms will mean that there will be a time-lag of about two months between the goods going out and the cash coming in. The anticipated income is consequently likely to be around £320,000 in Q.1, £325,000 in Q.2, £350,000 in Q.3, and £400,000 in Q.4—making £1,395,000 in all.

A.5 In addition to the Sales Manager's forecast for an additional £20,000 in respect of sales administration salaries, and another £5,000 for other 'third-party' expenses, the finance and administration areas forecast that a further £20,000 will be needed to cover additional salaries and other expenses. This all adds up to an overall increase of £45,000 over the Year 5 total of £180,000, making £225,000 in all: £150,000 of which will be salaries and other 'direct' costs, and £75,000 of which will be 'third-party' costs. The salaries and 'direct' costs will be £30,000 during the first quarter, rising to £40,000 per quarter over the remainder of the year.

A.6 Depreciation of fixed assets in the production areas will go up from £35,000 in Year 5 to £40,000 in Year 6, and depreciation in the non-production areas will have to be doubled: from £5,000 p.a. to £10,000.

A.7 Loan interest should remain steady at £20,000, although it is hoped that we shall be able to double our Year 5 dividend to £60,000.

A.8 Taking into account the capital allowances mentioned in Note A.3 above, the total amount of Corporation Tax anticipated to be chargeable in respect of Year 6 is £76,000, of which £26,000 will be Advance Corporation Tax associated with the dividends forecast in Note A.7 above.

Getting ourselves organized

This exercise puts us back into the same sort of situation that we were in when we were preparing the Andco forecasts for This Year in Chapter 8, and we shall again be using the transaction equation work sheet as our central assembly document.

All the details that we shall need are—believe it or not!—contained in the three budget scenarios that we have just been given. We shall start by concentrating only on the annual figures, and when we have completed the stock movements and cost of goods sold schedule and the profit and loss forecast, we shall then be able to finish off the work sheet. This will enable us to complete the balance sheet and the quarterly cash flow forecast. We could also, if we wished, then compile a forecast source and application of funds statement, but we shall not bother with that, since the cash flow forecast will be sufficient to enable us to see what is likely to happen to Matthew Grimble's cash flow during the course of the forthcoming year.

So that's our strategy—we now have a plan for evaluating a plan! We have decided against the provision of a complete set of blank forms for you to write in, because that would only be repeating exercises that we have already done before, but you may nevertheless be interested in checking the figures through for yourself before you read the step-by-step guide which follows. That would be a good way of finding out which parts you find most easy to understand, and which ones may still be a little obscure, so why not give it a try, and see how you get on? The form references are as follows:

Figure 11.5—Stock movements and cost of goods sold forecast
Figure 11.6—Profit and loss forecast
Figure 11.7—Funds flow forecast
Figure 11.8—Forecast balance sheet
Figure 11.9—Quarterly cash flow forecast

Stock movements and cost of goods sold forecast—Figure 11.5

The first things to fill in here are the four opening stock balances, taken from the Year 5 balance sheet in Figure 11.1; after which we should be able to rely on the production manager to supply most of the information we need. He does not tell us what his cost of goods sold is going to be, so we shall have to work down to this through the cost of goods manufactured, starting off at the top of the sheet with consumable stores. According to P.6, his usage of these is going to be £5,000 more than it was in Year 5, which makes this figure £35,000, and his closing stock (P.1) is also going up to £5,000 higher than the Year 5 level of £20,000; so his purchases must, by deduction, be (35,000 + 25,000 − 20,000 =) £40,000.

His forecast raw material usage is going to be £255,000 (P.2/1) and he considers that these stocks are going to increase to £65,000

£'000		Year 6 Forecast
(a) CONSUMABLE STORES		
Opening stock		20
Purchases		40
		60
Less: Closing stock		25
Usages (to work-in-progress)		35
(b) RAW MATERIALS		
Opening stock		55
Purchases		265
		320
Less: Closing stock		65
Usages (to work-in-progress)		255
(c) WORK-IN-PROGRESS		
Direct labour		265
Overheads:		
Indirect labour	155	
Production administration	45	
Power and light	50	
Depreciation	40	
Rates and insurance	40	
Consumable stores	35	
Total		365
Charges during year ('Activity')		885
Opening stock b/fd		65
		950
Less: Closing stock c/fd		70
COST OF GOODS MANUFACTURED		880
(d) FINISHED GOODS		
Opening stock b/fd		180
		1,060
Less: Closing stock c/fd		210
COST OF GOODS SOLD		850

Fig 11.5 Matthew Grimble's stock movements and cost of goods sold forecast for Year 6

(P.1), so that his raw material purchases will therefore be (255,000 + 65,000 – 55,000 =) £265,000.

Direct labour and indirect labour are straightforward at £265,000 (P.2/2) and £155,000 (P.2/3) respectively, and production administration costs are likely to go up by £10,000 to £45,000 (P.2/4). He then tells us that power and light will be 'quite significantly' higher than Year 5: at £50,000 (P.2/5).

We have to turn to the accountant's notes to find out how much to include for depreciation and rates and insurance, and we can see from these—A.6—that depreciation will be £40,000, and that rates and insurance will also go up quite significantly from £30,000 in Year 5 to £40,000 in Year 6.

Production overheads therefore total up to £365,000, so that the total charges—or production 'activity'—for the year will be (255,000 + 265,000 + 365,000 =) £885,000. The production manager feels that work-in-progress stocks are likely to be 'adequate' at their present volume levels (P.1), so that his increased valuation from £65,000 to £70,000 is obviously accounted for by higher prices and costs, and this means that the cost of goods manufactured will be (885,000 + 65,000 – 70,000 =) £880,000. Also according to P.1, the stocks of finished goods will need to be increased to £210,000, so that the cost of goods sold must consequently be (880,000 + 180,000 – 210,000 =) £850,000.

The profit and loss forecast—Figure 11.6

Turning to the profit and loss forecast, we can now transfer the cost of goods sold, and deduct this from the sales revenue of £1.45 m forecast by the Sales Manager in S.1, and this gives us a gross trading profit of (1,450,000 – 850,000 =) £600,000.

Product promotion is going to go up to £160,000 (S.2) and the Sales Manager also wants a further £25,000 to cover increased selling and administration costs. But that is not all, because the Accountant also needs a further £20,000 for his own salaries and administration budget (A.5), which means that Year 5's total spend of £180,000 is going to have to go up to (180,000 + 25,000 + 20,000 =) £225,000, of which £150,000 will be salaries and other 'direct' costs, and £75,000 will be third-party costs. Depreciation of non-production assets is going to be doubled to £10,000 (A.6).

The total fixed operating costs of the business will consequently be (160,000 + 150,000 + 75,000 + 10,000 =) £395,000, giving us

£'000		Year 6
Sales		1,450
Less: Cost of goods sold		850
Gross trading profit		600
Product promotion	160	
Selling and administration		
Employee costs	150	
Third party costs	75	
Depreciation (non-production)	10	
Total selling and administration costs		395
Operating profit/(loss) before interest and tax		205
Interest payable on loan capital		20
NET PROFIT BEFORE TAX		185
Taxation		76
Profit after tax		109
Dividends		60
RETAINED PROFIT		49
Number of employees		79

Fig 11.6 Matthew Grimble's profit and loss forecast for Year 6

an operating profit before tax of (600,000 – 395,000 =) £205,000, from which we then have to deduct the non-operational finance costs—the interest on loan capital—of £20,000 (A.7), to arrive at a net profit before tax of £185,000.

We have decided to accept the Accountant's word that £76,000 will be needed to cover the anticipated Corporation Tax liability, so that the profit after tax will be (185,000 – 76,000 =) £109,000, out of which it has apparently been targeted to allocate a dividend payment of £60,000; thus leaving (109,000 – 60,000 =) £49,000 to be retained in the business as reserves.

The transaction equation work sheet—Fiture 11.7

So we can now get down to compiling the funds flow forecast, and, as always, our first step must be to fill in the opening balance sheet

Year 6 (£'000)	F. Ass. @ cost	Depreci-ation	Total stocks	Trade debtors	CASH	=	Share capital	Res'vs	Loan capital	Trade cred'rs	Tax due	Div'nds due	Loan int'rst due	Profit and loss
1 Opening balance equation	400	−120	320	210	16	=	200	281	150	110	35	30	20	:
2 Clearance of b/fd liabilities:														
Tax due—Advance Corp'n Tax	:	:	:	:	−13	=	:	:	:	:	−13	:	:	:
Net mainstream tax	:	:	:	:	−22	=	:	:	:	:	−22	:	:	:
Dividends due	:	:	:	:	−30	=	:	:	:	:	:	−30	:	:
Loan interest due	:	:	:	:	−20	=	:	:	:	:	:	:	−20	:
3 Stock movements and cost of G.S.														
Consumables purchased	:	:	40	:	:	=	:	:	:	40	:	:	:	:
Raw materials purchased	:	:	265	:	:	=	:	:	:	265	:	:	:	:
Direct labour	:	:	265	:	−265	=	:	:	:	:	:	:	:	:
Indirect labour	:	:	155	:	−155	=	:	:	:	:	:	:	:	:
Production administration	:	:	45	:	:	=	:	:	:	45	:	:	:	:
Power and light	:	:	50	:	:	=	:	:	:	50	:	:	:	:
Depreciation	:	−40	40	:	:	=	:	:	:	:	:	:	:	:
Rates and insurance	:	:	40	:	:	=	:	:	:	40	:	:	:	:
4 Profit and loss														
Sales revenue	:	:	:	1,450	:	=	:	:	:	:	:	:	:	1,450
Cost of goods wold	:	:	−850	:	:	=	:	:	:	:	:	:	:	−850
Product promotion	:	:	:	:	:	=	:	:	:	160	:	:	:	−160
Sell/Admin—Third party	:	:	:	:	:	=	:	:	:	75	:	:	:	−75
—Added value	:	:	:	:	−150	=	:	:	:	:	:	:	:	−150
Loan interest	:	:	:	:	:	=	:	:	:	:	:	:	20	−20
Depreciation (non-prod'n)	:	−10	:	:	:	=	:	:	:	:	:	:	:	−10
5 Fixed assets purchased	90	:	:	:	:	=	:	:	:	90	:	:	:	:
6 Intermediate balance equation	490	−170	370	1,660	−639	=	200	281	150	875	:	:	20	185
7 Payments by debtors	:	:	:	−1,395	1,395	=	:	:	:	:	:	:	:	:
8 Payments to creditors	:	:	:	:	−735	=	:	:	:	−735	:	:	:	:
9 Tax due—Advance Corp'n Tax	:	:	:	:	:	=	:	:	:	:	26	:	:	−26
Net mainstream tax	:	:	:	:	:	=	:	:	:	:	50	:	:	−50
10 Dividends due	:	:	:	:	:	=	:	:	:	:	:	60	:	−60
11 Transfer to reserves	:	:	:	:	:	=	:	49	:	:	:	:	:	−49
12 Closing balance equation	490	−170	370	265	21	=	200	330	150	140	76	60	20	:

Fig 11.7 Matthew Grimble's transaction work sheet for Year 6

equation, the details for which we can obtain from the Year 5 balance sheet in Figure 11.1. After that, we must clear the opening balances on current liabilities, but without worrying at this stage about the actual timings of the payments specified by the accountant in his Note A.1. The amount of tax actually payable during the year in respect of Year 5's operations is going to add up to £35,000—£13,000 of which will be in respect of Advance Corporation Tax—and these transactions will involve a reduction in both the amount of cash available, and in the amount of tax due.

All the stock movement and production cost details can be taken from the stock movements and cost of goods sold forecast that we have just completed in Figure 11.5, with one side of each transaction equation being added to the value of stocks, and the other side of all third-party purchases going to creditors. Wages and salaries are all cash items, while depreciation naturally has to come out of the depreciation column.

Similarly, one side of all the profit and loss transactions affects the profit and loss column, with the other side of sales revenue going to debtors, and the cost of goods sold coming out of stocks. Selling and administration expenditure is split between third-party credit purchases, and wages and salaries, etc., which will be cash transactions. Notice, incidentally, that the term 'added value' is introduced into the funds flow analysis here, although we shall leave a full discussion of this topic until later. The actual figures required for this item are as noted in A.5.

Note A.2 also tells us that there is still £90,000 outstanding on the recent plant expansion programme, so this transaction will be between fixed assets and creditors. When this item has been logged, we can rule off the columns in order to obtain the totals for a trial balance, which enables us to check our balances down to this point, at which the profit and loss balance should agree with the net profit before tax figure of £185,000 shown on the profit and loss forecast we compiled in Figure 11.6. It does—so we're all right so far!

In this exercise, we do not have a known closing balance equation to agree to, so we shall have to complete our remaining entries from the budget information provided. We have already processed all the information available on fixed assets, depreciation and stocks, so we must assume that our intermediate balances can be carried straight down to the closing balance line in these columns.

The next column to check is debtors, which has an intermediate balance of (210,000 + 1,450,000 =) £1,660,000. The sales manager forecasts that this balance is likely to be up to £265,000 by the end of the year (S.1), which means that total anticipated receipts over the year should be (1,660,000 – 265,000 =) £1,395,000. This transaction will be between debtors and cash.

We then want to see how much money is going to be needed to pay the company's creditors, where the intermediate balance is shown as £875,000. The Accountant forecasts in Note A.2 that these balances are likely to increase from £110,000 to £140,000 by the end of the year, which means that payments will amount to (875,000 – 140,000 =) £735,000; of which £90,000 will be in respect of the capital project, and (735,000 – 90,000 =) £645,000 will consequently be payable to trade creditors.

This then leaves us with the tax, dividends, and retained profits to transfer out of profit and loss to tax due, dividends due, and reserves, thus clearing the profit and loss column to zero, and enabling us to total all of the columns to produce the closing balance equation.

The forecast balance sheet for Year 6—Figure 11.8

The figures from the closing balance equation on the transaction equation work sheet are the ones that we need for the forecast balance sheet, so all we have to do is to transfer them across to Figure 11.8—and that's that!

The cash flow forecast—Figure 11.9

We can now press straight on with the cash flow forecast, which can be started by completing the Annual Total column from the figures in the Cash column of the transaction equation work sheet in Figure 11.7, starting with the opening balance, and progressing via the brought-forward Year 5 liabilities, the payroll and other 'direct' cash payments, followed by the receipts from debtors, payments to creditors, and down to the closing balance.

This is exactly the same as the process we went through when we prepared Andrew's cash flow forecast in the previous chapter, and our initial impression of the annual cash flow is somewhat similar, with everything looking quite satisfactory and straightforward. There is admittedly no great fund of ready cash available at the beginning of the year, but the forecast Grimble income exceeds expenditure overall, and the company should eventually end up

£'000	Year 5		Year 6	
Fixed assets at cost:				
Land and buildings		120		140
Plant and machinery		280		350
Total cost		400		490
Less: Depreciation to date		120		170
Written down book value		280		320
Stocks:				
Consumable stores	20		25	
Raw materials	55		65	
Work-in-progress	65		70	
Finished goods	180		210	
Total stocks	320		370	
Trade debtors	210		265	
Cash/bank	16		21	
Current assets	546		656	
Trade creditors	110		140	
Tax due	35		76	
Dividends due	30		60	
Loan interest due	20		20	
Current liabilities	195		296	
NET WORKING CAPITAL		351		360
NET ASSETS		631		680
Share capital		200		200
Reserves		281		330
Shareholders' funds		481		530
Loan capital		150		150
CAPITAL EMPLOYED		631		680

Fig 11.8 Matthew Grimble's balance sheet for Year 5 and forecast balance sheet for Year 6

with £5,000 more in the bank at the end of the year than they had at the beginning. That does not seem to be too bad.

Now let's get down to the quarterly analysis and see what

£'000	Q.1	Q.2	Q.3	Q.4	Annual total
1 Opening balance b/fd	16	−59	−99	−57	16
2 Clearance of Year 5 items					
Tax paid—Year 5 A.C.T.	:	:	−13	:	−13
Year 5 M.C.T.	:	:	:	−22	−22
Dividends due	:	−30	:	:	−30
Loan interest	−20	:	:	:	−20
3 Payment of salaries					
Direct labour	−60	−65	−70	−70	−265
Indirect labour	−35	−40	−40	−40	−155
Selling and administration					
4 Receipts from debtors	320	325	350	400	1,395
5 Payments to creditors					
Year 6 trading	−180	−170	−145	−150	−645
Fixed assets	−70	−20	:	:	−90
6 Closing balance c/fd	−59	−99	−57	21	21

Fig 11.9 Matthew Grimble's quarterly cash flow forecast for Year 6

happens. The opening balance for Q.1 is obviously going to be £16,000, and we have to look at the accountant's notes to find out exactly when the Year 5 liabilities are going to be cleared. Note A.1 tells us that loan interest is payable during Q.1, and that dividends are payable in Q.2, so we can enter these figures as negative quantities—outflows of cash—in the appropriate quarters. The tax payments are split into two parts, with the A.C.T. of £13,000 being payable in Q.3, and the Mainstream Tax of £22,000 being payable in Q.4.

Next we come to salaries and other 'direct' cash items, the first of which is direct production labour. According to Note P.2/2, the Production Manager expects to spend a basic £60,000 in Q.1, £65,000 in Q.2, and £70,000 in each of the other two quarters, which consequently gives us a distribution of:

$$-60{,}000 - 65{,}000 - 70{,}000 - 70{,}000 = -265{,}000$$

Indirect labour (P.2/3) goes up from £35,000 in Q.1 to £40,000 in Q.2 onwards, so that:

$$-35{,}000 - 40{,}000 - 40{,}000 - 40{,}000 = -155{,}000$$

The Accountant has gathered together all the selling and administration forecasts (A.5), and he reckons that the total projected bill for salaries etc. of £150,000 under this heading will be broken down to £30,000 in Q.1, and £40,000 per quarter thereafter:

$$-30{,}000 - 40{,}000 - 40{,}000 - 40{,}000 = -150{,}000$$

He also gives us, in Note A.4, his forecast for the inflow pattern of cash receipts from debtors, so these figures—320,000, 325,000, 350,000 and 400,000—can be entered straight into the cash flow forecast.

The last set of allocations is the payments to creditors, and the first thing to deal with here is the clearance of the £90,000 still outstanding on the capital project (A.2), of which £70,000 is due for payment during Q.1, and £20,000 during Q.2. Total payments to trade creditors amounted to £645,000, and Note A.2 also tells us that £180,000 of this will be paid in Q.1, £170,000 in Q.2, £145,000 in Q.3, with the rest during Q.4, so that the Q.4 payment will be (645,000 − 180,000 − 170,000 − 145,000 =) £150,000.

So our cash flow allocations are now complete, and we can total each quarterly column in turn, carrying the closing balances of each quarter up to the opening balance line of the next, checking to ensure that the closing balance for Q.4 is the same as that for the Annual Total column.

Now comes the moment of truth, because we can see that, despite the end-of-year forecast of £21,000 in the bank, the intermediate picture looks extremely gloomy—even more gloomy than Andco's, in fact!

Management reaction

We must now look at these figures from a practical point of view. They should not be regarded as merely the net result of a number-shuffling exercise: we should try to put ourselves into the shoes of the accountant who has just prepared his evaluation and co-ordination of the joint budget projections of his colleagues, and imagine what his reactions would be. You couldn't expect him to be too enthusiastic about the prospects that he could see ahead of him over the next few months! So what questions would you, as that accountant, want to discuss with your colleagues in this situation?

How confident is the sales manager that he can really expect to achieve a 16 per cent growth in sales volume within the coming year, especially when combined with a 10 per cent price increase? Is the forecast promotional spend going to be adequate to achieve this target—or should he have been slightly less ambitious? Are additional staff really needed to cope with the extra work, and what are those 'additional third-party costs' supposed to cover which require an extra £5,000? Can anything be done to help reduce the existing level of expenditure before we start talking about increasing it?

It may not seem unreasonable that the production manager should talk about higher stock levels to help support the anticipated extra sales demand, but how does he justify the need for *present* levels, let alone higher ones? Are we satisfied that the proposed new production schedules are going to require the engagement of one more process worker *and* another production supervisor *and* another progress control clerk—or could the existing labour force be employed more efficiently?

And what about the 'further £20,000' that the accountant has included to cover 'both salaries and other expenses'? This all sounds rather vague, and there is no reason for the accountant to think that he has a divine right to ask questions of everyone else, and not expect to have to justify his own position.

All in all, the dilemma in which this company seems to have found itself is very similar to that of Andrew Coe's. Recent expansion plans have got to be paid for, and additional sales volumes cannot be achieved until the production facilities are available. These are needed to satisfy the demand that is due to be created as a result of the forthcoming promotion drive. All of this is going to cost a lot of money before the rewards come flowing back in.

These are some of the questions we should ask, and the points we should consider, if we were responsible for the management of Matthew Grimble Ltd. They are not questions that can all be answered by one man sitting in his own office; they are questions which need to be discussed very seriously among all the managers concerned. They must all be aware of the situation that their company is in, so that they can all have an opportunity to recommend any remedial action that may be appropriate to the particular circumstances. Then, having reached a joint decision, they can all accept their share of the responsibility for ensuring that the agreed strategy is followed.

So what would we do in their position? Would we cross our fingers and hope—or would we modify our original plans? Well, we obviously do not know the full background of the case, so we can only hazard a guess; but the chances are that we would probably suggest a few changes to the plans *as we have seen them.* It could be, though, that revisions to original plans have already been made, and that the figures that we have worked through are the final version of a number of revised strategies. Perhaps the whole management team is aware of what lies ahead, and of how careful they are going to have to be to ensure that they do not spend one penny more than they absolutely have to—especially during the early part of the year.

Let us assume that this is what has happened, because, although Matthew would be the first to admit that he is much more of an electronics expert than he is an accountant, he insists that he has considerable faith in the technical abilities of his management and staff. We must therefore conclude that the accountant has already negotiated short-term overdraft facilities up to the £100,000 that he will need by the end of the second quarter, and that the cost of this is included in that 'further £20,000' that he mentioned in his Note A.5.

At this point, we might have asked you to put another hat on! In your new capacity of bank manager, it would have been interesting to know what your reaction would have been when the chief accountant of Matthew Grimble Ltd arrived in your office to discuss the possibility of negotiating short-term overdraft facilities of £100,000? Would you have regarded his company as sufficiently stable to justify this amount of support, and, if so, on what information would you have based your decision?

For the moment, we must assume that Matthew has looked thoroughly into the whole question of viability before he embarked on the current expansion programme—back in Year 5, or even Year 4. He should have formed a pretty good idea of the probable cash flow pattern then, but if our confidence is misplaced, and he did not do either of these things, then he had better call his team together as soon as possible to work out some modifications to their strategies. Perhaps they should slow down the promotion and production forecasts in order to reduce the early outlays, although they would have to appreciate that this may, in turn, reduce their later revenues.

The accountant couldn't expect to leave it all to the others, any more than they could expect to be able to leave him to solve all the problems. Whatever is done would have to be a team effort, with the accountant's contribution coming in the form of trying to obtain extended credit from his suppliers—with the help and support of the purchasing manager, of course!—while at the same time putting his foot just a little more firmly on the accelerator marked Debtors.

So we are beginning to think of all these financial statements as something that we can use as a foundation upon which to build the strategic commercial decisions which are the keystone of management's role in business. We shall follow this up with some further practical examples in our next chapter, but now is the time to sum up the points covered during the last few pages.

Summary

We have now started to think of financial statements in the practical context of a company budget, or forward corporate plan. We have seen how the individual functional forecasts can be evaluated and co-ordinated into exactly the same sort of presentations that we have been discussing in earlier chapters, but the main difference lies in the fact that we are now looking forward to the future, rather than backwards into history. We are using the conventional format of the balance sheet, the profit and loss statement and the other financial statements to help us assess the possible outcome of future commercial strategies.

We started the chapter with a complete set of Matthew Grimble's figures for Year 5— his latest completed year of operations—and progressively worked our way through the evaluation of his sales, production and administration forecasts for Year 6 in order to produce a comparative set of figures for that year. The overall result certainly looked encouraging, although it did seem that the risks involved in achieving these results were rather high, since the company was committing itself to a lot of expense in the increased promotion and production of their products for quite a while before they could expect to see any return. This sort of situation is not unusual in real life, and our example helps to explain how some companies can suddenly find themselves face to face with financial disaster, simply because they cannot afford the expansion that their business may need in order to survive! They are, in a sense, victims of their own success.

12

Management, information and ratios

Introduction

We have come a long way since Andrew Coe picked four winners in a row on Derby Day. In fact, if we were to list the topics which have come under discussion, you might be quite surprised to see how much ground has already been covered. The general headings include:

— Money and investment
— The balance sheet
— The profit and loss statement
— Profit, taxation and interest
— The source and application of funds
— The cash flow forecast

We have also looked at how an accountant settles down to tackle his job of double-entry book-keeping, and we have constructed a set of financial budgets from the forecast data created by managers from different functional backgrounds—so we haven't done too badly!

We now need to stand back and look at the wood as a whole, rather than at the individual trees, because it is one thing to *assemble* information, and something else again to *interpret* it. As we pointed out at the very beginning, the work we have done so far has been essential, because no one can be expected to interpret information intelligently if they don't know what it is supposed to mean; on the other hand, there is not really a great deal of point in finding out what it all means if you don't know what to do with it when you've got it.

How much information do we need?

In our last chapter, we went through the process of evaluating Matthew Grimble's sales, production and administration forecasts, and ended up with a set of financial statements which looked exactly like all the other statements that we had discussed earlier, so there should not have been anything startling or alarming about them.

Take the profit and loss forecast in Figure 11.6, for example. That looks simple enough, so let's take the first figure we come to: sales revenue. We all know what that means: it is the sales value of the grimbles that Matthew hopes to sell, and his sales manager reckons that this is going to amount to £1.45 m.

Well, so what? Is that a good figure, or a bad one? How can we tell? The answer is that we can't, because a figure in isolation like that doesn't tell us anything, apart from the fact that, to most of us, it sounds like a whole lot of money. In order to assess whether it is 'good' or not, we need to relate it to something else; otherwise, it is no different from looking at a tiny spot in the middle of a picture, or a full-stop in the middle of a page of print. If all we can see is one small dot, and that one dot is one of a line of dots, how can we tell in which direction the line is heading? We have to be able to see at least two or three—and preferably more—in order to judge the relationship which exists between one and the others.

Exactly the same principle applies to financial data, so the first thing that we had better do now is to compare the Year 6 sales revenue with the sales revenue for Year 5 in Figure 11.3. This at least shows us that the £1.45 m forecast for Year 6 is ($1.45/1.13 \times 100 =$) 128 per cent of the £1.13 m revenue achieved during Year 5.

This helps to introduce a certain sense of perspective into the figures, although we are still rather restricted in our ability to draw any firm conclusions, because we have so far only been able to compare one piece of forecast data with one year's actual historical data, so we cannot be sure that even that comparison is valid. As yet, we are still unable to judge the management capability of the company, since our only clue to their achievements so far is what we can see in the Year 5 accounts.

So we could do with even more information! All right, then—how much more? One year? Two years? How about the whole set of financial statements for Matthew Grimble's company since he started up in business five years ago? Pages 200–207 contain exactly that, together with the Year 6 forecast figures that we have just prepared. We can't be fairer than that, can we?

Your references are:

Figure 12.1—Balance sheets
Figure 12.2—Stock movements and cost of goods sold
Figure 12.3—Profit and loss statements
Figure 12.4—Source and application of funds statements

The source and application of funds statements are presented in the 'official' SSAP format, although we have included a set of these statements arranged in accordance with our unofficial alternative version in the Appendix (page 358). The individual transaction analyses for each year have also been omitted, although the analysis for Year 6 was reproduced in Figure 11.7 (page 188). The complete set of all the analyses, together with details of the tax calculations and all of the above statements, are also included in the Appendix at the end of the book for ease of reference, so that you can trace all the figures through for each year if you wish.

The measurement of growth

This is usually the point where data-indigestion sets in! However essential information may be, the sight of too much of it can be guaranteed to put anybody off, so we must be careful to keep our heads, and take just one step forward at a time. So, now that we have started looking at sales figures, perhaps we should stay with them, and measure the extent to which they have grown over the years?

We have already compared the forecast sales revenue for Year 6 with the actual revenue for Year 5, and found that the Year 6 figures represented a 28 per cent increase over Year 5. This is an absolute comparison, and is in fact the way in which most people would measure the relationship between one period and another. Some would argue that this method of calculation does not represent a true measure of the *rate* of growth, however, and that the way in which this should be done is to relate the *difference* between two sets of comparative data to the *average* of the two.

The more legitimate formula for the calculation of growth rate can consequently be expressed as follows:

$$\text{Growth rate (\%)} = \frac{L - E}{\frac{1}{2}(L + E)} \times 100$$

where L = selected data for the later period, and
E = comparative data for the earlier period.

£'000	Year 1		Year 2	
Fixed assets at cost:				
Land and buildings		40		60
Plant and machinery		60		95
Total cost		100		155
Less: Depreciation to date		10		25
Written down book value		90		130
Stocks:				
Consumable stores	5		5	
Raw materials	20		30	
Work-in-progress	15		30	
Finished goods	50		65	
Total stocks	90		130	
Trade debtors	75		105	
Pre-payments (ACT)	4		:	
Cash/bank	50		23	
Current assets	219		258	
Trade creditors	35		40	
Tax due	4		25	
Dividends due	10		15	
Loan interest due	8		8	
Bank overdraft	:		:	
Current liabilities	57		88	
NET WORKING CAPITAL		162		170
NET ASSETS		252		300
Share capital		120		120
Reserves		72		120
Shareholders' funds		192		240
Loan capital		60		60
CAPITAL EMPLOYED		252		300

Fig 12.1 Matthew Grimble's balance sheets

Year 3		Year 4		Year 5		Year 6	
	75		85		120		140
	155		225		280		350
	230		310		400		490
	50		80		120		170
	180		230		280		320
10		15		20		25	
35		45		55		65	
40		50		65		70	
100		140		180		210	
185		250		320		370	
135		175		210		265	
:		:		:		:	
:		88		16		21	
320		513		546		656	
60		80		110		140	
34		32		35		76	
20		30		30		60	
8		20		20		20	
15		:		:		:	
137		162		195		296	
	183		351		351		360
	363		581		631		680
	120		200		200		200
	183		231		281		330
	303		431		481		530
	60		150		150		150
	363		581		631		680

£'000		Year 1		Year 2
(a) Consumable stores				
Opening stock		:		5
Purchases		15		15
		15		20
Less: Closing stock		5		5
Usages (to work-in-progress)		10		15
(b) Raw materials				
Opening stock		:		20
Purchases		130		130
		130		150
Less: Closing stock		20		30
Usages (to work-in-progress)		110		120
(c) Work-in-progress				
Direct labour		75		105
Overheads:				
Indirect labour	45		55	
Production administration	10		15	
Power and light	15		20	
Depreciation	10		10	
Rates and insurance	15		15	
Consumable stores	10		15	
Total		105		130
Charges during year ('Activity')		290		355
Opening stock b/fd		:		15
		290		370
Less: Closing stock c/fd		15		30
COST OF GOODS MANUFACTURED		275		340
(d) Finished goods				
Opening stock b/fd		:		50
		275		390
Less: Closing stock c/fd		50		65
COST OF GOODS SOLD		225		325

Fig 12.2 Matthew Grimble's stock movements and cost of goods sold statements

Year 3		Year 4		Year 5		Year 6	
	5		10		15		20
	25		30		35		40
	30		40		50		60
	10		15		20		25
	20		25		30		35
	30		35		45		55
	175		195		230		265
	205		230		275		320
	35		45		55		65
	170		185		220		255
	155		200		230		265
80		100		120		155	
20		25		35		45	
25		30		35		50	
20		25		35		40	
20		25		30		40	
20		25		30		35	
	185		230		285		365
	510		615		735		885
	30		40		50		65
	540		655		785		950
	40		50		65		70
	500		605		720		880
	65		100		140		180
	565		705		860		1,060
	100		140		180		210
	465		565		680		850

£'000		*Year 1*		*Year 2*
Sales		450		595
Less: Cost of goods sold		225		325
Gross trading profit		225		270
Product promotion	55		65	
Selling and administration				
Employee costs	55		75	
Third party costs	25		25	
Depreciation (non-production)	:		5	
Total fixed costs		135		170
Operating profit/(loss) before interest and tax		90		100
Interest payable on loan capital		8		8
NET PROFIT BEFORE TAX		82		92
Taxation		:		29
Profit after tax		82		63
Dividends		10		15
RETAINED PROFIT		72		48
Numbers of employees		38		48

Fig 12.3 Matthew Grimble's profit and loss statements

Year 3		*Year 4*		*Year 5*		*Year 6*	
	805		950		1,130		1,450
	465		565		680		850
	340		385		450		600
80		100		130		160	
95		100		120		150	
35		50		60		75	
5		5		5		10	
	215		255		315		395
	125		130		135		205
	8		20		20		20
	117		110		115		185
	34		32		35		76
	83		78		80		109
	20		30		30		60
	63		48		50		49
	62		68		73		79

£'000	*Year 1*		*Year 2*	
Sources of funds:				
Operating profit before interest and tax		90		100
Add back: Total depreciation		10		15
Total funds generated from trading operations		100		115
Additional share capital	120		:	
Additional loan capital	60		:	
Total funds from other sources		180		:
TOTAL FUNDS GENERATED		280		115
Application of funds:				
Interest on loan capital	:		8	
Dividends paid	:		10	
Tax paid—ACT/offset	:		4	
—Mainstream tax	:		:	
Purchase of fixed assets	100		55	
Total		100		77
Increase/(decrease) in working capital				
Increase/(decrease) in stocks	90		40	
Increase/(decrease) in debtors	75		30	
Increase/(decrease) in cash	50		−27	
(Increase)/decrease in creditors	−35		− 5	
Net increase/(decrease)		180		38
Total application of funds		280		115

Fig 12.4 Matthew Grimble's source and application of funds statement

Year 3		*Year 4*		*Year 5*		*Year 6*	
	125		130		135		205
	25		30		40		50
	150		160		175		255
:		80		:		:	
:		90		:		:	
	:		170		:		:
	150		330		175		255
8		8		20		20	
15		20		30		30	
− 4		:		:		:	
29		34		32		35	
75		80		90		90	
	123		142		172		175
55		65		70		50	
30		40		35		55	
−38		103		−72		5	
−20		−20		−30		−30	
	27		188		3		80
	150		330		175		255

The mere sight of a formula like this is another thing which can be almost guaranteed to switch people off, but it is quite simple to see the way in which it works if we replace the alphabetic variables with some actual figures. In our Matthew Grimble example, the anticipated growth in sales revenue during Year 6 would consequently be:

$$\frac{1.45 - 1.3}{\frac{1}{2}(1.45 + 1.13)} \times 100$$

$$= \frac{0.32}{1.29} \times 100 = \underline{24.8\%}$$

This is somewhat lower than the 28 per cent increase that we obtained by simply measuring the Year 6 forecast sales against those of Year 5, but this 'smoothing' effect is inherent in the method of calculation.

Neither figure is completely valid in this instance, however, since we have not been comparing like with like. Forecasts should not be compared with actual historical figures in this way unless they are suitably and adequately qualified to ensure that the reader fully appreciates that the figures under examination relate to *forecast* growth rate. Normally, this calculation is applied to historical data in order to produce an index of proportional growth rate over the last few years, and one of the merits of the formula is its ability to condense the rate of growth over a number of successive years into one single index figure.

A span of three years is the period to which this measurement is commonly applied, and the result is obtained by taking an average of each period's growth rate (over the previous year). Once again, the formula is quite simple, as you can see from Figure 12.5, because all it does is to calculate the growth rate over each pair of neighbouring years, and then take the average of the two results.

$$\text{Growth } \textit{rate} \text{ (\%)} = \frac{\dfrac{L - M}{\frac{1}{2}(L + M)} + \dfrac{M - E}{\frac{1}{2}(M + E)}}{2} \times 100$$

where: L = Latest Year's data
M = Middle Year's data
E = Earliest Year's data

Fig 12.5 The growth rate formula

Now let us take a look at Figure 12.6, in which we have calculated the sales revenue growth rate for the grimbles over Years 3–5:

$$L = 1{,}130 : M = 950 : E = 805$$

$$\text{Growth } \textit{rate} \ (\%) = \frac{\dfrac{1{,}130 - 950}{\frac{1}{2}(1{,}130 + 950)} + \dfrac{950 - 805}{\frac{1}{2}(950 + 805)}}{2} \times 100$$

$$= \frac{\dfrac{180}{1{,}040} + \dfrac{145}{897.5}}{2} \times 100 = \frac{0.173 + 0.165}{2} \times 100$$

$$= 16.9\%$$

Fig 12.6 Matthew Grimble's sales revenue growth rate for Years 3 to 5

Figure 12.6 tells us that the Year 4–5 growth rate was 17.3 per cent, following a rate of 16.5 per cent between Years 3 and 4, giving an average growth rate of 16.9 per cent over the three years. This is obviously quite an encouraging start to our analysis of the Grimble performance, and we can now link this piece of information to the projection of 24.8 per cent that we have already calculated for Year 6 to see that the company is obviously hoping for some very significant expansions in the market place in the very near future.

There would be nothing to stop us, if we so wished, calculating a growth rate index for the whole of the five-year operating period. This would merely mean calculating the four individual growth rate percentages for Years 2 to 5, and then taking the average—just like this:

$$\frac{\overset{\textit{Year 2}}{0.277} + \overset{\textit{Year 3}}{0.300} + \overset{\textit{Year 4}}{0.165} + \overset{\textit{Year 5}}{0.173}}{4} \times 100$$

$$= 0.228 \times 100$$

$$= \underline{22.8\%}$$

This series of indices tells us that sales over the first three years forged ahead at a higher rate of growth than they did in subsequent years, so something seems to have happened in Year 4, and the Grimble team are apparently hoping that Year 6 is going to bring them back up to their previous levels of progress.

Sales revenue is by no means the only factor that we might want to measure in terms of growth rate. Profit levels could certainly be another, so let us now see what the growth rate was in Matthew Grimble's profit before tax over the same span of Years 3 to 5 (Figure 12.7):

$$L = 115 : M = 110 : E = 117$$

$$\text{Growth } rate\ (\%) = \frac{\dfrac{115 - 110}{\frac{1}{2}(115 + 110)} + \dfrac{110 - 117}{\frac{1}{2}(110 + 117)}}{2} \times 100$$

$$= \frac{\dfrac{5}{112.5} + \dfrac{-7}{113.5}}{2} \times 100 = \frac{0.044 + 0.061}{2} \times 100$$

$$= -0.0085 \times 100$$

$$= \underline{-0.85\%}$$

Fig 12.7 Matthew Grimble's growth rate in profit before tax

Here we have a much less encouraging picture, because the growth rate in the company's profit before tax was negative—a shrinkage, in fact—so we have now established that the growth rate of 16.9 per cent in sales revenue was achieved at the expense of a decrease in profit before tax of 0.85 per cent, which is certainly not the sort of news that is guaranteed to produce a wave of enthusiasm in the boardroom.

Both the growth rate calculations that we have shown so far are based on the profit and loss statements, but it is also possible to apply the same approach to the balance sheet, and Figure 12.8 shows the degree to which Grimble's capital employed 'grew' over the same period. (Figure 12.1 contains the details we need.)

$$L = 631 : M = 581 : E = 363$$

$$\text{Growth } rate\ (\%) = \frac{\dfrac{50}{606} + \dfrac{218}{472}}{2} \times 100$$

$$= \frac{0.082 + 0.462}{2} \times 100$$

$$= 0.272 \times 100$$

$$= \underline{27.2\%}$$

Fig 12.8 Matthew Grimble's growth rate in capital employed

The picture now begins to fill out even more. When we compare this growth rate index figure with our previous ones, we can see that Matthew's company needed to invest a higher proportional amount of capital in its business than it achieved in proportional increases in sales revenue over the last three years, and that, even then, the profit position worsened.

Notice that we have been extremely careful throughout this particular section to emphasize that our calculations have been aimed at the measurement of the *rate* of growth between two or more sets of comparative data. This has involved smoothing out the differences by comparing average figures, but we should stress that there is nothing wrong in measuring the absolute comparisons of the figures themselves—provided that you appreciate the meaning of the results. This method of calculation would give you a measurement of *growth*, rather than of growth *rate*, and there is a subtle difference between the two.

Management information ratios

Let us now pause for a moment to consider the implications of what we have been doing. Taken individually, our three growth-rate calculations have each taken one piece of data from the financial statements of a company, and converted their progression over a period of time into a single index figure. In our example, this has been a period of three years, and is equivalent to taking one of the summary schedules at the beginning of this chapter, and tracing a line from left to right across the columns of annual figures, as illustrated in Figure 12.9:

£'000		← *Absolute values*		→		*Growth*
		Year 3	*Year 4*	*Year 5*		*rate (%)*
Profit and loss statement						
Sales	(12.6)	805	950	1,130	→	16.9
Profit before tax	(12.7)	117	110	115	→	− 0.9
Balance sheet						
Capital employed	(12.8)	363	581	631	→	27.2

Fig 12.9 The horizontal dimension of growth rates

This method of interpretation can therefore be regarded as looking at the 'horizontal dimension' of the figures, and is indeed extremely relevant, although it was not long before we started to compare one growth rate with another. We commented that the sales growth had been achieved 'at the expense of a shrinkage in profit', for example, and that a 'higher proportional amount of capital' was employed in the company than was achieved in terms of growth in sales revenue from its use.

These are 'vertical' comparisons, because we are no longer looking simply at the behaviour of one piece of data over a period of time; we are considering the relationship which exists between two (or more) different pieces of data during the same period of time. We are comparing different *lines* of data from within the same *column*—or period—of information.

These relationships are nothing more nor less than ordinary ratio calculations, although they generally rejoice under the rather grand and impressive title of Management Information Ratios, because they can, if used properly, provide extremely valid and significant management information.

Look at those sales figures of Matthew's, for instance. Forget about his Year 6 budget figures for the moment; just look at the Year 5 figure of £1.13m. As we said earlier, £1.13m is just a figure, which doesn't mean anything until you relate it to something else. But the one thing Matthew wouldn't want to do—unless he had a king-sized inferiority complex!—would be to compare his sales revenue of £1.13m with that of one of our big industrial giants like ICI or Unilever. That would only prove how small his company's sales were compared with these other companies, and that would be like trying to compare chalk and cheese.

What he is much more likely to do is measure the amount of profit that his company managed to generate out of each pound of sales revenue it achieved, and then compare *that* with the profit margins of the other companies, because that would be a perfectly meaningful and logical comparison to make.

Management information ratios can be divided into three main groups:

1 *Investment ratios*, which show how the financial results of a company relate to the shareholders' stake in the business.
2 *Financial status ratios*, which measure the company's financial stability, distinguishing between their long-term ability to meet their liabilities—their *solvency*—and their short-term ability, or *liquidity*.
3 *Performance ratios*, which measure how successfully the company

is being run, or how well its management is utilizing the assets for which it has been made responsible.

Some ratios are relevant to more than one of these headings, but, when one considers the vast number of potential permutations of data combinations that it would be possible to obtain from the various headings that are incorporated into the financial statements we have prepared, it will be obvious that an in-depth study of this subject is a complete—and often fascinating—topic in its own right. For the purposes of our present discussion, however, we shall restrict our references to a few of the most relevant and commonly-used ratios.

Profit margin

A few moments ago, we made a reference to Matthew Grimble's profit margins, although we did not actually calculate what they were. The profit margin is the relationship which exists between the amount of profit—*before* the deduction of loan interest and tax—that a company makes, and the amount of sales revenue needed to achieve it. Matthew Grimble's margins are calculated, and charted in profile, in Figure 12.10.

If we were to compare the Year 6 forecast figures with those of Year 5, we would no doubt be quite encouraged to think that this company is about to increase its margins from 11.9 per cent to 14.1 per cent. However, one can't help having a few reservations about the prospects of achieving this target when we can see that the trend has been progressively downwards from its starting point of 20.0 per cent in Year 1.

One explanation may be that the company started out with the introduction of a new product into a new market, and was able to pitch its prices deliberately high because of non-existent competition. High margins will naturally attract competition, however, so the strategy would then have been to reduce prices in an established market of increasing volumes, in order to keep the competition at bay. If margins get too low, though, one has to consider the amount of profit generated in relation to the value of assets utilized in the business, and to the amount of capital employed. It may well be that, if sales volumes are sufficiently high, a low margin may not necessarily be a cause for concern, which is really another way of saying that one ratio in isolation is not very much more informative than a single piece of data.

$$\text{Profit margin} = \frac{\text{Profit before interest and tax}}{\text{Sales revenue}}$$

(£'000)	*Year 1*	*Year 2*	*Year 3*	*Year 4*	*Year 5*	*Year 6*
Sales revenue	450	595	805	950	1,130	1,450
Profit before tax	90	100	125	130	135	205
Profit margin (%)	20.0	16.8	15.5	13.7	11.9	14.1

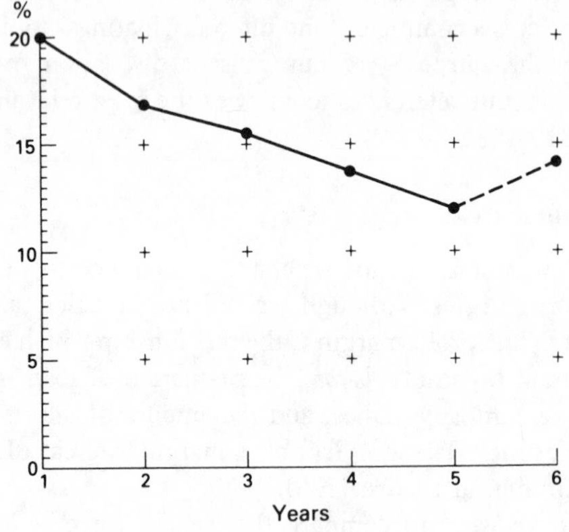

Fig 12.10 Matthew Grimble's profit margins

Return On Capital Employed (ROCE)

We mentioned the two main 'profitability' ratios very briefly when we were discussing the profit and loss statement in Chapter 6. One is actually called the 'profitability ratio'—and we shall discuss that one in a moment—whilst the other is called the return on capital employed. Let us take the return on capital employed first, since this is the one that has tended to be in the background of most of our discussions. This is one of the most reliable and widely-used measures of a company's performance, measuring as it does the amount of profit generated out of each pound invested in the company. Performance in this context is therefore interpreted from the point of view of utilization of funds, rather than of the generation of sales, or of the modernization of plant.

In this situation, we are not really concerned with the capital structure of the business, or with how much of the capital employed is share capital, as distinct from loan capital. So we are interested in the level of profit *before* the deduction of loan interest and tax, since the amount of loan interest involved is directly linked to the way in which the company's capital is structured.

Matthew Grimble's return on capital employed is calculated and profiled in Figure 12.11.

$$\text{Return on capital employed} = \frac{\text{Profit before interest and tax}}{\text{Capital employed}}$$

(£'000)		*Year 1*	*Year 2*	*Year 3*	*Year 4*	*Year 5*	*Year 6*
Profit before interest and tax	(12.3)	90	100	125	130	135	205
Capital employed	(12.1)	252	300	363	581	631	680
Return on capital employed	(%)	35.7	33.3	34.4	22.4	21.4	30.1

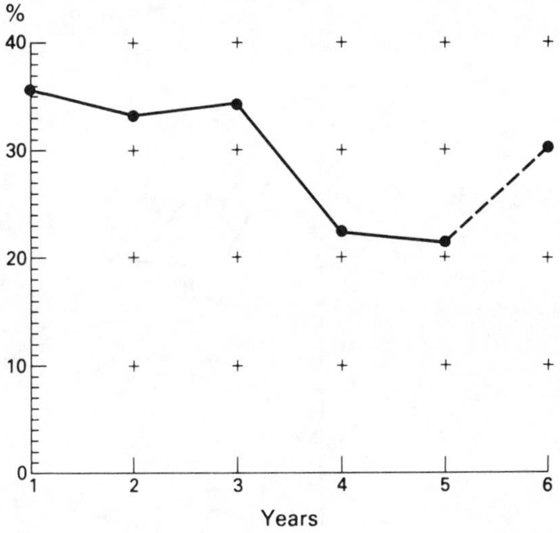

Fig 12.11 Matthew Grimble's return on capital employed

These figures show that the grimbles only generated 21.4 pence profit in Year 5 out of every pound invested in the business, compared with 35.7 pence in Year 1, which proves that the decreasing profit margins were not compensated by increased sales volumes. The sharp decline in Year 4 is a direct reflection of the increase in capital employed that year, and we can see from the balance sheets in Figure 12.1—and from the source and application of funds statements in Figure 12.4—that Matthew introduced a further £80,000 of share capital and £90,000 in loan capital at that time, obviously in order to finance his expansion plans.

Return on shareholders' funds

This ratio fits very solidly into the category of investment ratios, in that it indicates the rate of return that the shareholders are getting

$$\text{Return on shareholders' funds} = \frac{\text{Profit after interest and tax}}{\text{Shareholders' funds}}$$

(£'000)	*Year 1*	*Year 2*	*Year 3*	*Year 4*	*Year 5*	*Year 6*
Profit after tax (12.3)	82	63	83	78	80	109
Shareholders' funds (12.1)	192	240	303	431	481	530
Return on Sh'drs funds (%)	42.7	26.3	27.4	18.1	16.6	20.6

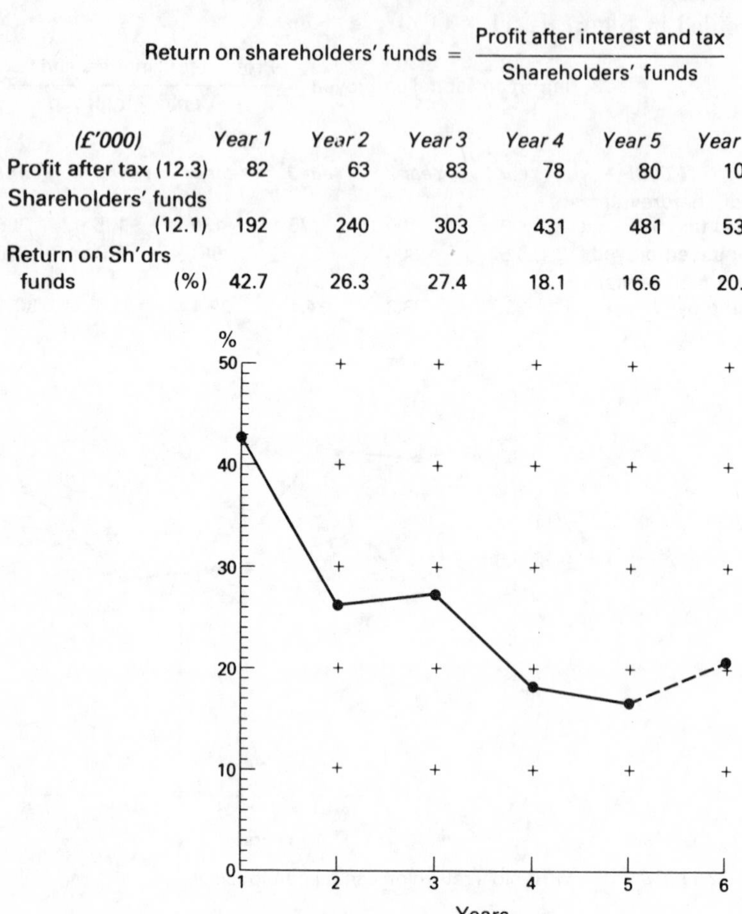

Fig 12.12 Matthew Grimble's return on shareholder's funds

on the capital that they have invested in the business. The 'level' of profit with which we are concerned here must therefore be *after* the deduction of both loan interest and tax, since the only decision left to be made is how much of this profit is to be taken out of the business in the form of dividends, and how much is to be left in for the purposes of expansion and growth. The rates of return for Matthew Grimble are set out in Figure 12.12.

Once again, we can see a dramatic tumble in 'investment performance' over the five years, and the impact on these figures of the injection of additional capital in Year 4 can again be clearly seen. The projection for Year 6 shows a marked improvement over Year 5, but the stark fact of the situation is that the shareholders' rate of return for Year 5 was only 40 per cent of that achieved in Year 1!

Profitability

From a purely mathematical point of view, the return on capital employed that we looked at a moment ago might just as well have been called the Return on Net Assets, because the figures used would have been exactly the same. The implication of the two terms is somewhat different, however, because, on the one hand, we are focusing on the effectiveness of a company's *capital* utilization—or its *commercial* performance—while, on the other hand, the accent is on the effectiveness or efficiency of its *asset* utilization, which is much more a question of *management* performance.

One of the main responsibilities of management is, as we have said before, the efficient use of the company's assets which have been entrusted to its control. In this context, it is often argued that the profitability ratio is more relevant as a measure of management performance than the return on net assets. Since the operational management of a company has no direct responsibility or concern for capital structure, the profit level in which we are interested here is again *before* interest and tax, and the difference between the two ratios is that, whereas the return on net assets relates this profit to the *net* assets of the business, the profitability ratio uses the company's *total* assets figure as its base.

What we are aiming for here is the amount of profit generated by management out of every pound invested in the *total* assets for which it is responsible. Let us see, in Figure 12.13, whether the operational performance of Matthew's management team looks any better than the results enjoyed by the shareholders. You can check the figure for total assets from the balance sheets in Figure 12.1, either by adding the current liabilities to net assets, or by adding the current assets to the fixed assets.

The Grimble profitability profile follows the same declining pattern as all the other ratios we have looked at so far, so it is beginning to look as if we may have some general cause for concern about the management policies that are being applied.

$$\text{Profitability} = \frac{\text{Profit before interest and tax}}{\text{Total assets}}$$

(£'000)		*Year 1*	*Year 2*	*Year 3*	*Year 4*	*Year 5*	*Year 6*
Profit before int/tax	(12.3)	90	100	125	130	135	205
Total assets	(12.1)	309	388	500	743	826	976
Profitability	(%)	29.1	25.8	25.0	17.5	16.3	21.0

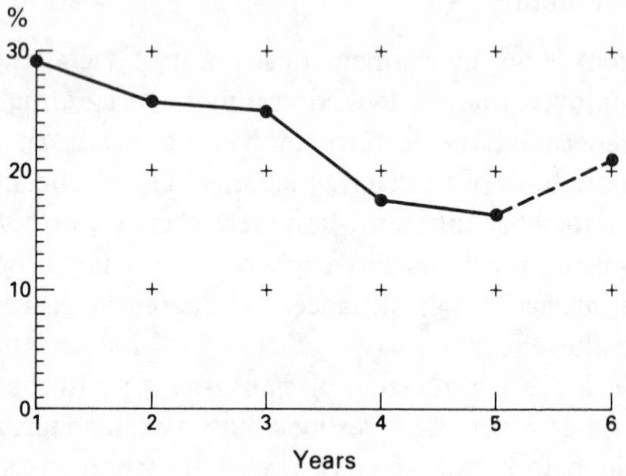

Fig 12.13 Matthew Grimble's profitability ratios

Asset utilization, or capital usage

The next thing that we should look at is the company's asset utilization ratio, which relates sales revenue—rather than profit—to total assets. This will show us the amount of revenue the company is generating out of each pound invested in its assets, so this is obviously another key ratio in the assessment of its management's operational efficiency. The higher this ratio is, the more efficient is the use of the assets; so let us now look at Figure 12.14 to assess how Matthew Grimble stands up to this test of asset utilization, or capital usage.

Well, at last we seem to have got the sort of picture we have been looking for. Apart from the dip in Year 4 caused by the introduction of quite a significant amount of additional capital, the trend in this ratio is reasonably encouraging. One thing we do have to remember here, though, is that the value of assets is depreciated each year in the accounts, so that, apart from any additional assets which may be introduced during the course of a year, the denominator of each successive ratio will, by the very nature of things, be reduced.

$$\text{Asset utilization (Capital usage)} = \frac{\text{Sales revenue}}{\text{Total assets}}$$

(£'000)		*Year 1*	*Year 2*	*Year 3*	*Year 4*	*Year 5*	*Year 6*
Sales Revenue	(12.3)	450	595	805	950	1130	1450
Total assets	(12.1)	309	388	500	743	826	976
Asset utilization	(*x*)	1.46	1.53	1.61	1.28	1.37	1.49

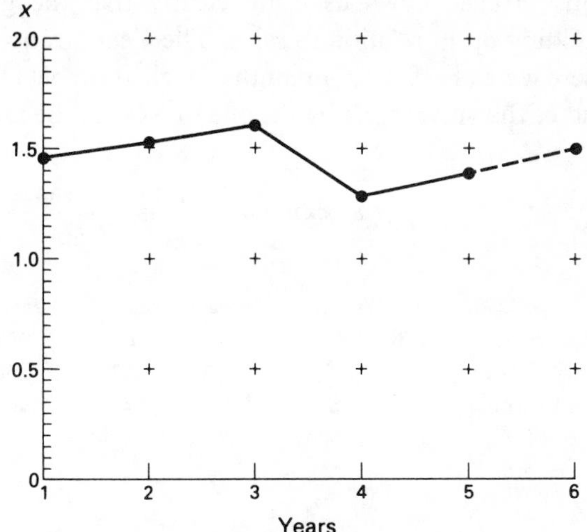

Fig 12.14 Matthew Grimble's asset utilization or capital usage ratios

Turnover ratios

The asset utilization ratio that we have just looked at is the principal one of a whole group of 'turnover' ratios—so called because they measure the relationship between sales revenue and various asset classifications, and thus indicate the number of times that these assets have been 'turned over' during a period.

Asset utilization measures total assets turnover—Matthew's were turned over 1.37 times during Year 5, for example—and this is the 'principal' ratio of this group because it measures the turnover rate of the company's *total* assets—and you can't get higher than that! It is also useful, however, to measure the turnover of net assets, fixed assets, stocks and debtors, because these help to pinpoint the causes for any deviations or trends in the 'main' asset utilization ratio.

Turnover ratios are very useful in comparing utilization performances between different companies, or between different divisions of the same company. The two that are of particular relevance are the two that measure the turnover of stocks and debtors. These are of particular importance because they relate to the working capital area of the business.

Stock turnover—Figure 12.15

This profile shows us quite clearly that the grimble stocks are building up in relation to sales. The Year 1 ratio of 5.0 tells us that there were (12/5 =) 2.4 months' stock available in the pipeline at the end of the year; while by the end of Year 5, the ratio had dropped to

$$\text{Stock turnover} = \frac{\text{Sales Revenue}}{\text{Stocks}}$$

(£'000)		Year 1	Year 2	Year 3	Year 4	Year 5	Year 6
Sales revenue	(12.3)	450	595	805	950	1130	1450
Stocks	(12.1)	90	130	185	250	320	370
Stock turnover	(x)	5.0	4.6	4.4	3.8	3.5	3.9

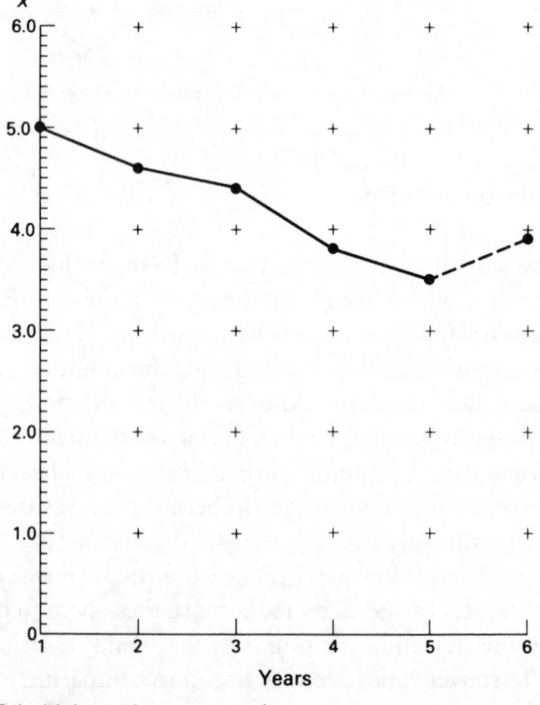

Fig 12.15 Matthew Grimble's stock turnover ratios

3.5, which is equivalent to (12/3.5 =) 3.4 months in terms of stock-holding. Our first question must then be to ask why an additional one month's stock should have been considered necessary, when all it was doing was locking up capital which may well have been urgently required for something else, like reducing the level of overdraft that the accountant has got to go out and negotiate—and pay for!—during the early part of Year 6, for instance.

There are two things to be pointed out about the way in which we have calculated this—and other—turnover ratios. The first is that we have taken an easy option in our calculations here, and related *year-end* stocks to sales turnover, whereas the ratio is often based on the rather more legitimate figure of *average* stock levels. The main thing to watch, though, is consistency, so that you can always be satisfied that you are comparing like with like.

The second point to note is that we have been measuring *cost* against *revenue*—the *cost* of stocks against the *revenue* realized as a result of their sale. Once again, this can be criticized, because it could be argued that true stock turnover figures should really relate the value of stocks to the cost of goods sold. Nevertheless, we have to remember that this ratio is one of a 'family' which all use sales revenue as their common element; this is another instance where the consistency of measurement criteria is of fundamental importance.

Credit period—Figure 12.16

The second working capital turnover ratio mentioned just now relates to debtors, and since we are currently thinking in terms of turnover, we might expect that the ratio coming up next would be the one which measures the number of times that the company's outstanding debtors' balances are 'turned over' during a year. This would obviously be the debtors' turnover ratio, and there is nothing to stop us working this out, if we want to. However, a more practical way of looking at this figure is to turn the ratio upside down, and multiply the answer by 365, because this will give us the average number of days that it takes to recover debts. This is obviously a very critical factor to control, since it has a direct influence on cash flow; and the objective must always be to peg the ratio back to the lowest possible realistic level. As with the other ratios in this category, the really legitimate basis for measurement should be the *average* level of debtors, rather than the year-end figures, which tend

$$\text{Credit period (days)} = \frac{\text{Outstanding debtors}}{\text{Sales revenue}} \times 365$$

(£'000)	*Year 1*	*Year 2*	*Year 3*	*Year 4*	*Year 5*	*Year 6*
Outstanding debtors (12.1)	75	105	135	175	210	265
Sales revenue (12.3)	450	595	805	950	1130	1450
Credit period (days)	61	64	61	67	68	67

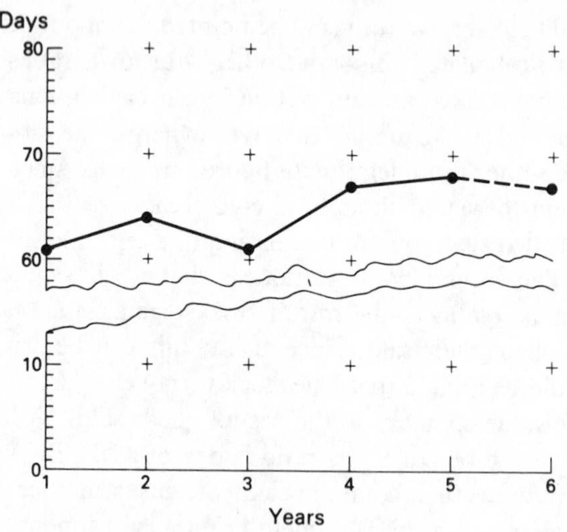

Fig 12.16 Matthew Grimble's credit period profile

to result in a rather more erratic profile. Consistency is again the key-word though, and we have chosen to follow the easier—and quite common—course of using the year-end figures.

Figure 12.16 gives us an opportunity to see what Matthew's accountant has been doing to tackle this problem, and the answer unfortunately appears to be 'Not a lot!'. The ratio has crept up quite steadily from the very first year of operations, and it does not seem as if he has any contingency plans for cutting the figure back to any significant degree during Year 6, even though we already know that he could really use some of the money that is sitting around in some of his customers' bank accounts!

Liquidity ratios

The stock turnover and credit period ratios give us vital clues relating to the management of two of the three principal categories of a company's current assets. The other category is cash—the stuff that is needed to settle the Current Liabilities as and when they become due. The ratios that are most commonly used to measure a company's capacity to settle those debts are the Current Ratio and the Acid Test Ratio.

The calculation of both ratios is quite simple. In the case of the Current Ratio, the current assets are related directly to current liabilities. One problem with this ratio is the inclusion of stocks in its evaluation, since their degree of 'liquidity' can be so varied that they will almost certainly not all be readily convertible into cash during the short term. A harsher way of measuring liquidity is consequently to relate only the liquid assets—current assets minus

$$\text{Current ratio} = \frac{\text{Current assets}}{\text{Current liabilities}}$$

$$\text{Acid Test Ratio} = \frac{\text{Liquid assets}}{\text{Current liabilities}}$$

(£'000)		*Year 1*	*Year 2*	*Year 3*	*Year 4*	*Year 5*	*Year 6*
Current assets	(12.1)	219	258	320	513	546	656
Liquid assets	(12.1)	129	128	135	263	226	286
Current liabilities	(12.1)	57	88	137	162	195	296
Current Ratio	(*x*)	3.84	2.93	2.34	3.17	2.80	2.22
Acid Test Ratio	(*x*)	2.26	1.45	0.99	1.62	1.16	0.97

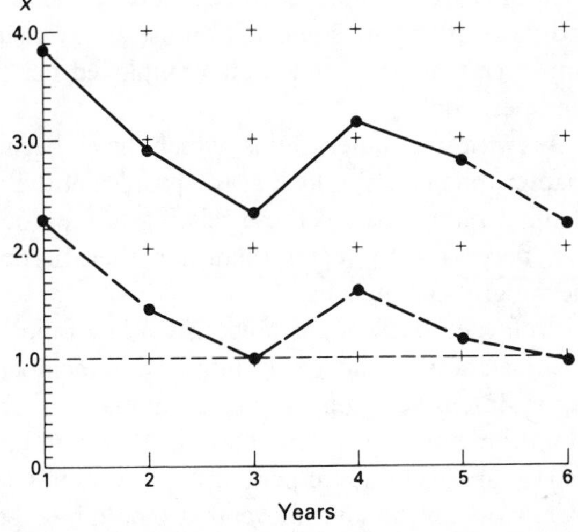

Fig 12.17 Matthew Grimble's Current Ratio and Acid Test ratio profiles

stocks—to current liabilities; in this situation, a ratio of 1.0 would be regarded as the 'Plimsoll line'. This ratio is quite appropriately called the Acid Test Ratio—or 'Quick Ratio'—and Figure 12.17 gives us an opportunity to assess both of these Grimble ratios together.

The picture that emerges here is that the current ratio is high—almost uncomfortably high, in fact!—whereas the acid test ratio is obviously taking a lot of pounding, declining as it has from a high level of 2.26 in Year 1 to 1.16 in Year 5.

The wide gap between Matthew Grimble's current ratio and his acid test ratio is also explained by the high levels of stocks that seem to be carried, but even more disturbing than that is the indication given by the Year 6 ratio to the effect that the accountant does not seem to have noticed that the acid test ratio is heading straight for the rocks. If he had, then he should surely have been sending out some 'red alert' signals to his colleagues about the potential liquidity crisis that is looming over the horizon. Short-term overdraft facilities to cover foreseen situations over a few months is one thing, but this could be something much more serious.

Employee ratios

Another way of looking at a company's performance is to measure its results in relation to the number of people that it employs. Profit, sales and capital employed are the three main reference points here, and three other ratios in common use are average remuneration per employee, and sales and capital employed per pound of employee remuneration.

As with the other ratios which have been discussed in this chapter, one needs to look at the profiles of the ratios over a period of time, rather than at those relating to a particular year, and it is also necessary to relate them together in order to draw very meaningful conclusions.

Profit per employee is obviously a key ratio to watch under any circumstances, although it must be remembered that the more capital-intensive a company or an industry is, the higher this ratio would be expected to be. It would therefore be necessary to refer also to capital employed per employee, and to sales per employee, in order to assess the sort of level that should be expected for 'profit per employee'.

For instance, if profit per employee is considered to be low, but sales per employee is good, then the profit margin is going to be low, and this could either be due to high production costs, or to low utilization of assets—or both. If, on the other hand, profit per employee is low, and sales per employee is also low, but asset utilization is good, then the explanation could well be that outdated plant is being used, and capital employed per employee should be checked to confirm this diagnosis. If profit per employee, sales per employee and asset utilization are all low, then the company is more than likely to be operating well below its optimum production capacity.

One cautionary note that should be made about this group of ratios is that the 'number of employees' quoted in the directors' report that is filed with each set of annual accounts refers to the average number employed over the year, and it is possible for this figure to be distorted in cases where an unusually high number of part-time employees are engaged. This is where the ratios for sales or capital employed per pound of employee remuneration can be more reliable barometers of performance than those based purely on employee numbers.

The only part-time employees engaged in Matthew Grimble's company were a canteen assistant and a cleaner, so his figures will not be distorted too much by them. The set of statements prepared for our case study contains all the details we need to illustrate these ratios, and this information is all pulled together in Figure 12.18.

These figures tell us quite an interesting story. The average remuneration ratio gives us a very fair indication of the sort of salary increases that Matthew has awarded over the years (assuming that the mix of senior to junior staff has remained fairly constant) and the trend in sales per employee also looks encouraging. The sales per pound of employee remuneration shows us very clearly, however, that salary levels were rising at a proportionately higher rate than sales revenue over the first four years, although this trend was halted in Year 5, and, in common with most of Matthew's other ratios, is apparently expected to improve quite dramatically during Year 6! The profit per employee ratio shows a sharp forecast improvement during Year 6, although the steady downward trend over Years 1 to 5 is hardly likely to make anyone rub their hands in confident anticipation.

So we really are beginning to build up some sort of picture out of all those charts full of figures with which we started this chapter—

£,000		Year 1	Year 2	Year 3	Year 4	Year 5	Year 6
1 Employee remuneration							
Direct labour	(12.2)	75	105	155	200	230	265
Ind. prod'n lab.	(12.2)	45	55	80	100	120	155
Selling/admin.	(12.3)	55	75	95	100	120	150
Total		175	235	330	400	470	570
2 No. of employees	(12.3)	38	48	62	68	73	79
3 Average remun'n	(£/ea)	4,605	4,895	5,323	5,882	6,438	7,215
4 Prof. bef. int/tax	(12.3)	90	100	125	130	135	205
5 Sales revenue	(12.3)	450	595	805	950	1,130	1,450
6 Capital employed	(12.1)	252	300	363	581	631	680
7 Employee ratios	(£/each)						
Profit	(4/2)	2,368	2,083	2,016	1,911	1,849	2,594
Sales	(5/2)	11,842	12,395	12,983	13,970	15,479	18,354
Capital emp.	(6/2)	6,632	6,250	5,855	8,544	8,644	8,608
8 Employee remuneration ratios							
Sales	(5/1)	2.57	2.53	2.43	2.37	2.40	2.54
Capital emp.	(6/1)	1.44	1.28	1.10	1.45	1.34	1.19

Fig 12.18 Matthew Grimble's employee and employee remuneration ratios

simply by selecting relevant items of data, relating them, and studying the trend of these figures and ratios over a period of time. We shall have a few words to say in the next chapter about the ways in which all this information can be used as a basis for the formulation of strategic decisions, but, before we do that, we ought to pause here to marshall our thoughts, and to summarize the new definitions that have been introduced.

Summary

Information is no good to you unless you know how to interpret it—as Andrew Coe would have been able to tell you many years ago when he became interested in racing, and bought his first *Sporting Life* newspaper. Some years later, when he became interested in rather more serious forms of investment, he bought his first *Financial Times*, and got the same feeling! Pages of figures that you are unable to interpret—or have not the time to read—can very often be even worse than no figures at all, and the only conclusion that can be drawn from this is that, if one accepts the premise that information is an essential ingredient in the process of decision-making, then an equally essential ingredient must be the ability to interpret it.

We started this chapter with a complete set of financial statements relating to the five-year span of Matthew Grimble's business operations. We felt that we needed this because we were unable to assess his forecast figures for Year 6 simply on the evidence of his Year 5 results.

We found that one figure in isolation told us nothing. It had to be related to some other figure or figures before we were able to get any impression of movement, direction or trend, so we traced the movement of the same data element over a period of time, and calculated its relative *rate* of growth. This is rather different from the *absolute* growth, which merely measures the relationship between one comparative set of data and another, i.e., $(B/A \times 100)\%$. The normal time-span for the growth *rate* calculation is three years, and the formula that we used was:

$$\text{Growth } rate\ (\%) = \frac{\dfrac{L - M}{\frac{1}{2}(L + M)} + \dfrac{M - E}{\frac{1}{2}(M + E)}}{2} \times 100$$

where: L = Latest Year's data
M = Middle Year's data
E = Earliest Year's data

In simple terms, the *rate* of growth over two consecutive periods is calculated by relating the *difference* between two sets of comparative data to the *average* of the two. The rate of growth over a number of consecutive years is consequently established by calculating the growth rate over each consecutive pair in the series, and then dividing the sum of these rates by the number of pairs in order to find the average rate over the whole period.

It was not long before we found that, while these growth rate indices were useful, we needed to compare them with each other in order to introduce the extra dimension of knowledge that we needed. So we moved on to the subject of management information ratios, which are calculated by relating one data element to another. This meant that we were no longer thinking of items like sales revenue in purely numeric terms: we were calculating such things as the amount of profit that had been generated out of each pound of revenue achieved.

There are three commonly acknowledged 'groups' of ratios:

1 *Investment ratios*, which show how the financial results of a company relate to the shareholders' stake in the business.
2 *Financial status ratios*, which measure the company's financial stability, distinguishing between its ability to meet its long-term commitments—its solvency—and its ability to meet short-term commitments—its liquidity.
3 *Performance ratios*, which measure how successfully and efficiently the company is being run, or how well its management are utilizing the resources that have been entrusted to their control.

When one considers the number of permutations that it would be possible to pair from the many data elements included in our financial statements, it is evident that there are a great many possible combinations which might be considered. We have only been able to deal with a few of the key relationships here, and the ones that we have discussed are summarized below:

- *Profit margin (%):*

$$\frac{\text{Profit before interest and tax}}{\text{Sales revenue}} \times 100$$

The amount of profit generated out of every pound of sales revenue.

- *Return on capital employed (%):*

$$\frac{\text{Profit before interest and tax}}{\text{Capital employed}} \times 100$$

The amount of profit generated out of every pound invested in the business. This is consequently one of the most reliable and most widely used measured of a company's performance from the point of view of utilization of funds.

- *Return on shareholders' funds (%):*

$$\frac{\text{Profit after interest and tax}}{\text{Shareholders' funds}} \times 100$$

This measures the return that the shareholders obtained on the capital that *they* invested in the business. This ratio differs from the return on capital employed to the extent that loan capital is excluded from the denominator.

- *Profitability (%):*

$$\frac{\text{Profit before interest and tax}}{\text{Total assets}} \times 100$$

A prime measure of management performance, in that it measures the amount of profit generated in relation to the total value of assets for which they are responsible.

- *Asset utilization (Capital usage):*

$$\frac{\text{Sales revenue}}{\text{Total assets}}$$

Another key test of operational efficiency, in that it measures the amount of sales revenue generated out of each pound's-worth of assets for which management are responsible.

- *Stock turnover:*

$$\frac{\text{Sales revenue}}{\text{Stocks}}$$

This is a very important measure of the liquidity of a company's stocks, in that it measures the number of times that they are 'turned over' during a year.

- *Credit period (days):*

$$\frac{\text{Outstanding debtors}}{\text{Sales revenue}} \times 365$$

This is a 'turned over' turnover ratio, and measures the average number of days that it takes the company to collect its debts—a useful clue to the care with which it watches its cash flow. This figure may be significantly affected by the proportion of export business handled by the firm, and an Export Ratio, which measures the relationship between exported and total sales, can be a useful factor to consider in conjunction with the credit period.

- *Current ratio:*

$$\frac{\text{Current assets}}{\text{Current liabilities}}$$

  A commonly used measure of a company's liquidity, which measures the relationship between its immediate, or short-term, debts and the value of the current assets out of which these debts will have to be satisfied. This ratio is often known as the 'liquidity ratio'.

- *Acid test ratio:*

$$\frac{\text{Liquid assets}}{\text{Current liabilities}}$$

  Sometimes referred to as the 'quick ratio', this is a more stringent test of liquidity than the current ratio, because it assumes that stocks cannot necessarily be regarded as readily convertible into the liquid funds which are needed to discharge a company's short-term liabilities.

- *Employee ratios:*
  These relate key elements, such as profit, sales revenue or capital employed to the number of people employed by a company, in order to get a set of 'labour utilization' indices. These figures can sometimes be distorted if a company happens to employ a high proportion of part-time workers, in which case ratios based on the level of employee remuneration would be regarded as more relevant and meaningful.

13 Bases for decision

First impressions of the grimbles

In the last chapter, we selected a number of key management ratios, and with their help started to piece together a picture of the way in which Matthew Grimble Ltd had conducted its trading operations during the five years for which we have historic financial information. Some of the points that we noticed can be summarized as follows:

Figure 12.9 The rate of growth in sales revenue over Years 3 to 5 was 16.9 per cent—an encouraging rate of expansion until you compare it with the rate of growth in profit before tax and in capital employed, when you find that the increased revenue was achieved at the expense of a 0.9 per cent shrinkage in profit, and a 27.2 per cent increase in capital employed. This message is confirmed by the profit margin profile in Figure 12.10, which traces a steady decline from 20.0 per cent in Year 1 to only 11.9 per cent in Year 5.

Figure 12.11 Declining profit margins combined with increased capital employed had the inevitable consequences of reducing the return on capital employed (Figure 12.11) and the return on shareholders' funds (Figure 12.12). But these are investment indices, and while they are of paramount interest and importance to the company's shareholders, we are currently rather more concerned with internal measures of management performance. The profitability ratio (Figure 12.13), which relates profit before interest and tax to the total value of the assets entrusted to the management's care, is more relevant here, and this shows a steady decline from 29.1 per cent in Year 1 to 16.3 per cent in Year 5.

Figure 12.14 The next thing that we checked was the asset utilization, or Capital usage ratio, which showed us the amount of sales revenue generated out of each pound invested in total assets. This profile was rather more encouraging, because apart from the dip in Year 4 created by the impact of increased capital investment, the trend was slightly upwards. This enthusiasm should, however, be tempered with the reminder that the progressive reduction in asset values resulting from the effects of the depreciation calculation is bound to emphasize this effect.

Figure 12.15 We then turned our attention to the working capital area of the business, and looked at the stock turnover and the credit period ratios. The stock turnover profile was disturbing, in that the value of stocks had risen from the equivalent of 2.4 months' sales in Year 1 to 3.4 months' in Year 5. This raises the very practical question of why this should be necessary. Especially in view of the expanded and presumably improved facilities with which he has been provided, the production manager should be asked to explain why he considers that all this extra lead time should be required in order to ensure the satisfaction of marketing requirements.

We can easily work out what this means in terms of money that is being locked up on the shelves of his warehouse instead of in the bank, where the accountant would dearly love to see it. The Year 1 stock turnover was 5.0, and the Year 5 sales revenue was £1.13 m, which means that if the Year 5 stock turnover had remained at the Year 1 level, then the amount of stock needed to sustain that level would have been (1,130,000/5.0 =) £226,000. This is (320,000 – 226,000 =) £94,000 less than the value of stocks carried at the end of Year 5, and that is almost exactly the amount that the accountant is going to have to go out and borrow, and pay interest on, in order to see him through the next few months!

Figure 12.17 Mind you, the accountant needs to keep his eyes open as well! His control of the debt collection does not appear to be all that exceptional, although it is rather difficult to judge that too positively at the moment, and the acid test ratio profile demonstrates quite clearly that he has never been completely free of liquidity problems.

The overall impression is that of a company facing declining profitability, which is seriously affecting its liquidity, and its consequent chances of survival. This situation is not being helped at all by the apparently high stock levels which are being held, and the employee ratios suggest that productivity could, and should, be improved. This is not a particularly encouraging scenario, but at least the application of a selected series of ratio analyses has enabled us to reach this diagnosis with comparatively little effort. Once we have identified the problem, it is easier to formulate a strategy with which to tackle it, and that is what we want to do now—after all, we can't stand by and watch a great little product like the grimble disappear from the face of the earth without making some effort to ensure its survival!

Interrelationship of ratios

We have looked at quite a number of ratios during our analyses, and we could obviously have calculated many more. There is no need to complicate the issue unnecessarily by the introduction of too many figures, but it is very important to retain our sense of perspective, and we want to concentrate our attention now on ways in which the various data elements and ratios link together into a comparatively small number of groups. In Figure 13.1, we have prepared a composite chart of the main elements of the profit and loss statement and balance sheet. You will see that we have joined these together at the point where the retained profit from the trading period is regarded as being part of the reserves on the liabilities side of the balance sheet. The other categories of liabilities are added in to build up to total liabilities/total assets, and we then go down the 'other side' of the balance sheet, splitting Total Assets down into its various sub-classifications as we go.

The dotted lines with the circled numbers indicate the elements which are linked together in the ratios that we discussed in Chapter 12, and we can see that these fall into four main groups:

(A) Profit and loss only

1 Profit Margin, which relates profit before interest and tax to sales revenue.

(B) Profit and loss/balance sheet

2 Profitability/Return Ratios, which measure profit before interest and tax in relation to shareholders' funds, capital employed/net assets, and total assets.

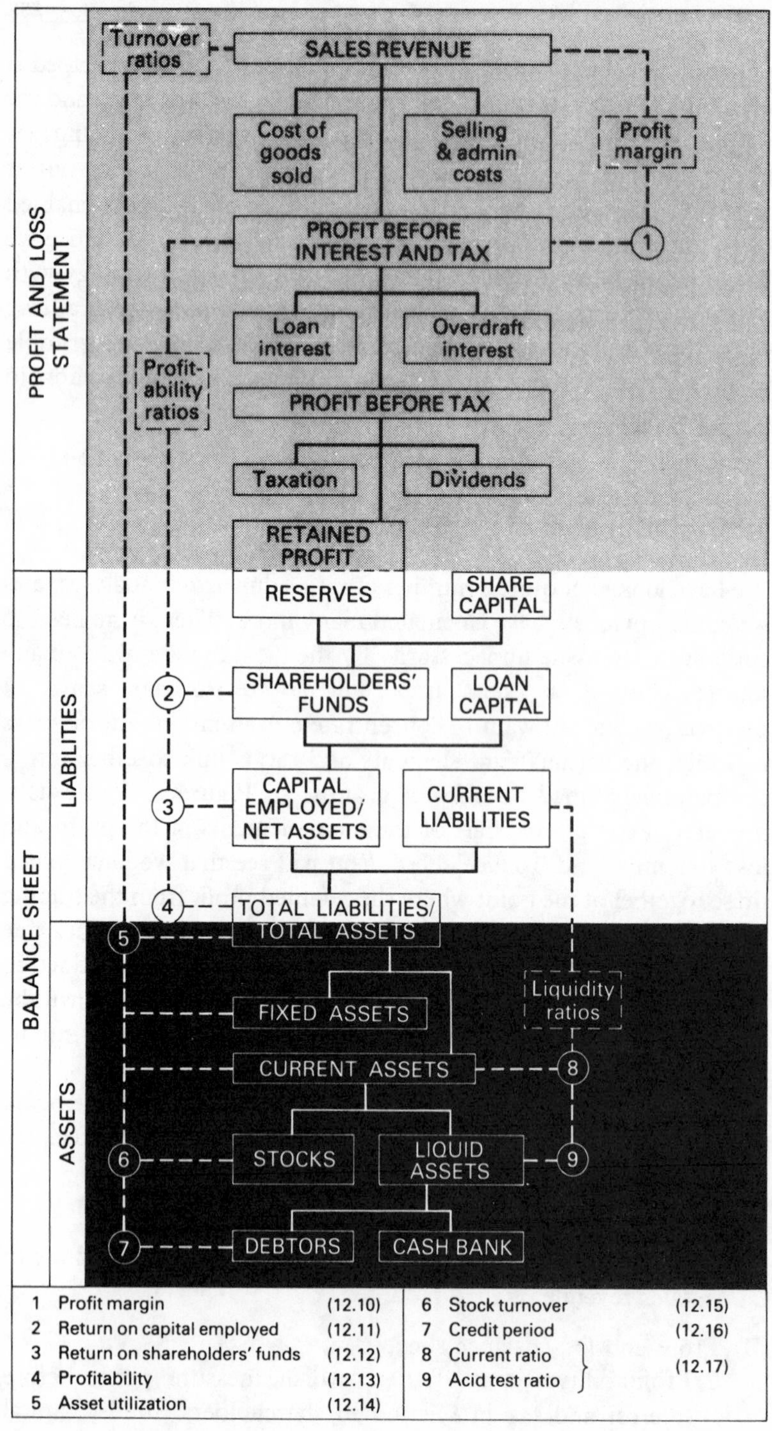

Fig 13.1 The interrelationship of ratios

3 Turnover Ratios, which measure the number of times that the various classifications of assets have been 'turned over' during a period. We have only selected three key ratios from this group for discussion, although many companies would compile turnover ratios for other asset categories, such as fixed assets, current assets etc.

(C) Balance sheet only

4 Liquidity Ratios, which are used to assess the amount of readily-convertible assets that a company has available to meet its short-term debts.

Identification of three key ratios

This chart helps up to see quite readily that there are three data elements which dominate the suite of ratios which we have selected—namely sales revenue, profit and total assets. This should be no surprise when one considers that one of the main responsibilities of management is the generation of as much revenue, and as much associated profit as possible, from the effective use of the assets for which it has been made responsible.

The development of this line of thought leads us to another observation, which is that these three data elements can be linked together by three 'key' ratios, although, as Andrew pointed out, he has always been aware that, when you perm any two from three, you invariably end up with three 'doubles' bets! We have already met the three ratios concerned, so if we accept the fact that, for the purposes of this discussion, we shall be defining 'profit' as being 'profit before interest and tax'—let us identify the ratios concerned, and see how they relate together in Figure 13.2.

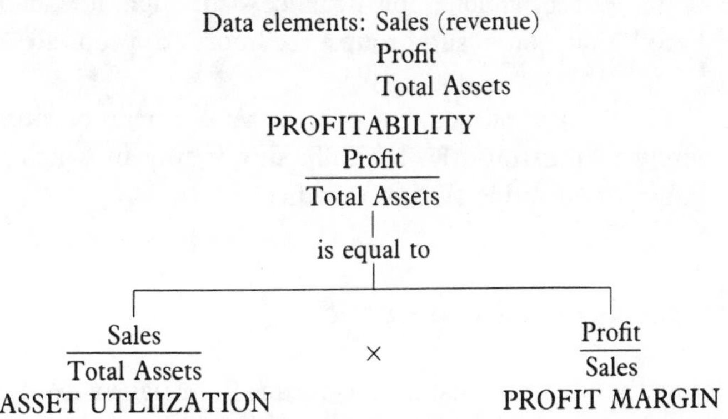

Fig 13.2 The interrelationship between the three key management ratios

This is no mysterious accident, of course. We would have obtained the same sort of relationship from any group of three ratios made up from three basic data elements; but, having identified the three elements which are most relevant to the management objectives which we have defined, this exercise does at least help us to focus on the three key ratios to watch.

If we were looking at a company from the point of view of investment, rather than of management performance, we would be likely to be more interested in the return on capital employed than in the profitability ratio, in which case we could get the same sort of 'three-cornered' relationship by using net assets turnover as the relevant turnover ratio, rather than asset utilization, since:

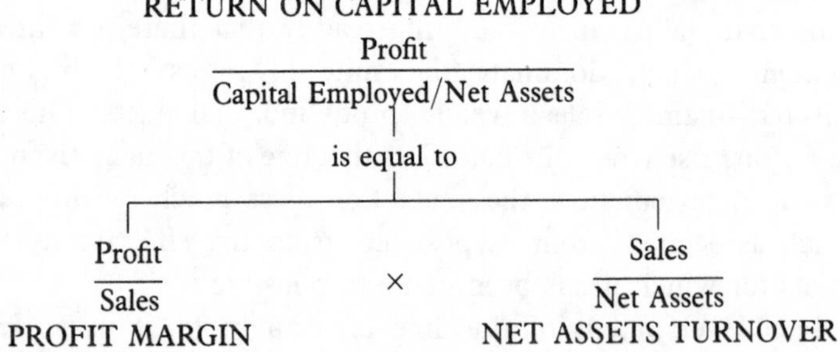

The two small pyramids of ratios we have just built up may be linked together through the common element of profit margin, and we have shown the result of this in Figure 13.3, in which the two principal turnover ratios are each subdivided into their main subordinate ratios. Each of the asset classifications we have identified here can be broken down further into smaller sub-groups as appropriate—we have already looked at the stocks and debtors elements of current assets, for instance—although it should be remembered that some sub-groups are more 'appropriate' than others.

We do not want to pursue that point here; our main purpose has been merely to illustrate the basically simple way in which these rather grand-titled ratios all link together.

The strategic decision pyramid

Now let us think about what all this means to management. It is all very well playing around with figures, but that doesn't necessarily

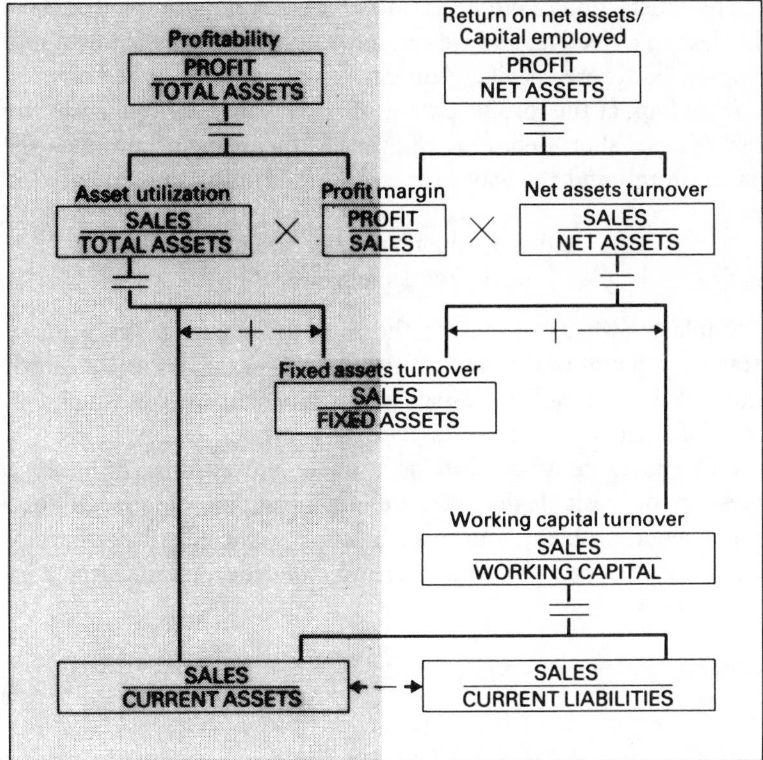

Fig 13.3 The key ratio pyramids

get you very far unless you can achieve some practical benefit or advantage out of the exercise.

We will start with profitability—the amount of profit generated out of each pound invested in the company's total assets. There can be no argument about the claim that one of the main objectives of management must be to get this figure as high as possible; so suppose we look at this objective from the purely mathematical point of view, and then consider the sort of strategies which enable it to be satisfied.

Our ratio for the measurement of profitability is:

$$\frac{\text{Profit}}{\text{Total assets}}$$

Looking at this in pure, basic terms, there are two ways in which we can increase this ratio. We can:

either (a) increase the profit,
or we can (b) reduce the value of the assets

The satisfaction of either or both of these conditions will achieve the desired objective, and we can now break the problem down into smaller, but more specific elements.

If we look at the 'profit' element first, we are very well aware by now that the short definition of profit is 'the excess of revenue over expenditure', and the way to increase profit must consequently be to:

either (a) increase sales revenue,
or (b) reduce expenses

Similarly, when we look at the second element of the primary strategy—to reduce the value of the assets—we can break this down into a whole range of subclassifications, the main ones of which will be fixed assets and current assets.

There is nothing revolutionary about any of this. It is all a question of basic logic. We are organizing our approach to a fundamental problem, and this has led us to the effective construction of a 'strategic decision pyramid', like the one illustrated in Figure 13.4.

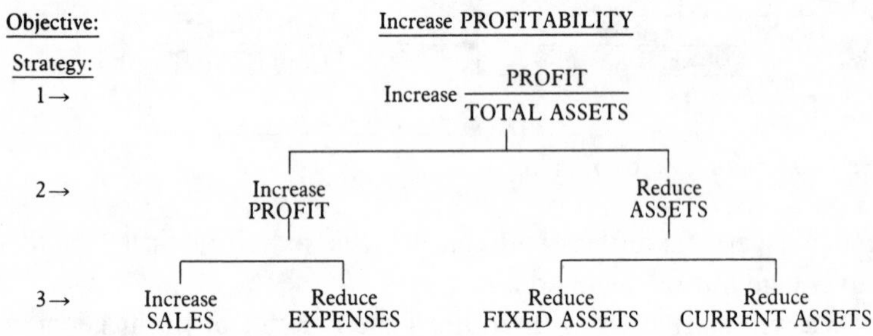

Fig 13.4 The strategic decision pyramid

Once again, the successful implementation of any or all of these strategies will ensure that the primary objective is achieved. And this is where everyone can get involved—including the accountant.

Many suggestions could be made about possible strategies which might be adopted in order to achieve each of these individual 'third level' objectives. We shall list a few of them here, although you will almost certainly be able to think of several more:

(1) *increase sales revenue:* This might be achieved by:
- — Reconstructing the pricing policy
- — Investing in more market research
- — Product and packaging design changes

— Re-assessment of advertising policy
— Re-assessment of contract terms
etc. etc.

(2) *reduce expenses:* Consideration should be given to:
— Siting (or re-siting) of the factory
— More efficient and up-to-date plant
— Research into improved production methods
— Maintenance policies
— Industrial relations
— Productivity schemes
— Purchasing economies
— Expenditure control

(3) *reduce fixed assets:* Consider the following points:
— possibility of increasing utilization of existing plant
— sale of obsolete plant
— improve planned maintenance schedules to reduce down-time

(4) *reduce current assets:* Discuss ways in which:
— stock levels can be reduced
— production lead-times can be cut
— outstanding debts can be recovered more quickly, possibly by reviewing credit terms

This last area is one where managers may feel that they have more scope for some positive action, because in many ways, current assets are more easy to control than fixed assets. One generally has more flexibility in influencing the control of stock levels than in the control of most types of fixed assets, for example, and reaction times are also generally much less. The only trouble is that there is a limit to how far one can go in reducing stocks and credit limits, and, although this is a *vital* area to watch, it should never be regarded as the *only* area to watch.

Business development strategies

We can now begin to imagine our management team meeting to discuss the best ways of achieving their common objective of improving their company's profitability—each manager with a few ideas of his own about the contribution that he is potentially capable of making. They must now analyse the various options open to them when formulating their business development strategies. What are the relative advantages and disadvantages of these options, and how can they be combined into an effective corporate strategy?

This is obviously a very complex problem, and one that needs to be broken down under a number of separate headings, such as:

1 Sales Strategy
2 Production Strategy
3 Investment Strategy
4 Finance Strategy

In fact, the agenda for this meeting might well read something like this:

1 SALES STRATEGY

1.1 Increase Price This would have a direct effect upon Revenue, provided that sales volumes are not affected, but demand may well be reduced.

1.2 Increase Volume We would need to establish whether or not there is a potential market, and what would need to be done in order to increase our share, and then to satisfy the demand.

1.3 Develop New Products Getting in on a new market could be really profitable, but investment in research and development and new plant could be heavy, and potential competition might be high.

1.4 Cease Trading No more worries? Certainly no more income, and the disposal of our assets might involve us in serious losses.

Each of the last three options would need to be linked to an appropriate investment strategy.

2 PRODUCTION STRATEGY

2.1 Revise Schedules Production schedules are likely to need revision in order to meet the requirements of increased sales forecasts and inventory policies. These revised schedules must be achieved smoothly, and with the minimum impact from 'stop/go' decisions. (A targeted reduction in stock levels, for instance, could well reduce production pressure in the short term, even if sales volumes increase).

2.2 Planned Maintenance It may well be advisable to schedule the shut-down of production, assembly and packaging plant on a rotating basis for routine maintenance checks, rather than wait for breakdowns to disrupt an urgent production programme.

3 INVESTMENT STRATEGY

3.1 Modify Existing Plant A comparatively small capital investment could conceivably result in considerable cost savings and more efficient production.

3.2 Expand Production Capacity Perhaps the capacity of the existing plant could be expanded, but, if so, at what cost? If new plant is needed, where should it be sited?

If there are a number of different possibilities available, the advantages and disadvantages of each must be measured against the others.

If expansion is the chosen option, but will involve the expenditure of more capital resources than are readily available, the various methods by which the additional resources can be obtained must also be considered.

4 FINANCIAL STRATEGY

4.1 Obtain Additional Capital How much can be made available from existing sources, and how much extra should we borrow?

Where shall we get it, and how much will it cost?

4.2 Obtain Maximum Benefit from Existing Capital

— Control of working capital
— Balance competition for scarce resources, and establish priorities
— Cash flow planning and control
— Transfer pricing policies
— Budgetary control
— Expenditure control
— Financial reporting and management reaction.

This all adds up to quite a lengthy agenda, and it is not just coincidence that puts the accountant at the end of the list. He is obviously unable to evaluate strategies if there are no strategies to evaluate, although his management colleagues must be given as fast an analysis as possible of the forecast financial impact of the various options under discussion. This is an aspect of his job which could be compared with that of an air traffic controller advising pilots about landing conditions.

Neither is it coincidence that the word 'control' appears so often under the part of the discussion devoted to financial strategy, because no strategy can succeed if it is not controlled. There is no point in paying lip-service to a system of budgetary control, for example, if all that happens is that all the budgets are tucked away in a drawer and forgotten until next year. Progress must be monitored, and any deviations from the chosen course plotted, reported and corrected; this, as you may remember, is another essential part of the 'management accounting' function to which we referred early on.

One of the more innocent-looking items under financial strategy refers to the 'control of working capital', and it is quite possible that, by the time the managers have got to that one, the managing director will realize that it must be getting on for lunchtime, and put that item back for the next meeting—or even for a differently constituted meeting altogether. This is not necessarily a bad thing, because it is a topic that fully deserves a meeting of its own—probably one with a wider attendance that that which would normally gather for a senior management meeting. We have already stressed the need to minimize the amount of resources tied up in working capital, and this is an appropriate point to set out some of the reasons again.

The control of working capital

Almost every functional area of a company contributes in some way to the control of its current assets and current liabilities, whether it be in the form of planning, market research, produce development, stock control, credit control, or whatever. 'Control' in this present context means 'minimizing', since cash invested in working capital is locked away, and does not earn any profit until sales have been made and revenue has been received. This is unlike cash invested in fixed assets, which can be employed to produce more goods for eventual conversion into more cash.

Working capital has been described as the physical expression of lead-time—or money converted into time instead of into profits. For example, if it takes two months to store and to convert raw materials into finished goods, which themselves have to be held in stock pending sale, then each week's sales has to be propped up by two months' stock of raw materials. The longer the lead-time, or the larger the 'safety cover', the more 'dead' capital will be needed to support the sales. So, if lead-time can be reduced, so can the working capital, and the less working capital we have, the less we have to control: less stocks, fewer outstanding debts, and so on. Or—looking at it another way—if we can support an increase in demand with no increase in the amount of working capital required, then we should be employing the same investment to earn more profit than before.

The amount of working capital used to support each pound of sales must therefore be minimized. If we do this, any future expansion can be financed at the lowest possible cost. Flexibility would then be increased, because new products could be produced faster; the consequences of obsolescence would be less costly, and our vulnerability would be reduced. What better motives could there be? It certainly ties in with all we have been saying so far—effective use of capital, maximization of return, and so on—but who should be made responsible for the control of such a project, and how would they set about it?

Should it be the purchasing manager? He knows how long it should take for his suppliers to react to an order, so if he did his job properly, he should be able to guard against the luxury of holding five weeks' stock of an item that can be readily obtainable within two weeks. Provided, of course, that the production manager remembers to let him know what his anticipated requirements are likely to be.

In fact, the production manager could well be another candidate for the job. He should have his finger sufficiently on the pulse of the business to be able to keep Purchasing informed of his production plans, and he obviously is not going to keep breaking into his production schedules any more than he can help just in order to satisfy unforeseen panic requirements. Not any more than he can help—but what happens if the Marketing people don't keep him up to date with their plans for special promotional campaigns?

Normally they would, of course, but we know that it is not always easy to guarantee complete infallibility in pressure situations such as these, so maybe it would be easier if we put the marketing manager in charge instead. If anyone knows what's going on, it's got to be him!

Maybe it has, but we've met his sort before, haven't we? In Chapter 10, to be exact. Wasn't he the one who filled the warehouse up with so much stock in his anxiety to be able to satisfy every conceivable customer requirement at a moment's notice that the lads couldn't find anywhere to plug in their electric kettle? Or perhaps that was his predecessor—at least, if he has read this far, our present one should, we hope, appreciate some of the problems associated with the holding of too much stock!

But is he fully in touch with the length of time that some of his customers are taking to pay their bills? Perhaps they have read this book too—we certainly hope they have, anyway!—and are extending their credit, not to mention their luck, right up to the limit. That is rather more in the accountant's area, though, and he would be the first person to make a fuss if the Marketing people started sending out goods to customers who hadn't yet paid for the things they had three months ago.

On that basis, then, there might be a case for putting the

accountant in charge of working capital. Or would there? Apart from all those invoices being held up by the buyers in Purchasing Department, how many sales invoices are being delayed, either in preparation or in the post-room, and how often and how firmly are the late payers being chased up? Money we are waiting for to come in from somebody else is just as effectively locked away out of our reach as all that cash that is still tied up as stock in the warehouse—we can't use it until we can get our hands on it.

So, all in all, it wouldn't be a very good idea to put any one of these managers in sole charge of working capital. It just wouldn't be fair, because its sphere of influence spreads far beyond the functional areas of responsibility of any one division of the company. The only person who should perhaps be considered for this appointment is the marketing manager, because, in his capacity of forecaster, he is the one who makes the future marketing plans that will influence inventories, production schedules, purchasing and cash-flow requirements. But, unless he keeps his colleagues in the picture about the plans that he has been busy formulating, he might just as well not bother about making them in the first place. The right stocks won't be in the warehouse, and production schedules will be breaking down all over the place because the purchasing manager has been buying all the wrong things—assuming, of course, that the accountant has managed to lay his hands on money with which to pay for them.

It is very easy to paint a picture of chaos, simply by depicting a group of managers who do not talk to each other. But get them all together—*communicating*—perhaps as members of a working capital committee with joint responsibility for its minimization, and it is another story altogether. They will all know what is going on, they will all feel part of a cohesive team, and they will all feel as if they are making a positive contribution to the management of a *proper* business. It *must* be worthwhile.

Asset utilization and profit margin

The discussion that we have developed over the last few pages all arose out of the profitability ratio. However, this is arguably the most important single business ratio of them all—although we have stressed the point several times that it is generally advisable to assess the *relativity* of ratios rather than risk jumping to wrong conclusions on the basis of the possibly misleading evidence of one ratio alone. This is because most 'good' ratios will be regarded as satisfactory, while 'poor' ratios will require some further explanation, and our other two 'key' ratios of asset utilization and profit margin are no exceptions. A high profit margin will normally be regarded as 'good' under any circumstances, and a high asset utilization ratio will suggest that the company is using its assets efficiently. Combine them, and it could well be an occasion for drinks all round, but it is useful to know the sort of things to look for if either or both of these conditions do not prevail. Figure 13.5 may help to give a few leads.

Asset utilization	*Profit margin*	*Possible diagnosis*
Low	Low	The company may be operating below optimum level. Consider increasing sales promotion, or reduce investment in assets.
Low	Reasonable/ average	Sales may be low, or investment high. Check credit period and stock turnover to establish whether funds can be released.
Low	High	Productivity could be low, or capital intensity—i.e. the value of Total Assets per pound of employee remuneration—may be high, indicating inefficient use of labour, or high levels of stock, debtors, plant, etc.
Reasonable	Low	Selling prices may be low, or costs may be high. A positive economy drive could be indicated.
High	Low	Not necessarily bad if sales are high, but this condition could result from a high proportion of leased, or of old and under-valued assets.
High	Reasonable/ average	This is generally a satisfactory situation.
High	High	Fill the ice-buckets, and polish up the glasses!

Fig 13.5 Diagnostic matrix of asset utilization and profit margin ratio combinations

This table identifies some of the factors which could give rise to the various possible ratio combinations that might be encountered, although there may also be other factors involved which will have to be considered. A declining asset utilization ratio may be due to a falling sales demand, for instance; so the sales growth rate should be checked if such a trend is spotted, to ascertain whether this is so. If it is, then another one of those meetings should be set up to consider what extra effort may be needed to retrieve the situation—either by a change in promotional strategy, or by the development and introduction of new products.

In fact, sales growth can tell quite a few stories of its own, because a low growth rate could indicate:

(a) a poor performance by the marketing department
(b) a failure to satisfy demand as a result of poor management, inefficient labour, material supply problems, etc.
(c) unrealistically high selling prices, resulting in demand being switched to competitors.

A high growth rate in sales revenue would generally be regarded as a good thing to have, although, here again it should be cross-checked; if it happens to be going hand-in-hand with a low profit margin, the reason may well be that the company's products or services are under-priced, and their customers have recognized a bargain when they saw one. This would be a situation where the return on capital employed would be a further very relevant factor to be taken into consideration.

Finally, a low asset utilization ratio may not necessarily be a sign of difficulty, since it may simply indicate that a company is more capital-intensive than its competitors. In such a situation as this, we would want to see a high profitability ratio and favourable employee ratios in order to satisfy ourselves that all is as well as it appears to be on the surface.

The 'third dimension' of inter-company comparisons

Quite a number of references have been made during the course of this chapter to 'high', 'reasonable' and 'low' ratios. This is all very well, but, once you've put the book down and started to work out a few ratios of your own, you will very soon come face to face with the problem of deciding which category your results fall into. We are back to the same problem of degree, and the identification of 'norms' against which any ratio can be realistically compared.

Provided you had the time to spare, and the computer facilities available to process the data, it would conceivably be possible to compare the ratios of any individual company with those of any other company, or group of companies—or even with those of all the UK companies, whose accounts are filed at Companies House. But it is doubtful whether anyone would take the trouble to do this, simply because of the prohibitive cost and time that would be involved in collecting, processing and analysing the data—only to risk that dreadful death by data indigestion at the end of it all.

Nevertheless, it is vital to have comparative data available if you hope to stand any chance of assessing how any particular company rates alongside an accepted 'norm'—whether that company be your own, or one of your competitors', or possibly that of one of your potential customers or suppliers. This would help tremendously by adding an invaluable 'third dimension' to the two that we have already discussed: the first being that of Time, and the second being that of Data Element. Figure 13.6 helps to illustrate the dimensional concept that we have in mind.

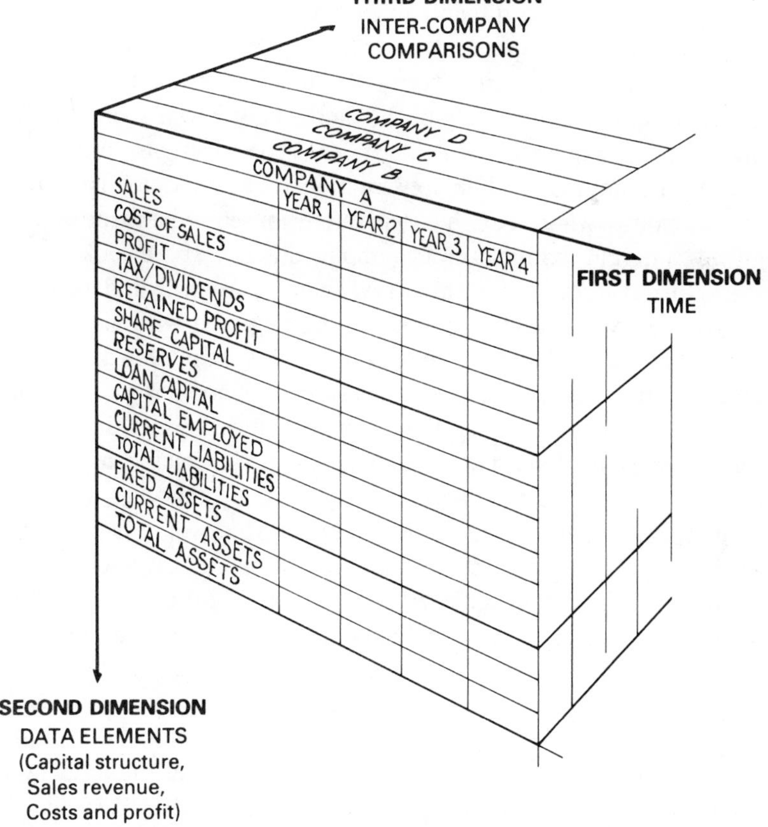

Fig 13.6 The three-dimensional concept of ratio analysis

Fortunately, all is not lost, because specialist information services exist which provide just such data: all collected, processed, sifted and categorized into the formalized type of presentation that is so essential for reliable interpretation. Dun and Bradstreet is one well-known company which provides a Management Ratios service, among many others. Another such company is Inter Company Comparisons Ltd—ICC—to which we are greatly indebted for its enthusiastic help and encouragement in the provision of open access to its data files and reports, and for its permission to use any details or extracts which may be relevant to the content of this book.

ICC specializes in the provision of inter-company and inter-sector ratio comparisons, including in its reports and publications all of the ratios to which we have referred during the course of these chapters. Its data files contain annually updated records of over 12,000 leading UK companies, divided between 150 trading sectors in the manufacturing, merchandizing/distribution and service industries, so it should not prove too difficult to find a relevant and realistic base against which to compare any individual company results.

The sector analyses are a very important and valuable feature of this service, because a study of the global figures will soon indicate the degree of diversity which can exist between one industry's 'norm' and another's. The construction industry sector is a good case in point, where ICC has separated housebuilders from ready mixed concrete manufacturers (among others). If we look at the stock turnover ratios for these two sectors, we will find that the average for housebuilders is about 1.3, compared with about 21.0 for ready mixed concrete! The reasons for this are not too difficult to find, because the very nature of these two industries is so different, even though they are both quite logically included under the general classification of construction industry. The normal construction cycle in the house-building industry is such that heavy stock-holding is inevitable, whereas we all know what would happen to a ready-mixed concrete lorry if it did not unload its cargo on time!

Suppose, then, that ICC decided to make a sub-group out of its construction industry sector which consisted only of housebuilders and ready mixed concrete manufacturers. Assuming that the overall 'sizes' of both sectors were the same, the average stock turnover ratio would be $[(1.3+21.0)/2=]$ 11.2, which would be a pretty meaningless base against which to measure either of the individual industry figures. It would be pointless to maintain that one is 'good' and the other is 'bad'—or even that one is 'better' than the other.

Even as it is, the average ratio for the whole of this particular ICC group of construction industries is 4.5 (the average for the whole of UK industry is 5.5) and this would still not be particularly helpful to managers in either of the industrial sectors that we have quoted. What they need in order to make a valid and realistic assessment of their own company's 'performance rating' is a summary of ratios relating to as many companies as possible—provided that they relate to similar-sized companies engaged in the same, or closely similar, industrial or commercial activity.

This is exactly the sort of service that is provided by the Business Ratios Division of Inter Company Comparisons Ltd, although, for

Matthew Grimble:	*Year 1*	*Year 2*	*Year 3*	*Year 4*	*Year 5*
UK Sectors:	*1975/76*	*76/77*	*77/78*	*78/79*	*79/80*
(1) Matthew Grimble (12.15)	5.0	4.6	4.4	3.8	3.5
(2) Electronic comp. mfrs	4.6	4.7	5.2	5.6	5.4
(3) UK manufacturing	:	:	4.9	4.9	4.8
(4) UK – all sectors	:	:	5.5	5.6	5.4

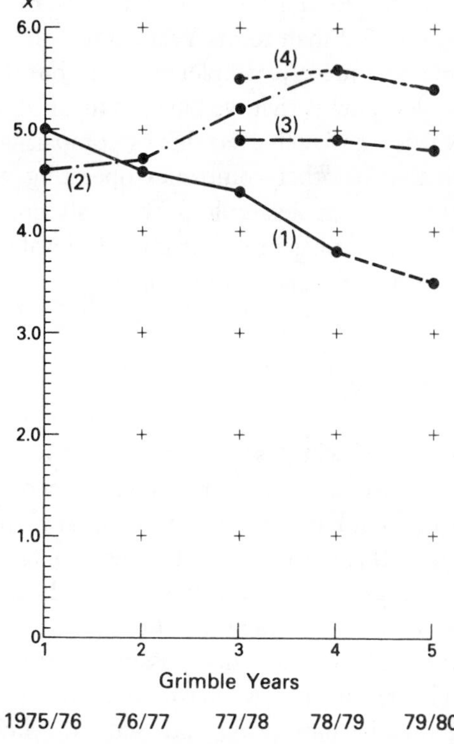

Fig 13.7 Matthew Grimble's stock turnover ratios in perspective

some reason best known to itself, the division does not appear to have a Grimble Manufacturing Sector on its files. Since we have just been looking at one or two Stock Turnover ratios, though, and have already expressed some concern about the apparently low rate of turnover in Matthew's company, it would not be a bad idea to relate his figures to one or two others. In Figure 13.7, we have selected the electronics component manufacturers sector as being probably the most realistic comparison that we are likely to find. The average ratios for all manufacturing industries, and for all sectors combined, are also shown in this chart.

This really does add in that extra dimension which is so helpful in enabling us to grade the Grimble figures as good, bad, or just average. Unfortunately, in this case our earlier misgivings appear to have been justified. We can see from this chart that the average stock turnover ratio for manufacturing industries (3) is somewhat below that for all industrial sectors combined (4), but that the electronics components manufacturers (2) are above the average for manufacturers as a whole. If our comparisons are valid, we could have expected Matthew's stock turnover to be much nearer his Year 1 ratio of 5.0 than to his Year 5 ratio of 3.5. Our earlier comments were consequently completely valid, but the big difference between then and now is that we have established a justification for making them. We have achieved this by comparing Matthew's performance with that of other companies operating within a similar environment. This one example is obviously not completely conclusive in isolation, but has been introduced in order to demonstrate the need for such comparisons to be made.

Summary

Our objective in this chapter has been to explain and to illustrate the ways in which a selection of management information ratios can be used to build up a picture of a company's performance over a period of time. It is rather similar to a series of tests that would be taken at a medical examination, at the end of which the doctor would be in a position to provide a pretty shrewd diagnosis of any illnesses that are going to need treatment—possibly in order to save the patient's life.

The ratios that we have used in our examples are all linked together in some way, and, with the help of the chart that was reproduced in Figure 13.1, we were able to identify the three key data elements in our analyses as being sales revenue, profit and total assets. The three ratios which link these elements together are profitability, profit margin and asset utilization, and we consequently regarded these as being the three key performance ratios.

We then defined the maximization of profitability as being one of the prime measures of management performance or efficiency; and we broke the profitability ratio down mathematically into four 'strategic objective' elements, the achievement of any or all of which would result in an increase of profitability. The four strategic decision elements were:

1 Increase Sales Revenue
2 Reduce Expenditure
3 Reduce the value of Fixed Assets
4 Reduce the value of Current Assets

We found that the achievement of these objectives called for the development of a set of businesss strategies affecting sales, production, investment and finance—consequently involving the concentrated and concerted attention and expertise of managers from all walks of corporate life, rather than from just one area alone. It follows from this that, if managers are given the task of 'improving productivity', they should not only be aware of exactly how this term is defined, but also of the sort of influence that their own experience and effort can exert on its successful achievement.

One of the main areas in which most managers can exert a fairly quick and positive influence is the working capital area of the company, and it is not by accident that we have returned once again to stress the sensitivity and importance of this area—whether it be through tighter stock or expenditure control, credit control, purchasing policies, or whatever.

We finally turned our attention to the 'third dimension' of ratio analysis: that of inter-company comparisons. Although the trends in a company's ratios over a period of time are vital statistics to watch, it is not easy to assess whether they should be regarded as 'good', 'bad' or 'indifferent' unless they can be compared with similar ratios relating to other companies. Such comparisons need to be made with great care, since it is vitally important to ensure that like is being compared with like. Circumstantial and environmental differences between industries mean that legitimate comparisons can only really be made between companies of similar size in a similar industrial or commercial activity sector. In this field the services of such companies as Dun and Bradstreet and Inter Company Comparisons Ltd can be invaluable.

Only one new term has been introduced into our glossary during the course of this chapter. This is a 'productivity ratio' called *capital intensity*, which relates the value of total assets to employee remuneration in order to provide an indication of a company's labour/capital relationship: the higher the ratio, the more capital per pound of labour cost, and hence the greater the capital intensity.

14 Productivity and added value

Introduction

During the course of the last chapter we made the occasional passing reference to 'productivity'. Added value has also cropped up under the general heading of taxation.

At first sight, the strong links which exist between these two topics may not be readily apparent, but we have now arrived at the point in our discussion where it is appropriate to take another, longer look at both of them. We shall start with added value—or value added, as it is equally correctly called—and then move on to consider some of the ways in which it can be used as a very valuable measure of productivity.

The added value concept

Until fairly recently, one might almost have been forgiven for thinking that the balance sheet, the profit and loss statement, and the source and application of funds statement between them provided all that anyone could require by way of historical financial information. And then something happened a few years ago which resulted in the birth of a new concept called added value. This can be defined as 'the difference between the price that a company pays for the goods and services that it buys, and the price at which it sells the goods or services that it produces'.

As consumers, we generally tend to feel that all we ever see is the wrong end of it, because Value Added Tax is nearly always tagged on at the bottom of our purchase invoices or receipts as a rather tiresome surcharge of 15 per cent—or whatever the rate may be when you happen to be reading this—on the value of the goods or services we have just paid for. Sometimes we won't notice it on small items, or it might be incorporated into the overall price that we pay, but it can often come as a bit of a shock when we find it added on to the price of our new car, or video system, or whatever.

This point happened to crop up one evening when we were enjoying one of our social encounters with Andrew. He had just returned from the bar with his round of drinks, wondering why he should have to pay an extra 15 per cent of their cost to the government when the Chancellor had never offered to buy him a drink in return. We decided to cite the table that we were sitting around as our illustration of the principles involved, and asked him to imagine the table as it was when it started off in life: as a tree growing in a plantation in Canada, or somewhere.

At that point, it had cost nothing. All it had done was stand there, minding its own business, and growing a bit larger each year. And then, one day, along came a tree-feller to cut it down so that he could cut it up into logs and sell them to a saw-mill down the road. In so doing, the feller had added value to the tree by converting it into logs that the mill could use. The difference between the original cost (or value) of the tree—which we shall assume for the purpose of this example was nothing—and the cost at which the logs produced from it were sold is therefore equivalent to the value added to the tree by the feller as a result of his conversion labour. The cost of these logs to the mill is called a 'third-party' cost, because it is an 'invoiced' cost paid to a third party: to someone from outside their own organization.

Apart from the cost of the logs themselves, the mill will also incur some other third-party costs, such as electricity, insurance, telephone, postage or miscellaneous supplies, and all of these will be associated with the conversion of the logs into planks or veneers. The difference between the total of their third-party costs—or purchases of goods and services from outside suppliers—and the price at which the planks are sold to their customers will represent the value that has been added to the logs by the mill.

The planks and veneers will then be taken on the next stage of their journey, to be converted into matches, pit-props, bar tables, goal-posts, or whatever. To the manufacturers of these items, the price paid to the saw-mill for the planks will be part of their third-party costs, and the value added by them will be the difference between this cost—plus all their other third party costs—and the price at which they sell their own products. This difference consequently represents the value that has been added as a result of their own company's efforts during the conversion process from purchased materials and services into the products and services that are then passed on for sale to somebody else.

Elements of added value

In order to create this added value, the manufacturer will generally have to employ labour to assist him in the conversion process. He may have had to borrow capital to help finance the business, and the interest that he pays on this capital will be part of his finance costs—sometimes referred to as capital services costs. The depreciation of his fixed assets will also be an 'internal' cost, and then, if he makes any profit, some of this will immediately, or almost immediately, be spirited away by the taxman, as we have already seen.

Finally, some of the profit that is left will be divided among the shareholders as a return on their investment in the business, and the rest will be retained in the business as reserves. This picture is summarized in Figure 14.1, and Figure 14.2 illustrates how these principles would apply to Matthew Grimble's business.

Sales revenue Cash received from customers in return for the products or services sold.

– *Purchases from third parties* Cash paid to the suppliers of goods and services that are needed for conversion into the products or services sold.

= GROSS ADDED VALUE This is made up of:

(1) *Employee Costs* Cash paid to the employees for the work they do, to the government for payroll taxes and social security contributions, and to pension funds, etc.

(2) *Capital Usage Costs* The depreciation of assets charged against profits to provide for their future replacement.

(3) *Finance Costs* Cash paid as interest to people who have lent money to the owners of the business in order to help them get started, and to banks as interest on overdrafts, etc.

(4) *Taxation* Cash paid to the government out of the company's trading profits to help fund the provision of all the national and local services and amenities that are needed to satisfy community requirements.

(5) *Dividends* Cash paid to shareholders as a return on the capital that they have invested in the business, which is the reward they receive in return for the risks they have taken.

(6) *Retained Profit* Money put aside for future expansion in the business, and to help combat the effects of inflation.

Fig 14.1 The elements of added value

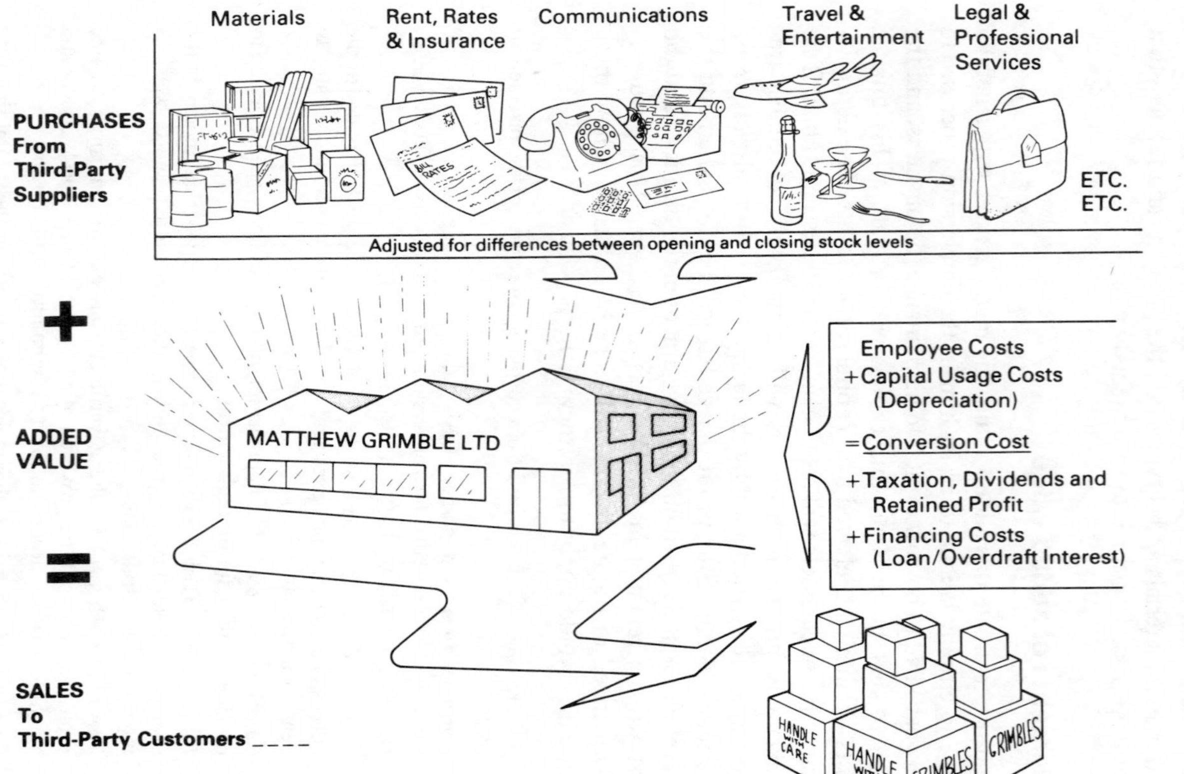

Fig 14.2 Matthew Grimble's added value analysis

Value added tax

We mentioned in an earlier chapter that value added, or 'turnover' taxes were one of the government's main sources of tax income. It is simple in concept, and basically quite simple to operate—unless you happen to be a small businessman who has to spend so much of his time form-filling instead of getting on with the things that he is really in business to do, like earning more money!

Every company with more than a certain level of sales revenue has to pass on to its customers a VAT surcharge, calculated as a percentage on the net total of its sales invoice. This VAT surcharge then has to be passed back to the government, net of any VAT surcharges that have in turn been passed on to the company by its own suppliers. The net effect of all this is that each company pays to the government a tax based on the 'value' it has added to its purchased goods and services during their conversion into the products or services that it has provided to its customers.

The value added statement

If we look down the list of added value elements that we have just prepared, we can see that most of them can be lifted straight out of the profit and loss statement. This will not show us the split between third party and employee costs, although, with any luck, we should be able to get to this quite easily by referring to the Notes to the Accounts, since all companies must now disclose details of their total employee remuneration and the average number of employees throughout the year.

We may also need to refer to the balance sheet in order to ascertain the total amount of depreciation charged for the period, but things aren't really as difficult as you might think at first sight. Let's have a look at Figure 14.3, which provides some relevant extracts from the documents concerned.

These pieces of information are really all that we need to enable us to get back to the value added elements that we specified in Figure 14.1, and the first thing that we want to do now is to work out the gross added value, which is merely the total of the items listed in the abridged profit and loss statement in Figure 14.3, plus the employee remuneration included in the Notes to the Accounts,

£'000		Year 5
(a) PROFIT AND LOSS STATEMENT		
Sales revenue		1,130
Trading profit		135
Less: Interest charges		20
Trading profit before tax		115
Less: Taxation		35
Profit after tax		80
Less: Dividends		30
Retained profit		50
(b) BALANCE SHEETS or Notes to the Accounts (extracts only)	*Year 4*	*Year 5*
Total fixed assets at cost	310	400
Less: Depreciation to date	80	120
Net book value	230	280
Stocks	250	320

(c) NOTES TO THE ACCOUNTS
'The average number of employees during the year was 73, and the total employee remuneration was £470,000'

Fig 14.3 Extracts from the published accounts of Matthew Grimble Limited for Year 5

and the total depreciation charge for the year of (120,000 – 80,000 =) £40,000.

	£'000
Employee remuneration	470
Total depreciation	40
Loan interest charges	20
Taxation	35
Share dividends	30
Retained profit	50
Gross added value	645

We now have to convert the gross 'value of sales' to a 'value of production' figure by adjusting for the difference between opening and closing stock values of (320,000 – 250,000 =) £70,000. Since the stock values have increased, the 'value' of production must have been that much more than the 'value' of sales—or (1,130,000 + 70,000 =) £1,200,000. All that remains to be done now is to deduct the gross added value from this figure in order to arrive at the total third party costs of (1,200,000 – 645,000 =) £555,000. The value added statement will consequently be as illustrated in Figure 14.4.

£'000		*Year 5*
Sales revenue		1,130
Less: Net third party purchases		
Total third party	555	
Increase in stocks	– 70	
Net purchases		485
Gross added value		645
Total employee costs		470
Finance cost—(Loan interest)		20
Capital usage costs—(Total depreciation)		40
Taxation		35
Dividend		30
Retained profit		50
Gross added value		645

Fig 14.4 Matthew Grimble's value added statement for Year 5

Diagrammatic presentation

Another way of looking at the subject is to use some sort of diagrammatic illustration, rather similar to those used in some of our earlier chapters. As you might imagine, we were able to find exactly what we were looking for in Matthew's Employee Report for Year 5, and his artistry is reproduced in Figure 14.5. The more formalized value added statements for all of Years 1 to 5—plus the forecast for Year 6—are shown in Figure 14.6. As we have not given you copies of the relevant extracts from the Notes relating to any of the early years, we have built up the employee cost figures in these statements from the analyses provided in the stock movements and cost of goods sold schedules in Figure 12.2 (pages 202–203), and from the profit and loss statements in Figure 12.3 (pages 204–205).

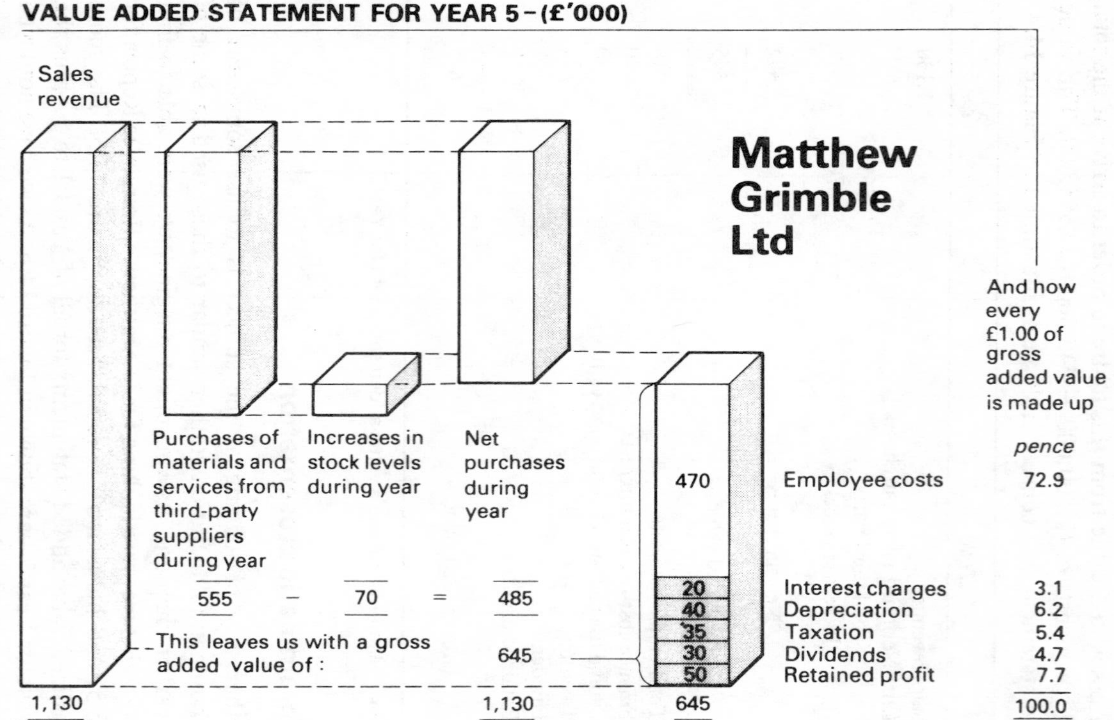

Fig 14.5 A diagrammatic representation of Matthew Grimble's value added statement for Year 5

VALUE ADDED STATEMENT

£'000		Year 1		Year 2		Year 3		Year 4		Year 5		Year 6	
Sales revenue			450		595		805		950		1,130		1,450
Less: Net third party purchases													
Total third party (b/d)		265		285		380		455		555		675	
(Incr.)/Decr. in stocks		−90		−40		−55		−65		−70		−50	
Net purchases			175		245		325		390		485		625
GROSS ADDED VALUE			275		350		480		560		645		825
Employee costs:													
Direct process labour	(12.2)		75		105		155		200		230		265
Indirect labour	(12.2)		45		55		80		100		120		155
Selling and admin.	(12.3)		55		75		95		100		120		150
Total employee costs			175		235		330		400		470		570
Loan interest			8		8		8		20		20		20
Depreciation (total)			10		15		25		30		40		50
Taxation			0		29		34		32		35		76
Dividends			10		15		20		30		30		60
Retained profit			72		48		63		48		50		49
GROSS ADDED VALUE			275		350		480		560		645		825

Fig 14.6 Matthew Grimble's value added statements for Years 1 to 6

The added value of added value

Having defined the principles of added value—or value added, if you really prefer—we should now consider its purpose in life, because it is not intended to be just another excuse for re-shuffling all the financial data of a company into yet another form of presentation.

The main difference between the value added statement and the profit and loss statement is one of emphasis and focus. Whereas the profit and loss statement is a reflection of the whole spectrum of trading and other income and expenditure during a period, the value added statement represents the difference between the prices paid to suppliers *outside* the company, and the prices paid by customers *outside* the company. In other words, it focuses attention completely on what is happening *inside* the company, and it is for this reason that it has been described as a tool which helps to concentrate the manager's mind on the things that he is in the best position to control.

Added value ratios

We can apply the same logic of interpretation to added value figures as we can to any other financial data. Many people contend that management information ratios based on added value are more relevant to the positive management of a company than the ones based on sales revenue, simply because of the sharper focus that they provide on the company's operational efficiency.

Under this philosophy, the three key ratios of profitability, asset utilization and profit margin that we identified and related together in Figure 13.2 would be replaced, or supplemented, by the pyramid shown in Figure 14.7, into which we have also incorporated the Matthew Grimble calculations.

Added value analysis

The first comparison to make here is that between profit/added value and the profit margin. If charted alongside each other, these two series of ratios would produce quite similar profiles, although this is not the aspect that we want to develop. The significant point is the way in which the proportion of profit to added value has fallen off over the years, so we would want to know which other elements of added value have increased, and eaten into this profit.

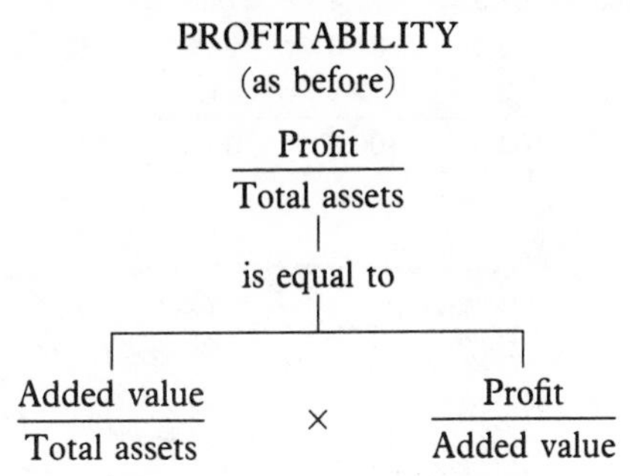

£'000		*Year 1*	*—2*	*—3*	*—4*	*—5*	*—6*
(A) Gross added value	(14.6)	275	350	480	560	645	825
(P) Profit BIT	(12.3)	90	100	125	130	135	205
(T) Total assets	(12.1)	309	388	500	743	826	976
Added value/total assets (A/T)	(×)	0.88	0.90	0.96	0.75	0.78	0.84
Profit/Added value (P/A)	(%)	32.7	28.6	26.0	23.2	20.9	24.8
Sales/Total assets	(12.14)	1.46	1.53	1.61	1.28	1.37	1.49
Profit margin	(12.10)	10.0	16.8	15.5	13.7	11.9	14.1

Fig 14.7 Matthew Grimble's key added value ratios

Using the value added statements reproduced in Figure 14.6, we can break these figures down into four main elements:

1 Employee costs
2 Capital usage costs (depreciation)
3 Profit (tax, dividends and retained profit)
4 Finance costs (loan interest etc.)

The percentage values of each of these elements to the total—or gross—added value are shown in Figure 14.8, into which we have also incorporated the 'ingredient profiles'.

This chart shows us very clearly what has been going on—the profit proportion of the company's added value has been progressively eroded by increasingly high proportions of conversion costs. By far the greater portion of these are employee costs, which have eaten away nearly 10 per cent of the company's added value over the five years to date, but it is also interesting to note how the

(% of gross A.V.)	*Year 1*	*Year 2*	*Year 3*	*Year 4*	*Year 5*	*Year 6*
1 Employee costs	63.6	67.1	68.8	71.4	72.9	69.1
2 Capital usage costs	3.7	4.3	5.2	5.4	6.2	6.1
Total conversion cost	67.3	71.4	74.0	76.8	79.1	75.2
3 Profit	29.8	26.3	24.3	19.6	17.8	2.4
4 Finance costs	2.9	2.3	1.7	3.6	3.1	2.4
TOTAL	100.0	100.0	100.0	100.0	100.0	100.0

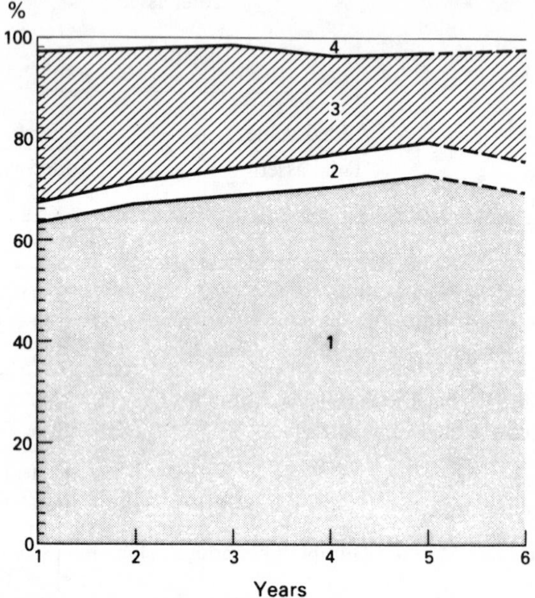

Fig 14.8 Matthew Grimble's added value analysis

percentage of depreciation has crept up from 3.7 per cent in Year 1 to 6.2 per cent in Year 5. This must surely indicate that the company is not getting such an effective 'return' from the money invested in its assets as it was a few years ago—a fact borne out by the profitability ratios that we calculated in Figure 12.13, but here represented in another, rather startling dimension.

Productivity

The implication of the steadily increasing proportion of employee costs to added value is that the company's 'productivity' has been falling off quite seriously over the years. In this context, we are defining productivity as 'the relationship between employee costs and the added value generated by each pound spent on them'. This is what productivity really means, because if increases in a company's bill for employee remuneration are not matched by an equivalent—or preferably by a better—proportional increase in added value, then the productivity ratio of added value to employee remuneration will go down, and the pay rises will not have 'paid for themselves'.

As we have mentioned before, the comparative interpretation of any ratios based on employee numbers or employee remuneration must also take into account the capital intensity of the business, or the amount of capital invested in the company per pound of employee remuneration—which is another aspect of the point that we made just now about depreciation costs. These two ratios link together quite easily through the added value 'version' of asset utilization, which we intend to refer to as the Asset Usage Ratio, in order to avoid confusion with the ratio that we discussed earlier. This pyramid of key productivity ratios is illustrated in Figure 14.9, in which we have again included some sample calculations based on the Matthew Grimble figures.

And it looks as if poor old Matthew could be in trouble again here! Although the trends in capital intensity and asset usage are

PRODUCTIVITY

$$\frac{\text{Added value}}{\text{Employee remuneration}}$$

is equal to

$$\frac{\text{Total assets}}{\text{Employee remuneration}} \times \frac{\text{Added value}}{\text{Total assets}}$$

CAPITAL INTENSITY ASSET USAGE

£'000		*Year 1*	—2	—3	—4	—5	—6
(A) Added value		275	350	480	560	645	825
(E) Employee remuneration		175	235	330	400	470	570
(T) Total assets		309	388	500	743	826	976
1 Productivity	(A/E)	1.57	1.48	1.45	1.40	1.37	1.44
2 Capital intensity	(T/E)	1.76	1.65	1.51	1.85	1.75	1.71
3 Asset usage	(A/T)	0.88	0.90	0.96	0.75	0.78	0.84

Fig 14.9 Matthew Grimble's key productivity ratios

quite encouraging—due to the depreciating values of the company's assets—the productivity ratio shows a steady decline, and this must be because the increases in average remuneration, as shown in Figure 12.18, were not compensated by corresponding increases in added value. Put another way, Matthew's generosity in awarding quite high wage increases has not been rewarded by a corresponding increase in productivity, or efficiency, by his employees.

This may not necessarily have been their fault. This decline could have resulted from inadequate sales volumes, a failure to achieve realistic price increases, an unjustified increase in manning levels, or just plain bad management. We are not in a position to answer all these questions from where we stand, but the figures speak for themselves, and the sooner Matthew settles down to sort things out, the better.

The productivity ratio of added value to employee remuneration is obviously the reciprocal of the employee remuneration/added value relationship that we plotted in Figure 14.9, and that chart illustrates quite clearly how any increases in the proportion of added value taken up by employees' remuneration can only result in a smaller share being available for capital usage costs—depreciation—and profits. And the smaller the proportion left for profit, the smaller the proportion available for distribution as dividends, and for reinvestment in the business. Conversely, the smaller the proportion spent on employee costs, the more there will be available to the owners of the business for expansion.

This most certainly does not mean that wage increases are out—provided that productivity increases are in! The really enterprising and successful firms are the ones that would be able to demonstrate how increasing wage levels can be coupled with a falling proportion of employee costs to added value—i.e. with increasing productivity. The principles involved here are basically very simple and straightforward, and it is this quality of simplicity which has made the added value concept of productivity such a fruitful basis for wage negotiations over recent years.

Productivity incentives and payment in advance of results

The problem with negotiations, of course, is that you have to be talking about the future, whereas all the data that we have collected have been based on what happened in the past—so what sort of guarantee can there be that future targets or forecasts can be achieved? Well, we have been over this ground already, and the answer is that you can never make any guarantees. The best you can do is select the most relevant and reliable bases for assessment and projection.

In practice, this is another one of those things which is not quite as easy as it may sound, since no company will have the final 'Year 5' results available before it starts talking about how much it will be paying its employees in 'Year 6'. One of the things that this means is that it will have to base its negotiations on its forecast figures up to the end of Year 5, although this should not be too difficult, provided that the accountant keeps his work up to date.

The other point to consider is that any one year may be known to be exceptionally good or exceptionally bad, so it may not necessarily be realistic for the forecast results of the current trading year to be used as the sole base against which the following year's awards should be made. The way in which many companies overcome this problem is by using a rolling two-year period for both the base and the forecast periods, which helps to smooth out any unusually good or bad results. In Matthew's case, he could use Years 4 and 5 combined as the base period for his negotiations in respect of a wage-rate settlement for Year 6, and Years 5 and 6 as his combined forecast period.

Gross and net added value

You may have noticed that throughout this chapter we have often used the term 'gross' added value, as distinct from just plain and simple 'added value'. Added value has been defined as the total of all the costs that are incurred in actually running the 'conversion' operations of the business, and it has been shown that part of this added value can relate to the company's financing costs—the interest that they pay on the capital which has been borrowed to get the business under way, or to keep it going.

This brings us back to the question of whether or not these financing, or capital services costs should be regarded as being part of the operational costs of the business, since they really relate to its capital structure. Whichever way you look at it, they are certainly a part of added value, but the point here is that the *total* added value, inclusive of these financing costs, is often called gross added value, in order to distinguish it from the 'net' figure of added value exclusive of these costs. This net figure is—not surprisingly—referred to as *net* added value, so the whole structure of added value can be summarized quite simply as follows:

Employee costs
+ Capital usage costs (depreciation)
= CONVERSION COST
+ Profit (made up of taxation, dividends and retained profit)
= NET ADDED VALUE
+ Financing, or capital services costs (interest on loan capital, bank overdrafts etc.)
= GROSS ADDED VALUE

It is sometimes claimed that the net added value figure is the one which should be used as a basis for ratio calculations, instead of the gross figure we have used in our illustrations throughout this chapter. This is not such a bad idea, since it can actually act as a spur to management—and also, of course, to everyone else concerned—to keep an eye on the capital structure of the company, rather than purely on its (gross) operational performance.

Suppose, for example, that the company had—dare we quote Matthew Grimble Ltd as an example?—been putting on too much working capital 'fat', by allowing stocks to rise too high, or by investing too much capital in fixed assets which were not being economically used. Either of these situations may lead to the need to borrow more capital, or to take on higher overdraft facilities, which would in turn result in higher interest charges to pay for their use. If a net added value base is used for the calculation of the productivity ratios, this calculation base would be depressed by the additional amount of interest paid, and there is a fair chance that the pressure would soon be on to remedy this situation as quickly as possible!

Let us take another look at the productivity ratios that we calculated on the gross added value base in Figure 14.9, and see—in Figure 14.10—how these compare with those measured against a 'net' base. The (literally) depressing effect of the increased interest charges associated with the injection of additional loan capital in Year 4 can be clearly seen in this example. The reason for this emphasis lies in the fact that, in the 'gross' calculation, the financing costs are incorporated into the 'non-conversion' area of added value, which consequently does not affect either the gross amount or the

(£'000)	*Year 1*	*Year 2*	*Year 3*	*Year 4*	*Year 5*	*Year 6*
(G) Gross added value	275	350	480	560	645	825
(N) Net added value	267	342	472	540	625	805
(E) Employee remuneration	175	235	330	400	470	570
Gross productivity (G/E)	1.57	1.48	1.45	1.40	1.37	1.44
Net productivity (N/E)	1.52	1.45	1.43	1.35	1.32	1.41

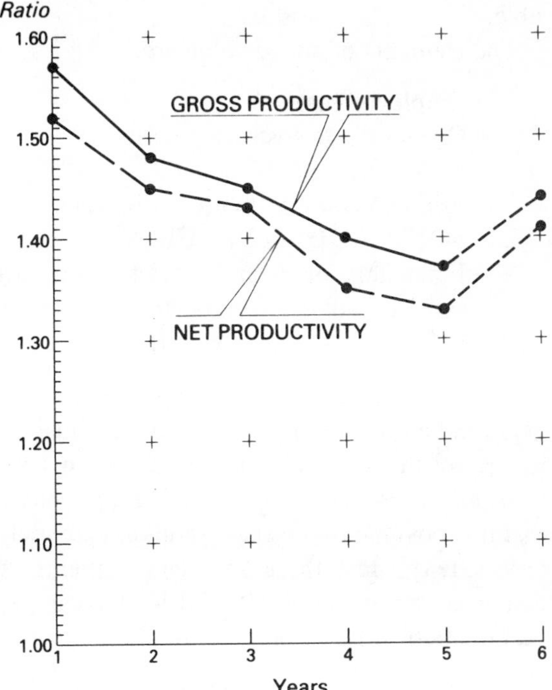

Fig 14.10 Matthew Grimble's gross and net productivity ratios

employee remuneration element, whereas, in the 'net' calculation, its exclusion has a direct negative influence.

Summary

It is only comparatively recently that the concept and name of added value were introduced into the financial vocabulary. The concept has been described as one in which a company's sole purpose in life is to take in supplies of goods or services from suppliers *outside* the company at one end, and to sell their products or services to customers *outside* the company from the other end. What happens during the conversion process *inside* the company consequently 'adds value' equivalent to the difference between the amount of money paid out to the suppliers, and the amount of money collected in from the customers. It is a widely held view that added value helps to concentrate the manager's mind by focusing more sharply on the internal operations of the business for which he is responsible.

The elements of added value are:

Employee costs
\+ Capital usage costs (depreciation)
= CONVERSION COSTS
\+ Profit (including taxation, dividends and retained profit)
= NET ADDED VALUE
\+ Financing, or capital services costs (interest paid on loan capital, bank overdrafts etc.)
= GROSS ADDED VALUE

Management information ratios constructed out of added value data can be linked together to provide valuable control information in exactly the same way as the more conventional 'turnover' and 'margin' ratios that we examined in previous chapters. We found that it is possible to use these ratios as extremely useful measures of productivity. The three key data elements of added value (A), employee remuneration (E) and total assets (T) can be linked in a permutation series to provide the three key ratios of:

Productivity = A/E
Capital intensity = T/E
Asset usage = A/T

The productivity ratio itself, which relates added value to employee remuneration, is a measure which is quite commonly accepted as a clear, reliable and fair basis for salary negotiations related to productivity levels. The concept of added value is consequently one from which everyone can benefit, because it enables executive managers and employees alike to concern themselves with, and to enjoy joint benefit from, improvements in productivity and efficiency. It is a concept that can be readily understood, and consequently readily accepted, by all concerned; and this in itself should lead to a wider understanding and appreciation of the use and interpretation of financial information for the development of positive—and it is to be hoped successful—business strategies.

There must be plenty of scope and justification for the wider use of value added statements as a routine part of financial reporting, alongside the rest of the conventional statements that we have discussed throughout the course of this book. How long it will take for this to happen will depend upon one of the key words emphasized in our earlier chapters—*communication*.

15 Accounting for inflation

Introduction

One of the final items for discussion on our agenda is the subject of Inflation Accounting. You may remember that we touched on this very briefly back in Chapter 7, when we suggested to Andrew that the Profit After Tax of £13,000 that his company reported Last Year might well have been turned into a loss of £22,000 if the company had been following the UK type of current cost conventions instead of the traditional historic cost conventions which have formed the basis of all our discussions and illustrations so far.

Andrew had to dash off to keep an appointment with his tax consultant at the time, but we did have an opportunity to go into the subject in much more detail at a later date. Our first inclination was to take him step by step through each and every one of the conventions associated with the UK system of Current Cost Accounting—or 'C.C.A.', as it is often more conveniently called—as recommended in the guidelines published in 1980 by the Accounting Standards Steering Committee in their Statement of Standard Accounting Practice (SSAP 16), and with which all professional accountants are expected to comply. On reflection, however, we felt that this would perhaps not be the most sensible way to approach the subject.

Our reasons for this were that the British C.C.A. approach is only one of several methods which have been recommended and experimented with worldwide, and that no system has so far managed to survive its trial period unscathed by criticism from the accountancy bodies and other professions in the countries concerned. We consequently felt that it would be wise to focus our discussion more on the principles involved than on a detailed description of a methodology which may well change, or even be discarded over time. Andrew agreed, and reminded us that 1980 also happened to be the year in which Henbit won the Derby—just a little more than an hour after Pontin Lad had 'started it all' . . ..

Background to inflation accounting

Accounting traditions and conventions have their roots firmly established in an historical cost base. This decrees that every item of expense or revenue should be recorded in the accounts of a company, and reflected in its financial statements, at the exact number of monetary units that were involved in the transaction, although one major deviation from this rule did stipulate that stocks should be valued at the lower of cost or realizable market value. Companies pay their accountants a lot of money to ensure that this convention is followed with meticulous accuracy, and then they pay their auditors a lot more money to make sure that the accountants did their job properly, and to vouch for the fact that the resulting accounts represent a 'true and fair view' of the company's financial situation. Any accountant who tried to record a £1,000 purchase as £1,100, just because he happened to feel that 'that was what the goods were really worth, Your Honour', would very soon be 'up the street' with his cards.

We have already defined profit as being a measure of the growth or shrinkage arising out of the operational activities of a business for whatever period of time we choose. It follows from this that, under the historic cost conventions, profit will be the excess of actual historical revenue over the actual historical cost of the goods or services sold.

There is no problem about this in times of relative price stability, but no one is going to pretend that prices have been anywhere near stable over the past several years. High rates of inflation bring with them a proportionate fall in the value of money. Consequently some of the profit calculated under the historic cost conventions needs to be retained in the business in order to provide the *increased* number of monetary units—whether they be pound notes, dollars, francs, or whatever—that will be required to finance the replacement of the *same* volume of assets, measured in real terms.

In Chapter 7, we demonstrated to Andrew that if his fixed assets had been valued at current replacement cost instead of at historic cost, then the value at which they would have been shown in Last Year's balance sheet would have gone up from £962,000 to £1,412,000—an increase of (1,412,000 – 962,000 =) £450,000. This would inevitably have resulted in the depreciation charged against trading for the year being increased, and we estimated that this increase would probably have been in the region of £35,000, thus converting his £13,000 historic cost profit to the £22,000 current cost 'loss' that we mentioned. This £35,000 additional depreciation charge is a measure of how much of his reported 'profit' should really have been kept in the business purely in order to maintain the value of its assets in real terms.

The value of stocks will be affected in a similar way, and it follows from this that the cost of goods sold should also be adjusted to reflect increasing purchase prices and production costs. The cost at which these are charged against the revenue for a period should therefore be the same number of monetary units that are required to replace them, rather than the number for which they were historically purchased and produced. If prices rise, and the volume of business remains constant, it also follows that the 'current' value of outstanding debtors and creditors will be different from that shown in the books at 'historic' value.

In all of these situations, a company will require an increasing amount of capital in order to finance its existing level of activity, and—unless the shareholders are prepared and able to put more money into the business—the only place from which this capital can be obtained is from the company's historic profits. In periods of rapid inflation, a business which uses a large volume of assets will need a proportionately large amount of historic profit to plough back into the business—simply to support the same level of activity.

It would be very convenient if adjustments for the effects of inflationary pressures could be achieved simply by a percentage reduction to historic cost profits of all companies, at the same time maintaining a valid comparison between industries and between different companies in the same industry. Unfortunately, the extent to which historic cost profits have to be adjusted depends upon a number of factors, the impact of which will differ widely from one company to another.

These factors are:

(a) The pattern of price rises relating to the fixed assets and stocks used and held by the company; not only in the current trading period, but also since the oldest assets held at the start of the period were originally purchased.

(b) The age profile of the company's fixed assets, which will directly affect the amount of depreciation charged against the trading revenue for the period.

(c) The average time during which stocks are held—the value of stocks held at any moment being a function of this time factor—and the rate at which these stocks are consumed.

(d) The mix of assets held, made up of fixed assets, stocks and monetary items—the monetary items being mainly debtors less creditors, and

(e) When looked at from the point of view of the shareholders, the way in which the net assets used in the business are financed—whether by borrowings or by shareholders' funds.

From such a list as this, it is not difficult to appreciate that companies which may appear to be *relatively* profitable on an historic cost basis could easily slip significantly down the league table as a result of the differential adjustments involved during the conversion to current-cost profitability.

In fact, a survey undertaken by a firm of London stockbrokers revealed that businesses whose results are least affected by the adjustments required to reflect the impacts of inflation—in other words, the less capital-intensive sectors, such as the major retail stores—have consistently out-performed those companies more seriously affected. The implication is quite clear: inflation can have a very draining effect on any company, and failure to recognize this can be lethal.

The brief examples that we have thought about so far have tended to focus on the effects that increased depreciation charges resulting from the revaluation of fixed assets can have on the profits of a company, as reflected in its profit and loss statement. This is obviously a vital factor, and one to which we shall return very soon, but the best way to keep this discussion in perspective is to follow the example that we set earlier in the book, and to start with the balance sheet . . ..

The historic cost balance sheet

What we want to do is to try to establish the amount of additional capital that would be required in order to maintain the physical identity and trading value of a company's assets or business investments during periods of inflation. This is very reminiscent of our earlier discussion of the balance sheet—that snapshot of the financial structure of a company taken at a particular moment in time—except that in this case the values of the assets are not looked at from the point of view of their historical cost, but from the point of view of their current replacement cost, or 'value to the business'. It is no longer a case of 'where the money went to', but of 'how much would be needed to replace all the existing assets from scratch?'

Let us go back to basics for a moment, and think about the way in which we discussed the various problems associated with the effects of inflation on asset values a page or two ago. We approached the problem by identifying a company's assets under three main headings, namely,

1 *Fixed assets*
2 *Stocks*
3 *Monetary working capital*—or the net value of cash and bank balances, plus debtors, and minus creditors

Each of these elements has distinct and different characteristics; and these differences become particularly apparent when one tries to assess the varying impacts of inflation upon each one in turn, and the resulting impact on the company as a whole. The end result will depend initially upon the individual constitution of each of the elements, and then on the overall mix of the elements within the company, so that it would be impossible to find a single index figure capable of representing the 'impact of inflation' on any company—or any industry—over any given period of time. In order to measure the overall impact, we must consequently attempt to measure each of the three main asset classifications separately and in their own right, and then sum the individual results. Let us try to visualize this by looking at Figure 15.1, in which Matthew Grimble's historic cost balance sheet for Year 5 is represented in chart form.

Revaluation of fixed assets

We can now start to think about the sort of changes we would need to make to each of the balance sheet elements in turn in order to make it reflect the current replacement value of the assets, and the corresponding changes that will apply to the company's liabilities.

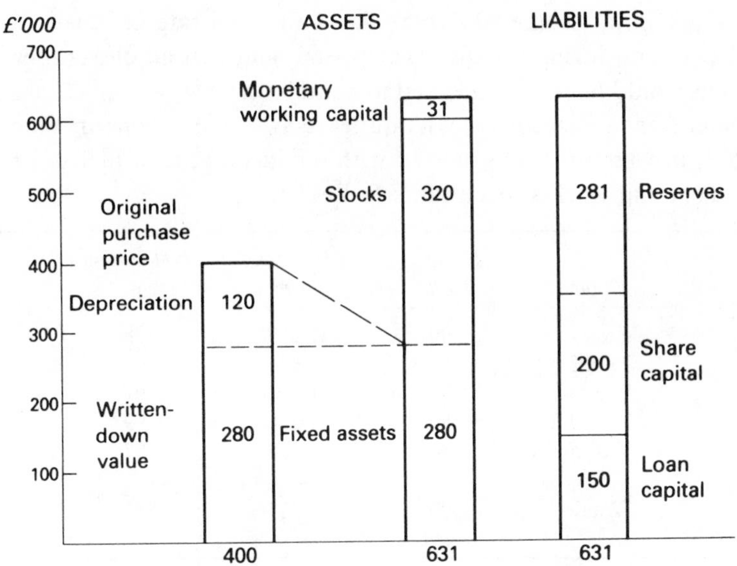

Fig 15.1 Matthew Grimble's historic cost balance sheet for Year 5

The first, and by far the most important, element is fixed assets. These are different from current assets within the context of the present discussion, because, by their very nature, they are meant to last longer. This is why their 'usage cost' is depreciated over a period of several years, but it also means that their 'age profile' can be a significant factor in any revaluation calculation. The older the assets, the higher the revaluation factor that will need to be applied.

Perhaps we should have a look at the age profile of Matthew's fixed assets, and see how his total expenditure of £400,000 was spread over the five years' life of his company. These details are readily available from his balance sheets as set out in Figure 12.1 (pages 200–201), and his source and application of funds statements listed in Figure 12.4 (pages 206–207), and they are reproduced here in Figure 15.2.

	←— *Purchases* —→			*Written down*
£'000	*Year*	*Cumulative*	*Depreciation*	*historic value*
Year 1	100	100	10	90
Year 2	55	155	25	130
Year 3	75	230	50	180
Year 4	80	310	80	230
Year 5	90	400	120	280

Fig 15.2 The age profile of Matthew Grimble's fixed assets at historic cost

If we now assume that there was an annual rate of inflation of 15 per cent during this five-year period, and that all of Matthew's assets would have been affected to a similar degree, we can calculate the current replacement costs quite easily. This is done in Figure 15.3, in which we have started with a mid-year factor of 1.075 for Year 5, and worked backwards to Year 1.

£'000	*Historic cost*	*Inflation factor*	*Replacement cost*
Year 1	100	1.879	188
Year 2	55	1.634	90
Year 3	75	1.421	107
Year 4	80	1.236	99
Year 5	90	1.075	97
Total	400	1.453	581

Fig 15.3 Inflated cost of Matthew Grimble's fixed assets, assuming an annual rate of inflation of 15 per cent

So far, so good. That wasn't too difficult, and the vital piece of information that emerges from these calculations is that the value of Matthew's fixed assets should be increased by an *overall* forty-three per cent in the balance sheet in order to arrive at a realistic inflated value, based on the way in which the general purchasing power of money has declined over the period. If the expenditure over Years 1 and 2 had been switched around, however, the inflated value of his Year 1 purchases would have been (55,000 × 1.879 =) £103,000, and his Year 2 purchases would now cost (100,000 × 1.634 =) £163,000 to replace. The total inflated value over the five years would then have been (103,000 + 163,000 + 107,000 + 99,000 + 97,000 =) £569,000. This would have given an overall inflation factor of only 42.2 per cent—purely as a result of changing the age profile of the historic actual expenditure.

We have also made a very simple basic assumption in this example by taking a regular annual rate of inflation of 15 per cent, although it would not have made the mathematics any more difficult if we had taken a different rate overall, or even a different rate for each year. The only trouble is that things do not quite work out like that in real life. That total historic value of £400,000 is made up of £120,000 spent on land and buildings, and £280,000 spent on plant and machinery, and it is only realistic to accept that each of these asset classifications would have been subject to quite different inflationary pressures over the years. Indeed, each main classification would contain a number of subclassifications—each one of which could have been affected to a different degree.

There are four main ways of looking at the problem, namely:

1 *Price indices*, which is the method that we used in our example just now. Either these can be linked simply to a central index related to the general purchasing power of money, or different indices can be used for each asset classification, as and where appropriate and available.
2 *Current replacement cost*, in which suppliers' current price lists would be used as a reference for 'off the shelf' items which are still available from stock.
3 *Independent valuation*, where the current values of assets would be assessed by (preferably independent) 'experts'.
4 *Value to the business*, which is defined in the UK SSAP 16 as:

'(a) Net current replacement cost, or, if a permanent diminution to below current replacement cost has been recognized,
(b) recoverable amount, which is the greater of the net realizable values of the assets and, where applicable, the amount recoverable from its further use.'

General purchasing power (G.P.P.) accounting

General purchasing power accounting is the method by which the figures in financial statements are adjusted for changes in *general* price levels. This is the method that we adopted to calculate the 'inflated' values of Matthew's fixed assets in Figure 15.3, and is basically the same as that recommended by the United Kingdom Accounting Standards Steering Committee in the provisional SSAP—No. 7—issued in 1974, in which it was referred to as the 'Current purchasing power', or 'C.P.P.' method of accounting.

These recommendations were later rejected by the Inflation Standards Committee, under the leadership of Lord Sandilands, on the grounds that the application of *general* indices was not appropriate to the valuation of *specific* assets, and that the method involved expressing accounts in terms of 'purchasing power units' rather than money. Conceptually, therefore, it could be argued that the C.P.P. approach attempted to tackle the problem from the point of view of the *shareholders*, who were obviously interested in the extent to which their 'purchasing power' had been affected by inflation over time, while the Sandilands Committee felt that the matter should be looked at from the point of view of the *management* of the business, and its concern for maintaining the value of the company's assets in real terms.

It could also be argued that the term 'general purchasing power' —G.P.P.—is more legitimate than 'current purchasing power' accounting for this type of 'general index' approach. In fact, this is the term now used in the USA, where the method was also recommended for adoption during the early 1970s. In that case, it was originally introduced under the name of 'general price-level accounting', but the recommendations were no more enthusiastically received there than they were in the UK, largely because, as we have already pointed out, there could well be a significant difference between the G.P.P. cost of an asset—converted from its historic cost via a general price index factor—and its current replacement cost or value.

One of the other problems with the G.P.P. method is that it involves the updating of previous periods' reported figures in order to reflect the situation as it is 'now', as distinct from what it was when the accounts were originally compiled. This consequently makes it difficult to reconcile 'This Year's' opening balances with 'Last Year's' closing balances. It is very much a 'shifting sands' approach to accounting, and it is hardly surprising that the method has never received universal acclaim as a reliable and comprehensible reporting system.

What do we mean by value?

The current cost accounting method advocated in the British SSAP 16 does enjoy the advantage of being able to relate each year's accounts consistently back to the previous year. It advocates the use of price indices in cases where more positive valuations are not available, but it places much more emphasis on specific valuations—especially in cases where this can be accepted as a practical approach.

Here, though, the emphasis is on the fact that valuation, by its very nature, can indeed be a very subjective process, because it so often depends upon an 'expert's' assessment or judgement of a particular set of circumstances, as we have already noted in earlier chapters. Oscar Wilde probably put his finger on it when he once defined a cynic as someone who 'knows the price of everything, but the value of nothing'. In much more recent times, Stirling Moss is quoted as saying that it had taken 'thirty-three years and a bang on the head to get his values right'.

A lot of people like going to auctions, and will bid for things which take their fancy. The price to which they are prepared to bid will be determined by how much they consider a particular lot to be *worth*. If they are lucky enough to be able to get it for less, then they will consider that they have got good 'value' for their money. Given the time to do so, most people will shop around for the cheapest prices they can find for the items on their shopping lists, and many people will comb through the stalls of a market or a rummage sale in the hope of spotting an occasional 'bargain'. So we all know what we mean in that sort of context: 'value' is a measure of one's assessment of worth; invariably, therefore, a very subjective measure indeed.

A team of judges at an ice-skating championship might mark a performance with anything between, say, 5.2 and 5.9 points out of six, depending upon how they 'saw' it. In many ways, this is not a great deal different from a team of experts being invited into a company to 'value' a particular building or piece of machinery, or—perhaps more correctly—to estimate how much it would be likely to cost the company to replace it with a new one of equivalent power, capacity or capability. They could very easily end up with a whole range of answers, the 'accuracy' of which will be entirely dependent upon a series of subjective judgements, and it is consequently none too easy for companies to place a 'true' value on some of their assets. The best they can hope to do will be to make an educated 'guesstimate'.

The fourth 'current valuation' alternative that we mentioned a couple of pages ago was 'value to the business', as defined in the SSAP. This can be illustrated by taking the example of a chemical company which invested a fortune in the design and installation of a new chemical plant some years ago. As a great deal of this expenditure would have been on custom-built buildings and plant which would never have been available 'off the shelf', the use of general industrial indices may well be the only way in which original costs could be converted to current costs.

But we now have another question. The economic climate may have changed, and the market may have been depressed as a result.

Perhaps the main product is now in danger of being overtaken by obsolescence. The company now has to ask itself whether it would even want to repeat the investment if it had another opportunity to evaluate it under existing conditions. If, by the time it had charged the revised rate of depreciation against the trading results of the period—as it would be expected to do under any system of inflation accounting—an historic cost profit developed into a current cost loss, the answer is almost certainly going to be 'No!'. So, in this case, 'value to the business' could be lower than replacement cost, and would then be based on the 'recoverable amount'.

We do not need to go into the detailed revaluations of all of Matthew's fixed assets now, but since he is not the sort of person to cut too many corners on something as important as this, we shall assume that he did the job properly, and arrived at the following comparisons between historic cost and current replacement cost, as at the end of Year 5:

£'000	*Historic cost*	*Replacement cost*
Land and buildings	120	280
Plant and machinery	280	420
Total	400	700

This shows us that this company's fixed assets would have cost (700,000 – 400,000 =) £300,000 more to replace than they originally cost when new, although this is an overall figure which just happens to apply to this particular company, at that particular time. If we look at the separate items which combine to make these totals, we can see that land and buildings have increased by 133 per cent, and plant and machinery by 50 per cent, so that the overall increase of 75 per cent is entirely dependent upon the individual asset mix at that specific year-end.

These adjustments will obviously affect the structure of the balance sheet, so we now need to consider which part will be affected. If some of the assets were sold at a price higher than their written down 'value'—or the unamortized cost which appeared in the Balance Sheet—then the 'profit' on the sale would be transferred to the operating reserves, together with the rest of the company's trading profits. In this case, however, we are not dealing with 'retained profits'. Since no actual trading profits have been generated, it would be misleading to mix this sort of adjustment up with the fund of reserves arising out of trading operations.

Obviously, we are going to have to increase the 'value' of fixed assets, so we have the problem of retaining the 'balance' in the balance sheet. This should not be too difficult for us at this stage of the book, because this is exactly the same sort of situation we encountered with our earlier transaction equation examples. All we have to do is open up a new column, and the most appropriate name for us to use will be current cost reserve—and one of the reasons why it is so appropriate is that this is the name decreed in the C.C.A. conventions! Having got this new column, we shall find that it is an extremely convenient 'sink' for balancing out the rest of the adjustments we are going to have to make.

Therefore, in Matthew's case, the asset revaluation of £300,000 will be debited to fixed assets, and credited to current cost reserve. Since, as we have just pointed out, this adjustment has no impact at all on the trading results for the period, it is called an 'unrealized' adjustment. Any inflation adjustment to the accounting records which affects the trading results as reported in the profit and loss statement is called a 'realized adjustment', and one such adjustment is the one with which we opened this chapter: the depreciation adjustment.

Depreciation adjustment

When we looked at the additional amount of depreciation that we felt should be charged against Andrew's profits for last year, we were actually only looking at one part of the problem. We were focusing on an equitable charge that ought to have been made for the use of his company's fixed assets during a one-year slice of their anticipated useful working lives.

The point to emphasize here is that any revaluation process should involve an updated assessment of each asset's anticipated life-span. For example, it might be that, when an item was purchased, this life was estimated at four years, so that 25 per cent of its net cost would have been charged each year as depreciation. Two years later, when the asset was revalued, it might then have been decided that there was still another three years' life left in it. Its total life-span is increased to five years, and the equitable annual charge will then be only 20 per cent of its current replacement cost.

This brings us to the other part of the problem—what about the depreciation charges that have been made in previous years? This is called 'backlog depreciation' under the UK system of C.C.A.: it follows that any adjustments made to the accounting records in respect of fixed asset revaluation should be accompanied by a corresponding adjustment to the amount of depreciation which has already been charged for the use of these assets during the periods up to, but not including, the period in which the revaluation is made.

If we go back to that item with an initial four-year life that we mentioned just now, we could assume that its original cost was £4,000. This would mean that the depreciation charge for its use would have been set at £1,000 p.a., and that after two years its written-down value would have been £2,000. It was then revalued to £6,000, and given an estimated life expectancy of five years, so the revised annual depreciation charge should now be (6,000/5 =) £1,200. The implication of this is that, at this new rate, the accumulated depreciation up to the beginning of the current year ought to have been (2 × 1,200 =) £2,400, rather than the £2,000 actually charged, so there is still an adjustment of (2,400 – 2,000 =) £400 to be made. This is the backlog depreciation adjustment, which has nothing to do with the current year's profits, and has consequently to be recorded in the balance sheet as an unrealized adjustment.

In the case of this particular example, our first C.C.A. adjustment would therefore be the £2,000 revaluation of the assets, which we would record by increasing the values of fixed assets and current cost reserve. In our historic cost accounts, we charged £1,000 against profit in respect of depreciation, but now need to increase this to £1,200, so the transaction is to increase depreciation, and to reduce profit by £200. That will still leave us with the backlog depreciation adjustment of £400 to record, which we will do by increasing depreciation, and reducing the current cost reserve by this amount.

In order to follow through our example based on Matthew Grimble's figures for Year 5, we shall assume that, following the revaluation of his assets to £700,000, he found that the appropriate depreciation charge for the year would have been £55,000, instead of the £40,000 charged 'historically', and that the cumulative depreciation up to the end of Year 4 would have been £120,000 instead of the £80,000 actually charged. This would therefore have resulted in a depreciation adjustment of (55,000 – 40,000 =) £15,000, and a backlog depreciation adjustment of (120,000 – 80,000 =) £40,000.

The transaction equations we have created so far in order to comply with the C.C.A. requirements can be summarized as follows:

	← ASSETS →			← LIABILITIES →	
£'000	*Fixed assets*	*Depreciation*		*Current cost reserve*	*Profit and loss*
(1) Fixed asset revaluation	300		=	300	
(2) Depreciation adjustment		−15	=		−15
(3) Backlog depreciation		−40	=	−40	

One further point to mention in relation to depreciation adjustments is that in the UK they have no impact on the amount of tax charged, because tax is levied on the amount of profit made by a company *before* the deduction of depreciation, as explained in Chapter 7. In most other countries, including South America, where the rate of inflation has been running at appallingly high levels over recent years, the 'general purchasing power' principles are applied, and tax is based on profits *after* the deduction of depreciation charges which have, in turn, been adjusted to line up with the indexed purchasing power of money.

Revaluation of stocks

The second asset category we need to consider is that of stocks, which are just as much affected by inflation as are fixed assets. The big difference between the two is that, generally speaking, stocks do not stay around for so long, and their revaluation adjustments are consequently nowhere near as large. It is seldom practical, or even possible, to think in terms of tracing the current replacement cost of every single item in an inventory, although it might be practical to adopt this principle for the 'top few' high-value items. The commonly-accepted principle under the C.C.A. system of inflation accounting is to apply one—or possibly more—price index, which would be rather like the one we shall use to illustrate Matthew Grimble's stock revaluations in Figure 15.4.

Indices		114		118		121		124		128		132	
	=======		=======		=======		=======		=======		=======		====
Quarter	Q.3		Q.4		Q.1		Q.2		Q.3		Q.4		
	Year 4→				←		Year 5				→		

Fig 15.4 Matthew Grimble's stock valuation indices for Years 4 and 5

If we relate the value of Matthew's stocks (Figure 12.1) to his cost of goods sold (Figure 12.3) we can see that he was holding roughly six months' stock at the end of Years 4 and 5. (This should not be confused with his 'stock turnover' of 3–4 months that we calculated in Figure 12.15, when we were relating the value of stocks to *sales revenue*, rather than to *cost of sales*.)

On this basis, we could assume that the average 'age' of his stock was three months, which would mean that his historic cost valuation would be linked to the price index of 128 which was applicable to the end of the third quarter of Year 5. In order to calculate what the 'current' cost would be at the end of the year, when the index stood at 132, we must scale up the historic cost valuation by this proportion. The adjusted valuation is consequently [(320,000 × 132,000)/128,000 =] £330,000, and we shall therefore need to make a revaluation adjustment of (330,000 – 320,000 =) £10,000 to accommodate this.

This represents an increase of only 3 per cent, compared with the overall increase of 75 per cent we encountered on fixed assets, so it is hardly in the same league, although we have to remember that this relationship applies only to Matthew Grimble Ltd at the end of Year 5. Such comparisons as this are bound to vary quite considerably between one company and another, one activity sector and another, and between one period and another. This is consequently an adjustment that may still be very relevant in some companies, and should consequently not be ignored. It follows the same sort of route as the revaluation of fixed assets—i.e., an increase in stocks, balanced by an (unrealized) adjustment to current cost reserve.

Many companies have actually been providing for this sort of adjustment for many years via the use of a Standard Costing system, in which the prices and costs of materials and products are updated regularly to a current 'standard' cost level. This is beyond our scope at the moment, though, and, in any case, Matthew didn't use 'standards', but the 'old-fashioned' method of 'actual' historical costs. It is nevertheless worth pausing here for a moment to consider the sort of situation which could arise if a company failed to keep its stock records valued at up-to-date prices.

Just imagine a sales manager receiving an enquiry for a quotation on a product that is not among his company's main product range, and perhaps has not been in great demand for a while. He asks the accountant for a cost upon which to base his quotation, and the accountant works this out based on the latest historical information that he has to hand. He comes up with a unit cost of £5, so the sales manager sends off a quotation for £7, and doesn't think very much more about it.

The customer is beside himself with joy, because the only other potential supplier has quoted £9.50. The contract is signed, and in comes the order for several thousand of these things, which immediately throws the production manager into a spin, because he is nearly out of stock of the main ingredient, and will have to order some more. When the invoice for this material arrives, the accountant is amazed to discover that the price has gone up by 60 per cent since the last time they bought any. Apparently the material now has to be imported because the domestic supply has dried up, with the result that the new 'replacement' cost of this product works out at £6.80, instead of £5!

This is going to mean that a considerable part of the production capacity will now be committed to a very low-margin product, because business has been attracted by a price with which no one would want to compete. There is more than one reason for this—but one of them is bad communication. The sales manager did not tell the accountant how many units were involved in his enquiry, and the accountant did not ask! And nobody, it seems, took the original enquiry seriously enough to consider mentioning it to the production manager or the warehouse manager. On top of all this, the accountant also had a systems problem, because his historical cost records did not alert him to the potential effects of inflation on the replacement cost of this product.

This sort of thing may not happen in your present company, but, if it seems too unlikely a situation ever to have occurred in real life, just ask anyone who has ever had any practical experience in any of the areas involved in this example! . . .

Cost of sales adjustment

We next have to remember that, unlike fixed assets, stocks are a central part of the working capital area of the business—and they move. If we accept the principle that the value of stocks should be reflected in the balance sheet at their current replacement cost, it follows that, when they move out of the business, they should be charged under the same valuation criteria. Once again, this is no great problem if a system of standard costing is in use, because it is likely to happen anyway, but if, as in Matthew's case, actual historical costs are used as the basis for evaluating the cost of sales, this figure will need to be adjusted, and this, in turn, will affect profit.

Think of this in the context of any business—even in the context of the retail trade, where there are no manufacturing processes involved. For example, Andrew used to know a chap who ran a small retail business—from a stall in the local market, actually—so let us imagine that he buys 1,000 items of stock at £1 each, and sells them all for £1,500. He decides to spend all of his profit on a holiday, and, when he gets back, he goes off to buy another £1,000-worth of stock.

The only trouble is that the unit price has gone up to £1.25 in the meantime. So now he can only afford to buy 800 items, and his own profits are going to suffer as a direct result of the diminishing purchasing power of his £1,000 capital. He can put his own price up, of course, and hope that he will be able to generate the same sort of profit margin out of his £1,000 in the same sort of time-span; but the fact remains that, during a period of inflation, the continued recycling of his £1,000 in replacement stock is going to provide him with progressively fewer items to sell.

Your own local garage may well be another example. How many times over the last few years have you complained about the speed with which the garages put up their petrol prices every time a price or tax increase is announced? What about all that petrol in their storage tanks that they must have bought at the old price? They are all set to make a real killing on that, aren't they? The garage proprietor might explain very quickly—and politely, of course—that, in the sort of high-volume/low margin business that he is in, he has to make sure that he can pay for the next delivery of petrol when it arrives—and that is going to be at the new high price. He has to find the extra price on the quantity he has sold out of the last delivery, so his purchasing power has already been affected, and he would eventually find himself out of petrol altogether if he let the rest of his stocks go at the price that he originally paid for them.

Under a system of general purchasing power accounting, the 'current' cost of sales figure would be calculated by converting the opening and closing stocks, and the purchasing and production costs for the year, to the end-year index equivalents. We can take Matthew's Year 5 figures as an example. These are checkable from the stock movements and cost of goods sold schedule in Figure 12.2, and we have taken them into Figure 15.5, together with the relevant price indices from Figure 15.4.

These show us that the opening stock index is 114, as at Year 4/Q.3; the closing stock is at the Year 5/Q.3 level of 128; and we could assume that all purchases and production costs balance out at the Year 5 midpoint of 124. The 'current' index at the end of Year 5 is 132, so the 'general purchasing power' conversion factors for each of these points in time would be (132/114 =) 1.16; (132/128 =) 1.03; and (132/124 =) 1.06 respectively.

£,000		*Historic cost*	*Conversion factor*	*G.P.P. @ index 132*
Opening stock		250	1.16	290
+ Purchases (35 + 230 =)	265			
+ Production costs (excluding transfers from central stores)				
Direct labour	230			
Overheads	255			
		750	1.06	795
= Total activity		1,000		1,085
− Closing stock		320	1.03	330
= Cost of sales		680		755
Cost of sales (G.P.P.) adjustment (755 − 680 =)				75

Fig 15.5 Matthew Grimble's cost of sales adjustment for Year 5, evaluated under G.P.P. principles

This method of calculation assumes that all stock movements should be calculated at the *current* Year-end index rate, and, since the cost of sales is a ('realized') revenue item, the adjustments necessary to translate the value of movements throughout a whole year up to the year-end index level are bound to have a significant impact on the company's profits. In Matthew's case, this would amount to (755,000 − 680,000 =) £75,000, which is just about enough to soak up the whole of his historic-cost profit after tax, without any help at all from the depreciation adjustment!

There is another school of thought which argues that the index to which G.P.P. adjustments should be geared ought to be the mid-year rate, rather than the end-year one; this is, in fact, the principle defined in the C.C.A. guidelines. This would appear to be a much more reasonable argument, and is quite realistic, provided that there are no violent seasonal fluctuations in revenue and/or expenditure, and that the rate of inflation remains fairly steady throughout the period. One advantage of this approach is that the historic purchase and production costs can be used as they stand, because, on average, they can be assumed to balance out at around the mid-year index. All that has to be done, therefore, is convert the opening and closing stock figures to this index. In our case, this is 124, so that the opening stock conversion factor will be (124/114 =) 1.09, and the closing stock factor will be (124/128 =) 0.97. The calculation of the C.C.A. adjustment for cost of sales will therefore be as illustrated in Figure 15.6.

£'000	*Historic cost*	*Conversion factor*	*Current cost*
Opening stock	250	1.09	272
+ Purchases/Production costs	750		750
= Total activity	1,000		1,022
− Closing stock	320	0.97	310
= Cost of sales	680		712
Cost of sales (C.C.A.) adjustment (712 − 680 =)			32

Fig 15.6 Matthew Grimble's cost of sales adjustment for Year 5, calculated in accordance with C.C.A. principles

This is the sort of result that most people—including Andrew—would find much easier to accept than the G.P.P. adjustment of £75,000, so our next step will be to illustrate the accounting requirements of C.C.A. by setting up the transaction equations necessary to record the stock revaluation adjustment of £10,000, and the cost of sales adjustment of £32,000 that we have just calculated.

	ASSETS →		← LIABILITIES →	
£'000	*Stocks*		*Current cost reserve*	*Profit and loss*
(4) Stock revaluation	10	=	10	
(5) Cost of sales adjustment			32	−32

A current cost view of the balance sheet

Now let us see what we have done to that historic-cost balance sheet that we illustrated in Figure 15.1. On the assets side, we have increased the replacement value of fixed assets from £400,000 to £700,000, although, by the time we have deducted the revised cumulative depreciation of £175,000—from its historic level of £120,000—the net written-down value is (700,000 – 175,000 =) £525,000. Stocks have also been increased from £320,000 to £330,000.

These adjustments are balanced by the creation of a current cost reserve, the purpose of which is to reflect the net impact of inflation upon the company's financial structure. The asset revaluations that we have just mentioned do not affect the trading profits, although the current-year depreciation adjustment of £15,000—which formed part of the cumulative £55,000 adjustment relating to both backlog and current-year revaluations—and the Cost of Sales Adjustment of £32,000 most certainly do; so these are recorded by transferring the appropriate amounts from the (operating) reserves to current cost reserve. The effect of these two sets of adjustments is illustrated in Figure 15.7.

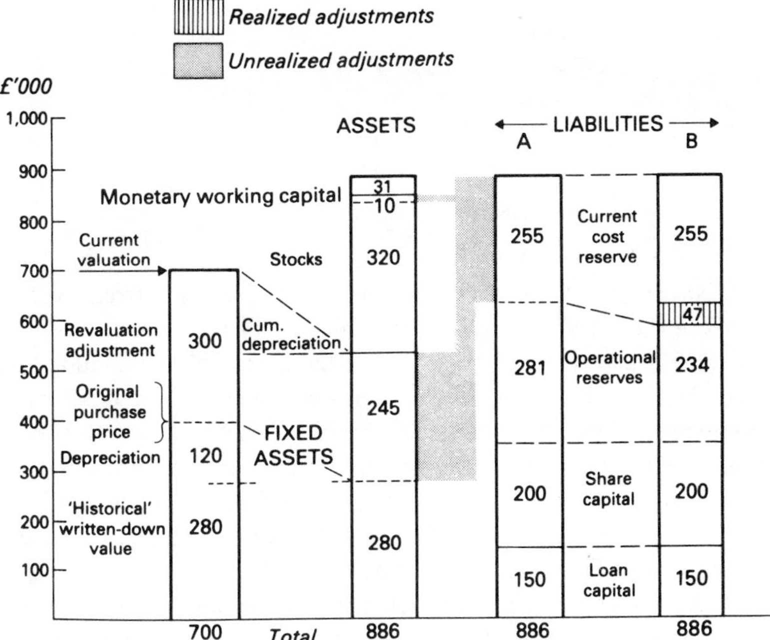

Fig 15.7 Matthew Grimble's current cost balance sheet for Year 5

This sort of illustration helps us to keep the situation in perspective. We can see at a glance from the (unrealized) current cost liabilities in Column A of the diagram that the main impact of inflation has been on the valuation of fixed assets, and that the revaluation of stocks was relatively insignificant by comparison. Column B shows us that the adjustments associated with the 'realized' aspects of current-year depreciation and cost of sales did not affect the overall 'size' of the business, but that they did transfer some of the trading reserves into the 'compound' set aside for the funds needed to maintain the company's level of activity.

Monetary working capital adjustment

The third asset category in Matthew's balance sheet is monetary working capital, and we saw in Figure 12.1 that this is made up of:

		£'000
Current assets (excluding stocks)		
Trade debtors		210
Cash		16
		226
Less: Current liabilities		
Trade creditors	110	
Other liabilities	85	
		195
Net monetary working capital		31

Cash is one thing that you cannot adjust for current value, because there it is, all ready and available for any current use that you might care to make of it. 'Other liabilities', which include tax, loan interest and dividends due, are also committed, and will take no further part in the company's activities, apart from actually being paid. This consequently only leaves debtors and creditors, and since they both affect the amount of funds needed to support working capital, they are considered to be eligible for adjustment under the conventions of inflation accounting.

The reasoning behind this is that, when sales are made on a credit basis, the business has to finance the changes in the selling prices between the time at which the sales are made and the payment is received, and that, conversely, when goods and services are bought on credit, any price changes up to the time of payment are financed by the supplier.

According to the rules of G.P.P. accounting, the closing balances will need no adjustment, and the opening balances will be converted to the end-year purchasing power index, while, under C.C.A., both balances will be adjusted to the mid-year index, after having taken the average 'age' of the balances into account.

This calculation is very similar to the cost of sales adjustment, so there is really no need to go through the process again here. The effect is also similar, in that the resulting current cost adjustment will be a transfer from profit and loss to the current cost reserve. The netting-off of debtors and creditors obviously depresses the value of this adjustment, and, in the majority of cases, it will not be very significant. Let us say that, in Matthew's case, it was worth £11,000 in Year 5, which would mean that the total 'realized'—or operating—adjustments to his historic profits would be made up as follows:

	£'000
Depreciation adjustment	−15
Cost of sales adjustment	−32
Monetary working capital adjustment	−11
Total operating adjustment	−58

We had to admit that Andrew had managed to remain remarkably quiet during our attempts to explain and illustrate the various factors which needed to be taken into account when one enters the realms of inflation accounting, and we were not the slightest bit surprised at the sigh of relief that came from his side of the table when we got to the part about 'total operating adjustments'. 'So that's it, then!' he said, concluding that, after all those 'realized' adjustments had been taken into account—and he felt bound to say that one or two of those working capital adjustments seemed to be far too nit-picking for his liking!—Matthew's historically retained profits of £50,000 for Year 5 should really be reduced by £58,000! Poor old Matthew seemed to be another one of those magicians who had managed to convert an historic cost profit into a current cost loss!

He was quite right, of course—apart from one thing. 'That' still wasn't quite 'it, then'!

Gearing adjustment

Under the rules of current cost accounting, there is still one more adjustment to make. This takes us back to the early part of the chapter, in which we referred to the point of view of the shareholders, and the way in which the net assets used in the business are financed.

If we look at the historic cost capital structure of Matthew's company in Figure 15.1, we can see quite clearly that £150,000 out of the total capital employed of £631,000, i.e. 23.8 per cent, was loan capital, and that the remaining 76.2 per cent was shareholders' funds. By transferring all the inflation adjustments to a current cost reserve, we are implying that the shareholders alone should be responsible for the whole of the extra costs of maintaining the company's assets during a period of inflation. However, as we have just seen, part of these assets is financed by loan capital, and it is not unreasonable to expect that the lenders of this capital would be prepared to lend further proportionate sums. The concept of the gearing adjustment is therefore to reduce the total operating adjustments—of £58,000, in our case—by a proportion equivalent to that which the average loan capital (if any) bears to the average net assets—or capital employed—as shown on the current cost balance sheets at the beginning and end of the year.

This again does nothing which affects the revised—or current—valuation of the company's net assets. It merely takes back some of the current year's profits which have been stashed away in the current cost reserve, and puts them back where they came from in the first place. In Matthew's case, it would have worked out at about £12,000, although Andrew was not particularly anxious for us to prove it. As far as he could see, having just converted Matthew's historic cost profit of £50,000 into a current cost loss of (50,000 − 58,000 =) £8,000, we were now giving him £12,000 back. This presumably meant that he had now managed to scrape together a £4,000 profit!

He just didn't like this one at all! He could see what we were getting at, but, in his opinion, it was nothing more nor less than playing around with the figures for the sake of it—especially since he thought that we had already agreed that the capital structure of a company had nothing to do with the way in which the profit margin was calculated!

This was true, and he had touched on one of the main points of criticism that has been directed at the current cost conventions ever since their introduction. We explained that the idea was to ensure that the realized adjustments incorporated into the current cost reserve should only relate to that proportion of the company's assets which were legitimately attributable to the shareholders, since it is assumed that those people who had loaned money on a long-term basis will be content to keep their proportion of the capital employed intact.

But he still wasn't convinced. He couldn't see why it should be considered necessary or appropriate to transfer back into the 'distributable' trading reserves of a company an amount which had only just a moment ago been earmarked as a current cost reserve against inflation, simply by saying that it was an amount equivalent to the proportion of the operating adjustments that were 'chargeable' to the lenders of the company's loan capital. That was tantamount to saying to the shareholders that they could, if they wished, distribute the whole of that amount as dividends, instead of retaining it in the business as they would have been advised to do if it had been related to their own invested share of the company's total capital employed. Or was it getting late, or something?

We had to admit that his interpretation was certainly one way of looking at it—all we were trying to do was to explain the guidelines as they had been prescribed.

Current cost reserve

Having illustrated our references to the SSAP on current cost accounting with the figures from Matthew Grimble's Year 5 accounts, it is only logical that we should draw them together into a final set of current cost statements. Figure 15.8 shows the current cost reserve account, in which you will be able to trace all the adjustments to which we have referred.

Current cost profit and loss

The sort of presentation recommended for a current cost profit and loss statement in the SSAP is illustrated in Figure 15.9. It should be

		£'000
(2) Depreciation adjustment c/d		15
(5) Cost of sales adjustment	32	
(6) Monetary working capital adjustment	11	
Total working capital adjustments		43
Current cost operating adjustment		58
(7) *Less:* Gearing adjustment		12
Net realized adjustments		46
(1) Revaluation of fixed assets	300	
(3) *Less:* Backlog depreciation	40	
	260	
(2) *Less:* Depreciation adjustment b/d	15	
Net revaluation of fixed assets	245	
(4) Revaluation of stocks	10	
Net unrealized adjustments		255
Total current cost reserve		301

Fig 15.8 Matthew Grimble's current cost reserve account for Year 5

noted that the current cost operating adjustment and the gearing adjustment are shown separately in both the current cost reserve and in the current cost profit and loss statement, and that the gearing adjustment is shown bracketed together with the net interest payable and/or receivable in the profit and loss statement.

Andrew felt that this last 'bracketing' exercise didn't make very much sense, either, since the gearing adjustment was nothing more than 'creative' accounting, whereas the interest on Matthew's loan capital was something that he had to find in hard-earned, solid cash. So why on earth should they be netted off or added together? We couldn't even think of a satisfactory answer to that one!

The first 'level' of profit reported in the profit and loss statement is defined as 'before interest and tax on the historical cost basis', and this also leads on to the point that, whatever the current cost adjustments may have been, the taxation liability is always calculated on the basis of historical figures.

£'000	*Historic cost (12.3)*		*Current cost*
Sales revenue	1,130		1,130
Historic cost profit before interest and tax	135		135
Less: Current cost operating adjustments	:		58
Current cost operating profit	:		77
Gearing adjustment	:	12	
Net interest payable/receivable	−20	−20	
			− 8
Profit before tax	115		69
Taxation	35		35
Profit attributable to shareholders	80		34
Dividends	30		30
Retained profit:			
at historic cost	50		:
at current cost	:		4

Fig 15.9 Matthew Grimble's current cost profit and loss statement for Year 5

So we can at last see the net 'conventional C.C.A.' effect of inflation on Matthew Grimble's Year 5 trading figures. His profit after tax was more than halved—from £80,000 to £34,000—and by the time he had taken out the £30,000 for distribution as dividends, the retained (historic) profit of £50,000 had crashed to a retained (current) profit of £4,000. The interpretation of this must consequently be that his company needed £46,000 to combat the effects of inflation—simply to maintain the value of its assets—leaving him with only £4,000 with which actually to expand the scope of its operations. Mind you, Andrew still maintained that the £12,000 gearing adjustment was nothing more than a 'meaningless bit of number-juggling', and that in reality the figures should show that Matthew needed £58,000 to maintain the value of his company's assets. On that basis, one could therefore argue that he had actually made an £8,000 loss—but we have already been through all that . . ..

Current cost balance sheet

We can see what all these adjustments have done to the balance sheet in Figure 15.10, and it should be fairly evident by now that it would not have been easy to find a simple index figure with which to accomplish all the adjustments that we have considered over the last several pages. As we saw from Figure 15.7, we have finally achieved an overall increase of [(886 – 631)/886 =] 29 per cent in the capital employed in Matthew's company, but this is a composite of

£'000		*Historic cost (12.1)*		*Current cost*
Fixed assets at cost/revaluation		400		700
Less: Depreciation to date		120		175
Unamortized cost at end of year		280		525
Stocks	320			330
Debtors	210		210	
Cash	16		16	
Current assets	546			
Trade creditors	110		−110	
Other liabilities	85		− 85	
Current liabilities	195			
Net working capital		351		:
Net monetary working capital		:		31
NET ASSETS		631		886
Share capital		200		200
Reserves				
Current cost reserve (15.8)		:		301
Other reserves (Year 4 = 231)		281		235
Shareholders' funds		481		736
Loan capital		150		150
CAPITAL EMPLOYED		631		886

Fig 15.10 Matthew Grimble's current cost balance sheet for Year 5

[(525 – 280)/525 =] 47 per cent in the unamortized value of fixed assets, and only [(330 – 320)/330 =] 3 per cent in the value of stocks. The value of monetary working capital obviously has to remain unchanged, since this is not a replacement item, and—apart from bad debts—will eventually be realizable at face value.

It should also be noted that the current-cost value of 'other reserves'—i.e., retained profits—differs from the historic-cost balance sheet because of the different profit figures that have been transferred from the profit and loss statement. The historic-cost figure of £281,000 is made up of the opening balance of £231,000 plus the Year 5 historic-cost retained profit of £50,000; whereas the current-cost figure starts off with the same opening balance, but closes after the addition of only £4,000 current-cost retained profit. In Year 6, the current cost opening balance will consequently be £235,000, compared with the historic-cost opening balance of £281,000; and so on.

You will also notice that, in both the profit and loss statement and the balance sheet presentations in Figures 15.9, and 15.10, the historic cost figures have been 'supported', or supplemented by their current cost equivalents. The SSAP does not specify that this is a positive requirement; in fact, the opposite format—or even the current cost figures on their own—is acceptable. It is, however, suggested that the format that we have illustrated is the more practical option, since it links more logically with the source and application of funds statement and the value added statement. Both of these are essentially historically based, and are consequently not subject to any obligatory current cost modifications.

Current cost ratios

One of the reasons why inflation accounting as such has met with such a struggle for acceptance is that many companies were, rather naturally, reluctant to use current cost results as the basis for the calculation of performance indices, such as the ones discussed in our earlier chapters. Depressed profit figures obviously result in depressed ratios, and the shareholders and would-be investors were consequently likely to be far less impressed with current cost results than they would be with historic cost ones.

As a consequence of this reluctance, companies continued to use their historic cost figures as a base against which to measure their performance, and with which to justify the distribution of dividends. These often turned out to be dividends that they could, in reality, neither afford nor justify. Even at the time of writing, published dividend yields are based on historic cost data, although the reasons for this also stem partly from the difficulties inherent in the extraction of consistent and comparable current cost information.

	Historic cost	*Current cost*
(A) INVESTMENT RATIOS		
1 Return on capital employed (12.11)	$\frac{135}{631} = 21.4\%$	$\frac{77}{886} = 8.7\%$
2 Return on shareholders' funds (12.12)	$\frac{80}{481} = 16.6\%$	$\frac{34}{736} = 4.6\%$
(B) PERFORMANCE RATIOS		
3 Profit margin (12.12)	$\frac{135}{1,130} = 11.9\%$	$\frac{89}{1,130} = 7.9\%$
4 Profitability (12.15)	$\frac{135}{826} = 16.3\%$	$\frac{77}{1,081} = 7.1\%$
5 Asset utilization (12.16)	$\frac{1,130}{826} = 1.37$	$\frac{1,130}{1,081} = 1.05$

Fig 15.11 Comparison between Matthew Grimble's historic cost and current cost ratios for Year 5

We can demonstrate the drastic effects that the application of current cost conventions could have on performance indices by comparing some of Matthew's Year 5 historic ratios with what they would have been if based on the current cost figures. These are assembled in Figure 15.11.

These comparisons must surely speak for themselves, and yet one cannot deny which ones are actually the more realistic. Some companies which seem more efficient than their competitors may only appear to be so because their accounting methods only require them to charge historic cost depreciation against their profits. The fact that they may be running clapped-out plant into the ground could well mean that they are not nearly as efficient in practical terms as another company using, and depreciating, more up-to-date and much more expensive plant, which may well have the effect of making them look less efficient on paper. This is one comparison that would very quickly get into a more realistic perspective if the performances of both companies were to be expressed in current cost terms.

Conclusions

Some of the principles prescribed in SSAP 16 are now accepted by many as a fairly practical method of achieving its defined objectives, although much of the contention that surrounded their development and eventual introduction still persists to the present day. Most of the objections concerned the potential difficulties involved in the extraction of the data required, and the validity of any conclusions that may be placed on the resulting calculations, and Matthew was not the slightest bit surprised to hear that the gearing adjustment was a particular target for criticism.

The tax authorities have so far had to pretend that C.C.A. has not happened, because they could never accept profit figures for tax calculation purposes which were based so heavily on subjective judgements, as distinct from hard, historical fact; but at least the UK system of Capital Allowances helps to alleviate this particular problem by allocating tax relief at the actual time of the capital outlay, as distinct from spreading it throughout its period of amortization.

As we have just seen, a lot of companies also resisted the pressure to publish current cost accounting information because of the depressing effect that it inevitably had on their investment and performance ratios. The auditors' task was made much more difficult, because they are called upon to certify that the company's accounts reflect a 'true and fair view' of its financial situation, and current cost results based on so many valuation 'judgements' and assessments cannot be expected to provide the same solid, practical foundation for such a certificate as do so-called 'actual', checkable historical figures. This is a fair reason for recommending that the published presentation should show the historical figures supported by comparative current cost figures, since this does then provide a realistic 'memorandum' style of reporting, with the current cost figures 'outside' the actual accounts. We are thus able to see the 'true and fair' historical situation supported by 'what it would have been like if . . .', and, in that context, no one can deny the usefulness of this supplementary information.

One cannot help wondering whether the accountants have gone just that fatal bit too far in their endeavours to extract a precise evaluation of this acknowledged phenomenon, however. Inflation is essentially time-related, and constantly moving onwards, whereas financial statements can really only reflect a 'true and fair view' of a situation that actually existed in fact—that 'snapshot' taken at a particular moment in time. It is almost like showing someone two snapshots, and saying: 'This one is a picture of me taken when I was six, and this one is what I would have looked like if I had been seven'.

Current cost figures can only be estimates, and they have to be interpreted as such. An ever-increasing number of companies are coming to the conclusion that their published financial accounts are not an appropriate place for estimated data. Dixons Photographic Ltd is one company which, 'in common with a growing number of companies', omitted the C.C.A. figures from their 1981 accounts on the grounds that they 'provide undue scope for subjectivity and inaccuracy, and, as such, are of little meaning or relevance'.

These are strong words, and they may well be indicative of the approach that more and more companies may take in the future. But too much good work has been done for it all to be thrown away, and the effort will not have been in vain if managers, generally, can recognize the potential effects of inflationary pressures upon the decisions for which they are responsible. Most of them do already, but if some of the principles established in the various inflation accounting guidelines can help them to formalize their approach to the interpretation of historical figures, and to the projection of these into the future, then the effort will have been worth while.

Summary

During periods of inflation, the fall in the value of money means that not all the profit reported under historic cost conventions represents a real increase in the company's wealth. Some profit is needed just to keep up with inflation, or to preserve the 'real value' of the company's assets, and the more the capital needed to support a particular level of activity, the more profit will be needed in order to maintain that value.

Many attempts have been made over the last several years to devise a standardized method of reflecting the effects of inflation within the accounting systems of companies, and, in the UK, this was finally defined in the Statement of Standard Accounting Practice (SSAP) No. 16, on 'Current Cost Accounting'—C.C.A.—which was published in 1980 by the six major accountancy bodies acting on the proposals of the Accounting Standards Committee. The object of this Standard was to provide more useful information than had hitherto been available from historic cost accounts on such matters as the financial viability of the business, return on investment, pricing policy, cost control in general and gearing.

It sets out to achieve these objectives by including assets in the balance sheet—and the usage of these assets in the profit and loss statement—at their current replacement cost, or realizable value to the business. This is something that cannot be achieved through the use of a single index figure, however, since each type of asset is affected to a different degree, and must consequently be dealt with separately.

Fixed assets are revalued at their current replacement value to the business, and this also means that depreciation has to be recalculated, although only that portion which is deemed to be fairly attributable to a period can be charged against the profits for that period. Any excess, or 'backlog' depreciation that should have been appropriate to previous periods—if the current valuation had then been in use—is transferred to the current cost reserve, to be offset against the capital revaluation of the assets concerned.

Net revaluations of stocks are also transferred to current cost reserve—which has to be kept separate from operational reserves in the balance sheet—but any adjustments to the cost of sales and net monetary working capital are charged direct to the current cost profit and loss. The total current cost operating adjustment is then further adjusted, via a gearing adjustment, by a proportion equivalent to that which the average loan capital bears to the average current cost net assets, in order that the shareholders' funds should only reflect an equitable proportion of the net charge or benefit of the impact of inflation on the company as a whole.

These combined adjustments require an involved set of calculations to implement, and the UK 'Standard' has provoked a considerable amount of criticism on the grounds that the adjustments specified distorted the traditional 'true and fair view' that is supposed to be projected by the historic cost accounts.

We have also made an occasional reference to the 'Current Purchasing Power', or C.P.P. system, which was initially recommended for adoption in the UK in the early 1970s, but was later rejected by the Sandilands Committee in favour of C.C.A. on the grounds that the application of *general* indices was not appropriate to the value of *specific* assets. An almost identical method was also recommended for adoption in the USA at about the same time, under the rather more appropriate title of 'General Purchasing Power'—G.P.P.—accounting, and its reception was no more enthusiastic there than in the UK. The G.P.P. system differs in concept from C.C.A. in that all period figures are converted to a year-end indexed equivalent, whereas some C.C.A. transactions are geared to an 'average', or mid-year index. G.P.P. adjustments consequently tend to be far more drastic than those calculated under C.C.A. guidelines.

The results calculated under any inflation accounting system must inevitably be subjective by nature, but it is easy for the protagonists of historic cost accounts to forget how many non-factual judgements—of *possible* assets' lives, and *possible* eventual scrap values, etc.—have to be made in order to produce this so-called 'true and fair' historic-cost view. At least the various 'standards' have made some constructive attempt to isolate and evaluate the effects of inflation, and, however much we may dislike the tricky calculations involved, we cannot afford to ignore the message that they convey. Whether or not the results should be recorded as part of the published accounts is possibly another matter, but there can be no question whatsoever that inflation is a factor that every manager must build into the evaluation of his future plans and strategies. If some of the principles and methodology embedded in the C.C.A. Standards can provide a consistent and reliable basis for that, then the time spent on their development will not have been wasted.

Definition round-up

We have inevitably introduced quite a lot of new terms into this chapter, and it would be useful to assemble some of the definitions before we conclude. Most of the ones which follow are taken from the English SSAP 16.

- *General Purchasing Power (G.P.P.) accounting* is the term used to define the method of inflation accounting in which all period balances and transactions are converted to a year-end index based on the general purchasing power of money. This system is effectively the same as that recommended for use in the UK under the title of *'Current Purchasing Power' (C.P.P.) accounting*: a recommendation rejected by the Sandilands Committee on the grounds that the application of general price indices was not appropriate to the revaluation of specific assets. They consequently recommended the adoption of the *Current Cost Accounting (C.C.A.)* system, in which the accent is placed much more on the central principle of replacement values, which are not necessarily the same as the original purchase prices indexed upwards to reflect the diminution over time of the general purchasing power of money.

- *Current Purchasing Power (C.P.P.) accounting:* See *General purchasing power accounting.*
- *Net operating assets* comprise the fixed assets (including trade investments), stock and monetary working capital dealt with in an historic cost balance sheet.
- *The operating capability* of a business is the amount of goods and services which the business is able to supply with its existing resources in the relevant period. These resources are represented in accounting terms by the net operating assets at current cost.
- *Current cost operating profit* is the surplus arising from the ordinary activities of the business in the period, after allowing for the impact of price changes on the funds needed to continue the existing business, and to maintain its operating capability, whether financed by share capital or by borrowing. It is calculated before interest on net borrowing, and before taxation.
- *Current cost profit attributable to shareholders* is the surplus for the period, after allowing for the impact of price changes on the funds needed to maintain their proportion of the operating capability. It is calculated after interest, taxation and extraordinary items have been deducted.
- *Value to the business* is:
  (a) Net current replacement cost,
  or, if a permanent diminution to below net current replacement cost has been recognized,
  (b) Recoverable amount.
- *Recoverable amount* is the greater of the net realizable values of

an asset, and, where applicable, the amount recoverable from its further use.

- *Monetary working capital* is the aggregate of:

  (a) trade debtors, prepayment and trade bills receivable

  – (b) trade creditors, accruals and trade bills payable, in so far as they arise from the day-to-day operating activities of the business; as distinct from transactions of a capital nature.

  (*Note:* Strictly speaking the value of stocks 'not subject to a cost of sales adjustment'—i.e. consumable items, returnable containers, etc.—should also be included under this heading, but has been omitted from the above 'general' definitions in order to avoid confusion.)

  Bank balances or overdrafts may fluctuate with the volume of stock or the items in (a), (b) or (c) above. That part of bank balances or overdrafts arising from such fluctuations should be included in monetary working capital, together with any cash funds required to support day-to-day operations of the business, if to do so has a material effect on the current cost operating profit.

  In the case of banks and other financial businesses, this definition is extended to cover other assets and other liabilities in so far as they also arise from the day-to-day operating activities of the business, as distinct from transactions of a capital nature.

- *Depreciation adjustment* is the difference between depreciation calculated on an historic cost basis, and on a current cost basis.
- *Backlog depreciation* is the difference between the cumulative historic cost and current cost depreciation relating to periods up to, but not including, the current trading period.
- *Cost of sales adjustment* is the difference between the cost of sales calculated on an historic cost, and on a current cost, basis.
- *Monetary working capital adjustment* is the difference between monetary working capital (defined above) valued on an historic cost basis, and on a current cost basis.
- *Gearing adjustment* is an adjustment which is made to reduce the total operating—or 'realized'—adjustments by a proportion equivalent to that which the average loan capital, if any, bears to the average (total) capital employed as shown on the current cost balance sheets at the beginning and end of the year.

- *Current cost reserve* is a separate account shown under reserves in the balance sheet, into which have been transferred all non-realized current cost adjustments.
- *Realized current cost adjustments* are ones which affect the profit and loss for the period—i.e. depreciation adjustment, cost of sales adjustment and monetary working capital adjustment—and are directly chargeable to the period.
- *Unrealized current cost adjustments* are ones which do not directly affect the profit of a period, and get charged to the current cost reserve—i.e. revaluation of fixed assets, backlog depreciation and the revaluation of stocks.

16 The 1981 Companies Act

Introduction

Occasional references have been made throughout this book to the way in which certain things have to be reported in the financial accounts of a company in order to satisfy the rules of law. We have deliberately refrained from overplaying this aspect because our primary intention has always been to concentrate on the development of a proper understanding of the basic principles of accounting. Assuming that those objectives have been achieved, however, it should now be possible to turn our attention to the provisions which have been made to ensure that companies do, in fact, abide by the rules of the 'business game'. These rules are enshrined in the Companies Acts, and there have been many of these passed over the years—each one being readily identifiable by its year of publication.

The most recent one is the Act of 1981, and a high proportion of its provisions arises out of requirements specified by the EEC Fourth Directive, issued in 1978. This stipulated categorically the basic principles upon which the accounting data should be based, what financial information should be disclosed in company accounts, and exactly how it should be displayed. Member countries of the Community were asked to incorporate these requirements into Company Law, and this (among other things) is what the UK Companies Act of 1981 set out to achieve.

Andrew didn't like the sound of this too much, because he immediately felt that he was going to be put into a position of giving away too many of his well-protected business secrets, so we had to explain to him that these rules were primarily intended for larger companies than his—those whose shareholders had often had difficulty in understanding the accounts that were sent to them for acceptance at the Annual General Meeting. This struck an immediate responsive chord with Andrew, who had invested in a few shares himself over recent years, and fervently agreed that, before our series of discussions, he had hardly been able to understand a word of the accounts himself! We explained to him that the provisions introduced by the 1981 Act would make for greater standardization of detail and presentation, and would reduce the opportunities for companies to 'hide' information, or to present their accounts in a confusing manner. Andrew decided to reserve his judgement for the time being, and wait and see the extent to which the Act had been successful in achieving these objectives, but he would certainly be happy in the meantime to drink a toast to its future success! But then, as we have already said, he'd drink to almost anything!

Accounting requirements

One of the important provisions of the 1981 Act was to distinguish clearly between the accounts which have to be 'laid' before a company's shareholders at its A.G.M., and those which have to be 'filed' with the Registrar of Companies for public scrutiny. 'Members' accounts must comply with all the disclosure requirements of the Act (and this is enforceable via criminal sanctions on the directors), whereas they can submit rather less 'informative' accounts to the Registrar. The rules apply to *all* companies, large or small, subject to certain exceptions such as banking, insurance and shipping companies, to which separate rules apply. Some 'smaller' companies may also qualify for certain exemptions to the disclosure rules applicable to published (or 'filed') accounts, as we shall see later.

The Act then turns its attention to the way in which the information is required to be presented, and it offers a choice between two balance sheet formats and four profit and loss formats! This piece of information nearly made Andrew fall off his stool when we first mentioned it to him, but we explained that, once a company had selected the one balance sheet and one profit and loss format which best suited its own particular needs, it was thereafter obliged to stay with them in order to ensure consistency and continuity of information. An illustration of each of the prescribed formats is given at the end of this chapter in Figures 16.3 to 16.8, but, in general terms, the Balance Sheet 'Format 1' is equivalent to the 'Net' presentations that we have been using throughout this book, while 'Format 2' is equivalent to the 'gross' presentation. The main headings of each are compared in Figure 16.1.

Our examples and illustrations have also been based principally on the 'Format 1' option of the profit and loss statement, which takes the 'functional' route from Sales to Trading Profit via Cost of

	Format 1		*Format 2*
Fixed assets		xx	xx
Current assets	xx		xx
Prepayments and accrued income	xx		xx
	xx		:
Less (Short-term) Creditors: accounts falling due within one year	−xx		:
Net Current assets		xx	:
Total Assets *Less* Current liabilities		xx	:
Total Assets			TT
Capital and reserves (a)		:	xx
(Long-term) Creditors: amounts falling due after more than one year	−xx		:
Provisions for liabilities and charges	−xx		xx
Creditors—(Short-term and Long-term to be shown separately and in aggregate)	:		xx
Accruals and deferred income	−xx		xx
Less Total Long-term Creditors, Provisions and Accruals (b)		−xx	:
Net Assets (b)		TT	:
Capital and reserves (a)		xx	:
Capital Employed (b)		TT	:
Total Liabilities			TT

Notes: (a) The positioning of Capital and Reserves differs between Format 1 and Format 2

(b) No titles for these lines in Format 1 are actually defined in the Act

Fig 16.1 Basic balance sheet formats as prescribed in the 1981 Companies Act

Goods Sold, Distribution and Administration Expenses. 'Format 2', on the other hand, takes the 'type of expense' route through Materials, Staff Costs, Depreciation and Other Charges. This comparison is shown in Figure 16.2.

Formats 3 and 4 of the profit and loss statement are shown in Figures 16.7 and 16.8, although we have to admit that Andrew was

	Format 1		*Format 2*	
Turnover		xx		xx
Cost of sales		−xx		:
Gross profit		xx		:
Distribution costs	−xx		:	
Administration expenses	−xx		:	
Materials consumed	:		−xx	
Staff costs	:		−xx	
Depreciation	:		−xx	
Other operating costs	:		−xx	
		−xx		−xx
Trading profit		xx		xx
Investment income	xx		xx	
Interest receivable	xx		xx	
	xx		xx	
Less Interest payable	−xx		−xx	
		xx		xx
Profit on ordinary activities before taxation		xx		xx
Tax on Profit on ordinary activities		−xx		−xx
Profit on Ordinary activities after tax		xx		xx
Extraordinary items		−xx		−xx
Profit for the financial year		xx		xx
Appropriations:				
— Transfers to reserves	−xx		−xx	
— Dividends paid and proposed	−xx		−xx	
		−xx		−xx
Retained profit for the year		xx		xx

Fig 16.2 Basic profit and loss formats as prescribed in the 1981 Companies Act

rather relieved when we said that, in our opinion, they are unlikely to be very widely used.

We have only shown the major headings in Figures 16.1 and 16.2. These headings must all appear separately in the prescribed wording and in the prescribed sequence, whenever the item exists in either the current or the preceding year. Many of these major headings are further analysed under minor headings, and these, too, must also be used if and when appropriate. These headings can be rearranged to some extent if the 'special nature of the company's business' should render this desirable, and further analysis can be provided, if desired. However, categories can only be combined with the specific objective of providing an easier understanding of the accounts, and then the prescribed analyses have to be disclosed in separate Notes to the Accounts.

In particular, set-offs between income and expenditure items, or between assets and liabilities, are not allowed, so that something like 'Net Interest Received'—meaning Interest Received less Interest Paid—would not be acceptable. Similarly, amounts owed *to* and *by* group companies could not be set off against each other, since these are both to appear under their own separate main headings. Andrew seemed to think that this was taking things a bit too far, but we assured him that the whole aim of the Act—and, for that matter, of the EEC Fourth Directive—was to achieve a clearer and more detailed disclosure of corporate financial data.

Accounting rules and principles

The 1981 Act also differs from its predecessors in that, for the first time ever, it decrees not only which items must be disclosed, but also how they should be computed, and we had to agree with Andrew's comment here that, in this sense, it seemed to be moving into areas which had hitherto been regarded as the province of the accountants, as represented by the Accounting Standards Committee. However, the Act does not pretend to be a comprehensive reference on accounting principles and practice, and it has to be assumed that any topics not specifically covered by the Act will continue to be covered by the SSAPs—bearing in mind that, be it Act or SSAP, the overriding principle must always be to provide that 'true and fair view' of the company's financial situation that we have emphasized so many times already.

There are five fundamental accounting 'principles' defined in the Act with which the preparation and presentation of all company accounts are expected to comply. The first four of these correlate very closely with the four basic accounting 'concepts' defined in SSAP 2 'Disclosure of Accounting Policies', which was issued in 1971. The five basic accounting 'principles' can be identified as follows:

(a) going concern (b) consistency (c) prudence (d) accruals	Accounting 'policies' as defined in SSAP 2: *Disclosure of Accounting Policies*
(e) 'aggregation'	

The first two of these principles—or 'policies'—create no problem of interpretation, since it is a long-accepted principle that all UK company accounts should be prepared to represent the company as a 'going concern', and that the information should be consistently based between one year and another.

We have also touched on the concept of prudence, which decrees that revenues and profits should not be anticipated—they should only be included in the profit and loss account 'when realized in the form either of cash or of other assets, the ultimate cash realization of which can be assessed with reasonable certainty; provision (having been) made for all known liabilities (expenses and losses) whether the amount of these is known with certainty or is a best estimate in the light of the information available'.

These are the words used in SSAP 2, although the concept of prudence is defined somewhat differently in the Act, which says that 'only profits realized at the balance sheet date should be included in the profit and loss account'. Andrew wasn't too happy with this definition, since he felt that 'realized' in this context could quite legitimately be interpreted to mean 'received in cash', which was surely quite contrary to the concept of 'accrual' that was underlined in the extract from SSAP 2 that we had just quoted to him. We had to agree that this was a perfectly legitimate point to make.

We then came to the fifth accounting principle specified in the Act—that of 'aggregation'. The object of this was to emphasize how determined the legislators were to ensure that companies did not 'set off' unrealized losses on some items within an asset category against unrealized profits from others. We actually tried to explain this to Andrew by using the wording of the Act itself, which states that 'in determining the aggregate amount of any class, the amount of each individual asset or liability that falls to be taken into account shall be determined separately'—but this didn't achieve any reaction other than some unrepeatable recommendation about what they could do with their 'individual assets and legalistic jargon'!

Valuation of assets

This reaction was quickly followed by one of approval as we went on to explain that one of the accounting 'rules' incorporated into Section B of Part II of Schedule 8 of the Act relates to the valuation of various classes of assets, and that these rules follow the general conventions of historic cost accounting. 'So much for the gearing adjustment, then!', exclaimed Andrew triumphantly, and his face was wreathed in smiles until we mentioned that there was also a Section C to Part II of Schedule 8 which accommodated certain 'alternative accounting rules', and that these did allow for the valuation of tangible fixed assets and (fixed asset) investments to be included 'at a market value determined as at the date of their last valuation'.

'Ah! But that still doesn't mention anything about gearing adjustments!' said Andrew, who also felt that there was another indication of a move in the same direction when he heard that, according to Section B, current assets, for example, are to be valued at the lower of cost and net realizable value, and stocks may be valued under the principles of F.I.F.O., L.I.F.O., weighted average prices, 'or similar conventions'. So may 'fungible assets', including investments.

Andrew was very grateful for this piece of information, although he couldn't for the life of him understand what we were talking about! The only definition of a 'fungible asset' that he could think of was a mushroom, and he couldn't see why any Companies Act should go out of its way to classify those as investments. Well, he needn't have worried, because we had already anticipated that one! 'Fungible' is apparently a rather quaint mediaeval term meaning items which are indistinguishable one from another. 'Ah!' said Andrew, immediately grasping the point, 'You mean like a *pound* of mushrooms!' You've certainly got to hand it to him, sometimes! But back to the Act, and the valuation of assets . . . .

The valuation of all assets, fixed or current, must include all directly attributable production costs, together with a 'reasonable proportion' of indirect overheads incurred during the period of production. Interest on capital may consequently be capitalized during the development stage of a project, although development costs as such may only be included as part of the value of an asset in certain (undefined) circumstances. In such cases, the reasons for their inclusion and the period over which they are intended to be written off must also be disclosed. Research costs, on the other hand, must never be treated as assets.

Goodwill may only be included as an asset if 'acquired for valuable consideration'—it would hardly ever have been otherwise in the UK—and must never be written off over a period exceeding its 'useful economic life'. Such an inclusion must always be accompanied by a disclosure of what this period is, and the reasoning upon which this estimate is based.

Another item of interest concerns non-current investments, which *may* be written down in value if they suffer a *temporary* reduction in value, and *must* be written down if they suffer what is seen to be a *permanent* reduction in value. Andrew seemed to think that this represented a permutation of four possible combinations, but we decided not to pursue that line of thought.

New and amended disclosures

In addition to the various format and accounting rules indicated above, the 1981 Act incorporates certain disclosure requirements which are either additional to, or different from those defined by earlier legislation. Some of these have for long been regarded as 'best practice', and most have already been defined within the accounting 'standards', but this is the first time that they have been defined in law. The most convenient way to comment on these will be to do so under the appropriate balance sheet and profit and loss headings.

Balance Sheet Items

Fixed Assets must now be classified under separate main headings for intangibles, tangibles and investments, with further minor headings as shown in Figures 16.3 and 16.4. full details of opening and closing costs (or valuations) must be shown, together with details of all movements and amounts written off. Payments on account of assets, such as those in the course of construction, must also be shown. As a point of interest, fixed assets are defined within the Act as being those 'intended for use on a continuing basis in the company's activities.' Any other assets are strictly 'current'.

Investments This main category of fixed assets is subdivided into a number of minor categories—many more than were previously regarded as either necessary or appropriate—one of which is called 'Shares in Related Companies'. This term covers what used to be called 'Associated Companies', and can be defined as a 'non-group company in which a long-term vote-carrying holding of equity (however small) is held for the purpose of securing a contribution to the investing company's own activities by the exercise of any control or influence arising from that interest'. An Associated Company was previously defined as one in which 20 per cent or more of such equity was held.

A share-holding of 20 per cent or more in a non-group company is still a significant break-point, however, since that is the point above which the capital and reserves of the Related Company as at its latest balance sheet date—together with the profit or loss for the latest financial year—have to be given, provided that:

(a) the investee is an overseas company which has no place of business in Great Britain, and does not publish its accounts either here or abroad, and
(b) where the holding in it does not amount to 50 per cent of the total share capital.

'Current asset investments' have to be similarly analysed under the main heading of Current Assets, and, if the company is holding any of its own shares, their nominal value must also be shown.

Stocks The valuation of stocks has to include payments on account, or money received in advance in respect of stock not yet dispatched or handed over to a customer.

Debtors and Creditors Each subclassification of these two main categories has to be analysed between amounts falling due within one year of the balance sheet date, and any that may not be due until after one year.

Net current assets 'Format 1' is the only one of the two permitted balance sheet formats which brings out a subtotal to show the value of a company's net working capital, and is consequently likely to be the one most widely used in practice.

Long-term liabilities All categories of creditors, losses and accruals not due for repayment during the following year need to be separately identified, and individual details must be given of all instalments or repayments not due until after the end of the next five years. Similarly, specific details are to be furnished in respect of all secured and contingent liabilities.

Provisions 'Provisions for liabilities and charges' are now required to be shown under a separate main heading in the balance sheet, and need to be subdivided between pensions and similar obligations, taxation and other provisions. Beginning and end-year balances have to be shown, together with details of the source and destination of all amounts transferred in and out.

Profit and Loss Items

Turnover The 1981 Act defines—for the first time—turnover as being 'the amount derived from the provision of goods and services falling within the company's ordinary activities, after the deduction of trade discounts, VAT and any other taxes based on the amounts so derived'. An analysis of turnover and pre-tax profit has to be given for each substantially different class of the company's activities, and for each geographical segment of its overseas trading—provided that such disclosure is not regarded by the directors as seriously prejudicial to the interests of their business. If such grounds for omission exist, then this fact must be clearly stated.

Costs The gap which has traditionally existed between turnover and operating profit now has to be bridged. The way in which that is done will depend upon which profit and loss format is adopted—Formats 1 and 3 analyse costs by function, while Formats 2 and 4 analyse them by natural expense. Separate details also have to be provided in respect of amounts written off investments, interest payable on group or external investments, and similar charges.

Extraordinary items Income, expenditure and taxation liabilities arising out of extraordinary activities have to be shown separately from those relating to routine trading operations.

Employee details The Notes to the Accounts now have to include details of the average number of employees in total and by category—this used to be required as part of the Directors' Report—and total employee costs have to be analysed between wages and salaries, social security costs and other pension costs. This provision now applies to all companies—the previous exceptions relating to companies employing less than 100 staff and for wholly-owned subsidiaries having been abolished, together with the previous exclusion of overseas staff.

Group accounts

Generally speaking, the disclosure requirements specified under the Act apply to consolidated Group accounts in the same way as if they were individual companies.

Directors' Report

Auditors are made legally responsible for considering whether the information given in the Directors' Report relating to the financial year in question is consistent with the accounts. If they do not consider that this is so, then they have a duty to say so.

In addition to reviewing the principal activities of the company, the report now has to contain 'a fair review of the development of the business of the company and its subsidiaries'. This review should cover such matters as:

(a) particulars of important post-balance sheet events
(b) an indication of likely future developments
(c) an indication of any activities in the field of research and development, and
(d) a number of details about the company's own shares acquired by, or for it, or over which it has a charge.

Conversely, certain earlier disclosure requirements—such as directors' interests in the company's shares—have been dropped from the Directors' Report, since they are now covered by the disclosure requirements of the accounts or Notes to the Accounts. One incidental point of interest is that, under the Employment Act of 1982, the Directors' Report attached to the registered accounts of all companies employing more than 250 people must also state what action, if any, has been taken during the year to develop or improve the level of employee participation in the management of the company.

Exemptions for medium-sized and small-sized companies

Certain exemptions from the general disclosure rules are granted to medium-sized and small-sized companies—but *only* in so far as the accounts that they file with the Registrar of Companies is concerned. Accounts presented to shareholders have to comply with *all* the disclosure requirements defined in the Act.

For this purpose, the 'size' classification of a company would depend upon its ability to satisfy at least two of the following three conditions during both the current and the preceding financial year:

	'Medium'	'Small'
(1) Turnover not exceeding	£5.75 m	£1.4 m
(2) Total assets (as shown in the balance sheet) not exceeding	£2.80 m	£0.7 m
(3) Average number of employees not exceeding	250	50

The permitted modifications to the disclosure requirements are extremely limited for medium-sized companies in that they are allowed to omit only turnover and cost of sales information, and the analysis of turnover and profit among different classes of business and for different overseas markets. Permitted modifications for small companies are far more extensive, however, and cover the whole of the profit and loss account and the Directors' Report, and all but the major balance sheet headings. This may sound fairly insignificant, although, in practice, the absence of turnover and profit information will now make it impossible to obtain any meaningful ratio analyses relating to the performances of medium and small-sized companies which decide to take advantage of these concessions. From an analytical point of view, this is consequently rather an unfortunate loophole to have provided within the otherwise extremely comprehensive legislation.

Other matters

Other topics covered by the Act include the procedures to be followed during the actual process of publishing accounts, and what is required to be done by 'dormant' companies—or companies which have had no financial transactions during a period. Company mergers, and rules to be followed by companies buying their own shares were also defined, as were also the declarations required in respect of a 'substantial' (proportion of) shares held in another company by a company and/or its directors, and disclosures of directors' transactions with their own companies. Previous legislation relating to the 'availability, change and registration of' company names was also considerably simplified under the Act, as a result of which the old Registry of Business Names was disbanded.

Summary

The Companies Act of 1981 was a very significant piece of legislation in that, for the first time ever, it stipulated quite categorically not only what financial information had to be disclosed in both shareholders' and published accounts, but also exactly how this information is to be displayed. Its origins lay in the EEC Fourth Directive, which was published in 1978, and it was the vehicle via which the requirements of this Directive were incorporated into UK company law.

Five accounting 'principles' are defined in the Act, the first four of which very closely resemble the four accounting 'policies' defined in SSAP 2: *Disclosure of Accounting Policies*, and it also goes into a great deal of detail about the accounting 'rules' which are to be applied to the valuation and definition of almost all categories of assets, liabilities, revenues and expenses to be shown in the balance sheet and profit and loss statement.

The provisions of the Act will ensure that all companies should now apply consistent interpretations to the financial reports that they compile, although it is in many ways unfortunate that 'medium' and 'small' companies may qualify for reporting 'concessions' in their published accounts which will make realistic comparisons with the performance results of other companies virtually impossible.

COMPANIES ACT 1981
Balance Sheet—Format 1

A Called up Share Capital Not Paid (May be shown either here or under C (ii) 5)

B Fixed Assets

(i) Intangible Assets
1 Development costs
2 Concessions, patents, licences, trade marks and similar rights and assets (*If* acquired for valuable consideration *or* created by the company itself)
3 Goodwill (*Only* if acquired for valuable consideration)
4 Payments on account

(ii) Tangible Assets
1 Land and buildings
2 Plant and machinery
3 Fixtures, fittings, tools and equipment
4 Payments on account and assets in course of construction

(iii) Investments
1 Shares in group companies
2 Loans to group companies
3 Shares in related companies
4 Loans to related companies
5 Other investments other than loans
6 Other loans
7 Own shares (The nominal value shall be shown separately)

C Current Assets

(i) Stocks
1 Raw materials and consumables
2 Work in progress
3 Finished goods and goods for resale
4 Payments on account

(ii) Debtors (Amounts falling due after more than one year must be shown separately under each of the following headings)
1 Trade debtors
2 Amounts owed by group companies
3 Amounts owed by related companies
4 Other debtors
5 Called up share capital not paid (May be shown either here or under A)
6 Prepayments and accrued income (May be shown either here or under D)

Fig 16.3 Balance Sheet Format 1 as prescribed by the Companies Act of 1981 (contd over)

(iii) Investments
  1 Shares in group companies
  2 Own shares (The nominal value shall be shown separately)
  3 Other investments
(iv) Cash at bank and in hand

D Prepayments and Accrued Income (May be shown either here or under C (ii) 6)

E Creditors: Amounts Falling Due within One Year

1 Debenture loans (Value of convertible loans to be shown separately)
2 Bank loans and overdrafts
3 Payments received on account (In so far as these items are not shown as deductions from stocks)
4 Trade creditors
5 Bills of exchange payable
6 Amounts owed to group companies
7 Amounts owed to related companies
8 Other creditors including taxation and social security (With taxation and social security shown separately from other creditors)
9 Accruals and deferred income (May be shown either here or under J)

F Net Current Assets/(Liabilities)

G Total Assets *less* Current Liabilities

H Creditors: Amounts Falling Due after More than One Year

1 Debenture loans (The amount of convertible loans must be shown separately)
2 Bank loans and overdrafts
3 Payments received on account (In so far as these items are not shown as deductions from stocks)
4 Trade creditors
5 Bills of exchange payable
6 Amounts owed to group companies
7 Amounts owed to related companies
8 Other creditors including taxation and social security (With taxation and social security shown separately from other creditors)
9 Accruals and deferred income (May be shown either here or under J)

Fig 16.3 contd

I Provisions for Liabilities and Charges

1 Pensions and similar obligations
2 Taxation, including deferred taxation
3 Other provisions

J Accruals and Deferred Income (May be shown either here or under either E (9) or H (9))

K Capital and Reserves

(i) Called up share capital (Details of allotted share capital and paid up share capital must be shown separately)
(ii) Share premium account
(iii) Revaluation reserve
(iv) Other reserves
1 Capital redemption reserve
2 Reserve for own shares
3 Reserves provided for by the articles of association
4 Other reserves
(v) Profit and loss account

COMPANIES ACT 1981
Balance Sheet—Format 2

ASSETS

A Called up Share Capital Not Paid (May be shown either here or under C (ii) 5)

B Fixed Assets

(i) Intangible Assets
1 Development costs
2 Concessions, patents, licences, trade marks and similar rights and assets (*If* acquired for valuable consideration *or* created by the company itself)
3 Goodwill (*Only* if acquired for valuable consideration)
4 Payments on account
(ii) Tangible Assets
1 Land and buildings
2 Plant and machinery
3 Fixtures, fittings, tools and equipment
4 Payments on account and assets in course of construction
(iii) Investments
1 Shares in group companies
2 Loans to group companies
3 Shares in related companies
4 Loans to related companies
5 Other investments other than loans
6 Other loans
7 Own shares (The nominal value shall be shown separately)

C Current Assets

(i) Stocks
1 Raw materials and consumables
2 Work in progress
3 Finished goods and goods for resale
4 Payments on account
(ii) Debtors (Amounts falling due after more than one year must be shown separately under each of the following headings)
1 Trade debtors
2 Amounts owed by group companies
3 Amounts owed by related companies
4 Other debtors
5 Called up share capital not paid (May be shown either here or under A)
6 Prepayments and accrued income (May be shown either here or under D)

Fig 16.4 Balance Sheet Format 2 as prescribed by the Companies Act of 1981

(iii) Investments
  1 Shares in group companies
  2 Own shares (The nominal value shall be shown separately)
  3 Other investments
(iv) Cash at bank and in hand

D Prepayments and Accrued Income (May be shown either here or under C (ii) 6)

LIABILITIES

A Capital and Reserves

(i) Called up share capital (Details of allotted share capital and paid up share capital must be shown separately)
(ii) Share premium account
(iii) Revaluation reserve
(iv) Other reserves
  1 Capital redemption reserve
  2 Reserve for own shares
  3 Reserves provided for by the articles of association
  4 Other reserves
(v) Profit and loss account

B Provisions for Liabilities and Charges

  1 Pensions and similar obligations
  2 Taxation, including deferred taxation
  3 Other provisions

C Creditors: (Amounts falling due after more than one year must be shown separately under each of the following headings)
  1 Debenture loans (The amount of convertible loans must be shown separately)
  2 Bank loans and overdrafts
  3 Payments received on account (In so far as these items are not shown as deductions from stocks)
  4 Trade creditors
  5 Bills of exchange payable
  6 Amounts owed to group companies
  7 Amounts owed to related companies
  8 Other creditors including taxation and social security (With taxation and social security shown separately from other creditors)
  9 Accruals and deferred income (May be shown either here or under D)

D Accruals and Deferred Income (May be shown either here or under C 9)

COMPANIES ACT 1981
Profit and Loss Account—Format 1

(*Note:* Any provisions for the depreciation and diminution in value of tangible and intangible fixed assets must be disclosed in a Note to the Accounts)

1 Turnover
2 Cost of sales (After taking into account any necessary provision for depreciation or diminution in value of assets)
3 Gross profit or loss
4 Distribution costs (After taking into account any necessary provision for depreciation or diminution in value of assets)
5 Administration expenses (After taking into account any necessary provision for depreciation or diminution in value of assets)
6 Other operating income
7 Income from shares in group companies
8 Income from shares in related companies
9 Income from other fixed asset investments (Income and interest derived from group companies must be shown separately from that derived from other sources)
10 Other interest receivable and similar income (Income and interest derived from group companies must be shown separately from that derived from other sources)
11 Amounts written off investments
12 Interest payable and similar charges (The amount payable to group companies must be shown separately)
13 Tax on profit or loss on ordinary activities
14 Profit or loss on ordinary activities after taxation
15 Extraordinary income
16 Extraordinary charges
17 Extraordinary profit or loss
18 Tax on extraordinary profit or loss
19 Other taxes not shown under the above items
20 Profit or loss for the financial year

Fig 16.5 Profit and Loss Account Format 1 as prescribed by the Companies Act 1981

COMPANIES ACT 1981
Profit and Loss Account—Format 2

1 Turnover
2 Change in stocks of finished goods and work in progress
3 Own work capitalized
4 Other operating income
5 External (third party) charges incurred
   (a) Raw materials and consumables purchased
   (b) Other external charges
6 Staff costs
   (a) Wages and salaries
   (b) Social security costs
   (c) Other pension costs
7 Depreciation and diminution in value of assets
   (a) Amounts written off tangible and intangible fixed assets
   (b) Exceptional amounts written off current assets
8 Other operating charges
9 Income from shares in group companies
10 Income from shares in related companies
11 Income from other fixed asset investments (Income and interest derived from group companies must be shown separately from that derived from other sources)
12 Other interest receivable and similar income (Income and interest derived from group companies must be shown separately from that derived from other sources)
13 Amounts written off investments
14 Interest payable and similar charges (The amount payable to group companies must be shown separately)
15 Tax on profit or loss on ordinary activities
16 Profit or loss on ordinary activities after taxation
17 Extraordinary income
18 Extraordinary charges
19 Extraordinary profit or loss
20 Tax on extraordinary profit or loss
21 Other taxes not shown under the above items
22 Profit or loss for the financial year

Fig 16.6 Profit and Loss Account Format 2 as prescribed by the Companies Act 1981

COMPANIES ACT 1981
Profit and Loss Account—Format 3

(*Note:* Any provisions for the depreciation and diminution in value of tangible and intangible fixed assets must be disclosed in a Note to the Accounts)

A Charges

1 Cost of sales (After taking into account any necessary provision for depreciation or diminution in value of assets)
2 Distribution costs (After taking into account any necessary provision for depreciation or diminution in value of assets)
3 Administration expenses (After taking into account any necessary provision for depreciation or diminution in value of assets)
4 Amounts written off investments
5 Interest payable and similar charges (The amount payable to group companies must be shown separately)
6 Tax on profit or loss on ordinary activities
7 Profit or loss on ordinary activities after taxation
8 Extraordinary charges
9 Tax on extraordinary profit or loss
10 Other taxes not shown under the above items
11 Profit or loss for the financial year

B Income

1 Turnover
2 Other operating income
3 Income from shares in group companies
4 Income from shares in related companies
5 Income from other fixed asset investments (Income and interest derived from group companies must be shown separately from that derived from other sources)
6 Other interest receivable and similar income (Income and interest derived from group companies must be shown separately from that derived from other sources)
7 Profit or loss on ordinary activities after taxation
8 Extraordinary income
9 Profit or loss for the financial year

Fig 16.7 Profit and Loss Account Format 3 as prescribed by the Companies Act 1981

COMPANIES ACT 1981
Profit and Loss Account—Format 4

A Charges

1 Reduction in stocks of finished goods and work in progress
2 External (third party) charges incurred
   (a) Raw materials and consumables purchased
   (b) Other external charges
3 Staff costs
   (a) Wages and salaries
   (b) Social security costs
   (c) Other pension costs
4 Depreciation and diminution in value of assets
   (a) Amounts written off tangible and intangible fixed assets
   (b) Exceptional amounts written off current assets
5 Other operating charges
6 Amounts written off investments
7 Interest payable and similar charges (The amount payable to group companies must be shown separately)
8 Tax on profit or loss on ordinary activities
9 Profit or loss on ordinary activities after taxation
10 Extraordinary charges
11 Tax on extraordinary profit or loss
12 Other taxes not shown under the above items
13 Profit or loss for the financial year

B Income

1 Turnover
2 Increase in stocks of finished goods and work in progress
3 Own work capitalised
4 Other operating income
5 Income from shares in group companies
6 Income from shares in related companies
7 Income from other fixed asset investments (Income and interest derived from group companies must be shown separately from that derived from other sources)
8 Other interest receivable and similar income (Income and interest derived from group companies must be shown separately from that derived from other sources)
9 Profit or loss on ordinary activities after taxation
10 Extraordinary income
11 Profit or loss for the financial year

Fig 16.8 Profit and Loss Account Format 4 as prescribed by the Companies Act 1981

17 The last round

Time to reflect

We had now completed our series of discussions with Andrew on the range of topics that we considered to be appropriate to the improvement of his understanding of accounting, but it was only natural that we should arrange to meet at our favourite 'local' for a final celebratory session. The object of this was to review and assess the progress that we had made, and, to give him his due, Andrew had managed to stay the course pretty well. It was only towards the end, when we got on to the subject of C.C.A. adjustments, that things began to get a bit difficult—and even that hurdle seemed to be overcome when he discovered that the 1981 Companies Act didn't appear to think too highly of current cost accounting, either!

Andrew admitted that he felt a great deal happier about quite a number of things which used to puzzle him in the past, but the strange thing was that he now seemed to have more questions to ask than when we started! When you come to think about it, though, this should not be too surprising because, now that he was able to grasp the basic principles of cash flow, interest rates, taxation, added value, and the impact of inflation upon profits (among all those other things) he was able to develop new lines of thought and enquiry from the solid base that we had helped him to create.

So far as he was concerned (and he admitted that this was purely a personal reaction) he felt that the most interesting subjects were the ones dealing with budgets, management ratios and added value analysis. Once again, this wasn't too surprising because, in his capacity as a manager, these were precisely the subjects that he ought to be able to understand if he was going to stand much chance of being commercially effective in his job. He agreed, however, that he wouldn't have had much chance of understanding ratios if he hadn't first made sure what was actually meant by capital employed, equity, working capital, gearing, and so on.

Time to consolidate

Some people might feel that topics such as management ratios and added value are rather beyond the scope of a book concerned principally with the understanding of accounting, but Andrew agreed that the finished book should be capable of being used as a comprehensive volume in its own right, and not necessarily as part of a set. It is quite true that a book on 'management accounting' would probably need to include some, if not all of these subjects in even greater detail than we have dealt with them here, but that's another story.

Management accounting is a subject that needs much more than a couple of chapters, because it involves getting down to the basic analysis and interpretation of *data*, as distinct from pure financial accounts; and data can be interpreted to mean anything from physical quantities to man-hours, steam pressures, energy consumptions, machine utilization—to name but a few.

Among other things, the purpose of management accounting reports is to assist managers to assess and measure their actual results against those defined in their budgets. Managers also need to know how much their products have *actually* 'cost', compared with what they *ought* to have cost, and how much their future products are *likely* to cost. How much will they have to try and sell them for in order to make the sort of profit margin that they would want; and what sort of demand would there be at that sort of price at various levels of expenditure on promotion? We scratched the surface of this sort of thing when we were discussing business development strategies in Chapter 13, but there is obviously a great deal more to this than we had the time or the space to explore in that one chapter.

One of the subheadings in this particular section referred to 'investment strategy', and included under this subheading was an item called capital investment appraisal. This, in itself, is a topic that goes much deeper than some people might think. That is the area where managers gather together in small groups, exchange significant glances, and mutter all sorts of weird-sounding things to each other about 'D.C.F.s' and 'N.P.V.s'.

And then there's risk analysis. That could be a subject worthy of elaboration in these days when nobody can risk selling goods to customers who might not be able to pay for them. So how do we actually measure that sort of risk, and—come to think of it—how do we measure the risk status of our own company?

Andrew was also rather intrigued about this thing called 'financial modelling' that more and more people seemed to be talking about these days. Wasn't this something that he ought to know about, too? In these days of microcomputers, the answer is almost certainly going to be 'Yes!'.

Time to speculate

One of the things that had consistently intrigued him during the course of our discussions was this thing about the 'speculative nature of investment'. He knew how to read papers like the *Sporting Life*; and in a way, he reckoned that in his younger days he probably used to read a race-card and a betting forecast in very much the same sort of way that an investor would read a balance sheet and a profit and loss statement. But what about all those pages of figures on 'stock market information' that he had seen people reading in the *Financial Times*? How did all those figures relate to economic trends, and how did the Financial Times Index actually work? And, talking about speculation, how could you really assess when was the 'right' time to buy and sell which shares?

All of these things were subjects that he had heard about, and sometimes felt that he ought to know about, although they had always seemed to be a bit too obscure and out of his reach before. We could only hope that we had been able to help him take his first—and certainly his most important—step along the road of discovery which could lead him further in any of these directions, if he so wished.

What is an accountant?

Andrew was wearing his rather thoughtful expression again. 'You know,' he said, 'I'm beginning to think that there must be quite a lot more to this accounting business than I first thought. I often used to wonder what sort of people took up accountancy for a living—and I'm still not sure that I could give a straight answer. I know that we touched very briefly on the subject of definitions way back in our very first session, but, just as a matter of interest, how would you define an accountant, and describe the work that he does?'

This was certainly quite an interesting point, and seemed to qualify as a suitable topic with which to bring our discussions to a close. What is an accountant, and where should one go for the best definition?

As we mentioned in Chapter 1, the *Oxford Dictionary* is rather coy about this. It just says: 'The professional keeper and inspector of accounts'—although this is probably not the definition that many people might suggest!

One person who certainly held a very jaundiced view of them was Elbert Hubbard, who said many years ago that an accountant was: 'a man past middle age, spare, wrinkled, intelligent, cold, passive, with eyes like a cod-fish, polite in contact, but at the same time unresponsive, cold, and damnably composed as a concrete post or a plaster of Paris cast; a petrification with a heart of feldspar and without charm or a friendly germ, minus bowels, passion or a sense of humour. Happily they never reproduce, and all of them finally go to hell!'

Sir Miles Thomas, on the other hand, thought that a good accountant was 'someone who told you yesterday what the economists forecast for tomorrow'. This fits in very much more neatly with the message that we have been trying to convey in this book, because one of the accountant's responsibilities in business is to give his fellow managers as much early warning as possible about what is happening to the company's money in order that, as a team, they will be able to plan and develop their future strategies. To this extent, therefore, his role is to provide timely and accurate financial *information*.

It is rather strange how people build up an impression of things in their minds, and how individuals can get themselves type-cast into a sort of image mould, simply as a result of the type of work they choose to do, or the profession they choose to follow—and the accountancy profession is no exception.

These impressions can start at a very early age. Some years ago, for example, *Accountancy Age* conducted a survey among 10 to 11-year-olds at two London schools, asking them to say what they thought a typical accountant was like, and what it was that he did all day. Some of the replies were quite illuminating, and the spelling and punctuation of the following examples are exactly 'as wrote':

(David Green, aged 10): 'I think that an accountant add's up all the money which is given to him. And he has a very hard job counting up all the money. And he probably work nine hour a day and five days a week. He is a short stout man with trousers and a wast coat, with very plane black shoes. He works out how much money he can make in his spare time. And how much profit he can make.'

(Shirley Brodie, aged 11): 'An accountant is a man who counts and looks after the money. He wears black shoes and a nice white shirt to go with his tidy black suit and tie. He also wears a nice black bowler hat. He's favourite meal is jellied eels.'

(Jonathan Neates, aged 11): 'An accountant is a very unfriendly person because if you disturb him he loses his count and has to start again. He carries a brief case full of money and a umbrella. In his spare time he sells watches and counts his own money.'

(Terry Norbury, aged 10): 'An accountant is a person who counts the money and looks after the money. Who wears a suit with a bald head and a moustache and a beard he sits at a desk behind a counter. He is fat with two big teeth and a long crooked nose with two big brown eyes and one ear.'

One can't help wondering whether these young people still think the same way now as they did in those days! . . .

Accountants often chide themselves for their stuffy public image, and as part of an exercise which was claimed to be in commemoration of the centenary of the foundation of the Institute of Chartered Accountants in England and Wales, the (now defunct) *Accountants' Weekly* commissioned a special survey in an attempt to discover just how bad, or good that image really is. The results were published in their issue of 9 May 1980 and we are obliged to them for giving us permission to reproduce some of their conclusions here.

Two of the questions asked were: 'What do you consider to be the characteristics most likely to be found in an accountant?' and 'How highly do you rate the accountancy profession in relation to other professions?'. The conclusions to be drawn from the charts reproduced in Figure 17.1 are that, generally speaking, accountants seem to be regarded as clever and honest people, although hardly anybody expected them to demonstrate creativity, generosity, humour or vitality as part of their character.

There is also no doubt that the accountancy profession rates lower than doctors, solicitors or airline pilots in the public popularity polls—being somewhat on a par with architects, surveyors, bankers and engineers. In fact, the only profession out of those selected

What do you consider to be the characteristics most likely to be found in an accountant?

Cleverness	68%
Creativity	14%
Dryness	9%
Dullness	8%
Generosity	6%
Honesty	70%
Humour	15%
Meanness	4%
Shiftiness	4%
Stupidity	1%
Vitality	10%

How highly do you rate the accountancy profession in relation to other professions?

	Higher	Lower
Doctors	15%	73%
Solicitors	23%	47%
Architects	34%	39%
Airline pilots	31%	52%
Surveyors	38%	31%
Bankers	34%	37%
Engineers	39%	38%
Sales Managers	61%	24%

Fig 17.1 The accountant's image: reproduced by kind permission of *Accountants' Weekly*

against which the accountant came out significantly ahead was sales managers, which is rather ironic in a way, when one considers that the particular skills of the sales manager are exactly the ones that the accountants could perhaps turn more to their own advantage.

It has to be admitted that there is not a great deal of glamour involved in their day-to-day working lives, and this is no doubt responsible for the rather dull and uninteresting image that is so often conjured up in people's minds at the very mention of the word 'accountant'. A lot of people also appear to think that an accountant's job is restricted to auditing, preparing accounts, and 'working out tax'. In some cases, this is, of course, quite correct, although it is by no means the whole story.

There is, in fact, more than one 'type' of accountant. The people who tend to concentrate on auditing, preparing accounts, and 'working out tax' will almost certainly be Chartered Accountants, and it will also be a Chartered Accountant with an office in the High Street that the small trader will consult for help and advice in the preparation of his accounts. They are also to be found working in industry and commerce.

Certified and Corporate Accountants are generally to be found in local and public authorities, whilst Cost and Management Accountants will generally be employed in industrial and commercial organizations, providing their management colleagues with the costing and financial information they need in order to enable them to control their businesses.

The traditional accountant's role

Between them, accountants have quite a comprehensive range of duties to perform. If we turn our focus back once more to the needs of a business organization—large or small, it makes no difference—they have a range of responsibilities which could be classified as being their 'traditional' function:

(1) *Stewardship*

1.1 Maintain up-to-date records of every transaction that takes place, affecting each and every one of the company's assets and liabilities.

1.2 Conduct regular physical checks of the company's assets to ensure that they coincide with the information recorded in the company's books of account.

1.3 Establish, control and monitor effective procedures for the protection of the company's assets.

1.4 Monitor the company's asset and liability levels against 'standard' ratios, and investigate variations.

(2) *Book-keeping and preparation of accounts*

Maintain adequate records in order to satisfy the requirements of:

2.1 Company law: the balance sheet, profit and loss statement, and the source and application of funds statement.

2.2 Statutory returns: for the Inland Revenue, Census of Production, Customs and Excise, etc.

2.3 Internal management: periodic reports, etc.

(3) *Financial transaction*

3.1 Recording of all purchases, sales and cash flow details.

3.2 Maintenance of fixed asset records, including depreciation calculations, etc.
3.3 Payment of employees, suppliers and other creditors.

(4) *Credit control and debt collection*
Ensuring that all money owed to the company is collected in due time.

The management accounting role

In addition to these 'traditional' roles, which mainly affect the company's relationship and dealings with the 'outside world', there is also the management accounting role to be considered, which involves the accountant in playing his part as an active member of the management team. This is the role upon which we have tended to focus throughout this book, and the following list of responsibilities is a reiteration of the ones we defined in Chapter 1.

(1) The Management Accountant has to help his colleagues to plan and co-ordinate the preparation of budgets and forecasts, and ensure that these are both reasonable and acceptable.
(2) He then has to prepare timely, relevant and accurate management reports and accounts, and
(3) Hold regular performance reviews with his management colleagues to help them interpret past results and update future forecasts and strategies.

What skills should a good accountant possess?

In order to be effective in the performance of these roles, a good accountant should not only be literate and numerate; he must also possess the ability to communicate. This is another prime function of management to which we have made many references, and which the Institute of Cost and Management Accountants endorses very forcefully by listing a number of personal skills that its members are expected to be able to display. These are:

(1) An enquiring mind to probe problems.
(2) An ability to analyse facts and figures.
(3) An ability to convey recommendations clearly and simply.

(4) An ability to express ideas clearly.
(5) An ability to 'get on' with people.
(6) A practical turn of mind.
(7) An ability to grasp principles of technical and mechanical processes.

In an article published in *Accountants' Weekly* on 18 April 1980, Richard Wilson, Director of the Post-Graduate Programme in Accounting and Financial Management at the University of Sheffield, listed the following attributes of effectiveness that accountants should concentrate on if we accept that basic aptitude and personality characteristics are essentially genetically determined, and if we see narrow technical skills as being inadequate for the task.

(1) A sense of identity—a knowledge of and insight into the role, aims and functions of the employing organization if it is to be made effective.
(2) Adaptability—the ability to identify and devise solutions to problems, and thereby react with flexibility to changing environmental demands.
(3) A capacity to test reality—the ability to search out, accurately perceive, and correctly interpret the real properties of the environment (rather than relying on precedent, assumptions, conventions, etc).
(4) A concern with 'truth'—the recognition that the major propositions of an empirical discipline should be open to refutation (which presupposes that criteria of acceptability exist, and that practitioners would recognize 'truth' if they saw it).
(5) An ability to integrate and to synthesize ideas—the capacity to transfer technical knowledge in a creative way from one situation to another.
(6) The ability to model socio-economic processes in a way that isolates the key variables in a problem situation as a necessary prelude to measurement and solution.
(7) A capacity to educate other managers about financial realities.
(8) An ability to manage one's own learning and development, rather than relying wholly on conventional wisdom etc.
(9) An ability to evaluate what one is doing, with an awareness of one's own value judgements.

These criteria put the accountant right into the middle of the management team where he belongs. This time he is cast rather in the role of an interpreter who brings together the knowledge and expertise of his fellow managers, in order to help them to translate their judgements into the common commercial language of finance. It consequently behoves all accountants to ensure that they are well qualified and capable of displaying these skills; and it behoves their colleagues to ensure that the accounting expertise at their disposal is employed to the maximum possible benefit and effective advantage of their company.

Time, gentlemen, please!

And that was really all we could say for the moment. In any case, it was already past 'last orders' time, and the landlord was beginning to show rather obvious signs of restlessness.

'Ah, well! A nod's as good as a wink to a blind horse!' said Andrew, who was probably as good an authority on the subject of blind horses as anybody, judging from the results of some of the racing 'information' that he had been known to pass on from time to time. 'And, by the way,' he added, as we made our way towards the door, 'talking of horses—did I ever tell you the story of how I first started my Andycab business? It all began in the summer of 1980, when I happened to be taking a few days' holiday at home. It was Derby Day, so I decided to watch the racing on television, and have a bet on the four televised races. It was a horse called Pontin Lad that started it all . . .'

Which just goes to show! We had always maintained that it was an Italian monk called Paccioli! In 1494! . . .

Appendix
Andco Ltd: case study

£'000		Last Year		This Year
FIXED ASSETS				
Land and buildings		530		530
Plant and machinery		312		445
Office furniture and equipment		120		120
Total at original cost		962		1,095
Less: Depreciation to date		245		332
Current written-down value		717		763
WORKING CAPITAL				
Current assets:				
(a) Stocks				
Consumable stores	82		55	
Raw materials	260		185	
Work-in-progress	120		227	
Finished goods	72		200	
Total:	534		667	
(b) Debtors				
Trade	298		241	
Prepayments	25		30	
Investment interest	2		2	
Total:	325		273	
(c) Short-term investments	20		20	
(d) Cash at bank and in hand	110		284	
Total current assets	989		1,244	
Current liabilities				
Trade creditors	110		95	
Loan interest due	20		20	
Taxation due	94		202	
Dividends due	5		30	
Total current liabilities	229		347	
NET WORKING CAPITAL		760		897
NET ASSETS		1,477		1,660
Share capital		800		800
Reserves		477		660
Shareholders' funds		1,277		1,460
Loan capital		200		200
CAPITAL EMPLOYED		1,477		1,660

Fig A.1 Andco Ltd: Balance sheets

£,000		Last Year		This Year
(a) Consumable stores				
Opening stock		82		82
Purchases		57		65
Total available		139		147
Less: Closing stock		82		55
Usages (transfers to work-in-progress)		57		92
(b) Raw materials				
Opening stock		120		260
Purchases		589		640
Total available		709		900
Less: Closing stock		260		185
Usages (transfers to work-in-progress)		449		715
(c) Work-in-progress				
Direct labour		245		365
Production overheads:				
Indirect labour	95		144	
Power and light	70		110	
Depreciation	64		77	
Rates and insurance	20		25	
Consumable stores (b/d)	57		92	
Total:		306		448
Charges during year (activity)		1,000		1,528
Opening stock		123		120
Total available		1,123		1,648
Less: Closing stock		120		227
Cost of goods manufactured		1,003		1,421
(d) Finished goods				
Opening stock		427		72
Total available		1,430		1,493
Less: Closing stock		72		200
Cost of goods sold		1,358		1,293

Fig A.2 Andco Ltd: Stock movements and cost of goods sold schedules

£'000		Last Year		This Year
Sales revenue		1,770		2,098
Less: Cost of sales		1,358		1,293
Gross profit/(loss)		412		805
Selling, distribution, and administration costs	277		342	
Depreciation (non-production)	10		10	
Total fixed costs		287		352
Operating profit/(loss)		125		453
Interest received from short-term outside investments		2		2
Profit before interest and tax		127		455
Interest payable on loan capital		20		20
Profit before tax		107		435
Tax on operational activities		94		202
Profit after tax		13		233
Dividends		5		50
Retained profit		8		183

Fig A.3 Andco Ltd: Profit and loss statements

	£'000	£'000	£'000
Sources of funds			
Operating profit before interest and tax			453
Adjustments for items not involving the movement of funds:			
Depreciation			87
Total funds generated from trading operations			540
Funds from other sources:			
Interest received from outside investments			2
Total funds generated			542
Application of funds			
Interest on loan capital		20	
Dividends paid:			
Last Year total	5		
This Year interim	20		
		25	
Tax paid		94	
Purchase of new plant		133	
			272
			270
Increase/(decrease) in working capital			
Increase in stocks		108	
Reduction in trade creditors:			
Charged to This Year (110 – 95)	15		
Pre-payments	30		
		45	
(Decrease) in debtors		–57	
Increase in net liquid funds (110 to 284)		174	
			270

Fig A.4.1 Andco Ltd: Source and application funds statement for This Year (SSAP 10 version)

£'000		Year 5
Sales revenue		1,130
Operational expenditure		955
Funds generated from trading operations		175
Financing costs		
Interest paid on loan capital	20	
Tax paid on Year 4's operations	32	
Share dividends paid	30	
		82
Net funds available for use		93
Net movements in circulating capital		
Increase in stocks	70	
Increase in debtors	35	
(Decrease) in cash	−72	
(Increase) in creditors	−30	
		−3
Operating funds available for long-term investment		90
Investment in new buildings and plant		−90
Additional capital required for investment		0

Fig A.4.2 Andco Ltd: Source and application of funds statement for This Year (recommended version)

£'000	*Q.1*	*Q.2*	*Q.3*	*Q.4*	*Total*
(1) Opening balance	110	−48	−48	−35	110
(2) Sales revenue	450	450	520	735	2,155
(3) Conversion costs					
Employee costs	−135	−175	−175	−175	−660
Third-party costs	−320	−270	−240	−221	−1,051
(4) Non-operational expenditure					
Loan interest	−20	:	:	:	−20
Div's (Last Year)	:	−5	:	:	−5
(This Year)	:	:	:	−20	−20
Tax (Last Year)	:	:	−94	:	−94
(5) Interest from outside investment	:	:	2	:	2
(6) Purchase of new plant	−133	:	:	:	−133
(7) Closing balance	−48	−48	−35	284	284

Fig A.5 Andco Ltd: Cash flow forecast for This Year

	ASSETS								LIABILITIES							
	Fixed assets	*Depreciation*	*Stocks*	*Trade debtors*	*Pre-payments*	*Investment interest*	*Outside investments*	*Cash/bank*	*Share capital*	*Reserves*	*Loan capital*	*Trade creditors*	*Loan int. due*	*Tax due*	*Dividends due*	*Profit and loss*
(1) Opening balance sheet equation	962	− 245	+ 534	+ 298	+ 25	+ 2	+ 20	+ 110	= 800	+ 477	+ 200	+ 110	+ 20	+ 94	+ 5	+ —
(2) Payment of liabilities:																
Loan interest								− 20 =					− 20			
Tax due								− 94 =						− 94		
Dividends due								− 5 =							− 5	
(3) Transfer of pre-payments			25		− 25											
(4) Interest received						− 2		+ 2								
(5) Trading operations																
Taxation														+ 202		− 202
Dividends															+ 50	− 50
Retained profits										+ 183						− 183
(6) Intermediate balance sheet equation	962	− 245	+ 559	+ 298	—	—	+ 20	− 7	= 800	+ 660	+ 200	+ 110	—	+ 202	+ 50	− 435
(8) Purchase of new plant	133							− 133								
(9) Depreciation of fixed assets		− 87						=								− 87
(10) Increase in stocks			+ 108					− 108								
(11) Reduction in debtors				− 57				+ 57								
(12) Pre-payments					+ 30			− 30								
(13) Outside inv't interest due						+ 2		=								+ 2
(14) Reduction in creditors								− 15 =				− 15				
(15) Loan interest due													+ 20			− 20
(16) Payment of interim dividend								− 20 =							− 20	
(17) Transfer of cash generated from trading								+ 540 =								+ 540
(7) Closing balance sheet equation	1,095	− 332	+ 667	+ 241	+ 30	+ 2	+ 20	+ 284	= 800	+ 660	* 200	95	+ 20	+ 202	+ 30	

Fig A.6 Andco Ltd: Transaction analysis work-sheet for This Year

Appendix Matthew Grimble Ltd: case study

£'000	*Year 1*		*Year 2*	
Fixed assets at cost:				
Land and buildings		40		60
Plant and machinery		60		95
Total cost		100		155
Less: Depreciation to date		10		25
Written down book value		90		130
Stocks:				
Consumable stores	5		5	
Raw materials	20		30	
Work-in-progress	15		30	
Finished goods	50		65	
Total stocks	90		130	
Trade debtors	75		105	
Pre-payments (A.C.T.)	4		:	
Cash/bank	50		23	
Current assets	219		258	
Trade creditors	35		40	
Tax due	4		25	
Dividends due	10		15	
Loan interest due	8		8	
Bank overdraft	:		:	
Current liabilities	57		88	
NET WORKING CAPITAL		162		170
NET ASSETS		252		300
Share capital		120		120
Reserves		72		120
Shareholders' funds		192		240
Loan capital		60		60
CAPITAL EMPLOYED		252		300

Fig G.1 Matthew Grimble Ltd: Balance sheets

Year 3	*Year 4*	*Year 5*	*Year 6*
75	85	120	140
155	225	280	350
230	310	400	490
50	80	120	170
180	230	280	320
10	15	20	25
35	45	55	65
40	50	65	70
100	140	180	210
185	250	320	370
135	175	210	265
:	:	:	:
:	88	16	21
320	513	546	656
60	80	110	140
34	32	35	76
20	30	30	60
8	20	20	20
15	:	:	:
137	162	195	296
183	351	351	360
363	581	631	680
120	200	200	200
183	231	281	330
303	431	481	530
60	150	150	150
363	581	631	680

£'000		Year 1		Year 2
(a) Consumable stores				
Opening stock		:		5
Purchases		15		15
		15		20
Less: Closing stock		5		5
Usages (to work-in-progress)		10		15
(b) Raw materials				
Opening stock		:		20
Purchases		130		130
		130		150
Less: Closing stock		20		30
Usages (to work-in-progress)		110		120
(c) Work-in-progress				
Direct labour		75		105
Overheads:				
Indirect labour	45		55	
Production administration	10		15	
Power and light	15		20	
Depreciation	10		10	
Rates and insurance	15		15	
Consumable stores	10		15	
Total		105		130
Charges during year ('activity')		290		355
Opening stock b/fd		:		15
		290		370
Less: Closing stock c/fd		15		30
COST OF GOODS MANUFACTURED		275		340
(d) Finished goods				
Opening stock b/fd		:		50
		275		390
Less: Closing stock c/fd		50		65
COST OF GOODS SOLD		225		325

Fig G.2 Matthew Grimble Ltd: Stock movements and cost of goods sold schedules

Year 3		Year 4		Year 5		Year 6	
	5		10		15		20
	25		30		35		40
	30		40		50		60
	10		15		20		25
	20		25		30		35
	30		35		45		55
	175		195		230		265
	205		230		275		320
	35		45		55		65
	170		185		220		255
	155		200		230		265
80		100		120		155	
20		25		35		45	
25		30		35		50	
20		25		35		40	
20		25		30		40	
20		25		30		35	
	185		230		285		365
	510		615		735		885
	30		40		50		65
	540		655		785		950
	40		50		65		70
	500		605		720		880
	65		100		140		180
	565		705		860		1,060
	100		140		180		210
	465		565		680		850

£'000	*Year 1*		*Year 2*	
Sales		450		595
Less: Cost of goods sold		225		325
Gross trading profit		225		270
Product promotion	55		65	
Selling and administration				
Employee costs	55		75	
Third party costs	25		25	
Depreciation (non-production)	:		5	
Total fixed costs		135		170
Operating profit/(loss) Before interest and tax		90		100
Interest payable on loan capital		8		8
NET PROFIT BEFORE TAX		82		92
Taxation		:		29
Profit after tax		82		63
Dividends		10		15
RETAINED PROFIT		72		48
Number of employees		38		48

Fig G.3 Matthew Grimble Ltd: Profit and loss statements

Year 3		*Year 4*		*Year 5*		*Year 6*	
	805		950		1,130		1,450
	465		565		680		850
	340		385		450		600
80		100		130		160	
95		100		120		150	
35		50		60		75	
5		5		5		10	
	215		255		315		395
	125		130		135		205
	8		20		20		20
	117		110		115		185
	34		32		35		76
	83		78		80		109
	20		30		30		60
	63		48		50		49
	62		68		73		79

£'000		Year 1		Year 2
Sources of funds:				
Operating profit before interest and tax		90		100
Add back: Total depreciation		10		15
Total funds generated from trading operations		100		115
Additional share capital	120		:	
Additional loan capital	60		:	
Total funds from other sources		180		:
TOTAL FUNDS GENERATED		280		115
Application of funds:				
Interest on loan capital	:		8	
Dividends paid	:		10	
Tax paid—A.C.T./offset	:		4	
Mainstream tax	:		:	
Purchase of fixed assets	100		55	
Total:		100		77
Increase/(decrease) in working capital				
Increase/(decrease) in stocks	90		40	
Increase/(decrease) in debtors	75		30	
Increase/(decrease) in cash	50		−27	
(Increase)/decrease in creditors	−35		− 5	
Net increase/(decrease)		180		38
Total application of funds		280		115

Fig G.4.1 Matthew Grimble Ltd: Source and application of funds statements (SSAP 10 version)

Year 3		Year 4		Year 5		Year 6	
	125		130		135		205
	25		30		40		50
	150		160		175		255
:		80		:		:	
:		90		:		:	
	:		170		:		:
	150		330		175		255
8		8		20		20	
15		20		30		30	
−4		:		:		:	
29		34		32		35	
75		80		90		90	
	123		142		172		175
55		65		70		50	
30		40		35		55	
−38		103		−72		5	
−20		−20		−30		−30	
	27		188		3		80
	150		330		175		255

£'000		Year 1		Year 2
Sales revenue		450		595
Operational expenditure		350		480
Funds generated from trading operations		100		115
Financing costs				
Loan interest	—		8	
Tax paid	—		4	
Dividends paid	—		10	
		—		22
Net funds available for use		100		93
Net movements in circulating capital				
Increase in stocks	90		40	
Increase in debtors	75		30	
(Increase) in creditors	−35		− 5	
Increase/decrease in cash	50		−27	
		180		38
Operating funds available for long-term investment		− 80		55
Investments in buildings and plant		−100		−55
Additional capital required for investment		−180		0

Fig G.4.2 Matthew Grimble Ltd: Source and application of funds statements (Recommended version)

Year 3		*Year 4*		*Year 5*		*Year 6*	
	805		950		1,130		1,450
	655		790		955		1,195
	150		160		175		255
8		8		20		20	
25		34		32		35	
15		20		30		30	
	48		62		82		85
	102		98		93		170
55		65		70		50	
30		40		35		55	
−20		−20		−30		−30	
−38		103		−72		5	
	27		188		3		80
	75		− 90		90		90
	− 75		− 80		− 90		− 90
	0		−170		0		0

CASH FLOW FORECAST FOR YEAR 6

£'000	*Q.1*	*Q.2*	*Q.3*	*Q.4*	*Total*
1 Opening balance b/fd	16	− 59	− 99	− 57	16
2 Clearance of Year 5 items					
Tax paid—Year 5 A.C.T.	:	:	− 13	:	− 13
—Year 5 M.C.T.	:	:	:	− 22	− 22
Dividends due	:	− 30	:	:	− 30
Loan interest	− 20	:	:	:	− 20
3 Payment of salaries					
Direct labour	− 60	− 65	− 70	− 70	−265
Indirect labour	− 35	− 40	− 40	− 40	−155
Selling and admin.	− 30	− 40	− 40	− 40	−150
4 Receipts from debtors	320	325	350	400	1,395
5 Payments to creditors					
Year 6 trading	−180	−170	−145	−150	−645
Fixed assets	− 70	− 20	:	:	− 90
6 Closing balance c/fd	− 59	− 99	− 57	21	21

Fig G.5 Matthew Grimble Ltd: Cash flow forecast for Year 6

VALUE ADDED STATEMENT

£'000		Year 1		Year 2		Year 3		Year 4		Year 5		Year 6	
Sales revenue			450		595		805		950		1,130		1,450
Less: Net third party purchases													
Total third party (b/d)		265		285		380		455		555		675	
(Incr.)/decr. in stocks		−90		−40		−55		−65		−70		−50	
Net purchases			175		245		325		390		485		625
GROSS ADDED VALUE			275		350		480		560		645		825
Employee costs:													
Direct process labour	(12.2)		75		105		155		200		230		265
Indirect labour	(12.2)		45		55		80		100		120		155
Selling and administration	(12.3)		55		75		95		100		120		150
Total employee costs			175		235		330		400		470		570
Loan interest			8		8		8		20		20		20
Depreciation (total)			10		15		25		30		40		50
Taxation			:		29		34		32		35		76
Dividends			10		15		20		30		30		60
Retained profit			72		48		63		48		50		49
GROSS ADDED VALUE			275		350		480		560		645		825

Fig G.6 Matthew Grimble Ltd: Value added statements

CAPITAL ALLOWANCES						
	Years					
	—1	*—2*	*—3*	*—4*	*—5*	*—6*
(1) Current rate of capital allowances (%)						
(a) Plant and machinery						
First year allowance	100	:	:	:	:	:
(b) Industrial buildings						
Initial allowance	75	:	:	:	:	:
Writing down allowance	4	4	4	4	4	4
(2) Capital investment (£'000)						
(a) Plant and machinery	−60	−35	−60	−70	−55	−70
(b) Industrial buildings	−40	−20	−15	−10	−35	−20
Total:	−100	−55	−75	−80	−90	−90
(3) Value of allowances						
(a) Plant and machinery						
First year allowance	60	35	60	70	55	70
(b) Industrial buildings						
Initial allowance	30	15	12	7	26	15
Writing down allowance						
Year 1	2	1	2	1	2	1
2	>	1	1	:	1	1
3	>	>	1	:	1	:
4	>	>	>	:	1	:
5	>	>	>	>	1	1
6	>	>	>	>	>	1
Total	92	52	76	78	87	89

(*Note:* These calculations are based on the rates of allowances applicable prior to the publication of the 1984 Budget.)

Fig G.7 Matthew Grimble Ltd: Capital allowance schedule

CORPORATION TAX LIABILITY AND PAYMENTS PHASING

£'000	—1	—2	—3	—4	—5	—6
	Years					
(1) Profit before tax	82	92	117	110	115	185
(2) Depreciation added back	10	15	25	30	40	50
(3) (1 + 2)	92	107	142	140	155	235
(4) Capital allowances (G.7)	92	52	76	78	87	89
(5) (3 – 4)	:	55	66	62	68	146
(6) Prior-year losses utilized	:	:	:	:	:	:
(7) Taxable profit	:	55	66	62	68	146
(8) Corporation tax @ –52%	:	–29	–34	–32	–35	–76
(9) Maximum A.C.T. offset (–30% of 7)	:	–17	–20	–19	–20	–44
(10) Dividends distributed	–10	–15	–20	–30	–30	–60
(11) A.C.T. payable (3/7ths of 10)	– 4	– 6	– 9	–13	–13	–26
(12) A.C.T. offset c/fd (to match 11 to 9 when 11 < 9) Year 1 only	4	– 4	:	:	:	:
(13) Net offset (11 + 12)	:	–10	– 9	–13	–13	–26
(14) Net mainstream tax (8–13)	:	–19	–25	–19	–22	–50
(15) Phasing of payment liability (in Year Y + 1)						
A.C.T. (11) (within 3 months of dividend payment)	:	– 4	– 6	– 9	–13	–13
M.C.T. (14)	:	:	–19	–25	–19	–22
Total cash commitment	:	– 4	–25	–34	–32	–35

(*Note:* The calculations of the capital allowances in line 4 are based on the rates applicable before the publication of the 1984 Budget.)

Fig G.8 Matthew Grimble Ltd: Corporation Tax liabilities and payments schedules

Year 1 (£'000)	F. ass. @ cost	Depreci-ation	Total stocks	Trade debtors	Pre-payments	CASH	=	Share capital	Reserves	Loan capital	Trade cred'rs	Tax due	Div'nds due	Loan Interest due	Profit and loss
1 Opening balance equation	:	:	:	:	:	180	=	120	:	60	:	:	:	:	:
2 Clearance of b/fd liabilities:															
Tax due: Advance Corp'n tax	:	:	:	:	:	:	=	:	:	:	:	:	:	:	:
Net mainstream tax	:	:	:	:	:	:	=	:	:	:	:	:	:	:	:
Dividends due	:	:	:	:	:	:	=	:	:	:	:	:	:	:	:
Loan interest due	:	:	:	:	:	:	=	:	:	:	:	:	:	:	:
3 Stock movements and cost of G.S.															
Consumables purchased	:	:	15	:	:	:	=	:	:	:	15	:	:	:	:
Raw materials purchased	:	:	130	:	:	:	=	:	:	:	130	:	:	:	:
Direct labour	:	:	75	:	:	− 75	=	:	:	:	:	:	:	:	:
Indirect labour	:	:	45	:	:	− 45	=	:	:	:	:	:	:	:	:
Production administration	:	:	10	:	:	:	=	:	:	:	10	:	:	:	:
Power and light	:	:	15	:	:	:	=	:	:	:	15	:	:	:	:
Depreciation	:	−10	10	:	:	:	=	:	:	:	:	:	:	:	:
Rates and insurance	:	:	15	:	:	:	=	:	:	:	15	:	:	:	:
4 Profit and loss															
Sales revenue	:	:	:	450	:	:	=	:	:	:	:	:	:	:	450
Cost of goods sold	:	:	−225	:	:	:	=	:	:	:	:	:	:	:	−225
Product promotion	:	:	:	:	:	:	=	:	:	:	55	:	:	:	− 55
Sell/admin: Third party	:	:	:	:	:	:	=	:	:	:	25	:	:	:	− 25
Added value	:	:	:	:	:	− 55	=	:	:	:	:	:	:	:	− 55
Loan interest	:	:	:	:	:	:	=	:	:	:	:	:	:	8	− 8
Depreciation (non-prod'n)	:	:	:	:	:	:	=	:	:	:	:	:	:	:	:
5 Fixed assets purchased	100	:	:	:	:	:	=	:	:	:	100	:	:	:	:
6 Intermediate balance equation	100	−10	90	450	:	5	=	120	:	60	365	:	:	8	82
7 Payments by debtors	:	:	:	−375	:	375	=	:	:	:	:	:	:	:	:
8 Payments to creditors	:	:	:	:	:	−330	=	:	:	:	−330	:	:	:	:
9 Tax due—A.C.T./offset	:	:	:	:	4	:	=	:	:	:	:	4	:	:	:
—Mainstream tax	:	:	:	:	:	:	=	:	:	:	:	:	:	:	:
10 Dividends due	:	:	:	:	:	:	=	:	:	:	:	:	10	:	− 10
11 Transfer to reserves	:	:	:	:	:	:	=	:	72	:	:	:	:	:	− 72
12 Closing balance equation	100	−10	90	75	4	50	=	120	72	60	35	4	10	8	:

Fig G.9.1 Matthew Grimble Ltd: Transaction analysis work-sheet for Year 1

Year 2 (£'000)	F. ass. @ cost	Depreci-ation	Total stocks	Trade debtors	Pre-payments	CASH	=	Share capital	Reserves	Loan capital	Trade cred'rs	Tax due	Div'nds due	Loan Interest due	Profit and loss
1 Opening balance equation	100	−10	90	75	4	50	=	120	72	60	35	4	10	8	:
2 Clearance of b/fd liabilities:															
Tax due: Advance corp'n tax	:	:	:	:	:	− 4	=	:	:	:	:	−4	:	:	:
Net mainstream tax	:	:	:	:	:	:	=	:	:	:	:	:	:	:	:
Dividends due	:	:	:	:	:	− 10	=	:	:	:	:	:	− 10	:	:
Loan interest due	:	:	:	:	:	− 8	=	:	:	:	:	:	:	− 8	:
3 Stock movements and cost of G.S.															
Consumables purchased	:	:	15	:	:	:	=	:	:	:	15	:	:	:	:
Raw materials purchased	:	:	130	:	:	:	=	:	:	:	130	:	:	:	:
Direct labour	:	:	105	:	:	−105	=	:	:	:	:	:	:	:	:
Indirect labour	:	:	55	:	:	− 55	=	:	:	:	:	:	:	:	:
Production administration	:	:	15	:	:	:	=	:	:	:	15	:	:	:	:
Power and light	:	:	20	:	:	:	=	:	:	:	20	:	:	:	:
Depreciation	:	−10	10	:	:	:	=	:	:	:	:	:	:	:	:
Rates and insurance	:	:	15	:	:	:	=	:	:	:	15	:	:	:	:
4 Profit and loss:															
Sales revenue	:	:	:	595	:	:	=	:	:	:	:	:	:	:	595
Cost of goods sold	:	:	−325	:	:	:	=	:	:	:	:	:	:	:	−325
Product promotion	:	:	:	:	:	:	=	:	:	:	65	:	:	:	− 65
Sell/admin: Third party	:	:	:	:	:	:	=	:	:	:	25	:	:	:	− 25
Added value	:	:	:	:	:	− 75	=	:	:	:	:	:	:	:	− 75
Loan interest	:	:	:	:	:	:	=	:	:	:	:	:	:	8	− 8
Depreciation (non-prod'n)	:	− 5	:	:	:	:	=	:	:	:	:	:	:	:	− 5
5 Fixed assets purchased	55	:	:	:	:	:	=	:	:	:	55	:	:	:	:
6 Intermediate balance equation	155	−25	130	670	4	−207	=	120	72	60	375	:	:	8	92
7 Payments by debtors	:	:	:	−565	:	565	=	:	:	:	:	:	:	:	:
8 Payments to creditors	:	:	:	:	:	−335	=	:	:	:	−335	:	:	:	:
9 Tax due—A.C.T. offset	:	:	:	:	−4	:	=	:	:	:	:	−4	:	:	:
—Advance corp'n tax	:	:	:	:	:	:	=	:	:	:	:	10	:	:	− 10
—Net mainstream tax	:	:	:	:	:	:	=	:	:	:	:	19	:	:	− 19
10 Dividends due	:	:	:	:	:	:	=	:	:	:	:	:	15	:	− 15
11 Transfer to reserves	:	:	:	:	:	:	=	:	48	:	:	:	:	:	− 48
12 Closing balance equation	155	−25	130	105	:	23	=	120	120	60	40	25	15	8	:

Fig G.9.2 Matthew Grimble Ltd: Transaction analysis work-sheet for Year 2

Year 3 (£'000)	F. ass. @ cost	Depreci-ation	Total stocks	Trade debtors	CASH	=	Share capital	Reserves	Loan capital	Trade creditors	Tax due	Div'nds due	Loan Interest due	Profit and loss
1 Opening balance equation	155	−25	130	105	23	=	120	120	60	40	25	15	8	:
2 Clearance of b/fd liabilities:														
Tax due: Net A.C.T./offset	:	:	:	:	− 6	=	:	:	:	:	− 6	:	:	:
Net mainstream tax	:	:	:	:	− 19	=	:	:	:	:	−19	:	:	:
Dividends due	:	:	:	:	− 15	=	:	:	:	:	:	−15	:	:
Loan interest due	:	:	:	:	− 8	=	:	:	:	:	:	:	− 8	:
3 Stock movements and cost of G.S.														
Consumables purchased	:	:	25	:	:	=	:	:	:	25	:	:	:	:
Raw materials purchased	:	:	175	:	:	=	:	:	:	175	:	:	:	:
Direct labour	:	:	155	:	−155	=	:	:	:	:	:	:	:	:
Indirect labour	:	:	80	:	− 80	=	:	:	:	:	:	:	:	:
Production administration	:	:	20	:	:	=	:	:	:	20	:	:	:	:
Power and light	:	:	25	:	:	=	:	:	:	25	:	:	:	:
Depreciation	:	−20	20	:	:	=	:	:	:	:	:	:	:	:
Rates and insurance	:	:	20	:	:	=	:	:	:	20	:	:	:	:
4 Profit and loss														
Sales revenue	:	:	:	805	:	=	:	:	:	:	:	:	:	805
Cost of goods sold	:	:	−465	:	:	=	:	:	:	:	:	:	:	−465
Product promotion	:	:	:	:	:	=	:	:	:	80	:	:	:	− 80
Sell/admin: Third party	:	:	:	:	:	=	:	:	:	35	:	:	:	− 35
Added value	:	:	:	:	− 95	=	:	:	:	:	:	:	:	− 95
Loan interest	:	:	:	:	:	=	:	:	:	:	:	:	8	− 8
Depreciation (non-prod'n)	:	−5	:	:	:	=	:	:	:	:	:	:	:	− 5
5 Fixed assets purchased	75	:	:	:	:	=	:	:	:	75	:	:	:	:
6 Intermediate balance equation	230	−50	185	910	−355	=	120	120	60	495	:	:	8	117
7 Payments by debtors	:	:	:	−775	775	=	:	:	:	:	:	:	:	:
8 Payments to creditors	:	:	:	:	−435	=	:	:	:	−435	:	:	:	:
9 Tax due: Advance Corp'n tax	:	:	:	:	:	=	:	:	:	:	9	:	:	− 9
Net mainstream tax	:	:	:	:	:	=	:	:	:	:	25	:	:	− 25
10 Dividends due	:	:	:	:	:	=	:	:	:	:	:	20	:	− 20
11 Transfer to reserves	:	:	:	:	:	=	:	63	:	:	:	:	:	− 63
12 Closing balance equation	230	−50	185	135	− 15	=	120	183	60	60	34	20	8	:

Fig G.9.3 Matthew Grimble Ltd: Transaction analysis work-sheet for Year 3

	Year 4 (£'000)	F. ass. @ cost	Depreci-ation	Total stocks	Trade debtors	CASH	=	Share capital	Reserves	Loan capital	Trade creditors	Tax due	Div'nds due	Loan Interest due	Profit and loss
1	Opening balance equation	230	−50	185	135	− 15	=	120	183	60	60	34	20	8	:
2	Clearance of b/fd liabilities:														
	Tax due: Advance corp'n tax	:	:	:	:	− 9	=	:	:	:	:	− 9	:	:	:
	Net mainstream tax	:	:	:	:	− 25	=	:	:	:	:	−25	:	:	:
	Dividends due	:	:	:	:	− 20	=	:	:	:	:	:	−20	:	:
	Loan interest due	:	:	:	:	− 8	=	:	:	:	:	:	:	− 8	:
3	Stock movements and cost of G.S.:														
	Consumables purchased	:	:	30	:	:	=	:	:	:	30	:	:	:	:
	Raw materials purchased	:	:	195	:	:	=	:	:	:	195	:	:	:	:
	Direct labour	:	:	200	:	−200	=	:	:	:	:	:	:	:	:
	Indirect labour	:	:	100	:	−100	=	:	:	:	:	:	:	:	:
	Production administration	:	:	25	:	:	=	:	:	:	25	:	:	:	:
	Power and light	:	:	30	:	:	=	:	:	:	30	:	:	:	:
	Depreciation	:	−25	25	:	:	=	:	:	:	:	:	:	:	:
	Rates and insurance	:	:	25	:	:	=	:	:	:	25	:	:	:	:
4	Profit and loss:														
	Sales revenue	:	:	:	950	:	=	:	:	:	:	:	:	:	950
	Cost of goods sold	:	:	−565	:	:	=	:	:	:	:	:	:	:	−565
	Product promotion	:	:	:	:	:	=	:	:	:	100	:	:	:	−100
	Sell/admin: Third party	:	:	:	:	:	=	:	:	:	50	:	:	:	− 50
	Added value	:	:	:	:	−100	=	:	:	:	:	:	:	:	−100
	Loan interest	:	:	:	:	:	=	:	:	:	:	:	:	20	− 20
	Depreciation (non-prod'n)	:	− 5	:	:	:	=	:	:	:	:	:	:	:	− 5
5	Fixed assets purchased	80	:	:	:	:	=	:	:	:	80	:	:	:	:
6	Intermediate balance equation	310	−80	250	1,085	−477	=	120	183	60	595	:	:	20	110
7	Payments by debtors	:	:	:	−910	910	=	:	:	:	:	:	:	:	:
8	Payments to creditors	:	:	:	:	−515	=	:	:	:	−515	:	:	:	:
9	Tax due: Advance corp'n tax	:	:	:	:	:	=	:	:	:	:	13	:	:	− 13
	Net mainstream tax	:	:	:	:	:	=	:	:	:	:	19	:	:	− 19
10	Dividends due	:	:	:	:	:	=	:	:	:	:	:	30	:	− 30
11	Transfer to reserves	:	:	:	:	:	=	:	48	:	:	:	:	:	− 48
12	Additional share capital	:	:	:	:	80	=	80	:	:	:	:	:	:	:
	loan capital	:	:	:	:	90	=	:	:	90	:	:	:	:	:
13	Closing balance equation	310	−80	250	175	88	=	200	231	150	80	32	30	20	:

Fig G.9.4 Matthew Grimble Ltd: Transaction analysis work-sheet for Year 4

Year 5 (£'000)	F. ass. @ cost	Depreci-ation	Total stocks	Trade debtors	CASH	=	Share capital	Reserves	Loan capital	Trade creditors	Tax due	Div'nds due	Loan Interest due	Profit and loss
1 Opening balance equation	310	− 80	250	175	88	=	200	231	150	80	32	30	20	:
2 Clearance of b/fd liabilities														
Tax due: Advance corp'n tax	:	:	:	:	− 13	=	:	:	:	:	−13	:	:	:
Net mainstream tax	:	:	:	:	− 19	=	:	:	:	:	−19	:	:	:
Dividends due	:	:	:	:	− 30	=	:	:	:	:	:	−30	:	:
Loan interest due	:	:	:	:	− 20	=	:	:	:	:	:	:	−20	:
3 Stock movements and cost of G.S.														
Consumables purchased	:	:	35	:	:	=	:	:	:	35	:	:	:	:
Raw materials purchased	:	:	230	:	:	=	:	:	:	230	:	:	:	:
Direct labour	:	:	230	:	−230	=	:	:	:	:	:	:	:	:
Indirect labour	:	:	120	:	−120	=	:	:	:	:	:	:	:	:
Production administration	:	:	35	:	:	=	:	:	:	35	:	:	:	:
Power and light	:	:	35	:	:	=	:	:	:	35	:	:	:	:
Depreciation	:	− 35	35	:	:	=	:	:	:	:	:	:	:	:
Rates and insurance	:	:	30	:	:	=	:	:	:	30	:	:	:	:
4 Profit and loss:														
Sales revenue	:	:	:	1,130	:	=	:	:	:	:	:	:	:	1,130
Cost of goods sold	:	:	−680	:	:	=	:	:	:	:	:	:	:	−680
Product promotion	:	:	:	:	:	=	:	:	:	130	:	:	:	−130
Sell/admin: Third party	:	:	:	:	:	=	:	:	:	60	:	:	:	− 60
Added value	:	:	:	:	−120	=	:	:	:	:	:	:	:	−120
Loan interest	:	:	:	:	:	=	:	:	:	:	:	:	20	− 20
Depreciation (non-prod'n)	:	− 5	:	:	:	=	:	:	:	:	:	:	:	− 5
5 Fixed assets purchased	90	:	:	:	:	=	:	:	:	90	:	:	:	:
6 Intermediate balance equation	400	−120	320	1,305	−464	=	200	231	150	725	:	:	20	115
7 Payments by debtors	:	:	:	−1,095	1,095	=	:	:	:	:	:	:	:	:
8 Payments to creditors	:	:	:	:	−615	=	:	:	:	−615	:	:	:	:
9 Tax due: Advance corp'n tax	:	:	:	:	:	=	:	:	:	:	13	:	:	− 13
Net mainstream tax	:	:	:	:	:	=	:	:	:	:	22	:	:	− 22
10 Dividends due	:	:	:	:	:	=	:	:	:	:	:	30	:	− 30
11 Transfer to reserves	:	:	:	:	:	=	:	50	:	:	:	:	:	− 50
12 Closing balance equation	400	−120	320	210	16	=	200	281	150	110	35	30	20	:

Fig G.9.5 Matthew Grimble Ltd: Transaction analysis work-sheet for Year 5

	Year 6 (£'000)	F. ass. @ cost	Depreci-ation	Total stocks	Trade debtors	CASH	=	Share capital	Reserves	Loan capital	Trade creditors	Tax due	Div'nds due	Loan Interest due	Profit and loss
1	Opening balance equation	400	−120	320	210	16	=	200	281	150	110	35	30	20	:
2	Clearance of b/fd liabilities:														
	Tax due: Advance corp'n tax	:	:	:	:	− 13	=	:	:	:	:	−13	:	:	:
	Net mainstream tax	:	:	:	:	− 22	=	:	:	:	:	−22	:	:	:
	Dividends due	:	:	:	:	− 30	=	:	:	:	:	:	−30	:	:
	Loan interest due	:	:	:	:	− 20	=	:	:	:	:	:	:	−20	:
3	Stock movements and cost of G.S.														
	Consumables purchased	:	:	40	:	:	=	:	:	:	40	:	:	:	:
	Raw materials purchased	:	:	265	:	:	=	:	:	:	265	:	:	:	:
	Direct labour	:	:	265	:	−265	=	:	:	:	:	:	:	:	:
	Indirect labour	:	:	155	:	−155	=	:	:	:	:	:	:	:	:
	Production administration	:	:	45	:	:	=	:	:	:	45	:	:	:	:
	Power and light	:	:	50	:	:	=	:	:	:	50	:	:	:	:
	Depreciation	:	− 40	40	:	:	=	:	:	:	:	:	:	:	:
	Rates and insurance	:	:	40	:	:	=	:	:	:	40	:	:	:	:
4	Profit and loss														
	Sales revenue	:	:	:	1,450	:	=	:	:	:	:	:	:	:	1,450
	Cost of goods sold	:	:	−850	:	:	=	:	:	:	:	:	:	:	−850
	Product promotion	:	:	:	:	:	=	:	:	:	160	:	:	:	−160
	Sell/admin: Third party	:	:	:	:	:	=	:	:	:	75	:	:	:	− 75
	Added value	:	:	:	:	−150	=	:	:	:	:	:	:	:	−150
	Loan interest	:	:	:	:	:	=	:	:	:	:	:	:	20	− 20
	Depreciation (non-prod'n)	:	− 10	:	:	:	=	:	:	:	:	:	:	:	− 10
5	Fixed assets purchased	90	:	:	:	:	=	:	:	:	90	:	:	:	:
6	Intermediate balance equation	490	−170	370	1,660	−639	=	200	281	150	875	:	:	20	185
7	Payments by debtors	:	:	:	−1,395	1,395	=	:	:	:	:	:	:	:	:
8	Payments to creditors	:	:	:	:	−735	=	:	:	:	−735	:	:	:	:
9	Tax due: Advance corp'n tax	:	:	:	:	:	=	:	:	:	:	26	:	:	− 26
	Net mainstream tax	:	:	:	:	:	=	:	:	:	:	50	:	:	− 50
10	Dividends due	:	:	:	:	:	=	:	:	:	:	:	60	:	− 60
11	Transfer to reserves	:	:	:	:	:	=	:	49	:	:	:	:	:	− 49
12	Closing balance equation	490	−170	370	265	21	=	200	330	150	140	76	60	20	:

Fig G.9.6 Matthew Grimble Ltd: Transaction analysis work-sheet for Year 6

Glossary of terms

Accelerated depreciation Any method of depreciation which charges higher amounts for the use of an asset during the early years of its life than is charged in later years.

Account A page in the book-keeping ledger onto which is recorded details of all the financial transactions relating to one individual supplier, customer, asset, liability, or type of expense or receipt.

Accounting The art of preparing accounting reports from book-keeping records in accordance with acknowledged methods and conventions.

Accounting policies The four accounting 'policies' defined in SSAP 2 *Disclosure of Accounting Policies* were:

(a) Going concern
(b) Consistency
(c) Prudence
(d) Accruals

They were all incorporated into the Companies Act of 1981 as 'accounting principles' to be followed, and each is defined in this Glossary under its appropriate heading.

Accounting principles There are five basic accounting 'principles' defined in the Companies Act of 1981, to which all companies are expected to adhere in the preparation and presentation of their accounts. The first four of these coincide with the four accounting 'policies' defined in SSAP 2 *Disclosure of Accounting Policies*, which was issued in 1971, and the fifth 'principle' is that of 'aggregation'. Each of the principles are defined in this glossary under its appropriate heading.

Accounts, nominal *See* Nominal accounts.

Accounts payable Money owed by a business to its creditors, or suppliers of goods or services.

Accounts, real *See* Real accounts.

Accounts receivable Money owed to a business by its Debtors, or customers.

Accrual Expense or revenue outstanding at the end of a trading period which needs to be 'accrued' for inclusion into the accounting records for the period.

Accrual accounting The accounting concept which decrees that all expenses and revenues should be taken into account as and when they become *due*, rather than when they are actually paid or received. It consequently represents a fundamental difference between 'cash' and 'expense'. The accruals concept is one of four accounting 'policies' specified in SSAP 2 *Disclosure of Accounting Policies*, issued in 1971, and was also defined in the Companies Act of 1981 as one of five accounting 'principles' to which all companies are expected to adhere during the course of preparing and presenting their accounts.

Accumulated profit *See* Retained profit

Acid test ratio A prime measure of a company's liquidity, of ability to meet its short-term debts. Sometimes referred to as the 'quick ratio', this is a more stringent test of liquidity than the current ratio, because it assumes that stocks cannot necessarily be regarded as readily-convertible into the liquid funds which are needed to discharge a company's short-term liabilities.

$$\text{Acid test ratio} = \frac{\text{Liquid assets}}{\text{Current liabilities}}$$

Activity ratios *See* Turnover ratios.

Added value The difference between the price that a company pays for the goods and services that it buys from suppliers *outside* the company, and the price at which it sells the goods or services that it produces to its customers *outside* the company. It consequently focuses attention on what is happening *inside* the company, and is made up of the following constituent elements:

Employee costs
\+ Capital usage costs (Depreciation)
= CONVERSION COST
\+ Profit (Made up of taxation, dividends and retained profit)
= NET ADDED VALUE
\+ Financing, or capital services costs (Interest on loan capital, bank overdraft, etc.)
= GROSS ADDED VALUE

Advance Corporation Tax (A.C.T.) A tax which is linked to (and paid shortly after) dividends are distributed to shareholders. The rate of tax is currently 3/7ths of the dividend paid. A.C.T. can be offset against the company's Corporation Tax liability for the year in which the dividend is paid, subject to certain restrictions. Any amount of A.C.T. which cannot be set off against that year's Mainstream Corporation Tax liability may be carried back or forward as appropriate.

Advance payments Payments made in one period for goods or services which are chargeable against the trading operations of a future period or periods. Usually included as part of the Debtors' balance in the balance sheet at the end of the period in which they are incurred.

Aggregation This is the fifth of the five accounting 'principles' stipulated in the Companies Act of 1981, with which all companies are expected to comply during the preparation and presentation of their accounts. The Act states that 'in determining the aggregate amount of any item, the amount of each individual asset or liability that falls to be taken into account shall be determined separately'. This is presumably intended to underline the ruling relating to setting-off—namely that, if corporate headings such as Stocks or Investments are used, unrealized losses on some items within the group cannot be set off against unrealized profits from others.

Amortization Similar to Depreciation, although 'amortization' is a term which is generally applied to intangible fixed assets, such as patents etc., rather than to machinery and equipment.

Application of funds Part of the *Source and Application of Funds Statement* which indicates the way in which a company has utilized the funds at their disposal during the year.

Asset base The total market value of a company's assets.

Assets Resources of value owned by a company. The use of these resources is called 'costs'. Assets can be subclassified between *fixed assets* and *current assets*, as defined elsewhere in this glossary.

Asset usage We have adopted this term to define the relationship between Added Value and Total Assets, in order to avoid confusion with the term of Asset Utilization that is often used.

Asset utilization A key test of operational efficiency, in that it measures the amount of sales revenue generated out of each pound's worth of assets for which the company's management is responsible.

$$\text{Asset utilization} = \frac{\text{Sales revenue}}{\text{Total assets}}$$

Associated company *See* Related company.

Audit The review of a company's accounting records by independent, outside—generally qualified—accountants.

Authorized nominal capital *See* Share capital.

Backlog depreciation The difference between the cumulative historic-cost and current-cost depreciation relating to periods up to, but not including, the current trading period.

Bad debt A debtor who fails to pay his outstanding debt to a company within a realistic and reasonable period, after which the balance is written off as a 'bad debt' expense against the trading activities of the business.

Balance sheet A financial statement which summarizes the balances from a company's asset and liability accounts. It will tell us where a company's money is invested, and where it came from, so that we can assess for ourselves what we consider the risk to be. It is a 'snapshot' of the company's financial situation taken at a (not necessarily representative) moment in time. There are basically two types of formal presentation—a *grossed-up* version, and a *net* version. The grossed-up version shows current liabilities included under total liabilities, and balances this total with that of Total Assets, whilst the 'net' version nets off Current Liabilities against Current Assets in order to evaluate Working Capital—to which is added Fixed Assets in order to arrive at Net Assets. This, in turn, balances with the total Capital Employed.

Balance sheet equation A method of presenting the subtotals from a balance sheet, so that the sum of the assets listed on the left-hand side of an 'equals' sign can be seen to be the same as the sum of the liabilities listed on the right.

'Below the line' Any items, other than dividends and retained profit, appearing below the 'Plimsoll line' of Profit after Tax in the profit and loss statement are called 'below the line' items. These would normally include extraordinary non-recurring items or items relating to previous years.

Bonds Long-term loans or debentures.

Break-even point The level of activity at which the total revenue equals the total costs of a business—or at which the total contribution equals the total fixed costs.

Budget The evaluated results of a co-ordinated management plan or business strategy for a future trading period.

Capital Cash that is invested in a business in order that it can commence—or continue—its trading operations.

Capital allowances These allowances, which are computed by reference to the level of capital expenditure undertaken, are deducted from a company's accounts profit when computing its taxable profit. A phasing-out of these allowances was initiated by the Chancellor in his 1984 Budget, but they were of three main types—namely 'first year allowances' in respect of plant and machinery, 'initial allowances' in respect of industrial buildings, and 'writing-down allowances' in respect of industrial buildings and certain types of equipment not eligible for first year allowances. Fuller details of each of these allowances may be found under their respective headings.

Capital employed The total funds invested in a business, made up of shareholders' funds and loan capital. It is consequently 'owed' by the company to the investors and lenders of its capital, and represents a measure of the company's 'limited liability' to the outside world. It is equivalent in value to the company's net assets.

Capital expenditure Expenditure on fixed assets, the net cost of which is to be 'capitalized', and depreciated over the anticipated useful working life of the assets.

Capital intensity The measure of total assets per pound of employee remuneration, which provides a guide to a company's labour/capital relationship. The higher the ratio, the more capital per pound of labour cost, and hence the greater the capital intensity.

Capital reserves Reserves of a non-trading nature, arising typically from such things as the sale of fixed assets at a profit, or from the issue of ordinary shares at a premium. They are not generally available for distribution as dividends.

Capital services cost Financing costs, such as the interest paid on loan capital and bank overdrafts, etc.

Capital stock *See* Share capital.

Capital surplus *See* Capital reserves.

Capital usage *See* Asset utilization.

Capital usage cost *See* Depreciation.

Cash flow The amount of money actually flowing into and out of a business during a period of time. It is not necessarily the same as the costs and revenues applicable to the same period.

Cash flow forecast A statement which analyses all cash receipts and payments over the periods during which the transactions are expected to take place, in order to anticipate any potential shortages or surpluses before they actually arise, and thus give sufficient time for appropriate remedial action to be taken.

Circulating capital Circulating capital is made up of stocks, debtors and cash, less creditors and overdrafts. They are continually recycled from cash into the raw materials, labour and services from which the finished goods are produced for reconversion into cash.

Common stock *See* Ordinary shares.

Companies Act 1981 The Companies Act of 1981 was a very significant piece of legislation in that, for the first time ever, it stipulated quite categorically not only what financial information had to be disclosed in both shareholders' and published accounts, but also exactly how that information had to be displayed. Its origins lay in the EEC Fourth Directive, which was published in 1978, and it was the vehicle via which the requirements of this Directive were incorporated into UK company law. Five accounting 'principles' were defined in the Act, together with detailed rules relating to the definition and valuation bases of almost all categories of assets, liabilities, revenues and expenses.

Consistency The accounting concept which decrees that all published accounting information should be consistently based between one year and another. It is one of the four accounting 'policies' defined in SSAP 2 *Disclosure of Accounting Policies*, issued in 1971, and one of the five accounting 'principles' stipulated in the Companies Act of 1981.

Contingent liabilities Obligations which may arise in respect of past or future events, such as the outcome of a patent infringement, etc.

Contribution The difference between revenue and variable costs. It is consequently essentially variable in nature, since it is related directly to the level of activity. A successful business must generate sufficient contribution to cover all of its fixed costs before it 'breaks even', and it is only thereafter that it starts to make a profit.

Corporation Company

Corporation Tax The tax levied on the accounts profit of a company after it has been adjusted for income and expenses or allowances recognized or ignored for tax purposes, but not for accounts purposes. The *mainstream* Corporation Tax is generally payable nine months after the company's year-end, but payment of part of that tax may be accelerated if dividends are paid. The *Advance Corporation Tax* linked to the dividend payment may be offset against the mainstream liability. The rate of Corporation Tax prior to the 1984 Budget was 52 per cent of the company's taxable profit, but was reduced to 50 per cent with effect from the date of that legislation—consequently applicable to the 1983 tax year—with a view to further and progressive reductions in successive years: i.e. to 45 per cent for the 1984 tax year, 40 per cent for 1985, and to 35 per cent for 1986. The ultimate objective of these changes was consequently to transfer the tax/allowance motivation for companies from a policy of continuing capital investment to one of profit stimulus.

Cost of goods sold The cost to the company of all goods sold during a trading period. It is not necessarily the same as the cost of production, since a business may produce more (or less) in a period than it actually sells.

Cost of production The outgoing costs of producing goods or services for sale during a trading period. This is not necessarily the same as the *cost of goods sold* (*cost of sales*) since the company may produce more (or less) in a period than it actually sells.

Cost of sales adjustment The difference between the cost of sales calculated on an historic cost, and on a current cost basis.

Costs The charge against profits made for the use or consumption of a company's resources during a trading period. It is not necessarily the same in value as the money actually spent during the period. Costs can be subclassified between *fixed costs* and *variable costs*, as defined elsewhere in this glossary. The Companies Act of 1981 provides for two alternative analyses of costs in published profit and loss statements: the first of which takes the 'functional' route from turnover to trading profit via cost of goods sold, distribution costs and administration expenses, and the second of which takes the 'natural type of expense' route through materials, staff costs, depreciation and other charges.

Credit To acknowledge the receipt of services rendered. An accounting entry which records the value of goods or services received in the account of the *creditor*—or provider of the goods or services received. The credit entry is always recorded on the right-hand side of the account, and represents a decrease in the value of a company's assets or expenses, or an increase in the value of its liabilities or revenues.

Creditors Suppliers to whom a company owes money for goods or services received, but for which they have not yet paid. This term is also defined within the Companies Act of 1981 to include debenture loans, bank loans and overdrafts, Bills of Exchange payable, amounts owed to group and related companies, and 'other creditors', such as taxation and social security liabilities. Each subclassification has to be analysed in the balance sheet between amounts falling due within one year of the balance sheet date, and any that may not be due until after one year.

Credit period This is a key management ratio which measures the average number of days that it takes for the company to collect its debts—a useful clue to the care with which it watches its cash flow. This figure can be significantly affected by the proportion of export business handled by the firm, and an *export ratio* (which measures the relationship between exported and total sales) can be a useful factor to consider in conjunction with the credit period.

$$\text{Credit period} = \frac{\text{Outstanding debtors}^{\star}}{\text{Sales revenue}} \times 365$$

* *Note:* Our examples throughout this book have all been calculated on year-end balances, although it is often considered more correct to base the calculation on average balances. Consistency in approach is really more important than the actual choice of base, however.

Current assets Things of value that are held for conversion into cash during the normal course of trading, such as stocks, debtors, short-term speculative outside investments, cash and bank balances, etc. According to the accounting 'rules' defined in the Companies Act of 1981, current assets should be valued in a company's balance sheet at the lower of cost and net realizable value.

Current Cost Accounting (C.C.A.) The method of accounting designed to reflect the effects of inflation within the accounting systems of companies, as defined in the Statement of Standard Accounting Practice (SSAP) No. 16, which was published in the UK in 1980 by the six major accountancy bodies acting on the proposals of the Accounting Standards Committee. The object of this Standard was to provide more useful information than had hitherto been available from historic cost accounts on such matters as the financial viability of the business, return on investment, pricing policy, cost control and gearing.

Current cost adjustments These are divided between *realized* and *unrealized* adjustments. Realized current cost adjustments are directly chargeable to the trading results of a period via Profit and Loss, and include the *depreciation adjustment*, the *cost of sales adjustment*, and the *monetary working capital adjustment*. Unrealized adjustments are ones which do not directly affect the profit of a period, and get charged to the Current Cost Reserve (i.e. the revaluation of fixed assets and stocks, and backlog depreciation).

Current cost operating profit This is the surplus arising from the ordinary trading activities of the business during a period, after allowing for the impact of price changes on the funds needed to continue the existing business, and to maintain its operating capability. It is calculated before interest on net borrowing, and before taxation.

Current cost profit attributable to shareholders This is the surplus for the period, after allowing for the impact of price changes on the funds needed to maintain their proportion of the operating capability. It is calculated after interest, taxation and extraordinary items have been deducted.

Current cost reserve A separate account shown under Reserves in the balance sheet, into which has been transferred all non-realized current cost adjustments. These Reserves should not be regarded as being available for distribution as dividends.

Current liabilities Debts that are currently owed to other people, and which will fall due for payment within a relatively short period (normally of less than twelve months).

Current Purchasing Power (C.P.P.) Accounting *See* General Purchasing Power Accounting.

Current ratio A commonly-used measure of a company's liquidity, which measures the relationship between its immediate or short-term, debts against the value of the current assets out of which these debts will have to be satisfied. This ratio is often known as the *liquidity ratio*.

$$\text{Current ratio} = \frac{\text{Current assets}}{\text{Current liabilities}}$$

Debit To charge. An accounting entry which records the value of goods or services supplied in the account of the debtor, or receiver of the goods or services provided or supplied. The debit entry is always made on the left-hand side of the account, and represents an increase in the value of a company's assets or expenses, or a decrease in the value of its liabilities or revenues.

Debtors People who owe a company money for goods or services which have been supplied to them, but for which they have not yet paid. The total amount of debt owed to a company. This heading is defined within the Companies Act of 1981 to include trade debtors, amounts owed by group and related companies, and 'other' debtors. Each subclassification has to be shown separately in a balance sheet, and has to be analysed between amounts falling due within one year of the balance sheet date, and any that may not be due until after one year.

Debt ratio Gearing

Deferred income Income received in advance of being earned. Generally reflected in the accounts as a current liability until the sale has been made and the income has been received.

Deferred tax A provision charged separately against accounting profits to reflect the difference between tax actually payable, and tax which would have been payable if the charge had been based solely on accounting profits. Not every difference between 'accounting' tax and tax deducted would be reflected in the deferred tax provision, however. The need to make such a provision is no longer obligatory.

Depreciation The 'using-up' cost of a company's fixed assets that is chargeable against its trading activities for a period. The initial purchase price of the fixed assets, less their anticipated eventual scrap or re-sale value, is known as their *net value*, and this net value is apportioned equitably over the number of periods in their anticipated useful working lives. Depreciation is an essential element of cost, but has absolutely nothing at all to do with Cash Flow, because the outlay of cash takes place at the time of the initial purchase. Depreciation is classified as a *fixed cost*, because its charging out is linked to a time base rather than to a level of activity. It is sometimes defined as the 'loss in value of an asset over a period of time', but this is not a definition that should be encouraged, since depreciation is a function of cost rather than of value, and the two terms are not necessarily synonymous. The Companies Act of 1981 stipulates four possible alternative methods of bridging the 'gap' between Turnover and Trading Profit in the Profit and Loss Statement, only two of which (Formats 2 and 4) isolate Depreciation as a separately identifiable natural element of cost. Formats 1 and 3 take the 'functional' route via Cost of Sales, Distribution and Administration Expenses, so that 'depreciation' is not separately identified, although, if either of these formats is used, a full analysis of the period's depreciation charges has to be detailed in the Notes to the Accounts.

Depreciation adjustment The difference between depreciation calculated on an historic cost basis, and on a current cost basis.

Development costs Costs incurred during the development stage of an asset. According to the Companies Act of 1981, these costs may only be included as part of the value of an asset in certain (undefined) circumstances, and, in such cases, the reasons for their inclusion and the period over which they are intended to be written off must also be defined. It is permissible, however, to capitalize interest charges on capital borrowed during the development stage of a project.

Development grants Cash grants made by the government to help defray the cost of capital investments made in certain designated areas of the United Kingdom.

Directors' Report A report which is appended to the published annual accounts of a company, and signed by the directors. It is a statutory requirement, and, according to the Companies Act of 1981, the company's auditors are made legally responsible for considering whether the information given in the Directors' Report relating to the financial year in question is consistent with the accounts. In addition to reviewing the principal activities of the company, the Report has also to contain 'a fair review of the development of the business of the company and its subsidiaries'. This review should include details of such matters as important post-balance sheet events, an indication of likely future developments, and of any activities in the field of research and development.

Dividends The amount of profit distributed to (or divided between) shareholders in proportion to the number of shares that they hold in the business.

Dormant company A company which has had no financial transactions during a period.

Double-entry book-keeping The method by which a company records details of each and every financial transaction that takes place between itself and the 'outside world'—and often between different sections of its own organization. An 'account', or transaction record, is maintained for every supplier, every customer, and every asset and liability owned by the company, and every transaction is recorded twice—the creditor (or *provider* of the goods or services received) is credited with the value of the transaction, and the debtor (or *receiver*) is debited, so that every debit is 'balanced' by a corresponding credit, and vice versa. The debit entry is always made on the left-hand side of the account, and represents an increase in the value of a company's assets or expenses, or a decrease in the value of its liabilities or revenues. Conversely, the credit entry is always recorded on the right-hand side of the account, and represents a decrease in the value of a company's assets or expenses, or an increase in the value of its liabilities or revenues.

Dual aspect *See* Double-entry book-keeping.

Earned surplus Reserves.

Earnings Income, profit.

EEC Fourth Directive A Directive issued by the European Economic Community in July 1978, relating to the information required to be disclosed in published company accounts, and the exact manner in which it should be displayed. All member countries of the Community were asked to incorporate these requirements into their own Company Law, and this was achieved in the UK via the Companies Act of 1981.

Employee costs Wages, salaries, insurance, pensions and all other associated costs incurred in connection with the payment of employed labour.

Employee details The Companies Act of 1981 stipulated that all companies were required to incorporate certain employee information into the Notes appended to their annual published accounts. This information is to include details of the average number of employees (in total and by category), and total employee costs analysed between wages and salaries, social security costs and other pension costs. This provision applies to all companies.

Employee ratios These relate key elements, such as profit, sales revenue or capital employed to the number of people employed by a company, in order to calculate a set of *productivity* indices. These figures can sometimes be distorted if a company happens to employ a high proportion of part-time workers, and, in this case, ratios based on the level of *employee remuneration* would be regarded as more relevant and meaningful.

Equity Shareholders' funds—what is left to the shareholders after all debts and liabilities have been met.

Expense Expenditure, including non-cash items, such as depreciation, which is properly chargeable to the trading activities for the period.

Export ratio A ratio which measures the relationship between exported and total sales. It can be a useful factor to consider in conjunction with the *credit period ratio*, since it is a commonly accepted fact that overseas debts will always take longer to collect than 'home' debts.

Extraordinary income/expenses A receipt or expense which is so far outside the normal trading activities of a company that it calls for completely separate treatment in its accounts. One example would be the profit received from the sale of a fixed asset. According to the Companies Act of 1981, all income, expenditure and taxation liabilities arising out of extraordinary activities has to be shown separately in the profit and loss account from those relating to routine trading operations.

F.I.F.O. The 'first-in/first-out' method of inventory valuation in which it is assumed that the first goods into stock will be the first to be issued for use or sale, as distinct from the *L.I.F.O.* (last-in/first-out) method, in which it is assumed that the last goods into stock will be the first to be issued for use or sale. Either of these two methods of stock valuation is acceptable under the accounting 'rules' prescribed in the Companies Act of 1981.

First Year allowance One of the three types of capital allowance, applicable to investments in plant and machinery. Prior to the 1984 Budget, these allowances used to be 100 per cent of the cost of all such investments, allowable—as the name implies—in the actual ('first') year of investment. The 1984 Budget reduced this rate to 75 per cent with immediate effect—i.e. as from the 1983 tax year—with further planned reductions to 50 per cent for the 1984 tax year, and to nil thereafter.

Fixed assets Things of value that a company intends to use on a continuing basis in the company's activities, such as land, buildings, plant and machinery, vehicles, furniture, etc., which are owned for the purpose of earning income. Also included under this heading are intangible assets (such as goodwill, patents, trade marks, etc.) and investments, including shares in, and loans to, group and related companies. The Companies Act of 1981 stipulates that full details of the opening costs (or valuations) of each separate category of fixed asset must be shown, either in the balance sheet itself, or in the Notes to the Accounts, together with all details of all movements and amounts written off. Payments on account of assets, such as those in the course of construction, must also be shown.

Fixed costs Costs which are linked to a time base, rather than to a level of activity. Examples would be rent, rates, insurance, etc.

Franked investment income Interest received from outside investments, and from which Corporation Tax has already been deducted. When received by another company, this income does not attract any further liability to Corporation Tax.

Funds The working capital resources of a business, consisting of stocks, cash, and debtors, less creditors. Any changes to the net value of working capital consequently has the effect of increasing or decreasing funds.

Funds flow analysis A method of analysing the movement of funds and other financial transactions, in which opening and closing balance sheet equations are linked together via a series of transaction equations which represent both 'sides' of the book-keeping entries.

Funds flow statement *See* Source and application of funds statement.

Funds transaction A transaction which leads to a change in the net value of working capital.

Fungible assets A category of assets, such as stocks or investments, in which individual items are indistinguishable from one another.

Gearing The proportion of a company's capital employed that is represented by loan capital. This term is also often used to define the relationship between loan capital and equity, although we have used the former definition. Both ratios are equally valid, but the essential thing is to ensure that all comparisons are made against a consistent base.

Gearing adjustment An adjustment which is made to reduce the total operating (or 'realized') current cost adjustments by a proportion equivalent to that by which the average loan capital (if any) bears to the average (total) capital employed as shown on the current cost balance sheets at the beginning and end of the year.

General Purchasing Power (G.P.P.) Accounting The term used in the USA to define the method of inflation accounting in which all period balances and transactions are converted to a year-end index based on the general purchasing power of money. This system was also recommended for use in the UK under the title of *Current Purchasing Power (C.P.P.) Accounting*, but was rejected by the Sandilands Committee on the grounds that the application of *general* price indices was not appropriate to the valuation of *specific* assets. They consequently recommended the adoption of the *Current Cost Accounting (C.C.A.)* system, in which the accent is placed much more on the central principle of replacement values, which are not necessarily the same as the original purchase prices indexed upwards to reflect the diminution over time of the general purchasing power of money.

General reserve *See* Reserves.

Going concern The accounting concept by which the financial reports of a business are prepared to reflect its anticipated continuation as a going concern, as distinct from being on the verge of liquidation. This is the first—and possibly the most important—of the four accounting 'policies' defined in SSAP 2 *Disclosure of Accounting Policies* issued in 1971, and is also decreed in the Companies Act of 1981 as being one of the five basic accounting 'principles' to be followed by companies in the preparation and presentation of their annual accounts.

Goodwill Essentially the difference between the price paid for the acquisition of a company as a 'going concern', and the total value of its net tangible assets, as shown in its balance sheet. It is classified as an *intangible* item under the heading of fixed assets in the balance sheet, and, according to the ruling of the Companies Act of 1981, it may only be included if it has been 'acquired for valuable consideration'. It must never be written off over a period exceeding its 'useful economic life', and such an inclusion must also be accompanied by a disclosure of what this period is, and the reasoning upon which this estimate is based.

Gross added value The sum of all the added value elements, including the financing costs which are excluded from *net added value*. *See also* Added value.

Gross profit/(loss) The difference between sales revenue and the cost of goods sold, before the deduction of the 'fixed', or time-based items, such as selling, distribution, administration, research and development costs, etc.

Growth rate The relative rate of growth of a data element over a period of time. The normal time-span for this sort of calculation is three years, and the formula is:

$$\text{Growth rate (\%)} = \frac{\dfrac{L-M}{\frac{1}{2}(L+M)} + \dfrac{M-E}{\frac{1}{2}(M+E)}}{2} \times 100$$

where: L = Latest Year's data
M = Middle Year's data
E = Earliest Year's data

Holding company A company which holds, directly or indirectly, more than 50 per cent of the equity capital of a subsidiary company, or controls the composition of the board of directors.

Income statement Profit and loss statement

Information Historical data that needs to be presented in a conventional, formalized way in order that it may be interpreted consistently by the user.

Initial allowance The first, and major, capital allowance that used to be available in respect of investments in industrial buildings. The pre-1984 rate of this allowance was 75 per cent, granted in the year in which the cost was incurred, but this was reduced to 50 per cent for the 1983 tax year, with further projected reductions through 25 per cent to nil in successive years.

Insolvency A company is 'technically insolvent' when it has sufficient assets to meet all of its financial obligations, but insufficient time to convert these assets into cash. It is 'legally insolvent' if it is in a situation of permanent cash shortage.

Intangible assets Assets which do not have a physical identity (such as goodwill, patents, trade marks, and unamortized research and developments costs, etc.) which are regarded as having some trading value to a company. Since they cannot be regarded as being readily convertible into cash, they cannot be classified as a current asset, and therefore come under the heading of fixed assets in the balance sheet.

Inventory *See* Stocks.

Investment An expenditure in cash or its equivalent in one or more time periods in the anticipation or hope of obtaining a net inflow of cash or its equivalent in some future time period or periods. It is speculative by nature. Investments can be shown in the balance sheet under either fixed or current assets, depending upon whether they are long-term (non-current) or short-term (current) in nature, and each main heading is subdivided into a number of minor categories, such as shares in or loans to group and/or related companies. According to the Companies Act of 1981, non-current investments *may* be written down in value in the balance sheet if they suffer a *temporary* reduction in value, and *must* be written down if they suffer what is seen to be a *permanent* reduction in value.

Issued share capital *See* Share capital.

Leverage Gearing.

L.I.F.O. The 'last-in/first-out' method of inventory valuation, in which it is assumed that the last goods into stock will be the first to be issued for use or for sale—as distinct from the *F.I.F.O.* (first-in/first-out) method, in which it is assumed that the first goods into stock will be the first to be issued. Either of these methods is acceptable as a basis for stock valuation, according to the accounting 'rules' prescribed in the Companies Act of 1981.

Liquid assets Things that can be almost immediately converted back into cash, such as cash itself, bank and debtors' balances—but *not* stocks. Liquid assets are consequently equivalent in value to current assets minus stocks.

Liquidity ratio *See* Current ratio.

Loan capital Money that has been loaned to the company on a long-term basis at a pre-arranged rate of interest to help finance the trading operations of the business. The lenders of loan capital do not (normally) share in the profits of a business.

Long-term liabilities Creditors, losses and accruals not due for repayment during the following year. The Companies Act of 1981 stipulates that all such liabilities must be separately identified in the balance sheet, and individual details must be given of all instalments or repayments not due until after the end of the next five years.

Mainstream Corporation Tax *See* Corporation Tax.

Management information ratios Ratios which measure the relationship between one data element and another. The data elements are generally of a financial nature, and there are three commonly acknowledged 'groups' of ratios:

1 *Investment ratios*, which show how the financial results of a company relate to the shareholders' stake in the business.

2 *Financial status ratios*, which measure the company's financial stability, distinguishing between their ability to meet their long-term commitments (their solvency) and their short-term commitments (their liquidity).

3 *Performance ratios*, which measure how successfully and efficiently the company is being run, or how well its management is utilizing the resources which have been entrusted to its control.

Medium-sized companies Defined in the Companies Act of 1981 as being companies capable of satisfying at least two of the following three conditions:

1 Turnover not exceeding	£5.75 m
2 Total assets (as shown in the Balance Sheet) not exceeding	£2.80 m
3 Average number of employees not exceeding	250

Medium-sized companies are permitted under the Act to omit turnover and cost of sales amounts, and turnover and profit analyses from the published accounts that they file with the Registrar of Companies.

Minority interest The equity interests of shareholders other than the holding company in the assets (and profits or losses) of subsidiary companies that are not wholly owned by the holding company.

Monetary working capital This is the aggregate of:

(a) trade debtors, prepayments and trade bills receivable
– (b) trade creditors, accruals and trade bills payable, in so far as they arise from the day-to-day operating activities of the business—as distinct from transactions of a capital nature.

(*Note:* Strictly speaking, the value of stocks 'not subject to a cost of sales adjustment'—i.e. consumable items, returnable containers, etc.—should also be included under this heading, but has been omitted from the above definition in order to avoid confusion.)

Bank balances or overdrafts may fluctuate with the volume of stock or the items in (a) or (b) above. That part of bank balances or overdrafts arising from such fluctuations should be included in monetary working capital, together with any cash funds required to support day-to-day operations of the business if to do so has a material effect on the current cost operating profit.

In the case of banks and other financial businesses, this definition is extended to cover other assets and other liabilities in so far as they also arise from the day-to-day operating activities of the business, as distinct from transactions of a capital nature.

Monetary working capital adjustment The difference between monetary working capital (as defined above) valued on an historic cost basis, and on a current cost basis.

Net added value The sum of a company's conversion costs plus profit, but excluding its financing costs. *See also under* Added value.

Net assets The value of a company's total assets, less its current liabilities—equivalent in value to its capital employed. It is a useful indication of the 'value' of the organization concerned.

Net borrowing This is the excess of:

(a) the aggregate of all liabilities and provisions fixed in monetary terms—(including convertible debentures and deferred tax, but excluding proposed dividends)—other than those included within monetary working capital, and other than those which are, in substance, equity capital.

over

(b) the aggregate of all current assets other than those subject to a cost of sales adjustment, and those included within monetary working capital.

Net current assets The term used in the Companies Act of 1981 to cover working capital.

Net income Profit after tax.

Net operating assets These comprise the fixed assets (including trade investments), stock and monetary working capital dealt with in an historic cost balance sheet.

Net working capital *See* Working capital.

Nominal accounts Temporary accounts for income or expense items which will appear in the profit and loss statement at the end of the period, prior to being transferred to reserves.

Nominal capital Authorized share capital. *See* Share capital.

Non-current investments *See* Investments.

Non-operational costs Costs not directly associated with the operational activities of a business, such as taxation, dividends paid to shareholders, and interest paid or received on loans or investments.

Normal sign The convention under which account balances are only marked with a minus sign if they are different from those normally associated with that 'class' of account. Thus, liability or revenue accounts—which one would normally expect to have credit balances—are only marked with a minus sign if they happen to show a debit balance. It can consequently cause some confusion if one is not aware that this convention is being used!

Notes payable Loans—often from banks—which are fixed both in amount and in period.

Operating capability The amount of goods and services which a business is able to supply with its existing resources in the relevant period. These resources are represented in accounting terms by the net operating assets at current cost.

Operating profit/(loss) Profit (or loss) arising out of the purely operational activities of a business, but excluding any non-operational expenditure or income, such as investment or loan interest, that may be incurred or received.

Operational costs Costs directly associated with the operational activities of a business.

Ordinary shares Shares which have the right to participate in all the profits and assets of a company after the rights of the prior fixed charges have been satisfied.

Outside investments Money invested outside the company in order to earn interest on the cash available. The short-term investment of temporarily surplus funds would be classified as a current asset, while long-term supportive investments or loans would be classified as fixed assets.

Paid-in surplus Share premium.

Paid-up capital The part of a company's issued share capital on which the nominal value of the shares has been received by the company, and on which, therefore, no further liabilities attach to the holders.

Participating preference shares A type of preference share, the holders of which are entitled not only to a fixed-interest dividend, but also to an additional distribution as may be defined in the terms of the issue.

Par value The 'nominal' value of a company's shares, as printed on the face of the share certificate. It is *not* to be confused with the current market value of the shares.

Preference shares Shares which have a priority claim on any profits available for dividend.

Prepaid expenses Advance payments.

Productivity The relationship between added value and employee remuneration—representing the amount of added value generated out of each pound spent on employee costs. It is a measure which is quite commonly used as the basis for wage negotiations linked to increases in productivity.

Profitability A prime measure of management performance, in that it measures the amount of profit generated in relation to the total value of assets for which they are responsible.

$$\text{Profitability (\%)} = \frac{\text{Profit before interest and tax}}{\text{Total assets}} \times 100$$

Profit after tax The net profit attributable to the shareholders of a company, after all operational and finance costs, and taxation, have been deducted. This is the amount that is left for allocation by the shareholders between dividends to be distributed to themselves as a return on their investment in the company, and the amount of money that they wish to retain—or reinvest—in the business as 'reserve'.

Profit and loss The measurement of growth or shrinkage arising out of the operational activities of a business for whatever period of time we choose. (*See also* Trading period.)

Profit before interest and tax The profit arising out of the 'actual business', which—as a separate entity—is not really concerned with its capital structure, since this is the concern of its shareholders and its loan-lenders. This is the 'level' of profit that is used to measure the company's 'profitability', return on capital employed and profit margin.

Profit before tax The net profit (or loss) arising out of the operations of a business before the deduction of tax, but after the deduction of all operational and non-operational expenses (such as loan interest, etc.) that may be involved.

Profit margin The relationship between a company's profit before tax and its sales revenue, which measures the amount of profit generated out of each pound of sales revenue.

$$\text{Profit margin (\%)} = \frac{\text{Profit before interest and tax}}{\text{Sales revenue}} \times 100$$

Provisions for liabilities and charges This is a main balance sheet heading as prescribed in the Companies Act of 1981, and covers such items as pensions and other obligations, taxation (including deferred taxation), and 'other provisions'.

Prudence The accounting convention under which revenues and profits should never be anticipated in the accounts of a company. It is one of the four accounting 'policies' defined in SSAP 2 *Disclosure of Accounting Policies*, which states that revenues and profits should only be included in the profit and loss account 'when realized in the form either of cash or of other assets, the ultimate cash realization of which can be assessed with reasonable certainty'. The Companies Act of 1981 also includes 'prudence' among the five accounting 'principles' to be followed by all companies during the preparation and presentation of their accounts, and says that 'only profits realized at the balance sheet date should be included in the profit and loss account.' If 'realized' in this context is interpreted to mean 'realized in cash', then this 'principle' could be seen to be at variance with the *accruals policy*, as defined in the SSAP, which states that, in arriving at the evaluation of revenues and profits, 'provision should be made for all known liabilities (expenses or losses), whether the amount of these is known with certainty, or is a best estimate in the light of the information available'.

Quick assets That part of a company's assets which is made up of cash and invested cash—such as outside investments, government securities, short-term deposits and tax reserve certificates, etc.

Quick ratio *See* Acid test ratio.

Real accounts Asset and liability accounts—all of which appear in a company's balance sheet.

Realized current cost adjustments These are adjustments which affect the profit and loss for the period (i.e., depreciation adjustment, cost of sales adjustment and monetary working capital adjustment) and are directly chargeable to the period.

Recoverable amount The greater of the net realizable value of an asset, and, where applicable, the amount recoverable from its further use.

Related companies This is the term used in the Companies Act of 1981 to cover what used to be known as *associated companies*. It can be defined as a 'non-group company in which a long-term vote-carrying holding of equity (however small) is held for the purpose of securing a contribution to the investing company's own activities by the exercise of any control or influence arising from that interest'. An associated company was previously defined as one in which 20 per cent or more of such equity was held.

A share-holding of 20 per cent or more in a non-group company is still a significant break-point, however, since that is the point above which the capital and reserves of the related company as at its latest balance sheet date—together with the profit or loss for the latest financial year—have to be given in the Notes to the holding company's accounts, provided that:

(a) the investee is an overseas company which has no place of business in Great Britain, and does not publish its accounts either in the UK or abroad, and

(b) where the holding in it does not amount to 50 per cent of the total share capital.

Research costs Costs associated with any product, operational or related research. The Companies Act of 1981 is quite specific about the fact that these costs must never be capitalized.

Reserves Trading profit which has been reinvested in the business in order to help fund future expansion, or to cushion the effects of inflation. The decision to reinvest this profit, instead of distributing it in the form of dividends, will have been made by the shareholders, and it therefore forms part of the shareholders' funds. It is just as much a part of capital as the original money invested in the company by its shareholders, or lent to them in the form of loan capital. *See also* Capital reserves *and* Current cost reserves.

Residual value The amount for which a fixed asset can be sold at the end of its useful working life. The anticipated residual value—often regarded as nil—is taken into account when calculating the amount of depreciation to be charged against profits for its use during this life.

Retained profit The amount of profit held back for reinvestment in the business by the shareholders as part of their 'reserve' capital.

Return Profit made from the investment of cash or its equivalent—generally related to the sum invested.

Return on capital employed One of the most reliable and widely-used measures of a company's performance from the point of view of its utilization of funds, in which its profit before interest and tax is related to capital employed in order to measure the amount of profit that has been generated out of every pound invested in the business.

$$\text{Return on capital employed (\%)} = \frac{\text{Profit before interest and tax}}{\text{Capital employed}} \times 100$$

Return on shareholders' funds A key management information ratio which measures the rate of return that the shareholders have obtained on the capital that they have invested in the business.

$$\text{Return on shareholders' funds (\%)} = \frac{\text{Profit after interest and tax}}{\text{Shareholders' funds}} \times 100$$

Revenue expenditure Money spent on the working capital area of the business with the object of eventually obtaining revenue—or of converting it back into cash.

Rights Entitlement. A 'rights issue' is an issue of shares to existing shareholders on a proportionate basis, generally at a price somewhat less than the current market price.

Risk capital Shareholders' funds—capital that is 'at risk' as a result of a company's trading operations.

Sales revenue The net sales of a business, i.e. gross sales less discounts and returns. It must not be confused with cash coming into the business, because the flow of cash will be interrupted by the 'debtors barrier', and is consequently likely to be out of phase with the value of goods and services actually 'sold' during a period.

Savings Money that is held for use at some future date without adding any value to it in the form of accrued interest—as distinct from *investment*, which is defined as 'an expenditure in cash or its equivalent in one time period or periods in anticipation of obtaining a *net inflow of cash* or its equivalent in some future time period or periods'.

Share capital The amount of money invested in a company by its risk-taking shareholders. The maximum amount of share capital that a company is authorized to issue is specified in its constitution, or Memorandum and Articles of Association. The issued share capital can never be more than this amount, and is often less.

Shareholders' funds The part of a company's capital which is owned by its shareholders. It is made up of share capital plus any trading profits that may have been reinvested in the business as reserves.

Share premium In the case of a new issue, shares may be sold at a price in excess of their nominal value. This excess is known as the share premium, and is treated in the company's accounts as a capital reserve, not available for distribution as dividends.

Small companies The Companies Act of 1981 defines a small company as one which is capable of satisfying at least two of the following three conditions during both the current and the preceding financial year:

1	Turnover not exceeding	£1.4 m
2	Total Assets (as shown in the Balance Sheet) not exceeding	£0.7 m
3	Average number of employees not exceeding	50

Small companies relief Relief granted to companies earning 'small' profits—defined in the Finance Act of 1978 as 'not exceeding £60,000'—by means of a reduced rate of Corporation Tax. This rate was adjusted to 30 per cent in the 1984 Budget, but may obviously be changed again at any time.

Source and application of funds statement This is a statutory document which has to be incorporated into a company's annual accounts and reports. Its purpose is to show the way in which funds have been generated and absorbed by the operations of the business, and the manner in which any resulting surplus of liquid assets has been applied, or any deficiency of such assets has been financed. It also has to show the funds used for the purchase of new fixed assets, as distinct from those used to increase the working capital of the company.

Statement of source and application of funds *See* Source and application of funds statements.

Stock movements and cost of goods sold schedule A schedule which traces the in and out movements and stock balances of various categories of stocks from raw materials, via work-in-progress to finished goods.

Stock relief An allowance against taxable profits introduced in the mid-1970s to help defray the cost of holding increasing levels of stock during periods of high inflation. This relief was finally abolished in the 1984 Budget.

Stocks Things of value which are for sale—or are for conversion into finished saleable products—during the course of a company's normal trading operations. One of the accounting 'rules' prescribed in the Companies Act of 1981 states that current assets (including stocks) are to be valued in the balance sheet under the principles of F.I.F.O., L.I.F.O., weighted average prices, 'or similar convention'. Valuations also have to include payments on account, or money received in advance of stock not yet dispatched or handed over to the customer.

Stock turnover A very important measure of the liquidity of a company's stocks, in which the value of stocks is related to sales revenue in order to establish the number of times that they have been 'turned over' during the period.

$$\text{Stock turnover} = \frac{\text{Sales revenue}}{\text{Stocks}}$$

Subsidiary company A company which is controlled by another (holding) company, where the holding company either owns, directly or indirectly, more than 50 per cent of its equity capital, or controls the composition of its board of directors.

Third party costs Payments to outside suppliers of goods and services purchased by a company for the purpose of converting into products or services intended for sale.

Total assets The total value of all assets held by a company—equivalent in value to its total liabilities.

Total debt The total of all of a company's liabilities to the 'outside world', i.e. the lenders of its Loan Capital, other long-term liabilities (such as deferred tax, etc.) and its current liabilities. It is equivalent in value to total liabilities minus shareholders' funds.

Total liabilities The total value of capital employed plus current liabilities, which thus represents a measure of a company's total liability to its long-term investors and lenders of capital, and to its short-term creditors. Equivalent in value to its total assets.

Trading period The period of trading between two successive publications of formal financial statements. This will normally be one year—partly because of the requirements of company law and taxation requirements—but the *financial year* will normally be broken down into smaller segments for purposes of internal management reporting and control.

Trading profit/(loss) *See* Operating profit/(loss).

Transaction equation An equation which records both the 'receiving' and the 'giving' sides of a financial transaction in a funds flow analysis.

Trial balance A list of all the balances on a company's ledger accounts. Such a listing is generally used as the first step in the preparation of the final published accounts, and its purpose is to prove that the total of all the debit balances is equal to the total of all the credit balances.

Turnover The Companies Act of 1981 defines turnover (for the first time) as being 'the amount derived from the provision of goods and services falling within the company's ordinary activities, after the deduction of trade discounts, VAT and any other taxes based on the amounts so derived'. An analysis of turnover has to be disclosed in the Notes to a company's accounts for each substantially different class of the company's activities, and for each geographical segment of its overseas trading—provided that such disclosure is not regarded by the directors as seriously prejudicial to the interests of their business. If such grounds for omission exist, then this fact must be clearly stated.

Turnover ratios A group of ratios which measure the number of times which a specified category of a company's assets have been 'turned over' during a trading period—generally one year. They are normally calculated by dividing sales revenue for the period by the average value of the assets as at the beginning and end of the period, although this calculation is often short-cut by using only the end-of-period value. Sometimes referred to as *activity ratios*.

Unrealized current cost adjustments Adjustments which do not directly affect the profit of a period, and get charged to the current cost reserve (e.g. revaluation of fixed assets, backlog depreciation and the revaluation of stocks).

Value added *See* Added value.

Value to the business In terms of current cost accounting, this is defined as:

(a) Net current replacement cost,

or, if a permanent diminution to below net current replacement cost has been recognized,

(b) Recoverable amount.

Variable costs Costs which vary roughly in proportion with the level of activity, such as raw materials, some labour costs, etc.

WIP *See* Work-in-progress.

Working capital The capital available for conducting the day to day operations of a business—normally the excess of its current assets over its current liabilities. The working capital area is often called the 'heart of a business'. The American definition for current assets less current liabilities is *net working capital*—Americans define working capital as being synonymous with current assets.

Work-in-progress (WIP) Any material, component, product or contract at an intermediate stage of completion.

Writing down allowance The writing down allowance on industrial buildings is currently 4 per cent, available from the date of investment, which means that this is the rate at which these assets may be depreciated in the accounts of a business for the purposes of calculating taxable profit. This allowance was not affected by the 1984 Budget, and is also applicable to plant and machinery which does not qualify for first year allowances. The rate of allowance for qualifying plant and equipment is 25 per cent, calculated on the reducing balance.

Index

Page numbers in bold type indicate illustrations.

Page numbers prefixed by the letter G indicate Glossary definitions.